Folk, Region, and Society

HOWARD W. ODUM

Folk, Region, and Society

SELECTED PAPERS
OF
HOWARD W. ODUM

Arranged and Edited by

Katharine Jocher, Guy B. Johnson,
George L. Simpson, and Rupert B. Vance

THE UNIVERSITY OF NORTH CAROLINA PRESS · CHAPEL HILL

In the midst of world change we cannot overlook the fact that the American South has repeatedly been summoned to embark upon social upheaval. Few such areas have undergone such drastic social change in so brief a historic period.

Not often does an intellectual with no footing in politics and no active leadership in a social movement project as clearly as did Howard W. Odum the course of history—"a history as it were without a country of its own."

Unlike many intellectuals, Odum had trained competence in a technical discipline—sociology—a discipline to which he devoted his life. It is the essence of this book that we have here an academic blueprint, as it were, of the changes the South has undergone and still must undergo.

Out of these experiences—from such empirical data, the scholar would say—Odum fashioned interpretation, generalization, and rounded out distinctive social theory.

In our title for these selected papers, Folk, Region, and Society, we have sought to suggest the range, complexity, and unity of Odum's thought as he moved from the Negro and his folksongs to the folk society and folk sociology, from race relations and the southern region to regionalism and regional-national planning, from the folkways to technicways and stateways, from social values to social action. The South of Odum's day may be represented as a passing phase, someday to be of interest only to historians. But as long as new regions and underdeveloped economies emerge from folk society to state society, as long as sectional conflict and national adjustment are with us, Odum's ideas will continue to interest the specialists and the generalists of social science.

Howard W. Odum
1884-1954

Howard W. Odum was born near Bethlehem, Georgia, May 24, 1884, and grew up as a farm boy in post-Reconstruction Georgia. The two family lines—his mother, descended from slave-owning families and his father, a small farmer four years her junior—are treated in *An American Epoch,* 1930. In 1897 the family moved to Oxford, Georgia, in order to send the children to Emory Academy and College.

Odum's education was secured in the classics—Greek, Latin, and English—and was achieved by benefit of hard work, borrowed money, and rural school teaching. After graduating at Emory College, A.B., 1904, Odum taught a rural school at Toccopola, Mississippi, 18 miles from the railroad. Fortunately it was only 21 miles from another Oxford, the seat of "Ole Miss." Here Odum taught as fellow, studied, collected folklore, observed and recorded Negro life, and earned an M.A. in the classics, 1906. Both at Emory and the University of Mississippi he encountered able teachers and colleagues who understood his combination of eagerness and timidity.

One fellow student was Stark Young; a teacher was T. P. Bailey, a recent Ph.D. in psychology from Clark University. It was Professor Bailey who helped Odum make the change to the social sciences and apply for a fellowship at Clark with G. Stanley Hall. Armed with a collection of Negro folk songs and studies of Negro town life, Odum took one Ph.D. in psychology with Hall at Clark in 1909 and another in 1910 in sociology at Columbia University with Franklin H. Giddings.

Odum wanted to go South to develop sociology, missed an appointment at Washington and Lee, and went instead to Philadelphia where he did a study of the Negro in the public schools of the city for the Bureau of Municipal Research. In 1912 he went to the College of Education at the University of Georgia and thence to Emory as Professor of Sociology and Dean of Liberal Arts. As chairman of the Committee of Deans he aided in Emory's move to Atlanta and its transition to university status. In 1920 he made his last and definitive move to the University of North Carolina, an academic home which was to witness 34 crowded years of achievement.

Odum joined the faculty in September 1920, just as the University was moving into a decade of its most notable development. At Emory, Asa Candler was reported to have said, "Odum wants to build a university overnight and to build it his own way." At Carolina he embarked on a period of brilliant promotion and organization of scholarly research and teaching.

Odum organized and staffed the new Department of Sociology. North Carolina had pioneered in the Nation in setting up a distinctive public welfare program and Odum organized the School of Public Welfare and became its first director in 1920. He founded and edited the sociological journal, *Social Forces* (1922—) and on the authorization of President Harry W. Chase and the Trustees, 1924, established the Institute for Research in Social Science. To his closest associates Odum occasionally recounted his meeting at a Charlotte hotel with Beardsley Ruml, director of the Laura Spelman Rockefeller Memorial. Evidently it represented a meeting of two first-class minds—an able promotor of scholarship vis-a-vis a shrewd judge of men.

Odum edited a Social Study Series for the University of North Carolina Press and a textbook series, the American Social Science Series, for Henry Holt.

To the casual observer Odum appeared to go from one administrative triumph to another. Elsewhere he has listed what he considered his major defeats: (1) the failure of his effort to locate a distinguished School of Public Administration at the University, (2) the depression's defeat of his effort to secure halls of Social Science and All American Culture at the Chicago Century of Progress World's Fair in 1933, (3) failure to develop a State Planning Board for

North Carolina, and (4) failure to secure acceptance of his report advising the reorganization of the State Prison System.

In all his activities Odum's sound training, his unlimited energy and enthusiasm, and his judgment and skill as an administrator were freely placed at the disposal of the University and aided it materially in the attainment of the status of a national institution. One of his last tasks was to help develop a Department of City and Regional Planning at the University, 1946. Organizations he founded were turned over to others to administer, for Odum never intended to give up his first love—creative scholarship.

In scholarship the complexity and integration of Odum's mental processes were apparent. His early studies of village life of Negroes in Mississippi showed him to be more than an avid collector of folk songs and folklore. Here also was the beginning of his interest in the South as a region and in folk sociology as a discipline. The opening sentences of his Clark dissertation stated a theme which he always kept in mind: "To know the soul of a people and to find the source from which flows the expression of folk thought is to comprehend in a large measure the capabilities of that people. To explain the truest expression of the folk mind and feeling is to reveal much of the inner consciousness of a race."

Odum had a wide range of research interests, but his first and most persistent interest was the field of Negro life and race relations. His earliest publications resulted from the collection of Negro folk songs which he began as a young school teacher in the Deep South. In 1909 he published a hundred-page article, "Religious Folk-Songs of the Southern Negroes," in *The American Journal of Religious Psychology and Education,* and in 1911 he had a lengthy article on "Folk-Song and Folk-Poetry as Found in the Secular Songs of the Southern Negroes" in *The Journal of American Folk-Lore.*

His real opus as a young man, however, was the volume entitled *Social and Mental Traits of the Negro,* published in 1910 in the Columbia University Studies of History, Economics and Public Law. In this work Odum was trying "to reach some insight into what the Negro appears to be and what he really is, what he may desire to be and what he may possibly become in his future development." The book was packed with factual details on the institutions and behavior of the Negro masses in the South, and it maintained what certainly must have seemed at that time an "objective" approach. However, Odum shared the then current "scientific" assumptions concerning racial differences, and his book was interlaced with them. For example, segregation was a taken-for-granted arrangement, the Negro was different, if not inferior, mentally and morally, and he should look for happiness not in the aspiration to become like white people but in the development of his own talents on his own level of civilization. It was a drastic picture of Negro life, realistically reported.

In the next twenty years science did an about-face on racial differences, and Odum became quite accustomed to sharp criticisms of his 1910 book. He was apparently little disturbed by them, for he rarely bothered to notice them, and he saw no reason for any formal "repudiation" of the book. In at least one instance he did suggest to the author of a critical footnote that he cite the date of publication of *Social and Mental Traits of the Negro,* as if to say, "After all, how many people are there who wrote on the Negro forty years ago and are still writing today?" To re-read today his chapter on Home Life and Morals in the light of changes is to reaffirm as Odum did continually one's optimism and faith in the Negro's development and destiny.

For about fifteen years after his early work on the Negro, Odum was busy making a living with teaching and administrative work, and his writing lagged. At North Carolina he came into the flowering of his creative scholarship. Again he was complex and many-sided, as the twenty-odd books and almost two hundred journal articles and brochures listed in the bibliography will show. North Carolina's public welfare program Odum saw as initiating the change in status of the underprivileged from clients of private philanthropy to citizens seeking the rights of social and economic security from the community. In adapting the new public welfare to the task of making democracy effective in the unequal places he edited a volume of the *Annals of the American Academy of Political and Social Science,* 1923, and with D. W. Willard wrote and edited *Systems of Public Welfare,* 1925, with his own prophetic last chapter on "The Movement for a Federal Department." In opening up the field of regional development he edited a symposium on *Southern Pioneers in Social Interpretation,* 1925, beginning with a sentence of unmistakable meaning: "Why, then, are the Southern States so barren of individual leaders who represent the highest achievement in their fields?" In collaboration with Guy B. Johnson, Odum returned to folk sources and in *The Negro and His Songs,* 1925, and *Negro Workaday Songs,* 1926, gave the Negro's secular songs a place alongside the spirituals.

These two books were happily timed to coincide with, if not initiate the rising tide of interest in Negro folk culture. Then came what he called his trilogy: *Rainbow Round My Shoulder,* 1928; *Wings on My Feet,* 1929; *Cold Blue Moon,* 1931. These portray the loves and sayings of a semi-fictional Negro named Left-Wing Gordon —prose poetry in the wanderings of a Black Ulysses. By now Odum's approach to the Negro folk character was so sympathetic and appreciative as to bring charges from certain upper-class Negroes that he was glamorizing crudity and immorality. He never let such complaints ruffle him, and his answer to the literary critics' speculation as to whether Left-Wing Gordon was real or fictitious was, "What difference does it make?"

After 1930 Odum's major research interests turned to regionalism and general sociology. With *Man's Quest for Social Guidance,* 1927, Odum published his first text and in the phrasing of the title showed his commitment to social science as a guide for social action. With Katharine Jocher he wrote *An Introduction to Social Research,* 1929, an early treatise on methods in the social sciences.

At the request of President Herbert Hoover, Odum was instrumental in setting up and securing the grant for the monumental *Recent Social Trends in the United States,* 1933, report of the President's Commission, and its 13 monographs. With William F. Ogburn he was Assistant Director of Research and helped edit the volumes. He also wrote the chapter on Public Welfare. By 1936 five years had passed without a major book from his pen. In working on *Recent Social Trends* Odum had faced the problem of accounting for national development in the divergencies of regional trends. In *Southern Regions of the United States,* 1936, Odum achieved the synthesis of his mature thought in regional theory, southern development, and a cultural-statistical approach to the analysis of regional divergence and national integration. For a work of such size and complexity the public's reception was little short of amazing. It became a basic book in courses and seminars, had an important impact on policy and thought, went through four printings and had books, commentaries, and pamphlets written about it. With Harry E. Moore he applied this analysis to the whole country and depicted the Nation's six major regions in *American Regionalism,* 1938. In retrospect regionalism represents the high point of Odum's achievement and influence. He had now become a public figure.

Odum's work went further than interpreting the South to the Nation and the Nation to the South. It pointed to one possible integration of social science; it projected trends of development for the South; and it cried aloud for implementation in social action and social planning. For all the reactions the new discipline met in the region, Odum never concealed the fact that he was a sociologist and that certain social theories implied certain appropriate social action. Odum's mature thought on regional-national integration was well stated in his paper, "The Promise of Regionalism," at the University of Wisconsin Centennial, *Regionalism in America,* 1951.

Odum's practical interests were as varied as his scholarly interests, and they found expression in his services to numerous official agencies and voluntary organizations. He shunned personal publicity, and many of his friends did not know that he advised presidents and governors or that at any given moment he was likely to be serving as chairman of half a dozen State and regional organizations. However, he was not a "joiner" or a "do-gooder." He saw organizations and offices as instruments which were good only if they contributed to the more efficient utilization of man's intelligence and capacity for progressive adaptation. He could rarely be persuaded to retain a chairmanship more than a year or two, because he felt that if he had any contribution to make he could make it within a short time. He kept out of the personal political conflicts which he found in many organizations, and it saddened him to see organizations becoming stale because their leaders had acquired strong vested interests. "Any organization," he said, "ought to know when to quit."

In *American Sociology,* 1951, his last major work to be completed, Odum made his first and only essay into the history and theory of sociology as such. The book told much about Odum and his personality. He could be starkly critical of movements but not of men.

Colleagues and scholars delighted to honor Odum. Four honorary degrees recapitulated both his biography and his contributions in public service and the arts: Emory University, LL.D., 1931; College of the Ozarks, Litt.D., 1935; Harvard University, LL.D., 1939; and Clark University, L.H.D., 1941.

He served as president of the American Sociological Society in 1930, received the Bernays Award for interracial cooperation in 1945, the Catholic Conference of the South distinguished service award in 1943, the American Jersey Cattle Club's award as "Master Breeder" in 1948, and the O. Max Gardner Award in 1953 to the member of the University faculty "making the greatest contribution to the welfare of the human race." He held distinguished positions as visiting professor or lecturer at Yale, Columbia, the Universities of Washington, Illinois, Southern California, Utah, and many others. At the time of his death he held a grant from the John Simon Guggenheim Memorial Foundation.

Odum left a mass of literary remains—work in progress. His manuscript, *Mid-Century South: The New Southern Regions of the United States,* is a statement of his maturing thought on regionalism and on the great social changes in the South from 1930 to 1950. His sociological system, left incomplete, reached its fullest statement to date in *Understanding Society,* 1947. Most lacking here is a definitive work on folk sociology, best outlined in relation to contemporary theory, in his *Social Forces* article of March 1953. Important for folk sociology, it also demonstrated the extent to which Odum kept abreast of developments in social theory. Also left unfinished was an autobiographical work, the *White Sands of Bethlehem.*

Howard Odum was a complex personality whose deceptively simple manner concealed neither his energy nor his scholarship. He played many roles and yet they were well integrated—teacher, sociologist, folklorist, prose poet, administrator, promoter, and breeder of pedigreed Jersey stock. Those who worked with Odum remember his desk as always piled high with books and papers. Yet, in what appeared a disorderly array, he could always in short time come up with a desired document. He was always busy but he always had time, it seemed, to see people who needed to see him. He also knew how to get rid of bores and long-stayers. There was always so much work to be done and so little time to do it, but he rarely gave the impression of being hurried. The speed with which he turned the pages of a book or manuscript always amazed his graduate students. Yet, when challenged, he could give a point by point outline of the contents of any page.

As a scholar he put in long hours of work through the night and then surprised colleagues with his vigorous teaching and gifts for promoting and administering the tasks of organized research. A true intellectual, he derided the intelligentsia to his students, extolling instead the values of the folk. He became a public figure in the development of the South and his advice and counsel were sought on many sides. He was a Master Breeder of pedigreed Jerseys—one of five in the United States acclaimed for the development of a genetic type by the American Jersey Cattle Club. Odum delighted to surprise his friends by saying that his bulls were worth more than his books. Withal he had especial gifts in the area of personal relations. Those who knew him realized that this quality went beyond the bounds of personal charm—a quality with which he was well endowed.

Contents

Folk, Region, and Society

PART ONE

The Negro and Race Relations

I speak the password primeval, I give the assign of democracy. By God, I will accept nothing which all cannot have their counterpart of on the same terms.

WALT WHITMAN

INTRODUCTORY NOTE

O dum's first and last great interest was the Negro. As a youth, he was fascinated by the folk Negro's songs, and as a young school teacher he began to collect Negro songs and to survey the Negro's community life. In 1909 appeared his first published work, "Religious Folk-songs of the Southern Negroes." In the excerpts presented below, Odum's characteristic style—vigorous, imaginative, poetic—showed forth clearly. He was one of the first scholars to collect the ordinary secular songs of the Negro, and his interpretation, as seen in the selection from a 1911 publication, is as fresh today as when he wrote it.

Years later, after having concentrated on regionalism and other subjects, Odum returned to his first love and wrote extensively on Negro folk life. From *Rainbow Round My Shoulder,* we have selected one of the many stories of Odum's "Black Ulysses." This book, together with *Wings on My Feet* and *Cold Blue Moon,* comprised what he liked to call his "trilogy." They were a compound of the real-life stories of a one-armed Negro wanderer called Left-Wing

Gordon and of Odum's own fertile imagination. When asked whether these stories were truth or fiction, he explained that, while many of the details were fictitious, the narratives all depicted the truth about the folk Negro. He wrote these three books with great verve and abandon, and one feels that he probably enjoyed this writing more than any other.

Paralleling his interest in the folk was Odum's interest in race and race relations. His best-known early work was *Social and Mental Traits of the Negro* (1910). It is not surprising that this book contained many of the then current assumptions about racial differences, yet it was permeated with a remarkable empathy and insight into the social condition of the Negro. To represent this early period of race relations research, we have chosen a lesser-known study, "Negro Children in the Public Schools of Philadelphia," (1913). In this we see Odum's deep concern for understanding the Negro and for giving him the opportunity to develop his talents to the fullest. His emphasis on environmental factors was prophetic. Odum was always fascinated by the problem of race differences—or "differentials," as he preferred to call them. This interest shows most clearly in his "Standards of Measurement for Race Development," (1915), a portion of which is presented here.

Although Odum insisted on "understanding the South," he was not an apologist for the South, and he could be a very harsh critic. This point is beautifully illustrated by the selection titled "Lynchings, Fears, and Folkways," in which, after explaining the white South's "folkways" as the key to understanding why southerners lynched Negroes, he suddenly ends with a stinging indictment of the practice of lynching.

Odum's productive research and writing covered a span of forty-five years, during which many dramatic changes took place along the color line. He grew along with the changing times, and the tensions of World War II and its aftermath drew him back again to the problem of race relations. His 1939 forecast of "The Position of the Negro in 1950" was a very perceptive piece, which can serve as an indicator of how far he had come since 1910. His *Race and Rumors of Race* (1943) was a remarkable collection of the rumors and gossip engendered by the changing status of the Negro during the war. From this work we have chosen the chapter titled "The South in Crisis," since it sets the stage for the whole book, and "The Romance of the Eleanor Clubs," because it illustrates so well the extreme reaction of the white South to the vanishing Negro servant.

The post-war conflict over segregation challenged Odum to state his matured analysis of the situation. He had in mind writing a book to be called *Agenda for Integration,* but six months after the momentous Supreme Court decision on school segregation in 1954 he was dead, and the book was not written. However, he had written what might be called a summary preview of such a book. This was the rather lengthy paper on school desegregation which was published in the Emory University *Journal of Public Law* in the spring of 1954. He referred to this as his "Agenda for Integration," and it is reproduced in full here because it embodies so much that was fundamental in Odum's thinking and self-expression. Here we see Odum's style of writing which suggests a blend of Walt Whitman, Thomas Wolfe, and William Faulkner; his determination to get into the record every conceivable "factor" or "assumption" needed to assess the changing racial situation; his deep involvement with the folkways as guardians of social continuity and slow evolutionary change, but his commitment also to the necessity of drastic change; his anxiety lest the pace of events might destroy something precious that ought to be preserved; and his communication of a sense of urgency about the writing, suggesting that perhaps he already had a premonition that time was short for him as well as for the South.

G. B. J.

1. The Negro Folk: Interpretation and Portraiture

Religious Folk-Songs
of the Southern Negroes [1909]*

To know the soul of a people and to find the source from which flows the expression of folk-thought is to comprehend in a large measure the capabilities of that people. To obtain the truest expression of the folk-mind and feeling is to reveal much of the inner-consciousness of a race. And the knowledge of those evidences which are most representative of race life constitutes the groundwork of a knowledge of social and moral tendencies, hence of social and moral needs. The student of race traits and tendencies must accept testimony from within the race, and in the study of race character the value of true expressions of the feelings and mental imagery cannot be overestimated. Thus it is possible to approximate knowledge of a race. To bring a people face to face with themselves and to place them fairly before the world is the first service that can be rendered in the solution of race problems.

To preserve and interpret the contributions of a people to civilization is to add to the science of folk-history. Posterity has often judged peoples without having so much as a passing knowledge of their inner life, while treasures of folk-lore and song, the psychic, religious, and social expression of the race, have been permitted to remain in complete obscurity. Likewise peoples have lived contemporaneously side by side, but ignorant of the treasures of folk-gems that lay hidden and wasting all about them. The heart and soul of the real people are unknown, science is deprived of a needed contribution, and the world is hindered in its effort to discover the full

* From *American Journal of Religious Psychology and Education*, III (July 1909), 265-365.

significance of the psychological, religious, social and political history of mankind. That which is distinctly the product of racial life and development deserves a better fate than to be blown away with changing environment, and not even remain to enrich the soil from which it sprang. Justice to the race and the scientific spirit demand the preservation of all interesting and valuable additions to the knowledge of folk-life. The successful study of the common development of the human intellect in primitive thought is thus advanced. The exact form of expression itself constitutes a contribution to knowledge and literature.

The value and importance of folk-lore are gladly recognized. Its successful study and a more comprehensive recognition of its worth have revealed new problems and new phases of thought. Not only its relation to civilization as an historical science and as it bears definitely upon peoples of modern cultural areas is recognized, but its essential value in the study of psychological, anthropological, and sociological conditions has called forth the most careful study that has been possible to give it. On the scientist's part, knowledge has been increased, while on the other hand, the peoples of the world have become more united in the appreciation of the kindred development of human thought. The vast contributions to folk-science and their relation to scientific interest, bear testimony to this truth. And perhaps even more with *folk-song,* a greater work is to be done. As a part of folk-lore it represents less of the traditional and more of the spontaneous. Its collection and study is now being pursued with more zeal and with marked success. And the hope may well be expressed that with the growing interest in folk-song may come an increased knowledge of all that is nearest and truest to the phyletic as well as the genetic concept of a people, and that with this knowledge may come effective efforts toward race adjustment and new aids in the solution of race problems.

. . . In revealing much of what he *is* rather than what he *appears to be,* the folk-songs of the Southern Negro are superior to any superficial study made from partial observations. The insight into Negro character gained from their folk-songs and poetry accompanied by careful and exhaustive concrete social studies may be accepted as impartial testimony. And on the other hand, the changing economic and educational conditions, the increasing influence of the white man upon the Negro, and the rapid progress that is being made on every hand in the South indicate that if the present-day folk-songs of the Negro are to be preserved, they must be collected now. Should they be permitted to become a lost record of the race?

. . . For the most part collections of Negro folk-songs in the past have been limited to the old spirituals. The present-day religious songs and the social productions are equally interesting and valuable. The particular nature and characteristics of these songs are discussed in connection with the examples. They are flexible and have various forms, they consist of broken and unbroken melodies, they have stately and rapid minor cadences. Musical notes can give only a skeleton of the real melody that accompanies the words; the peculiar qualification of the Negro singers to render their melodies defies art to exactly symbolize it. The words of the songs are given as they are sung, and the reader must needs employ an imagination kindred in vividness to that which is reflected in the songs themselves if he would comprehend their essential qualities. The characteristic quality is often found in an improvised arrangement of words which makes the dominant feeling that of mingling words and cadences successfully. The meaningless phrases and refrains do not hinder the expression of feeling through the minor chords. Simple emotion, inherent melody, and colloquial language are combined with fine and differentiating imagery and humor in an under-meaning common to the folk-song. An element of melancholia may be felt underlying many of the songs. But with all alike, vigor of expression, concreteness and naturalness of mental imagery, and simplicity of language and thought are combined with striking folk-art. The Negro's projective mental imagery assumes that the hearer's comprehension can easily grasp the full picture of description, moral maxims, and dramatic dialogues, all combined in a single verse, and that he can do it without confusion. Here may be seen much of the naked essence of poetry with unrefined language which reaches for the Negro a power of expression far beyond that which any modern refinement of language and thought may approach. Rhythm, rhyme, and the feeling of satisfaction are accompanying inherent qualities. The natural poetic spirit and the power of the imagination in the Negro are worthy of study.

In addition to these general qualities of the Negro folk-songs, it need only be suggested here that the best conception of his religious, moral, mental and social tendencies is reflected in them. That which the Negro will not reveal concerning his religion, his religious songs tell better than he could possibly do. His social nature and unconscious ideals bubble out from his spontaneous social songs. In the expression of his natural feelings and emotions he gives us the reactions of his primitive thought with environment. That which is subsequently treated at length may be anticipated in the approach to a careful consideration of the fullest spirit of the Negro folk-songs, namely, that it is important to note that the faculty of the Negro to think, not exactly as the white man, or to think in terms of modern science and literature, but in terms of his own psychological conditions, is pronounced. The Negro is a part of a nation at the same time that he is a distinct people; he, perhaps, has more anthropological importance than historical standing. His present status is an essential consideration of each of these relations to the civilization of today. The emotions, the religion, social aspirations and ideals—in fine, the character of a people is accustomed to be expressed in their literature. The Negro has no literature save that of his folk-song and story. May these not speak for him, both the good and the bad, in the following chapters?

The work here presented is not exhaustive but representative. The songs are not those of a single plantation, community or section of the Southern States. They are not the songs of the coast Negroes or of the river type. But they are sung popularly as much in Georgia as in Mississippi, as much in Florida as in Tennessee. They are distinctly the representative average songs that are current among the common mass of Negroes of the present generation. They belong to the Negroes who have been constantly in contact with the whites and to those who have had less association with the refinement and culture of the white man. They have been collected carefully and patiently under many difficulties. Many of them are sung only when the white man does not hear; they are the folk-song of the Negro, and the Negro is very secretive. Not only are they not commonly known by the whites but their existence is only recognized in general. They are as distinct from the white man's song and the popular "coon songs" as are the two races.

The scope of investigation is large and the field is a broad one; the supply of songs seems inexhaustible. Yet the student may not collect them hurriedly. He who has not learned by long observation and daily contact with Southern conditions the exact situation will make little progress in gathering valuable data. While all contributions to the total of Negro folk-songs have been very valuable, still it is true that they have been too long neglected and the studies made have been too partial. The nature of the Negro's songs is constantly changing; the number is continually increasing. They should be studied as the conditions of the Negroes are investigated. They are the product of our soil and are worthy of a distinct place in literature. . . .

Folk-Song and Folk-Poetry as Found

in the Secular Songs of the

Southern Negroes [1911]*

The songs in this collection are "Negro folk-songs," in that they have had their origin and growth among the Negroes, or have been adapted so completely that they have become the common songs of the Negroes. They are "folk-poetry which, from whatever source and for whatever reason, has passed into the possession of the folk, the common people, so completely that each singer or reciter feels the piece to be his own."[1] Each singer alters or sings the song according to his own thoughts and feelings. How exactly this applies to the Negro songs may be seen from the explanations which follow, and from the study and comparison of the different songs. It is not necessary, therefore, in order to classify the songs as Negro songs, to attempt to trace each song to its origin or to attempt to determine how much is original and how much borrowed. Clearly many of the songs are adapted forms of well-known songs or ballads; others, which in all probability had their origin among the Negroes, resemble very strongly the songs of other people; while still others combine in a striking way original features with the borrowed. In any case, the

* From *The Journal of American Folk-Lore*, XXIV (July-September 1911), 255-63.

1. Dr. John Meier, quoted by Professor H. M. Belden, *Journal of American Folk-Lore*, vol. xxiv, p. 3.

song, when it has become the common distinctive property of the Negroes, must be classed with Negro folk-songs. . . .

*   *   *   *   *   *

In studying the Negro's songs, three important aids to their inter-pretation should be kept in mind—first, facts relating to the manner of singing, and the occasions upon which they are sung; second, the general classes of Negro songs, and the kinds of songs within each class; and, third, the subject-matter, methods of composition, and the processes through which the songs commonly pass in their growth and development. The majority of songs current among the Negroes are often sung without the accompaniment of an instrument. The usual songs of the day, songs of laborers, of children, and many general care-free songs, together with some of the songs of the eve-ning, are not accompanied. In general, the majority of the songs of the evening are accompanied by the "box" or fiddle when large or small groups are gathered together for gayety; when a lonely Negro sits on his doorstep or by the fireside, playing and singing; when couples stay late at night with their love-songs and jollity; when groups gather after church to sing the lighter melodies; when the "musicianers," "music physicianers," and "songsters" gather to render music for special occasions, such as church and private "socials," dances, and other forms of social gatherings. Special instances in which a few Negroes play and sing for the whites serve to bring out the combined features of restrained song and the music of the instrument. The old-time Negro with his "box" (a fiddle or guitar), ever ready to entertain the "white folks" and thus be entertained himself, is less often ob-served than formerly. The majority of younger Negroes must be well paid for their music. In the smaller towns, such Negroes not in-frequently organize a small "orchestra," and learn to play and sing the new songs. They often render acceptable music, and are engaged by the whites for serenades or for occasions of minor importance. They do not, however, sing the Negro folk-songs.

Of special importance as makers and mediums for Negro folk-songs are the "music physicianers," "musicianers," and "songsters." These terms may be synonymous, or they may denote persons of different habits. In general, "songster" is used to denote any Negro who regularly sings or makes songs; "musicianer" applies often to the individual who claims to be expert with the banjo or fiddle; while "music physicianer" is used to denote more nearly a person who is accustomed to travel from place to place, and who possesses a combination of these qualities; or each or all of the terms may be applied loosely to any person who sings or plays an instrument. A group of small boys or young men, when gathered together and wrought up to a high degree of abandon, appear to be able to sing an unlimited number of common songs. Perhaps the "music physicianer" knows the "moest songs." With a prized "box," perhaps his only property, such a Negro may wander from town to town, from section to section, loafing in general, and working only when compelled to do so, gathering new songs and singing the old ones. Negroes of this type may be called professionals, since their life of wandering is facilitated by the practice of singing. Through their influence, songs are easily carried from place to place. There are other "music physicianers" whose fields of activity are only local. In almost every community such individuals may be found, and from them many songs can be obtained. From them and from promiscuous individuals, a "musicianer" may be influenced to obtain songs new to himself, which he, in turn, will render to the collector. Finally, a group of young Negroes, treated to a "bait" of watermelons or to a hearty meal, make excellent "songsters" in the rendering of the folk-songs. In addition to these special cases, it is a constant source of surprise to the observer to learn how many songs the average Negro knows; and they may be heard during work hours, or, in some cases, by request.

The great mass of Negro songs may be divided into three general classes, the last of which constitutes the folk-songs as commonly used, —first, the modern "coon-songs" and the newest popular songs of the day; second, such songs greatly modified and adapted partially by the Negroes; and, third, songs originating with the Negroes or adapted so completely as to become common folk-songs. The first class of songs is heard more frequently by the whites. All manner of "ragtimes," "coon-songs," and the latest "hits," replace the simpler Negro melodies. Young Negroes pride themselves on the number of such songs they can sing, at the same time that they resent a request to sing the older melodies. Very small boys and girls sing the difficult airs of the new songs with surprising skill, until one wonders when and how they learned so many words and tunes. The second class of songs easily arises from the singing of popular songs, varied through constant singing or through misunderstanding of the original versions. These songs appear to be typical of the process of song-making, and indicate the facility of the Negroes in producing their own songs from material of any sort. The third class of Negro songs is made up of the "folk-songs" proper; and while the variations of the songs of the first and second classes would constitute an interesting study, they are in reality not Negro songs. . . . In all of these the characteristic music and manner prevail, and the principal characteristics may be enumerated simply. The music may be reduced to a few combinations. The harmonies are made up mostly of minor keys, without reference to studied combinations or movement toward related keys. There is much repetition in both words and music. The song and chorus are adapted to an apparent mood or feeling. Verses are sung in the order in which they occur to the singer, or as they please the fancy. The great majority of the songs are made up of repetitions, but they do not tire the singers or the hearers. The Negro song often begins with one conception of a theme, and ends with another entirely foreign to the first, after passing through various other themes. This may be explained by the fact that when the Negro begins to sing, he loves to continue, and often passes from one song to another without pausing. In time he mingles the two or more songs. Most of the groups and "socials," and especially the dance, require continuous music for a longer period of time than the average song will last. It thus happens that the Negro could sing the great majority of his songs to a single tune, if the necessity called for it; although it is likely that the last part of his melody would scarcely be recognizable as that with which he began. In words, as in music, variation seems unlimited. As is pointed out subsequently, and as was true in the case of the religious songs, there is no consistency in the use of dialect. Perhaps there is less consistency in the social songs than elsewhere. It is common for the Negro to mingle every kind of song into one, or to transpose the one from its usual place or origin to any other position. Thus "coon-songs," "rag-times," "knife-songs," "devil-songs," "corn-songs," "work-songs,"—all alike may become love-songs or dancing "breakdowns." The original names given to such songs serve to distinguish them in the mind of the Negro, rather than to indicate their separateness. However, the distinctions are often made clearly enough for a definition of what the Negro means to be made.

The "musicianer" will play many "rag-times," which he carefully names, and calls off with pride. Usually they are not accompanied by words, but are represented on the fiddle or guitar. When he is through with these, he will offer to play and sing "some song." This he does to precisely the same music as the "rag-time." With the words, it is a song; without the words, it is a "rag-time," in which case the Negro puts more life into the music. Likewise the "knife-song" is by origin instrumental only, but it is regularly associated with several songs of many verses. Its name is derived from the act of running the back of a knife along the strings of the instrument, thus making it "sing" and "talk" with skill. Instead of the knife, Negroes often carry a piece of bone, polished and smooth, which they slip over a finger, and alternate between picking the strings and rubbing them. This gives a combination of fiddle and guitar. The bone may also serve as a good-luck omen. The knife, however, is more commonly used. The "musicianer" places his knife by the side of the instrument while he picks the strings and sings. He can easily take it up and use it at the proper time without interrupting the harmony. In this way the instrument can be made to "sing," "talk," "cuss," and supplement in general the voice and the ringing of the fiddle or the tinkling of the guitar. It is undoubtedly one of the Negro's best productions, and defies musical notation to give it full expression.

The "train-song" derives its name from its imitation of the running train. The most popular name for it is "The Fast Train." The Negro's fondness for trains and railroad life has been observed. . . . In no way is this spirit better portrayed than in the train-songs, which picture to the vivid imagination the rapidly-moving train. This imitation is done by the rapid running of the fingers along the strings, and by the playing of successive chords with a regularity that makes a sound similar to that of the moving train. The train is made to whistle by a prolonged and consecutive striking of the strings, while the bell rings with the striking of a single string. As the Negroes imagine themselves observing the train, or riding, the fervor of the occasion is increased; and when "she blows for the station," the exclamations may be heard, "Lawd, God, she's a-runnin' now!" or, "Sho' God railroadin'!" with others of a similar nature. The train "pulls out" from the station, passes the road-crossings, goes up grade, down grade, blows for the crossing, blows for smaller stations, blows for the operators at the stations, rings the bell for crossings and for stopping the train; this train meets the "express" and the mail-train, blows for the side-track, rings the bell; the mail-train in turn whistles, rings the bell, passes; both bells ring, and they continue on their run; the wheels are heard rolling on the track and crossing the joints in the rails. If the song is instrumental only, the man at the guitar announces the several stages of the run. If the song is one of words, such as the railroad-songs, . . . the words are made to heighten the imagination, and between the stanzas there is ample time to picture the train and its occupants. A study of the social songs current among the Southern Negroes shows that they have arisen from every-day life, and that they portray many of the common traits and social tendencies. The majority may be said to have sprung up within comparatively recent years. For the subject-matter of his songs, the Negro has drawn freely upon his favorite themes; and the growth and development of his songs have been spontaneous and natural. . . .

Changing Scenes and Broken Homes [1938]*

WITH *all his wanderings and waywardness, "Back Home" and "sweet old mommer" stand out as chief pictures to many a Negro on the road. In his songs, stories and philosophy, home and mother are themes of constant appeal in striking contrast to actual living experience and habits. The old spirituals magnified ideals of the Heavenly home as opposed to the earthly verdict that "This old world been a hell to me." This was considered logical and natural contrast. In his wanderer songs the Negro's wish-dream to be back home shows something of the same psychological quality. Childlike and wishful yearning, homesickness for home that never was, reflect the quick changing moods found in the Negroes' other changing scenes—in love and work and wanderings.*

> WHEN I LEFT HOME MY MOTHER WAS SICK,
> THE BES' FRIEND I HAVE IN THIS WORL'
> IS WAITIN' FER ME IN PAIN.
> TAKE, OH, TAKE ME BACK HOME,
> MY SISTER'S CRYIN', MY MOTHER'S DYIN',
> TAKE ME, TAKE ME BACK HOME.
> EVERY MAIL DAY I GETS LETTER
> SAYIN', SON, COME HOME.
> THAT OLE LETTER READ 'BOUT DYIN'.
> BOY, DID YOU EVER THINK 'BOUT DYIN'?
> THEN I CAN'T READ IT NOW FOR CRYIN',
> TEARS RUN DOWN, LAWD, TEARS RUN DOWN.

* From *Rainbow Round My Shoulder*, Chap. III, pp. 39-50. Copyright 1928 by The Bobbs-Merrill Company, 1955 by Mrs. Howard W. Odum, reprinted by permission of the publishers.

Again, the Negro woman and mother, chiefest of paradoxes in the white and Negro world. Faithful worker and stolid servant. Provider for large families. Revered "Auntie" and "Mammy" enshrined in memory and literature. Faithful, dependable, powerful in prepotency. The woman God forgot. Winner of long distance endurance tests. Yet again "Nigger woman," the lowest standard of personality to certain members of the white race. Considered as of old by white men and white women as not a person but a Negro. Storm center of race mixture. Battle-ground of Negro men, chief character in the Negro song life.

WOMAN IS A GOOD THING AN' BAD THING TOO,
THEY QUIT IN THE WRONG AN' START OUT BRAN' NEW,
DON'T NEVER GIT ONE WOMAN ON YO MIN',
KEEP YOU IN TROUBLE ALL THE TIME.
DON'T NEVER LET YO' WOMAN HAVE HER WAY,
KEEP YOU IN TROUBLE ALL YO' DAY.
DON'T NEVER HAVE ONE WOMAN FOR YO' FRIEND,
WHEN YOU OUT, 'NUTHER MAN IN.

Black Ulysses tells later on of his women and sweethearts, alike subjects and objects of his blues and loves and fights. Now he tells of his mother and her mother, types reflected in GOD'S TROMBONES *as guests of King Jesus.*

Bout this time mama an' us chillun all went to live with my grandfather and grandmother, bein' mama's papa an' mama, still livin' an' fine ole gray-haired citizens. Reason for us movin' was so mama could work-out better with white folks an' leave smallest chillun with her parents, an' reason she move at this time is long story how she have to lay her ole man on coolin' board.

My mother was mighty fine woman. Everybody say so, both white an' colored. She was handsome lady and strong and always helpin' other folks out. White folks always want her to help 'em out. She always stand well wherever she go. After we moved over to her mother's she git up 'fo' day an' go cook fer white folks an' leave us wid grandparents to take keer ourselves. Then she bring back washin' to do at home an' make us help her wash, totin' wood an' drawin' water an' hangin' out clothes. Then she go back and cook supper for folks an' come home after dark.

Sometime she have to hurry off to meetin' 'cause she was pillar in church. She help church folks same as she do everywhere else. When time come to make collections an' help build new church an' other things, mama was alway good stan'by fer the preacher an' the brothers and sisters. They sho' hold her in high 'steem. She respect herself too, she sho' did. She keep her house nice an' clean an' make us chillun move around like I done tell 'bout when she give us lickin's when we need it. I seen many day, too, when white folks sick she stay with 'em all time leavin' us to do best we could.

She was great singer, leader in church songs, an' always singin' at her work.

> *I wants to go to Heaven, jine de angels' ban',*
> *I wants to go to Heaven, stan' where de angels stan'.*
> *I wants to go to Heaven, have some angel wing;*
> *I wants to go to Heaven, see de Jesus King.*
> *I wants to go to Heaven, shout lak de angels shout;*
> *I wants to go to Heaven an' walk about.*
> *I wants to go to Heaven, set in de angels' seat;*
> *I wants to go to Heaven, eat what de angels eat.*
> *I wants to go to Heaven, weep when de angels weep;*
> *I wants to go to Heaven, sleep where de angels sleep.*

Mama was foolish 'bout us chillun in heap o' ways too, but she felt her duty to work fer white folks an' make good livin' fer us 'cause she couldn't git much from papa. An' she never pay no min' to wild niggers. Creepers didn't never bother wid her, leastwise mo' 'n one time. She sho' outstood 'em an' sent 'em on their way. Even when her ole man was so mean and no-'count she always faithful to him.

I remember one time when my father was away, one o' these high-steppin' 'fo'-day creepers keep comin' round to see mama. I heard him tell her she too sweet an' too han'some to be wastin' her time doin' drudgery an' workin' fer no-'count man like she got fer husband. He tell her he can make heap mo' money an' take her off to see the world where she will be some sister with the brothers an' sisters of big orders. She don't seem to pay him much min', goin' on 'bout her work and tellin' him to go about his'n. Then when that big buck up and tell her sweetly that she better let him have little money she save up so he can take keer of it fer her, she flew into rage and run that nigger clean out o' the place. Broom handle whut she use that time, but she tell him it be fohty-fo' next time. You ought to see us chillun laughin' at him an' we sorter skeered o' mama too. . . .

We mighty proud o' her. She was jes' like that an' make me cry now to think 'bout my po' mama done dead an' gone, a-sleepin' in her grave, an' nobody to think 'bout me like she used to.

> *I lef' my mother standin' in the door,*
> *Head hung down, tears fallin' to the floor.*
> *My sweet ole mommer dead an' gone,*
> *Nobody to tell my troubles to.*

My father I done told somethin' 'bout. He wasn't nothin' like mama. He was big, high-yellow, strappin', han'some man, too, but he was mean an' so rough the Lawd couldn't smooth him. I been told when he was comin' up from big city he an' my mama very han'some couple, an' seem mighty crazy 'bout each other. He sho' have fine clothes an' alway make mighty fine impression on women. He was one o' the laziest niggers I ever seen, too lazy to go on road even if he won't work. Only thing he ain't too lazy to do is quarrel an' fight and go 'cross other side town to git 'nuther woman treat him fine an' give him money an' liquor. Guess he sort of man we call got bad spirit, don't keer nothin' for nobody or hisself. Since he gittin' through the worl' don't keer whether he git from rich or poor, an' ain't got no feelin's 'scusin' what he want to satisfy hisself. Sometime he have to work little an' he make out like he doin' the whole worl' favor an' he raise ruckus with mama askin' her why'n hell she don't stay home an' have him good dinner.

> *I'm a havin' a hell of a time,*
> *Livin' with these two women o' mine.*
> *I'm goin' down to Georgia lan'*
> *Where women don't have jes' one man.*

He kept gittin' worse eve'y year an' when he sorter half set up wid whisky comin' home from other side o' town ain't nobody this side old Scratch hisself could put up with him. He come in 'busin'

mama an' she try startin' off patient. She say to him you mighty
sweet on me when you co'tin' me an' I turned down all them other
fine boys, an' las' week you seem mighty sweet like I think maybe
you goin' be good to me again. Then she ask him where he stay last
night, an' he say, "What the hell you got to do wid where I stay las'
night—I stayed 'tween two mountains my arms all round its brow."
Then she tell him he used to be mighty sweet on her till he git satis-
fied, then he started 'busin' her all over the place, an' jaw back at
her sayin' he guess lot o' women appreciate chance to satisfy him an'
they can lay lower than she can anyway, an' give him money besides.
Then he start beatin' her. Ain't nobody can stand that all time.

I hear my mama say many times ain't nobody can live with that
nigger. Whenever he work out or even be out loafin' he come home
night an' if mama ain't there to have his meals jes' right an' do
eve'ythin' jes' like he wants he start cuttin' up an' git so mad ain't
nobody an' nothin' respectable round him. Mean as he was he always 'cusin' mama of bein' wid other men when she out workin'
so hard. 'Nuther thing if mama won't stay home Sunday with him
he say he won't 'low her to work an' make money an' he ain't got
none to give her. Mama say he want her to be po' so he could lawd
it over her, but she say she likes to keep her money so he can't boss
her round so much.

But I'm tellin' you mama was match fer him when she did git
started. He'd come home some night an' start something an' fust
thing they knowed they was fightin' like cats an' dogs. Sometimes
he'd git through fightin' with nothin' on much but his skin, an' it was
pretty badly ruffed up. Reason they quit fightin' was so wore out
couldn't hardly stand up.

Then one night he got so mad after they went to bed he got up
an' hid gun which they kep' in room. But my mama she watch him
out corner her eye an' seed where he hid it. Then, nex' day she took
that gun an' hid so he couldn't find it. So that night he come home
an' pick a fuss an' they got to fightin' little rougher'n ordinary. So
he goes to fin' pistol where he hid an' when he can't find it he gits so
mad he beside hisself an' start to hunt that gun and mama git scared
an' grab it an' pull trigger. An' so that handsome yellow man fell
dead.

Turn me over, baby, turn me over slow,
May be las' time, I don't know,
It's all you got daid an' gone.

She sent for doctors, doctors all did come,
Sometimes they walk, sometimes they run,
An' it's one mo' rounder gone.

Nex' thing, mama takes littles' baby under her arm an' pistol in other han' an' goes straight to police station. She say to policemens to come on down to her house an' git man she done killed. They look at her startle' like an' ast her what man an' when she done kill him. An' she tells 'em jes' minute ago she kill him wid pistol she have in her han', an' she tell 'em to take the pistol 'cause she done done mo' with it already than she want to. So they taken pistol an' ast her about the killin' an' she tole 'em xactly how it was.

Sunday she got 'rested, Tuesday she was fined,
Wednesday she pleaded for all life trial
An' it's all she got done gone.

Lilly say to jailer, "How can I sleep?
All roun' my bedside lovin' Paul do creep,
It's all I got done gone."

Lilly said to jailer, "How can it be
Feed all prisoners, won't feed me?
Lawd have mercy on yo' soul."

Jailer say to Lilly, "I tell you what to do
Go back in yo' dark cell an' sleep some mo'."
An' it's all she's got done gone.

Well, the Law takes mama an' then they have trial and cause lot excitement in neighborhood. 'Course eve'ybody like mama an' know she was a good lady, an' nobody don't think much o' papa, sayin' never did 'spect much of han'some yellow man come from big city. So the courtroom was crowded with all sorts an' kinds of folks both colored an' white. Mos' all colored folks was there an' some good white folks come down testify to good life of my mother. White folks sho' did stan' by her an' jedge in stan' an' lawyers with big books in their hands and jury all settin' roun' tryin' her for her life.

Seem like that was hard times, but she stan' up under trial jes' like she did everything else an' talk straightfo'ard to all of 'em. An' they ast her lot o' questions 'bout what she suffered for fifteen or twenty years an' eve'ybody seem sorry for her an' they let her off an' jury file in verdict in few minutes sayin' she was not guilty. So she was sad an' wurried, an' so we change our home an' go live with her father an' mother.

> *Troubles makes me weep an' moan,*
> *Goin' where troubles be no mo',*
> *Good Lawd in Heaven, I'm troubled.*
>
> *Troubles meet me at the do'.*
> *Goin' where troubles be no mo'.*
> *Good Lawd in Heaven, I'm troubled.*

2. *Race and Race Relations*

Negro Children in the Public Schools of Philadelphia [1913]*

The scope of this inquiry included all the elementary schools of the Philadelphia public school system as organized during the months from September, 1910, to January, 1911, the information concerning enrollment and attendance being obtained at that time, and the experiments being made during that period and subsequently. The total number of pupils enrolled in the elementary schools was 154,125, of which 8,192 or 5.3 per cent were Negro children. This enrollment was made from a total number of enumerable children of 241,623, of whom 9,758 were Negroes; and they were enrolled in the 238 elementary schools with their several annexes. The larger study thus includes this total number and the larger comparisons are made between total children and Negro children. The larger group is again variously divided. There were two principal groups of Negro children, those who attend mixed schools for whites and Negroes, and those who attend schools in which only Negro children are enrolled. Again, smaller groups are made the basis of special experiments and minute study, the effort being to approximate in all cases, so far as possible, similar conditions for both white and Negro children, with experiments made uniformly by the same person.

*   *   *   *   *   *

* Summary from a special study of Negro children in the public schools of Philadelphia made for the Philadelphia Bureau of Municipal Research. *Annals of the American Academy of Political and Social Science,* XLIX (September 1913), 186-208. Reprinted by permission.

Conclusion

Further tests and measurements of white and Negro children might have been carried to an almost indefinite extent with profit. But the limit of this study, bounded by the facilities at hand, had been reached, and sufficient data obtained to permit brief summaries, conclusions and discussions of the relative differences between white and Negro children in their school environment.

In considering the data given it must be remembered that they apply to Negro children as they are found today, the product of inheritance and environment, and that the question of inherent *race* traits, in the strictly anthropological meaning, is entirely apart from the present discussion. It is hoped that researches into race differences will be aided by the facts reported in this study, but that is not the main object of this inquiry. If the cumulative influence of immediate and remote ancestry on the one hand, and immediate and remote environment on the other, has been such as to bring about present conditions, it is essential to analyze these conditions and undertake to determine what further influences will bring the best results from continuing inheritance and environment. There can be no doubt as to the problem from the practical viewpoint of efficiency in education or from the viewpoint of accepted principles of education, psychology, and anthropology.

It may be repeated that in a problem of such long-developed standing and complexity, both in itself and in its relation to environment, final conclusions cannot be reached at once. Dogmatic assertions and hasty recommendations should be avoided and the full force of study and recommendation be directed toward further research and the application of knowledge and means now available.

With these qualifications in mind, conclusions may be reached which will be of value in attempting to solve the pedagogical and administrative problems involved and in placing the entire question on a scientific basis. The study has shown conclusively that there are distinct differences between white and Negro children in all three of the aspects studied, namely, environment, school conditions and progress, and in mental and physical manifestations. The study of home environment shows that Negro children are at a disadvantage, in social and moral influences and in actual physical conditions, comprising food, drink, sleeping accommodations, and general hygienic conditions. In addition to the general social influences of crowded conditions and lower standards, the children are handicapped by poor air, water, food and irregular exercise and rest. Finally they receive little intelligent supervision and cooperation at home in maintaining a continuous connection with school and mental effort, and when leaving school face restricted opportunities for obtaining a livelihood.

The differences in school attendance and progress are equally large. Negro children show much greater retardation measured by both age and progress; a much lower percentage of attendance and higher percentage of irregularity; a lower percentage of promotion and a lower average of class standing. Great as these differences are, the influence of environment alone seems to be sufficient to account for the majority of the results. It appears, therefore, that injustice would be done to Negro children if harsh judgment be passed upon them because they do not maintain the standard of the white children. The fact that the records of a limited number of Negro children equal the records of the best white children gives indication of larger possibilities.

But the differences between the two groups do not end with environment and school progress. The exhaustive study of conditions of school progress indicated that there were differences in kind as well as in amount. The results of the tests, applied uniformly to white and Negro children, show that in their manifestation of general intelligence, Negro children, after the age of eight years, are behind the white children; that in single traits and processes these older children differ from the white children materially; that in comparison with white children the efficiency of Negro children varies inversely as the complexity of the process; but that in practically all instances the deviations for Negro children are larger than for the white children; and in many cases the individuals among the Negro children range as high as those among the white children. The white children tend always to conform to a normal curve of distribution, and the Negro children tend toward a flat, irregular, and not infrequently, multimodal curve. These facts apply to both normal and backward children.

As far as the data presented show, the differences in physical measurement of height, weight, neck and chest measurements, and temperature, respiration, and pulse, are much less and show less consistency in variation, and appear more traceable to the influence of immediate environment than do other differences.

That these facts are significant there can be little doubt. That they present certain complex problems is entirely consistent with the inevitable results of a long and varied race inheritance combined with an equally varying environment. If, as Professor Boas concludes, "Even granting the greatest possible amount of influence to environment, it is readily seen that all the essential traits of men are due primarily to heredity"[1] and if further "we must conclude that the fundamental traits of the mind . . . are the more subject [than physical traits] to *far-reaching* changes"[2] and "we are necessarily led to grant also a great plasticity of the mental make-up of human types,"[3] it would clearly be impossible for the Negro children to show the same manifestations of mental traits as white children, after having been under the influence of entirely different environments for many generations.

This conclusion also brings with it a great responsibility. The fact that such important differences exist between the white and Negro children and that they have arisen naturally through long periods of growth in different environment, brings with it an obligation to determine the exact nature of the differences, their specific causes, and the means by which a new environment and method may overcome such weaknesses as are found. The fact that the Negro children show great variability in all activities combined with the accepted theory of the plasticity of human types, gives indications of great possibilities in the development of the Negro. But it also characterizes all efforts to deny the existence of fundamental differences between the white and Negro children as inconsistent and harmful to the development of the Negro race, on the one hand, and to the permanent adjustment of conditions on the other.

* * * * * *

Responsibility does not end, however, with the effort to provide education which will ultimately develop the children into their highest capabilities. The present and immediate future must be provided for. The great majority of Negro children not only do not enter the

1. *The Mind of Primitive Man*, p. 76.
2. *Changes in Bodily Form of Descendants of Immigrants*.
3. *Ibid.*

high school but also fail to complete the elementary grades. Less than 2 per cent of the Negro children of school age reach the eighth grade. Furthermore, their training to the period of dropping out of school fits them neither for any special work in life nor for competing with the more fortunate and better fitted in society at large. The opportunities for employment of Negro children thus equipped are limited, and they are forced to continue the struggle under even more unfavorable conditions. Add to all the inequalities already mentioned the fact that the standard of excellence, toward which white and Negro children unconsciously strive, is often entirely different. An individual among the whites and an individual among the Negroes may each measure up to the maximum ideal of his habitual social and mental horizon and each deserve 100 per cent credit, and yet the objective measure of final achievement may be larger in the one case than in the other. What then, can the school and society expect of children to whom they give neither special training for life nor equal opportunity in the struggle? Here again the basis of improvement is found in the exact definition of conditions as they are and a recognition of their significance.

An Approach to the Negro Problem [1915]*

This paper purposes to consider very briefly and informally certain standards of measurement for race development. More accurately it may be said to present certain considerations concerning standards of measurement rather than to present the detailed methods themselves. . . .

At the outset it is well to emphasize the importance of the term "Race Development" *vs.* "Race Traits" and to emphasize the distinctive field of study offered by organized efforts for considering knowledge and problems of Race Development. For the purpose of this paper especially, the term "Race Development" is much more desirable than "Race Traits" or "Race Psychology." Likewise from the viewpoint of scientific study of races, with the information now at hand and from the viewpoint of practical problems of society, "Race Development" offers a field for much more tangible results. This is true for many reasons, some of which it is important to note here. "Race Development" offers a better medium for measurement; it assumes movement and progress; it assumes measurement of progress by differing and changing character rather than by fixed traits. It recognizes race character, group character, local character, chronological character, institutional character, and geographical and historical foundations. It enables the measurement of status and conditions without exclusive regard to cause; it recognizes fundamental differences in different groups; in fine, it is a term of evolution and of progress and in a very practical way leaves the question of

* Adapted from "Standards of Measurement for Race Development," *Journal of Race Development,* V (April 1915), 364-83.

original or innate race traits to the theoretical anthropologist. If we summarize development in human history as development in time; in space; in magnitude and scope of endeavor; in intensity of endeavor; in condition of adaptation; and in total social welfare; we may measure Race Development by ascertaining through objective methods the status or conditions of a given race of people at a given time or place, with reference to these several aspects of development. Thus our problem becomes a problem of measurement of condition or position compared with or removed from certain defined premises; with provisions for establishing a mode whereby one group or society may be compared with another; and in which the group or society compared may be a race.

Such measurement of conditions, however, is subject to numerous limitations. The whole question of measurement depends upon the standards by which measurement is made. The multiplicity and difference of viewpoints and standards make the problem most complex; make dogmatism out of the question and have given rise to a mass of conflicting data, opinions and so-called false science. The reported status of development of a race will vary in accordance with the several standards used, whether development in time, in space, in quality, in quantity or in general social adaptation be the measuring scale; or whether a single characteristic or group of characteristics be used as a standard of measurement; or whether there be one measuring agent or many. That modern society has made much progress in quantity of achievement is not doubted, but that the quality of Greek thought has ever been surpassed is entirely problematical. That the estimate passed upon the development of the Negro by the white race differs from that passed by the Negro race; or that passed by the South from that of the North; or that passed by a native American from that of a foreigner; or even that of one school of scientists from that of another school will not be questioned. The fallacies of false measurement and the desirability of accurate measurement will be pointed out in connection with subsequent suggestions, each of which will of course have its own limitation. Suffice it here to emphasize the importance in attempting to measure race development to determine as nearly as possible the predominating or sum total characteristics which distinguish the race or group from other groups or races; from other periods of its own development; and to compare this *ethos* or character with the best standards that are most commonly accepted by the best authorities.

Among the fallacies commonly met with in the study and discussion of the Negro problem, two may be discussed briefly as specifically important in connection with this presentation. The first fallacy leads both the students and the public to consider all facts relating to Negroes as characteristic of all Negroes. There are two aspects of this common fallacy which need emphasizing. The first has to do with the student or worker and the second with the public attitude at large. There has been not infrequently a tendency on the part of writers to consider, absolutely, characteristics of the Negro without distinguishing different groups or stating the scope to which their assertions might properly apply. Of the unreliability of this something will be said subsequently. On the other hand, efforts and studies are often limited in their effectiveness because of the haste with which specific problems and conditions are confused by the public with the total problem or with the Negro. It is therefore necessary for the student to avoid this fallacy by selecting specific problems and fields for experiment and study in order to reach conclusions just as he does in other broad research or public endeavor. It is also necessary for the public mind to accept his results without attempting to apply them to conditions with which they are only indirectly related, or without accusing him of gross inaccuracy because he has not portrayed specific conditions of one unit of work true to entirely different units. The student may not select as his work in the laboratory the Negroes in certain southern towns and apply his result to the Negro race everywhere. But after having selected this field and having made his investigations and defined his usage of the word Negro as applying only to that group, he may then give his results as a contribution to the whole subject. Or again, if he desires to make a study of Negro children in the schools, he may investigate and portray certain social and home conditions which these children have met. So far as this study is concerned his facts are essential and representative. But this does not mean that he has applied results to all Negro homes, or that he has exhausted his field of research here. He may desire to go further and investigate certain more general conditions of the Negro children's environment and so report certain groups of representative facts that are essential for his purpose, giving all the while their relation to the whole possible group of facts to be obtained. This does not mean that he applies the facts obtained to the whole group of Negroes. Indeed it is essential that he define from time to time the application of his results and note differences in other groups. This, however, does not detract from the essential value of the selected facts which he has been able to find as the necessary basis for this work.

Suppose we apply the principle of the above brief statement to a specific measurement of race development, as found in a concrete study of a large group of Negroes, as of Philadelphia, Pennsylvania. The Negroes constitute some 5 per cent of the total population of the city, but are segregated variously in groups so that in certain sections they form from 10 to 40 per cent of the population of these sections. They are further distributed throughout the city in contact with the whites. The total Negro community approximates 100,000; the Negro population is increasing more rapidly than the white with a tendency toward new segregations in the city. This increase of Negro population has averaged more than 50 per cent for each of the last two decades. Such a large increase is brought about, not by natural increase, but by congregate grouping chiefly of immigrants from nearby Southern States. The composition of the Negro population is further widely varied including the majority of the classes of Negroes found in the United States. This Negro population again has a preponderance of young people between the ages of fifteen and thirty years, with a small number of young people under fifteen years and children under five. The preponderance of females is even more abnormal and the largest excess is between the ages of fifteen and twenty-five years. Furthermore, irregular home and family conditions exist to a large extent; the families are relatively small and irregular; there is only a relatively small average overcrowding but many aggravated cases; the Negroes have to occupy inferior homes and pay relatively higher rents; they are limited in the scope of their occupations being restricted mostly to general labor and domestic services; while at the same time they often receive less wages than the whites who perform similar work. Living conditions and habits tend to increase the low standard of home life and to limit the products of good constructive living. The Negroes own little property, and property owners for the most part are engaged in the same sorts of occupations as non-property owners. Private and social habits, health conditions and crime are such as to involve almost endless difficulties in the progress of the Negroes and their relation to the whites about them. In all phases of life the Negro female is unusually prominent. The church constitutes the basis for a large part of social activities, supplemented by numerous organizations and miscellaneous means of amusement. From every possible standpoint of Negro life, conditions are especially difficult for the training of children and for the children themselves. Segregated thus in distinctly different conditions from the larger body of whites their environment may be said to be a separate environment. Other aspects of the social condition of the Negroes are important but cannot be included in a brief summary of the principal facts of population and general environment. These aspects include all the details of physical and social conditions of the Negroes and their larger economic, social, and political relation to the whites. Each furnishes in itself a field for special research and this statement shows the further complexity of any selected problem of the Negro. What of the results of social and political maladjustment? What of crime and pauperism? What of the details of diet, rest, recreation, sex life, and health? How much depravity really exists? What of heredity, insanity, feeblemindedness and suicide? How far can the causes for conditions be ascertained? Again the entire question of domestic service and efficiency, of race contact and admixture, of the rights and wrongs of discrimination enter largely into the full consideration of the Negro in the city. The political aspect itself constitutes a large problem. Again how much is the Negro discriminated against by charitable and religious institutions? What social forces from without are active in his behalf? What social forces can he bring to bear from within to give him social control? Such are the questions that suggest themselves almost without number. To answer only a part of these must not be confused with the sum total, nor confused with any broader theoretical consideration of traits, tendencies, both physical and mental. . . .

What may be termed a second fallacy is the tendency to believe the problems of the Negroes can be relegated to certain positions or transferred into certain dimensions at will. While the problem of

the Negro does involve separate and distinctive principles, thus making it a large and unique problem, it is not, nor can it ever be segregated as an unrelated problem of the commonwealth or society.
To assume only immediate and local aspects of the situation does
not alter the far-reaching significance of the problems involved. The
larger problem of the future is the problem with which the relief of
present difficulties should be correlated so far as is possible. This
does not mean that the future can be exactly foretold, but that the
study of and public policy toward the problem should be such as to
establish certain broad evidences of the ability and equity of the
American commonwealth to deal with a problem at once difficult and
cosmopolitan.

Lynchings, Fears, and Folkways [1931]*

A reading of recent lynching records in "Lynchings and What They Mean," the report of the Southern Commission on the Study of Lynching, recalls two elementary points of emphasis in the late Professor Giddings' theory of the evolution and behavior of human society. One of these points of emphasis was that the second most important objective of all social education is the emancipation of the human mind from fear, the first objective being akin to it— namely, the development of faith and confidence in fellow-beings in the social order and in the immediate social environment through which growth and development are conditioned. "One of the most significant characteristics of civilization," he said, "quite distinct from barbarism and other savagery, is the diminution of fear." And again, when fear is rampant, "the whole life of man has dropped back to a lower level."

The other point of Giddings recalled by a reading of the records concerning lynching—this "deadly harm and deadly injury" to human society—relates to effective laws and their enforcement.

With all our government activities [wrote Professor Giddings], all our legislation, everything we think we are doing with the power and finality and precision of government and law, . . . we discover that we are not doing it at all, that we get no result from it whatever unless we get the backing, the cooperation, and the loyal fulfilment of our wishes in and through the folkways. Every time, the folkways will defeat the stateways if they are against the stateways. . . . I have been unable to find any instance in history in which a law, a governmental enactment, has won its way against the folkways.

* The Nation, 133 (December 30, 1931), pp. 719-20.

These are not only important considerations to note at this time but they reflect two basic explanations of the situation as revealed in this study of recent American lynchings, which clearly indicates the problem to be a Southern and an interracial one. These basic points of theory interpret also the tragic consequences of lynching to the South, to the white man, to the Negro, and to the nation. Approximately 95 per cent of all lynchings in the United States during the last five-year period were in the Southern States, and nearly 90 per cent of the lynchings were mob murders of Negroes. There has been a very marked decrease in lynchings from about 187 cases a year during the late nineties to an average of less than 17 in the five years preceding 1930; but with an increase to 21 cases in 1930, and again a decrease in 1931. In the decade before 1899 the South's proportion of lynchings was 82 per cent, and in the decade from 1919 to 1929 it was more than 95 per cent. The States having the largest number of lynchings were Mississippi, Georgia, Texas, and Louisiana, while the highest rate of lynching per ten thousand of Negro population was in Florida, Oklahoma, and Arkansas. In the States with dense Negro population the rate is least in the old-black-belt counties, and the Negro is most in danger in sparsely settled areas and in newly developed territory.

In many of the lynchings there has been doubt as to the guilt of the persons lynched. This was true of more than three-fifths of those lynched in 1931, and while no complete study has been made of the last thirty years, it is evident that something of the same tragic double travesty has appeared. In addition to this there have been frequent attempts on the part of whites to fasten crimes of their own on Negroes by false accusations or by impersonating Negroes at the time of committing the crime, especially of robbery. Some of the mobs displayed unbelievable extremes of savagery. Their behavior was reminiscent of primitive orgy, maniacal frenzy, and holy combat. Burning, cutting, shooting, dragging of the body through the streets, disfiguring and dismembering the victim—surely such actions are a vivid demonstration of "the whole life of man dropping back to a lower level."

What do these facts, and many others as well, mean as far as the phenomenon of lynching in the Southern States is concerned? We assume various causes and irritants, such as economic competition and depressions, racial animosities and prejudices, lack of education, ignorance and limited social experience, a high crime rate for both Negroes and whites, elements of frontier society, and general historical background. But these exist in other regions without producing the same tragic results. We turn naturally, then, to inquire into special regional elements which, merging with these other factors, have produced these results.

First we come to the elemental factor of fear with its many ramifications. It is not primarily that the South is traditionally afraid of Negro domination. It might seem logical to assign this as an important factor in those regions where the Negro predominates numerically and where conceivably he might become master of voting and of control. But these regions are not the only ones where lynchings occur or where the most barbaric anti-social conduct is found. What, therefore, are the other phases of the fear-force which condition the region for this particular sort of anti-social behavior? It seems apparent that the general fear which lies at the basis of the lynching phenomenon involves many other features. The Negro is troublesome to our peace of mind, though we do not quite know how or why. He is making a great deal of progress in many different ways. He may become a different sort of person from what we now think he ought to be. He may become an intimate part of our civilization and culture. He may really be our equal. We may really be wrong in our estimates of him. We fear what will happen in the future. He has to be kept in his place. We are not really afraid of the Negro himself. We are afraid of the prospect. Our thought of it is beyond the control of anything except our emotional conditioning. What are we going to do about it? We are uneasy. But we let things drift along, and when something happens, the easiest way is the way of violence and emotional debauch. And we struggle with fear and misgivings and rage that we should get into such a fix. And the Negro must pay.

And then we are afraid of what we have done. Our conscience is the conscience of a religious people. It is written that we must protect our women and our race. It is written that the Negro is a hewer of wood and drawer of water. Written or not written, we have done right and will stand by it and see that the sacred whiteness of our race shall not be violated. We are dangerous to those who oppose us. We are hostile to those who reason. We are afraid, and it makes us mad.

Of this fear the great body of people who are horrified at lynching are afraid. In our turn, we are afraid to protest. We are afraid to legislate. We are afraid to enforce law and liberty. We are afraid to teach. We are afraid to preach. Afraid of the public, afraid of the demagogue, and, deep down, rationalizing amid the fear of fears, we are afraid to do anything. There are practically no exceptions. Teacher, preacher, doctor, lawyer, businessman, farmer, laborer, artist and craftsman, writer of poems, dreamer of dreams—we are all afraid. Among the Negroes fear, a normal conditioning factor of life, becomes stark terror. The Negroes are afraid to do anything. Why shouldn't they be afraid?

What is being done about it? Why can't more be done about it? The fear which militates against vigorous protest and action is of course a product of the folkways. *"Every time,* the folkways will defeat the stateways if they are against the stateways." The special report on lynchings says: "The lynching method is a recognized custom in many communities. Hence, church members and civic leaders, instead of taking a determined stand against mob violence, often yield to it either by silence or by apology." What the outside observer does not see is that the folkways are so strong that the enforcement of law by local or State forces would mean literally civil war in the community. The folkways have ruled continuously since the days of reconstruction. Progress is being made but it is in proportion as the folkways are being changed by education, publicity, civic appeal, and courageous leadership. One-half of the Negroes who have been lynched never got to the law; one-fourth never got as far as the jail; and one-fourth were taken from custody of the jail. Many lynchings have been prevented by officials and citizens and these are evidence of changing folkways and the diminution of fear. For what has been done and the reasons that no more has been done, I quote the report:

Although a few lynchers have been indicted, tried, convicted, and sentenced, the courts usually deal with them in the most perfunctory fashion. Between 1922 and 1926 grand juries investigated seventeen lynchings and indicted 146 persons. In 1922 ten were sent to the penitentiary; the next year two; in 1924 five were given jail sentences; the next year five received suspended sentences, one was put in jail, and fifteen were given indeterminate sentences of six months on the chain gang to eight years in the penitentiary; in 1926 eight were given sentences of four years, and a ninth a life sentence.

Of 1930's twenty-one lynchings, investigations resulted in grand-jury indictments of lynchers in five instances, forty-nine persons being indicted. In only one case, that of the second lynching near Thomasville, Georgia, were the lynchers dealt with as murderers. Here, life sentences were given two young white men. Not one of the lynchers indicted at Marion, Walhalla, or Chickasha was convicted. To date (October 15, 1931) but two of the Sherman lynchers have been convicted, one for arson, the other for rioting, each with a two-year sentence.

Although it is doubtless a good omen that courts investigate some of the lynchings, and that from year to year a few indictments are brought against the participants, with an occasional sentence, thus far lynchers have been comparatively safe from indictment and conviction. This immunity has been due to the lack of a disapproving public opinion and to the fact that State authorities have seldom made effective efforts to prosecute in such cases.

A third regional element which seems to enter into the situation is that of the high homicide rate in the South and especially in certain cities and counties. The report of the Southern Commission on the Study of Lynching pointed out the seasonal fluctuations in lynchings, with July, August, and June showing the largest number. This coincides with H. C. Brearley's study of homicide in the South. Furthermore, many murders of Negroes have been committed in such a way as to lead some students of the problem to classify them as in reality lynchings. There are those who affirm that one reason for the low rate of lynchings in the densely settled Negro areas is the custom there of murder by one or more individuals rather than by mob action, which is deemed unnecessary. The rate of murder reflects a lack of respect for human life and personality which gives rise to the accusation that murder is in the way of receiving institutional sanction in the South. The general "unwritten law," its special application to the Negro, and other "justifiable" grounds for homicide challenge the South to take stock anew of its prospects and tendencies.

Lynching attains none of the ends for which it has been defended. It proves no superiority. It clarifies no issues. It brings no happiness. It adds nothing to the richness of human living or the development of social personality. It accentuates devastating fear. It sets the folk-ways over against the stateways in lawless revolt. It cheapens human life and lessens respect for human liberty and personality. It defeats the ends of justice. It violates all the better traditions of Southern honor and ideals. It sets the strong brutally over against the weak. It negates the South's claim for excellence and genius in the science of politics. Its cost is frightful in money and in men. It drains off energies and resources. It blackens the reputation of every State. It cripples a race and handicaps a region. It intensifies racial animosities, isolates a section, sets people against people, and retards a wholesome integration of national culture.

3. Race Relations and Social Change

The Negro in 1950: A Forecast [1939]*

In the discussion of so important and so challenging a theme as the position of the Negro in the American social order in 1950, it must be clear that we have in mind more of promise and prospect than of prophecy; more of opportunity, needs, deficiencies, and the will to do than of pure prediction; and more of the realistic facing of facts than of that which tends primarily towards the Utopian picture. Nevertheless, there is no reason why we should not project boldly upon the screen a picture commensurate with the ideals and potentialities of the American scene and some estimate "of conditions which must obtain in order to achieve it."

The realistic approach to such a projected picture will somehow seek to ask and to answer some such questions as these: In terms of the American scene, what will be major assumptions of our civilization which will approximate the best possible attainable position of the Negro in the social order as we enter upon the second half of the 20th century? Compared with this, what are the realities of the society which we now have and what are its limitations? Next, what will it take to bridge the distance between what we want and what we now have? Then, how may we go about getting what it takes to bridge this distance? And, finally, what are next steps and the best procedures?

It seems to me that the assumption of a notable ten years, from 1940 to 1950, in American development in respect to the position of the Negro in the social order is a realistic one justified by both dilemma and promise. For here at the turn of the mid-century, we

* Adapted from "The Position of the Negro in the American Social Order of 1950," *Journal of Negro Education*, VIII (July 1939), 587-94. Reprinted by permission.

may well hope to integrate plans and approach new frontiers through the orderly process of cultural development. For instance, we can utilize a sort of super-census or social inventory of the nation which will be much needed and may be attainable at that time; we may realize upon whatever may be gained through the concept and practice of realistic social planning, American style; we may realize upon the mistakes and the tragedies of errors of race persecution in other lands; and we may realize on the great American characteristics of high motivation and celebration at certain stated periods. Our assumption that America will know by 1950 more of her new frontiers and will be well ready to start on new epochs implies both a timeliness and an urgency that this fundamental question of minority people shall have an increasingly natural and realistic development in the projected picture.

More especially, since greater numbers of Negro people now reside and will continue for sometime to reside in the South; and since the South and the nation are everywhere taking stock of how regional problems of economy and culture may be reintegrated into the national fabric to the enrichment of the South and the nation, it is especially important and timely that this projected program of the region shall assume the natural realities and contingencies which inhere in the Negro's position in its social order.

Again, it is of the greatest importance for the southern program to be well under way by 1950 for the reasons that unless this is true there will be irreparable loss to the South and the nation, and many of the techniques and procedures now available for a richer development of the South may be outmoded by that time. In view of the South's great deficiencies in both production and consumption of many farm commodities and of the lack of purchasing power basic to health, welfare, and prosperity, the assumption seems justified that the South might undertake an almost maximum production for a ten-year period without entailing the usual economic surpluses, provided its programs specialize upon consumption and distribution and the equalizing of its achievements more nearly with its resources. And since a chief trend of the Negro is towards the cities, thus pointing to a Negro-urban culture instead of a rural one, unless special programs are projected, it must be clear how important this ten-year reconstruction of the agricultural South is to the position of the Negro in the Southern social order as well as in that of the nation at large.

Now on the basis of these several premises, to what extent are we justified in the assumption of attaining by 1950 the desired characteristics of the social order with reference to the Negro's part and parcel in it? If we may be permitted to set up a series of general assumptions which will serve as premises for the purpose of coming to our final conclusions, I venture five such assumptions.

The first assumption is that we shall continue in America the general program of progress which has so signally marked the development of the American Negro, his culture, and his position in the social order. This means not only the extraordinary progress that the Negro himself has made in all phases of life, but also that orderly progress through which a great many admirable things have happened which a short time ago it was predicted could not happen. Thus, the record of achievement in education, public health, politics, economic development, interracial cooperation, and reduction of lynching. We must continue to take caution and to work against economic and social injustices, mob actions and exploitation, and provide realistic programs for attainable political development, culture representation, and educational advance. All of this assumes continuing normal and expanded programs of education, promotion, and action, but it seems to me we must go much further.

Our second approach, therefore, is a rather bold one, but a natural and logical assumption by the American people, and in particular by the Southern people, of a more realistic *fellowship* between the Negro people and the white people as our normal societal processes, development, and expansion continue. This means a diminution of the naïve arguments and quarrels about opportunity, equality, and justice, and the forthright *assumption* that equality, opportunity, and justice are already inherent in both the American democracy and in the capacity of the Negro. In other words, if there is developed a realistic sense of *fellowship* in all our processes, all these other products will be added in the logical processes which follow. Or, to put it differently, if we can attain the desired ends, it can be done only in this way.

A third assumption is like unto the first, namely, that in so far as action and achievements are concerned we naturally *assume* an increasingly larger *participation* by the Negro in those normal societal arrangements through which opportunity and justice are attained. It is inconceivable that these millions of Negro children and youth, representative of the most attractive personalities on this earth, shall not participate more and more in the normal work of education, politics, industry, the community. Here, again, we substitute logical assumptions of what is right and normal for arguments and conflict over irrational traditions.

A fourth assumption is that in the American social order there will be increasingly an emphasis upon race *differentials* rather than *differences,* the sub-assumption, . . . being that the earlier verdict of organic and composite race differences was wrong. Manifestly, this assumption is one which attempts a more effective technique of race relations than we have had. It must be clear that there is a great and cumulative mass of racial differentials due to explainable causes and often so numerous and powerful as to appear in reality to be fundamental differences. This distinction, therefore, between differences and differentials is of the utmost importance and assumes at once that races instead of being inherently different are *group products* of differentials due to the cumulative power of the physical and folk-regional cultural environment. Here, again, we propose to substitute working assumptions based upon adequate scientific conclusions for the tedious and tiring arguments about the question.

The approach to the further study of the premise is simple enough. There are on every hand numerous differentials in the environment, living standards, treatment, cultural backgrounds, which, when continued long enough, become powerful *mores* wrought out through cumulative *folkways,* such that they assume the proportions of tradition, authority, facts. It must be clear that the approach to the readjustment will be found in the elimination of separate units of differentials. . . .

A fifth assumption is that in spite of the psychological effectiveness of assuming these great fundamentals, after they have been accepted by leaders on the basis of facts, there must still be action, strategy, and hard work in the implementing of our assumptions and plans. The premise here is that more and more we shall minimize argument and debate about the old *folkways* and *mores* of race and shall introduce more and more the new social *technicways* which come through progress and science, education, government, and invention and which transcend and supplant in the modern technological world the older *folkways* and *mores*. This means that instead of conforming to the older inherited mores, often of fine and noble lineage, the new social order will provide *ways* and *means* of doing the thing that needs to be done in harmony with what is right and new and sound. Here again we substitute reality and action for words and symbols and shibboleths.

Now let us examine the situation to see to what extent we have realistic evidence to support these premises, upon which a more mature developing of the position of the Negro in the social order may be attained. . . .

Four general and international factors appear to make for these changing assumptions on the part of the American people. One is the general conclusion of the psychologists, sociologists, and anthropologists that evidence of inferior and superior races does not justify the world's previous appraisal and action in relation to races. We have already indicated the significance of the facts here. This factor, communicated to all races, contributes to the dark races' as well as to the white races' attitudes. A second factor has been the extension of learning and technology to all races and their consequent increasing use of common tools of economic and political development. A third factor is the increasing tendency toward racial and national consciousness. The fourth is the rapid rise and increasing articulation of the American Negro in contradistinction, on the one hand, to his earlier status, and, on the other, in relation to his proportionate part in Southern life. These factors, of course, have wrought a commensurate influence upon the attitudes of the white peoples and will continue increasingly to do so.

We have pointed out often the fact that predictions with references to the Negro in the United States have been peculiarly unreliable in the past. There is, however, at the present time a different situation from that which has existed in any of the previous decennial periods. The four basic factors upon which prediction must be made and plans developed seemed to be: First, the ratio of Negro population to the total population has been gradually decreasing and the experts estimate that this decline will be continuous until the maximum stabilization of population may occur. Second, the Negro population is being diffused throughout the nation, so that the problem is national rather than southern. Here, the Negroes often complain that the North is "going southern." The third factor is the changing nature of the Negro population as it relates to biological and cultural heritage. That is, there is growing up a "Brown America," a product of both selection and racial diffusion. The fourth element is found in the changing social character of the Negro as he expands his activities and increases his cultural stature to higher levels. The picture is such as to justify the conclusion that, if the Negro be given a fair opportunity with his remarkable powers of adaptation and his attractive personality, he will become increasingly one of the most important of the basic elements of American culture.

One of the most significant changes and trends that has come about within recent years bearing upon the reality of these new assumptions is what Dr. Charles S. Johnson has spoken of as the shift of focus:

. . . from the Negro as the South's economic problem number one, to a recognition of the complex of economic problems themselves as the South's major ill. This new focus presents the Negro problem as a phase of the South's broad economic and cultural problems. In spite of many acute psychological aspects of race contact and relations it is becoming increasingly evident to Southerners that the race problems are basically economic, and can only be soundly remedied by approaching them as such.

The sweep of this trend is indicated by the action of the Commission on Interracial Cooperation which has voted to expand this Commission into a Council on Southern Regional Development if it can be adequately supported. Such a Council would feature four points of tension in the South as race development and race relations, agricultural development and conservation, industrial development and security, political development and public administration. Thus, it is assumed over and over again that the Negro is part and parcel of all of these and, by the same token, each and every phase of the South's culture and economy implies its commensurate Negro participation.

It is important to note certain other fundamental facts. First, we must appraise continuously the influence of diffusion in the nation. There are three other regions than the Southeast in which more than a million Negroes reside. These exercise influence not only in their regions but back home in the South. Second, the Negro outside the South is almost wholly an urban inhabitant as compared to his rural heritage in the South. This is changing the isolation pattern and, as Dr. Johnson points out, is affecting the whole population. Third, the Negro has, as already assumed, in parts of the nation the balance of voting power in politics and has transferred from the Republican to the Democratic Party.

There is a rather profound situation which I think is usually over-looked with reference to the slow but sure evolution of the Negro race in the United States through the efficacy of its own great folk culture, in which the Negro *folkways* function within the *stateways* of the white nation. That is, whether in the rural South or in the urban North, the Negro survives and adapts and adjusts himself in spite of and in the midst of both his circumstantial and societal pressures. The poorer among the white people in the agrarian South are crushed more by the *stateways* of the economic and political order than are the Negroes, who, in spite of this and in the midst of it, continue their folk culture in which the Negro is making progress, and in many cases the whites tend to regress. This same great folk culture and the imple-mentation of *folkways* within the circumscribing state society is reflected also in the development of a high Negro culture and of pro-fessional opportunities and achievements. By the verdicts of all cultural history, this sort of thing must win an increasingly greater place for the Negro in the social order.

Another development of great significance, supporting to a con-siderable extent our assumptions, is the increasing emphasis upon regional-national instead of sectional-local attitudes and actions with reference to the Negro. A specific illustration of a real regional-national approach as opposed to the earlier narrow sectional may be found in the upbuilding of Negro institutions of higher learning in the South, in which southern institutions are being developed through inter-regional cooperation and aid, approximating mutual satisfaction to the South, the North, the Negroes, and the whites, as nearly as is possible under the circumstances. Thus the most eminent Negro men of science and letters in the nation have come to Southern Negro colleges to develop a new era. This new educational statesmanship is a maturer development than the earlier limitations set by the South, in which it sought little education for the Negro, on the one hand, and the missionary spirit of the philanthropists from the North, on the other. It also represents the best thought and effort of the Negro race, whose personnel, skill, and training are being brought more and more to bear upon the problems in hand. A similar illustration might be cited in the case of public and elementary education in many of the Southern States, in which such out-of-the-region funds as Rosenwald, Slater, and Jeanes have contributed to a richer regional culture and a broader inter-regional contact.

More noteworthy in recent years have been the development of such great Negro institutions as Fisk, Atlanta University, Dillard University, Tuskegee, and the others, and the increasing virility and effectiveness of many of the state institutions under the direction of distinguished Negro college and university presidents. Not only the best of the North and of the South, the white and Negro, are being cumulatively assumed in this work, but an extremely fine fellowship and esteem between educators of both races are being developed. There is no segment of the American people who will not esteem, admire, and follow to a great extent the brilliant and wholesome leadership of, let us say, a baker's dozen Negro college and university presidents.

Another more recent development is that of the application of Negroes for admission to the higher brackets of education and a United States Supreme Court decision as witness to the merits and reality of the case. This, again, is an inevitable and logical development. It is in line with the tenets of American democracy. The South is an increasingly important and hopeful region of the nation. It is not possible that the South can forever go on being different in many fundamental aspects of life, and it cannot maintain an isolationist policy. The South, like other regions or nations, must seek to find an adequate and reasonable solution of its major problems and crises. Surely no harm can come from facing the facts and seeing what they mean.

There are, however, many kinds of facts. Among the simplest of facts in the first series which we may examine are those relating to the Negro and his facilities for higher education. Concerning the Negro himself, there can be no doubt that individuals have shown, both by actual achievement and by tests, capacity to carry on in the upper brackets of education and culture, and they have shown furthermore a great deal of evidence of potential extension of their present achievement. The second set of facts here is that the Negroes do not have in any degree equal opportunity for higher education. Manifestly, then, here are facts, basic to a situation which cannot be enduring, calling for fair and equitable adjustment. Manifestly, here is a situation in which we do not need to set state against federal judgment, white against black, but rather the common-sense American assumptions of democracy stripped of the specialized race *folkways* and *mores*.

Yet, it is of the utmost importance to recognize the reality of the facts of race prejudice. . . . I have often pointed out that our problem is essentially, therefore, a societal problem of racial adjustment and a social problem of race relations. Adjustments, as we have pointed out, must be made on the basis of facts; yet facts are of two sorts, the one of race qualities and capacities and experience and the other of race prejudice and culture heritage. These constitute the factual basis of reality.

It is much more important for us frankly to assume race prejudices and understand them than to talk loftily, to satirize, and argue about their wrongness, . . .

Now, manifestly, we need something more than and in addition to the older, worn-out, stereotyped arguments and denunciations against ignorance, "crackers," morons, and that sort of thing, in so far as an appraisal and attack upon the white South is concerned. For these conditionings are almost literally physical and cannot be changed. Manifestly, therefore, the supreme approach is the substitution of ways and means coming within the framework of realistic planning, in which men everywhere assume that in the new transportation the Negro must have his right part; in the new redistribution of opportunity, of course, the Negro must have his part; in the new agriculture and economic arrangements, of course, provisions must be made for his adequate participation. And so for the newly equipped Negro citizen and leader in cultural opportunities, in political opportunities, and in all others, of course, any plans that are made will assume that he must have his pro-rata position in the social order.

This is what we mean when we speak of modern social *technicways* as transcending the old *folkways* and *mores*. The older *folkways* and *mores* are facts soundly grounded in traditional, racial, and cultural backgrounds. The newer *technicways* will become facts well grounded in the newer backgrounds of science, technology, skill, government, and the new reaches of democracy. In scores and scores of communities the Farm Resettlement Administration has set up with new opportunities many a Negro farmer whose chance is the pride of the community, the state, and the region. So, too, because of many of the trends towards planning for a better balanced economy, because of our new skills in communication, transportation, management, organization, development of new and old industries and other phases of modern technology, the premise is that we may transfer to the new order on the assumptions, on the one hand, of the Negro's capacity and, on the other, of his normal and natural fellowship and participation in the social order. On these assumptions, it seems to me we may look forward confidently to the ten years, 1940-50, as not only the supreme testing ground of American democracy and of American skill, but also as an era genuinely and realistically offering the greatest promise of any decade in the history of the nation.

The South in Crisis [1943]*

This is part of the story of the crisis of the South and of the Negro in the United States of America in the early 1940's—years of war tension and of another prospective post-war tragic era. It is a part of the story, therefore, of a national crisis as well. It is called *Race and Rumors of Race* because the measure and nature of the extraordinary crisis were reflected with such vividness in the mass of race rumors that swept, flood-like, upon us in the major areas of white and Negro relationships in the South, and thence as reflected in the rising tide of rumors and tensions in the hinterlands. They flooded even such cosmopolitan centers as the Nation's capital like flood waters suddenly released by a bomber's blast.

*   *   *   *   *   *

One of the first tasks was to explain why the crisis had developed so rapidly; why there was such sudden flare-up of emotions, tensions, and conflicts; and why, in both the South and the rest of the Nation, it so quickly assumed major proportions in the early war years. An understanding of the backgrounds and the immediate incidence of change and of the speed of change was essential to a preview of the crisis and what might be done about it. For, repeat and repeat, it was never a simple regional problem. And because it was a southern problem, an American problem, and because it was of the essence of world progress, it was therefore more difficult

* Adapted from *Race and Rumors of Race: Challenge to American Crisis* (Chapel Hill: The University of North Carolina Press, 1943), Chap. I, p. 3; Chap. II, pp. 13-21.

and would neither be isolated by the South nor "solved" by the Nation.

There had been, of course, a number of events, situations, and incidents which had accelerated the sweep of rumors and tensions, chiefest of which was the incidence of war with its attendant demands and opportunities and its philosophy of global democracy. These had all been logical and inevitable products of the time, reflecting the cumulative power and sweep of a logical long-time evolutionary process. While an adequate cataloguing and understanding of the mass of war episodes and influences constituted a first step, it was the portraiture of the reaction of the South and the explanation of the folk psychology involved that were essential, first, to understanding the situation and, second, to directing next steps. And by the same token the folk psychology of the rest of the Nation and of the Negro was part and parcel of the total picture.

A major element in the crisis was found in the South's vivid reaction to the total situation. More specifically was the role of reaction to outside criticism and war efforts to force her hand in making radical change of policies. Over against the outside verdict of denunciation, the South was thinking all along that it had made great progress toward better race relations; that it had attained a good deal of unity; and that perhaps it was finally on its way toward such interracial cooperation as would lead to the best possible adjustment.

There was, for instance, great pride in the Negro leaders and educators of distinction whose fellowship and participation in regional development were so highly valued. There were common gatherings and conferences between leaders of both races. There were meetings between the white and Negro college youth. Many things were being done, as a matter of fact, in racial fellowship which a short time ago would not have been considered. There was less and less violence and more and more inclination to increase the Negro's participation in all matters economic and cultural.

Furthermore, there were increases in appropriations for Negro education, often as much as fifty to one hundred percent. Teachers' salaries were more and more being equalized and special efforts were being made to develop Negro institutions of higher learning and to give the Negro increasingly greater opportunities in professional equipment. There had been such great strides in the reduction of lynching and mob action that already the hope was being expressed that a new era was in the making.

Then, suddenly, as it appeared to the South, there was a flood of criticism, denunciation, demand. Prospective measures of coercion were proposed which seemed to assume that the South was doing something new and quite bad in its whole pattern of biracial culture. It was as if there came the assumption that the South was initiating backward policies in which it boldly challenged the rest of the world in new reaches of injustice and discrimination. Instead, therefore, in the light of a normal and logical period of development, of being credited with substantial measures of progress, the South found itself, in wartimes, reflecting, relatively, retrogression in comparison with what was demanded and in comparison with the commitments of the American people to global democracy. And the South, hoping to achieve some measure of united patriotism, felt that the war crisis was no time to split the Nation again and to foment bitterness and violence.

Once again, it was as if the rest of the Nation, in particular the publicists, the intelligentsia, and the youth of other regions had suddenly discovered the structure of the South's biracial culture. They kept saying, "What is this new thing the South is doing to the Negro? What are we going to do about the South's treatment of the Negro?" Yet, it is not surprising that the new generation of the Nation, largely ignorant of the earlier backgrounds of national development, should know little or nothing of the tragedies of the South. There grew up quickly, therefore, a remarkable concern to save the South, to free the South, to take the occasion of war to purify American democracy. It was one of the most dramatic episodes in the long history of America's idealism.

What the South had done was, of course, nothing new. It was an old story except that the South was of the impression that it had actually made many concessions and had grown in stature through certain logical, advancing stages of development. The South was assuming, as it always had, a continuation of the economy and culture of a biracial caste culture and therefore appraised its progress as new gains. Who ever thought the South would abandon segregation anyhow? Hadn't the issue been settled over and over again? Was there not a powerful heritage of trial and error to make this sure? Had not every community or group of communities in the old days lived in the shadow of fear and in the relative disgrace of some racial tragedy? Was this to be done over again?

Yet because of the war and the revitalizing of America's ideology of democracy and freedom in global war, and because of the new discovery of the South by the Nation and consequently a new level of irresponsible agitation, even with the progress that the South had made, its culture economy reflected to its critics glaring inequalities that appeared neither right nor necessary. And even though there would be no inclination on the part of many southerners to deny the great distance between what the South was doing and what needed to be done, nevertheless the psychology of the sudden impact of criticism and accusation, when the South had thought it was going forward, was the key to the speed and intensity of reaction. The South, too, needed sympathy and understanding, the people thought, instead of denunciation and misunderstanding.

And here the South was following its standard folkways of resentment of outside criticism and Federal coercion. They were back again in united defense against outside aggression. "If outsiders," they began to react again, "would let us alone, we would work out our problem." "Mrs. Roosevelt and the New Deal," they would say, "are trying to make us discard the pattern of segregation." From the governors to the common man the refrain was that the southern people were quite capable of running their own government and would continue to do so. In the light of American experience, this was, of course, nothing new. Yet the South might very well have replied, "Well, of course, the rest of the Nation is still trying to make the South over; who said they were not? What of it? From their viewpoint, why wouldn't they? That, too, is an old story and we will not let it get us excited again." But that was not the way of the South, and so here again was basic soil for the multiplied rumors and rifts of a threatening crisis.

And then the Negro portion of the biracial culture was proceeding to assume attitudes and to initiate action in accordance with this new and radical freedom, whereas the white part of the South was not only not acquiescing but was finding a new unity in resisting, to the end that they went to extremes reminiscent of the old days of reconstruction. They did things and talked and listened to rumors that to the outsider could not be interpreted in terms of any logical and reasonable explanation. And because the rest of the Nation did not understand and because their verdict was primarily a "group" judgment, they advocated partial and unrealistic solutions, often advocating action without estimating the costs that might follow.

One of the first tasks, therefore, essential to the understanding of the situation and preliminary to the cataloguing and interpretation of what happened was to sense the realistic, living credo of the South with reference to the Negro and its relation to what might be called a symbolic credo of the rest of the Nation at large. The understanding of a folk psychology, which was committed to the defense of this credo at any cost, by the same token, was a first essential.

For, against this well-nigh universal southern credo came assumptions and demands that appeared to the South to be about as near the complete opposite as it would be possible to find. In substance, here was a sudden demand for the South, long conditioned in the Negro complex and southern loyalties, bottomed in the long heritage of race prejudice and cultural evolution, to change its whole structure of race relations overnight. And, equally vivid, from the outside regions was reflected what seemed an unreasonableness of the South in not being willing to conform to the larger American credo of democracy and the American dream of equality.

Now the bare statement of an organic credo, which would startle even most southerners, appeared crude and harsh. So, here again, it was important to repeat and repeat the question: Was it true that the South believed these things about the Negro? Or, if not, now that it was put down in black and white as the composite feeling and folkways of the South, what part of it was *not* true? Of course, no southerner ever wrote such a credo for himself and no one ever heard a southerner parading his credo as such. Yet, tested and checked in private life, in religious attitudes, in politics and law, and in the defense mechanisms of the region, in the great body of common folk, was this the South's credo and was it the heart of the whole drama?

Without an understanding of the South's organic feelings and beliefs it was not possible to explain such violent reactions to episodes and experiences which appeared to outsiders as mere commonplace behavior. Keeping in mind the variations of a composite credo and ratio of different groups of southerners who might dissent, and also the possible comparison with what people in the other regions held, it seemed important to ask again and again whether the white South would face the issue of its beliefs. Here, again, as always, there were paradox and contrast. While one group of leaders would protest the unfairness to the South of the presentation of such a credo, another large group would seem to say, "Sure, of course, that's what we believe. Why mention it? Everybody knows the Negro is just a Negro." Yet it was in many ways a startling credo that seemed to be the heart of the crisis. It seemed possible to count a score of units in the total and to ask again, Was it true that the South believed:

1. That the Negro was a Negro and always would be that and nothing more.

2. That, being a Negro, and different from the white man he therefore could not be expected ever to measure up to the white man's standards of character and achievement.

3. That, not being capable of full achievement and being of an inferior race, it was logical that he should be kept in an inferior place, which is "his place."

4. It followed that this was a white man's country, and that therefore the white man would dominate in about whatever way he chose. Laws and resolutions only made matters worse.

5. Political equality and equal educational opportunities, if given to the Negro, would lead to social equality and the mixture of races, which was contrary to all the major premises of the southern way of life.

6. Furthermore, political and social equality would lead to the domination of the white South by the Negroes and their northern supporters.

7. Discrimination and segregation, therefore, were necessary to keep the Negro in his place and protect the interests and integrity of the whites.

8. It was assumed, from this point on, by the best of the South, that the Negro, when kept within his rightful sphere, should not be treated unkindly or unjustly.

9. That he should be given fair trials and protected by law.

10. That he should be paid a living wage. Since, however, his

standards of living were lower, he could live on less than a white man could.

11. That if given too much pay, he would waste the money and get out of bounds to his own harm as well as to the detriment of the South.

12. That the Negro was by nature inclined to criminal behavior, partly because of his animal nature and partly because of his irresponsibility and immorality.

13. Moreover, the Negro was better off in the South where he was "understood" and where his best friends were.

14. That, while as a race the Negro was inferior and generally untrustworthy, as an individual he was often honest, loyal, lovable, capable, and even talented and distinguished. Yet this was the exception.

15. That his music, his carefree, patient disposition, his homely philosophy added interest and color and richness to the culture of the South.

16. That recognition should be given to the Negro for having made outstanding progress in many fields since being freed from slavery.

17. Yet the Negro in general was not capable of taking great responsibility or of assuming leadership.

18. That no self-respecting southerner would work under Negro supervision.

19. That if the New Dealers, northerners, and reformers would let the South and the Negro alone, peaceful adjustments of the race problem could be made.

20. That those who were inviting the Negro to discontent and trying to force his participation in industry and politics on an equal basis were fomenting race riots which would hurt both whites and Negroes and the total Nation in the long run.

21. And that, finally, this was not a debatable issue.

There were, of course, various self-evident facts with reference to such a credo. In the first place, there were some variations from the norm as indicated in this credo. Yet, for all practical purposes this made little difference, since it was the mode of southern attitude and folkways which gave rise to points of tension, conflict, and the like. This credo was presented, not because there was anything new in it, but rather in order to highlight and make more vivid the folkways of the South concerning the Negro. Such a bold and bald statement of a credo was so vivid that it was perhaps surprising to southerners and, therefore, might go a long way toward explaining why the other regions of the Nation have rediscovered a level of their own national life with which they were either not acquainted or which they had forgot. The credo was in such complete contradistinction to the urgings and demands that were being made on the South in the name of war and freedom and Americanism that the resulting tension and conflict were easily explainable. It had to be repeated often that the understanding of the realistic folkways of the South was necessary also to explain the reaction of so many people from other regions to what seemed to them arbitrary, unreasonable, and entirely unfair attitudes and procedures in the South with reference to the simplest, most common, everyday, reasonable expectations of the Negro for life, liberty, and the pursuit of happiness.

That is, unless the full meaning of the southern folkways concerning the Negro was clearly understood, most of the incidents, stories, and happenings that had been basic to recent race tension and conflict would themselves be unreasonable and unexplainable. On the contrary, to the South, sensing its concept of the biracial society, what had happened seemed so simple and logical as to need no other explanation than that it had happened.

The Romance of the Eleanor Clubs [1943]*

Perhaps the most remarkable of all the rumors were those relating to the Eleanor Clubs and to the activities and attitude of the First Lady of the Land. These rumors abounded in all their richness and variety wherever southerners abode. Not only in the South but in New York, in Los Angeles, in Chicago, vivacious southerners told the stories as they were told to them. The Eleanor Clubs struck deep at the heart of the South's whole domestic home economy. Basic causes were found in the opportunity for Negro women to work at higher wages, their organization into clubs and branches of organized labor, and the subsequent folk psychology of the South. That the Eleanor Club rumor seemed to reflect the "weakest" and most unfair perhaps of all the folkways of "servants," makes it all the more important as a chronicle of the era. The fact that the folkways of survival here were so strong as to lead the South to forget its manners was again evidence of crisis.

The slogan of the Eleanor Clubs was nearly always a variation of "A white woman in every kitchen by 1943." There were many variations of the same theme, and samplings were offered in abundance because of the richness of their details. Thus, from Mississippi it was reported that an Eleanor Club was found by the sheriff. "My cousin told me that the sheriff went down there and told those 'niggers' that they'd better get back to work, or else." In Georgia, they had heard

* From *Race and Rumors of Race: Challenge to American Crisis* (Chapel Hill: The University of North Carolina Press, 1943), Chap. IX, pp. 73-80.

a special version of the Eleanor Clubs as the "Royal House of Eleanor."

From Georgia it was reported that when an army camp was started "in my town and cooks were asked to cook for the soldiers, receiving as much as $15.00 a week, many housewives decided that this was a project of the Eleanor Clubs to get Negroes out of domestic service, and to give them higher pay." "Here was the way it was: 'Why, all the Negroes are getting so "uppity" they won't do a thing. I hear the cooks have organized Eleanor Clubs and their motto is: A white woman in every kitchen by Christmas.' " This was from North Carolina, where it was also heard that "all the colored maids at a hotel joined Eleanor Clubs and walked out in a body one day because their pay and hours did not suit."

Two major points of emphasis in the Eleanor Club stories were loyalty to the First Lady and her loyalty to the Negroes to the end that they would have better opportunities. Thus, a Negro girl left during the middle of a meal which she was helping to serve because one of the guests had said something she didn't like and "she had been instructed by the Eleanor Club to leave whenever she was insulted." So, too, a very common rumor was that a maid must resign whenever anyone spoke disparagingly of either the First Lady or the President. From Florida came the version that when a Negro applied for a job she first asked if the head of the house liked Eleanor Roosevelt. If not, she replied that she belonged to the Eleanor Club and couldn't work for her.

Another level of the Eleanor Club activities had to do with their influence. One story from North Carolina had it that by the time of the next presidential election the Eleanor Clubs would have enough strength and power to control the election. But always the heart of the situation was in the scarcity of help. Thus, it was said that in a community of two hundred families, who originally had cooks, but two of these families had a cook at that time. "This Eleanor Club is spreading like wildfire all over the South and their motto is 'a white woman in every kitchen.' " And again, "Eleanor Clubs are stirring up troubles that never should have arisen. Clubs are making the Negroes discontented, making them question their status." This was from Georgia, but again the crux of the trouble was reflected in the North Carolina verdict that before the appearance of the Eleanor

Club story, back in the early spring, probably in March, 1942, the community buzzed with the story that outside organizers were organizing the colored maids; that they were going to ask for a twelve dollar a week minimum in the wealthier residential section, and eight dollars a week in the middle-class residence area.

Still another type of story reflected the trend toward specialized labor. One woman's maid stopped bringing in any wood for the fire because the other maids in the neighborhood had "jumped on" her and told her that she could not belong to the Eleanor Club and bring in wood. That was not her job, and her employer would have to hire someone else to do the bringing in of the wood or she would have to do it herself. Likewise, the maids refused to wash any windows—that was a man's work—and the maids were to do only the lightest work. Again, a friend reported that "a friend had a maid who had been with them for fifteen years. She joined the Eleanor Club and told her mistress that she would have to leave as she could not work for less than a certain sum, which sum was much more than my friend was paying or could afford to pay."

That was a Florida story, and from Florida came also one telling of a woman who went to the "quarters to see why her maid had not showed up to work. She blew her horn in front of the cottage—no response. She could see there was someone in the place so went to the door. The colored woman was lying down, but said, no, she wasn't sick. When asked why she hadn't come to work, she said, 'because there had been a meeting of the Eleanor Club where they had been told to demand more wages.' The woman told her she would gladly have paid her more if wages had gone up but wanted to know why she hadn't come to tell her. That also had been forbidden. Also, the Club ruler had told them not to answer any more horn calls from a car."

The First Lady was held responsible for these developments and more, although she had appeared in very few towns. Yet a common saying was that in nearly every town in which she had occasion to speak, an Eleanor Club was formed by the Negroes soon thereafter. "They said maids walked out any time of the day with the excuse of going to an Eleanor's meeting."

A variation from South Carolina had it that "a Negro girl came in the front door of a white woman's house. The white woman asked why she came in the front door instead of the back door. The Negro's reply was that she had joined the Eleanor Club and she was supposed to come in the front door instead of the back." In Georgia, it was related that "Eleanor Clubs had drawn up a Black List of white employers and that several Negro servants had stopped working for people on this list. So, also, it was reported that Eleanor Clubs made a practice of investigating their employers and if they found a lack of sympathy for or had a dislike of Mrs. Roosevelt they quit their job and placed the employers' names on a Black List."

A Florida inquiry reported that "since the war started the Negro men had higher incomes and they could afford to have a higher standard of living. Therefore, their wives and children no longer had to cook for the whites. The Negroes had formed unions demanding higher wages and working conditions, so that it was almost impossible to find any help at all. It was thought that the First Lady had a hand in trying to organize the Negroes. It was also rumored in one community that the Eleanor Clubs intended to take an educational grievance to court and that they had money enough to 'fight it out.' It was reported that the money was given to the Eleanor Club by Mrs. Roosevelt who received it from one of her public lectures. They had, it was rumored, more money than one of the larger white high schools had for its entire budget that year."

Sometimes there was more comedy than pathos in the fantastic aspects of the Eleanor Club. A prominent businessman who had visited most of the States actually professed to believe there was some relation between the Eleanor Clubs and the zoot-suit young Negroes and their doings.

And in Alabama, they said that "whenever you saw a Negro wearing a wide-brimmed hat with a feather in it, you knew he was wearing the sign of the Eleanor Club." In North Carolina there was a story going around that the number and size of feathers in the new zoot-suit hats being worn by Negroes determined their position in the Eleanor Club. The larger the feather, the greater the number, and the brighter the color were symbols of rating. It was a long way from this to the other Alabama report that the Negroes called Mrs. Roosevelt the "Great White Angel" or the "Great White Mother," and made her sponsor for their Eleanor Clubs.

The intensity of the atmosphere in which the Eleanor Club rumors had grown up was indicated by the response of a very wealthy southerner who said that he would be willing to contribute substantially to a civic fund if it would stop the Roosevelts. His chief complaint was that his large organization could no longer work Negro women on the farm! From Florida came the story that "a gentleman of considerable wealth and position made this remark during a conversation, 'Thanks to Mrs. Roosevelt and the Eleanor Clubs, we're liable to have a race riot here in the South. Mrs. Roosevelt is poking her nose into a situation about which she knows nothing.'" A Louisiana householder reported that her cook at home had been attending meetings of the local Eleanor Club. "She said they promised the Negro to raise his standards of living as high as that of the whites as soon as the war was over. She spoke of the First Lady as Eleanor this, Eleanor that, and Eleanor the other. There were other rumors to the effect that Negroes in several places had said that they believed after the war there would not only be social equality but that the Negro would be the superior race. They believed that Eleanor Roosevelt would put them on this level."

From the mass of rumors, apparently abundant in all the Southern States, it was possible to learn not only the general theme but also the "rules" of the Eleanor Clubs. When it was recalled that the rumor was prevalent in most northern cities, especially in Detroit, it was not surprising that there were variations. Nevertheless, there was generally a common thread running through most of the stories, with the exception of the reference to the zoot suit. "White women were to be in the kitchen by Christmas, 1942, or January, 1943. Negro women were to be out of the kitchen. There must be more pay, more privileges, less hours. There must be no disparaging remarks about either Mrs. Roosevelt or the President. And Negroes must have equal opportunities with whites."

It was clear, of course, that the original Eleanor Clubs were not Eleanor Clubs at all, but new ventures in organization and talk. From these efforts and the accelerated demand for workers and especially Negro women workers, it was an easy step to follow some incidental local club tribute to Mrs. Roosevelt and spread the rumor far and wide. Unfortunately, it was not possible to determine the origin of the clubs with certainty. They appeared inspired by those seeking either to cause trouble or to disparage the President and his wife.

The earlier stages did not have the earmarks of the Negro folk story, although many of the later versions were genuine reflections of the folk tale. As a matter of fact, the ideals and aims of the clubs were irreproachable from the folk viewpoint, whether from the vantage point of the Negroes as genuine folk wishes and demands, or for perfect propaganda material, either for the Axis or against the Negro and the First Lady.

A few samplings indicated the range of rules and requirements as rumored. In addition to "Eleanor Clubs," the common designation, they were also called "Daughters of Eleanor," "The Eleanor Angel Clubs," "The Sisters of Eleanor," "The Royal House of Eleanor."

The clubs were, of course, named after the First Lady of the Land. The early slogan was the previously mentioned "A white woman in every kitchen by Christmas." The club's membership was made up of colored domestic workers. The members agreed not to work for less than a fixed amount a week, varying from rumor to rumor. The members agreed that if they heard any criticism whatsoever of Mrs. Roosevelt or the President they would immediately quit their jobs.

Another summary, featuring Virginia and North Carolina rumors, reported that the members of the Eleanor Clubs refused to work on Sunday. They would not serve extra people without a day's notice. They must be called "Miss" and "Mrs." and not just their first names. Servants must go to work by the front door of their employers' homes. Servants must strike for a dollar or more a day wages. Servants must take a bath in their employer's family bathtub before going home from work.

A South Carolina story reported that in an Army camp in the South a Negro maid was employed by an officer and his wife. "One day the wife entered the dining room and saw three places set at the table. She asked the maid if her husband had called and said he'd bring a friend home for lunch. The maid said, 'no.' The wife then asked what the extra place was for. The maid replied, 'In the Eleanor Club we always sit with the people we work for.' "

A North Carolina version had it that the clubs worked through the church. "When a maid quit work she handed the name of her employer to the church group to which she belonged. The name was read from the pulpit and no person's name which was read could expect to get a maid again. Other than remarks about Mrs. Roosevelt, the maids held grievances for low wages and unfair treatment."

Another summary emphasized the fact that Negro women could work at only one job. "That is, if they were to cook, that was all they were to do. They couldn't help with the house cleaning at all. There must be a butler to put the garbage out and mop the kitchen. A woman could do only one thing, such as wash, scrub, or clean house; the Eleanor Club would not allow her to do general work. The Eleanor Club consisted of Negroes who were going to better themselves and try to be equal to the white race. They believed that the First Lady was their white god and was setting them free. There was coming into existence a 'black list' made up of white employers for whom the Negroes refused to work. It was connected with the Negro women's membership in the Eleanor Clubs and seemed to be gaining ground."

And so the Eleanor Club rumors multiplied and competed with other stories that added to the humor of the era but also reflected an unbelievable abandonment by the South of its chivalry toward women.

Agenda for Integration [1954]*

It seems likely that—in the light of the critical nature of the problem of Negro segregation in the South, its interaction with major
segments of American life, and our limited knowledge and experience
which can be considered definitive—one of the best approaches to the
problem may well be through a series of assumptions which may
prove useful not only as premises to be studied and tested, but for
introducing next steps to all the people.

FIRST SERIES OF ASSUMPTIONS: A CONTEMPORANEOUS AMERICAN PROBLEM

1. The first series of assumptions relates to the identification of
the Southern regional crisis, emerging from prospective revolutionary
changes in patterns of Negro segregation, with the nation's critical
social problems. The assumption here is that once or more in every
few generations and in most periods of change and expansion, there
arise crises, emergencies, and situations which require not only re-
examination and inventory of public affairs and policies, but also
new ways of achieving desired ends.

2. The present is such a period; it reflects both a domestic and
an international crisis. More immediately, the assumption is that
the satisfactory readjustment of interracial relations, with special
reference to the Negro in America, constitutes the most crucial do-

* From "An Approach to Diagnosis and Direction of the Problem of
Negro Segregation in the Public Schools of the South," *Journal of Public
Law,* Emory University Law School, Atlanta, Ga., III (1954), 8-37.
Reprinted by permission.

mestic problem in the United States, dated at the mid-century point. Relevant to this assumption are two main facets. One is the dilemma at home of insuring equality and justice for all citizens commensurate with American ideals and national constitutional guarantees. The other is the role of the United States as potential leader of a new world society, in which the nation—obligated to become increasingly articulate for Western society and increasingly effective in interaction with oriental cultures—must square its professions with living reality.

3. Strategically, if the major premise is that the United States is a potential world leader, coming to terms with new world relations, and, specifically, with Eastern and Near Eastern cultures with their profound ethnic and folk cultures searching for the democratic way out of their dilemmas, the minor premise is clearly that of influencing the South to come to terms with the main consensus and to approximate an effective integration with the nation's policies and procedures. The specific dilemma of the South and the nation revolves around the conflict between powerful cultural traditions, and the resolving of the dilemmas of legislative and constitutional mandates, federal and state, in conflict with each other and seemingly with democratic and religious assumptions about freedoms and autonomy.

4. The inseparability of the Southern and national problem from the total world situation is reflected in the influence which Southern behavior has upon the nation's international leadership, on the one hand, and the national economy and defense, on the other. For the Southeast and Southwest to break away from the increasingly integrated national and regionally decentralized defense and production economy would seriously handicap the nation's leadership and bargaining power in the world of Eastern and Western culture. On the other hand, the South's failure to utilize its human resources adequately will handicap the nation in its aggregate achievements and limit the South greatly in its capacities. This, therefore, is a part of the nation's current efforts to renew its faith in American democracy and to seek solutions of its problems through orderly processes.

5. Crucial to the problem is the task of adjusting quickly to revolutionary social change which is both creator and creature of transitional periods of development. By the same token, the problem

must be identified with the necessity, arising from each new crisis or major problem, for effective ways of meeting needs through skills, techniques, movements, and statesmanship capable of bearing the burdens of the pressing problem.

One of the possible new aspects of the problem is reflected in the role of science and social science in the definition of the situation and their opportunity and obligation to function maturely in the realm of societal direction. The assumption is, therefore, that social scientists, educators, and public officials are obligated to make this dilemma a special order of business and to devise ways and means commensurate with the results needed, in relation to the magnitude of the disturbance desired. This assumption seems justified in that effective efforts here have neither been designed nor executed in any due priority schedule.

6. The requisites for adequate ways and means, commensurate also with both the most mature American strategy and the cumulative gains of science and social science, are several. To begin with, here, as elsewhere in any major problem, the first essential for diagnosis and direction must be information adequate for understanding the total situation. This means that the body of knowledge required, and its usefulness, will have three main foci: (1) the over-all scientific and theoretical inferences, (2) the specifical identification of the main problems, and (3) the concrete application of relevant data to diagnosis and direction.

7. Once again, each of these foci will need to be identified with a threefold *areal* setting: (1) the world situation, (2) the national social structure, and (3) the Southern regions of the United States— as the current arbiter of "destiny" in terms of response to challenge. That is, the United States must set the incidence for coming to terms with the world of diversified cultures and ideologies, and it must also come to terms with the South, even as the South must come to terms with the nation in its new role of world leadership.

8. More specifically, the assumption is that the concept and practice of regionalism offer the most effective *areal* approach to interstate, interregional, and national problems of discrimination against and segregation of the Negro people. Only through such regionalism, basic to cultural relativity and as the tool for research and administration, can we approximate the unity and integration of

diverse regions in the changing structure of American culture as part of the structure of world regionalism and world unity.

9. As the major regions of the United States concerned, the Southeast and Southwest—which have traditionally functioned as separatist sections—are challenged to do the best that they and the nation can do in readjusting to a potentially revolutionary culture-economy of nonsegregation, either enforced by federal authority or through a combination of reasonable voluntaristic cooperative effort with federally prescribed procedures for integration. The assumption is that neither the South nor the nation wants to face the alternative of failure.

10. A part of the crisis lies exactly in this possibility of failure, and a part is in the strategy of how the transformation can best be achieved. And a further part of the crisis is inherent in what will happen, if the transformation cannot be consummated. For here is something which much of the nation and most of the world are saying must be done; and most of the South and much of the nation that it cannot be done. Yet, it would not make sense if the South and the nation could not join hands in the most mature statesmanship and the most effective methods possible to solidify America's achievements at home and leadership abroad.

SECOND SERIES OF ASSUMPTIONS:
A VERY SPECIAL SOUTHERN PROBLEM

1. The second series of assumptions relates primarily to the task of identifying the specific problem of compulsory segregation in the public elementary and secondary school systems of the South within the total situation of discrimination, segregation, and civil rights as a crucial problem of race and region in the United States.

2. Although this very specific problem is an integral segment of the larger dilemma of the integration of minority groups, especially of the Negro, into the national fabric, it derives its special identification as the principal problem for both the South and the nation from several basic situations and forces. For one, the cumulative neglect by the Southern states of Negro public schools and the South's failure to live up to its obligations to provide equal facilities for the two races, have compounded educational deficits beyond the reason-

able limits of tolerance within the framework of constitutional mandates, democratic fair play, and moral obligations.

3. On another level, the South's crisis is accentuated by powerful cumulative pressures of social change, public opinion outside the South, the revivification of moral agitation, and mass propaganda by national voluntary agencies and the press. So, too, the influence of the new era of literary writing and many pressures from abroad, especially from Eastern cultures, have set the incidence for national and international demands—and for Southern acquiescence in radical changes in the culture-economy of the South. As such, the pressure is on the South.

4. More specifically, in the early 1950's, a number of suits before the United States Supreme Court awaited decisions, commonly anticipated as being critical, and setting the incidence for a twofold or alternative crisis for the South. On the one hand, the crisis can be identified with the dilemma of financial costs; on the other, of radical cultural readjustments inherent in the necessity to conform to judicial rulings and new legislation. If the Court rules in favor of "equal but separate" facilities, the specifications will be drawn to exact speed-ups toward equalizing the Negro schools. If the Court rules against the present system, the situation will require, in addition to greatly increased financial support and revised administrative strategy, revolutionary adjustment, even in the framework of liberal provisions for time and regional adaptations.

5. Quantitatively, the problem may be envisaged in terms of the actual number of state, county, city, and community administrative school units involved. For there will be, in addition to the eleven major state systems of the Southeast and Southwest, and of the border states, no less than 1,362 county systems, more than 1,300 city systems, and several thousand other special town and community schools affected. To these will be added, in case the Court rules against compulsory segregation, readjustments involved in upspringing private schools.

6. In terms of people, the problem involves them all, on various levels and in unevenness of distribution and situation. The 1950 census showed that 43,159,147 people, somewhat more than one-fourth of all the people in the United States, lived in the South. Of these, 32,722,598 were white and 10,436,549 were Negroes. Of

all these, a greater proportion, in relation to the rest of the nation, were under twenty years of age, of the white children, 37.7 per cent, and of the Negro children, 44.6 per cent, thus denoting an extra school load to be adjusted in the South.

7. The situation may be further envisaged in the prospect of revolutionary changes of crisis dimensions in specific areas. First, it will be necessary to eliminate state constitutional mandates which provide that no member of one race may attend the schools of the other, in order to set up the first broad provisions for permissive coeducation of the races under optional and defined administrative situations. Next, with the exception of a few newly constructed city school buildings and consolidated rural schools, the problem involves the changing of a situation in which Negro schools are grossly unequal, and in some instances less than half as good, to a status in which "equal" can be demonstrated in operational terms. This is the size of the job.

8. The most concrete measure of the dilemma is that of actually beginning the job. This may be envisaged in a threefold variation of change in the segregated systems. (1) There could be partially segregated systems. (2) There could be complete compulsory non-segregation. (3) And there could be mixed enrollment in individual schools. The ratio of Negro to white pupils would vary according to population ratios and community distribution, but there would be few schools in which no Negro children would want to enroll and few Negro schools to which white children might not be assigned.

THIRD SERIES OF ASSUMPTIONS: A PROBLEM INSEPARABLY
INTERRELATED WITH WORLD SITUATIONS

1. It must be constantly kept in mind that the definition of the problem, its identification with processes for the enforcement of court rulings and legislative mandates, and the subsequent fulfillment of stable educational obligations are inseparably interrelated with several major facets of the situation. One is the interaction between the South and the rest of the nation, and the inferences for national and international responsibilities and policies already emphasized. At the other end of the pole are the powerful conditioning factors of Southern tradition and culture patterns. Coordinate with these is the general role of social change and adjustment in transitional stages

of changing society and the main interacting forces and processes which go into the cumulative situation. All of these will constitute the framework of a score of series of assumptions that follow.

2. With reference to the interaction between the South and the rest of the nation, the assumption is that the South is the key to the nation's "destiny" in this particular area. There are many, perhaps most of the people, who believe that judicial and administrative decisions, and adjustment to those decisions, are crucial. This is an additional reason why this appears to be America's most critical domestic problem.

3. There is, however, one major facet of the situation which neither the nation nor the South has been able, or willing, to face in complete frankness, or to approach with adequate facts and statesmanlike strategy. This is the dilemma of discrimination and segregation and the successful integration of the Negro into the total cultural fabric. It is, again, both the South's and the nation's inability to come to terms with their moral obligation and with constitutional mandates, with reference to the Negro's participation in total American culture. Although the problems of discrimination are nationwide, it is in the South and border states that legal structures have backed the powerful folk traditions and practices of segregation. This regional situation constitutes an apparently insurmountable barrier to technically bridging the distance between the American ideal and the prevailing practices in much of the United States.

4. Further inferences, here, point to the fact that this problem is not primarily one of international identification, as it is of national complications. For, it is not only at home, but everywhere abroad, that this segment of undemocratic structure and practice is cited as an irreconcilable behavior pattern, in what is otherwise the nearest approximation to democracy the world has seen. Many say that it is futile for the United States to try to convert the world to democracy, until it has set its own house in order. Many say that the South can do nothing of the first order, so long as it is handicapped always with this dilemma. The nation itself, sensing the powerful historical and traditional backdrop of the situation, nevertheless appears to be tired of having the Negro-white problem injected into every issue and decision that has to be faced, in what is more and more being called another era of conflict. Yet, the obligation of the nation re-

flects a two-way responsibility. That is, if the nation owes it to the world, to which it is recommending its own democracy, to set its own house in order, it is obligated to do so without internal strife, if it is to set an example for world peace.

5. More specifically, the pressure upon the South to reform its undemocratic actions must also be identified with the nation's mid-century high motivation for the reaffirmation of its basic democracy. The rest of the nation complains that the South is retarding the whole nation's progress, and feels that the South owes it to the nation to match its great industrial development with commensurate advances in its race relations. Especially, there are powerful ideologies focusing upon freedoms and equality of opportunity for every individual and all groups everywhere. Most Americans outside the South feel strongly about the South's negations of the American ideal; and most Southerners, frustrated and worried, are moved to double their efforts toward reform.

6. Pressures from the world situation are also powerful. From many, in government service and out, comes the unusual consensus that the profession of the United States to show the world the way to democracy is greatly retarded—and often bitterly resented— abroad, because of the nation's reputation for discrimination against and segregation of its Negro citizens. Many feel embarrassed, and often disgraced abroad. Other pressures include the United Nations, with its Declaration of Freedoms, and the verdicts of other representatives of foreign nations. All this pressure from abroad is submitted as evidence, in briefs before the Supreme Court.

7. The conflicting dilemmas have been well-stated by the distinguished Negro author, Alain Locke, writing about the nation's "Unfinished Business":

For the moment, then, the paradox of race has become our democracy's great dilemma. But speeded on its way to solution, it could, by that very token, become a triumphant vindication. Clear credentials on this score would give America a passport to world confidence, especially in the eyes of that two-thirds of humanity who happen to be nonwhite. In its historic setting in the South, segregation means separate schools for Negroes, separate coaches for railway trains, separate sections on buses. It means separate libraries, hospitals, public parks and in small communities, complete exclusion from these municipal installations no less than from theaters—except in galleries. In its larger implications it means the denial of citizenship rights to the Negro. For it bars Negroes and whites from working together in the public service—state, municipal, and county. Hence positions become closed to Negro citizens since it is impracticable to divide all departments along lines of race and color. While recently a distinguished southern liberal, Mark Ethridge, general manager of the Louisville, Ky., *Courier-Journal,* made an eloquent plea for opportunities for Negroes to work in war industry, he was impelled to speak as follows: "All the armies of the world—both of the United Nations and the Axis—could not force upon the South the abandonment of racial segregation."

FOURTH SERIES OF ASSUMPTIONS:

IN THE SETTING OF SOCIAL CHANGE

1. Many other causal factors have operated to bring the South face to face with a new reality which is in conflict with the older traditions. Chief among these are the radical social changes which have transformed the national economy and challenged the biracial patterns of segregation. The startling potentialities of the atomic era are such as to relegate many of the petty prejudices and discriminations to a waning past, while the extraordinary inventions and scientific advances challenge the South to take advantage of its opportunities to minimize race in its accelerated industrial and economic strides.

2. Many situations are products of the flow of inventions, communications, and industrial society, which is no respecter of character and motivation of the people. In reality, social change, itself, is the first frame of reference in which may be found not only much of the explanation of the situation, but also the basic factors available for mature programs and policies likely to achieve enduring adjustment. Inherent in the potential catastrophic aspects of change may also be the genesis of a more mature mutual understanding of cultural dilemmas and an increasing cooperation to supplant the old traditional conflicts. Some such understanding, unity, and tolerance may be the supreme necessity of contemporary society.

3. Among the potent influences which have revolutionized the whole situation in contemporary society is that of new definitions and identifications of race, having been made more articulate by the biological and behavioral sciences and action agencies. There is con-

sensus that the traditional usages of the term "race" have been inaccurate and confused, and that the broader inferences of superior and inferior absolutes have long since been abandoned. In the realm of the behavioral sciences, race is no longer thought of as a biological phenomenon; rather, race is interpreted as a complex of societal conditioning, in which culture is considered to be a more dominant factor than biology. Although it is not possible to arrive at a composite definition of race acceptable to all, it is relatively easy to authenticate the general scientific consensus which constitutes the basis from which contemporary inferences and action programs stem.

4. Of special significance to the changing situation in the United States, has been the gradually evolving definition and identification of race and culture developed, over the two or three decades prior to 1950, by five major groups at work in the field of race and ethnic groups. These include sociologists, anthropologists, psychologists, biologists, and religious and social welfare groups, in conjunction with many agencies and movements looking toward the diagnosis and direction of intercultural relations and education. Selections from the writings of these scholars reflect a relatively uniform consensus on the meaning of race useful in current diagnosis and planning, as well as indicative of trends away from the earlier inflexible biological concepts of race and race differences. The changing concept of race and its almost universal dissemination has been a two-way force, operating both to accelerate the whole process of new adjustments and adaptations and to create a greater "tolerance" and understanding on the part of both segments of extremists in the area of racism and anti-racism, and of the academically and socially liberal-minded public.

5. Parallel to the revolutionary changes brought about by scientific concepts and identification of race with culture, what may prove equally powerful in influencing change in the past and providing specifications for structuring realistic theory and practice of the future, are the recent contributions of the behavioral sciences to research and theory in the realm of human relations. Research and theory concerning stratification and social structure, group dynamics and intergroup relations, personality and culture, attitudes and values, mass society and folk culture, social systems and community structure, demography, acculturation, and the impact of technology upon cul-

tural groups have set the incidence for new potentials in social adjustment as well as new influences in understanding society.

6. In addition, religion may be noted as a determinant in the contemporary consensus about race. It seems likely that, although the creeds of Christianity have long posited the basic assumption that the Negro, in the heart of the Christian's credo of the fatherhood of God and the brotherhood of man, has always been equal in the sight of God, the more recent teachings of the churches have also been influential in modifying the definitions of race, to which we have referred.

More specifically, both in the nation and in the South, the churches and religious groups within recent years have been almost uniformly active in the fight against racial discrimination. On the national level, the Federal Council, the Friends, the National Conference of Christians and Jews, the Catholic Church, and others have issued manifestoes and promoted special days, workshops, conferences, and programs on brotherhood. In the South, each of the major Protestant denominations has issued, through its social service committees or through special conferences, recommendations looking toward greater justice and equality for Negroes.

7. Still another influence accelerating social change has been the movement of intercultural education and community dynamics. One of the most important trends in this field is that of intergroup and intercultural relations. This, in turn, has two main segments. One focuses generally on analysis of relationships between ethnic and minority groups. The other segment of intergroup relations study was that of intercultural education, which is a separate area of its own.

FIFTH SERIES OF ASSUMPTIONS: SPECIAL CAUSAL FACTORS

1. Among other influences in the dynamics of social change, with special reference to the Negro, have been the fellowship programs of a number of foundations. Grants from the Rosenwald Fund and the Guggenheim Foundation resulted in the publication of many books and the training of leaders, whose work was to help reshape the Southern scene. The Social Science Research Council, the General Education Board, and the Carnegie Corporation made large contribu-

tions to the training of professional leaders, many of whom functioned in the area of race relations.

2. Still other forces have been the conferences, workshops, brochures, and programs designed for propaganda purposes by national and regional organizations. On the national level, among the most influential of these have been the Friends' Service Committee, Urban League, National Conference of Christians and Jews, American Jewish Congress, Anti-Defamation League, National Association for the Advancement of Colored People, and American Civil Liberties Union. During the two decades before mid-century, no less than 800 national agencies or groups were catalogued in the directories of social agencies which were interested primarily in the Negro and ethnic groups. At the regional level have been the Commission on Interracial Cooperation, the Southern Regional Council, and the Catholic Committee of the South. There have been, also, many *ad hoc* committees, civil liberties programs, and religious organizations continuously on the march.

3. In the 1940's, the Federal Government, itself, operated positively on a number of levels pertaining to race relations. Especially, the publications of two official groups, appointed by President Truman, were epochal in the bold and uncompromising conclusion presented to the public. One of these was *To Secure These Rights,* the report of the President's Committee on Civil Rights. Another was the six-volume report of the President's Commission on Higher Education.

4. Before that, the New Deal had exerted considerable pressures upon the South. First, perhaps, was the nation's "rediscovery" of the South. This was followed by the general labeling of the South as an example of backwardness and badness, followed by efforts to remake its culture overnight. The revival of the term "South," insofar as the national administration was concerned, and insofar as it began to be used universally by editors and critics, came about in two ways. One was typified in the now noted slogan that the South was the nation's "Economic Problem No. One." The South was Tobacco Road. It was again missionary territory. But, whatever it was, it was "The South." Secondly, the South came to be synonymous with conservatism or reactionary policies, because Southern senators and congressmen, state governors and leaders, opposed many New Deal policies. "What else could you expect? He is a Southerner,"

came to be a common refrain. And then the South, with its usual sensitiveness, revived with a vengeance the term "North," charging that section again with "trying to make over the South."

5. Then, between the New Deal and the later Truman era, World War II had a twofold influence. One was the interaction of the South with broader contacts, and the consequent re-examination by many Southerners of their framework of biracial culture. The other was the "discovery" of the South, and its limitations. And so there was the ever-recurring question, "What can be done about the South?" Increasingly, individuals and agencies, private and public, set themselves to the task of "making" the South change. This is a long story, which has already been touched upon.

6. Of the special pressures which contributed to social change, court decisions and prospects of others have been most dramatically operative within the years just before the mid-century. These decisions have been effective in the areas of higher education, transportation, community recreation, housing situations, and other civil rights. In fine, many observers rate such decisions as the most definitive of all the causal factors effecting change.

7. A constant factor has been the perennial advocacy of civil rights legislation—especially that designed to establish fair employment practices—in Congress, and its inclusion in the national political platforms.

SIXTH SERIES OF ASSUMPTIONS: SOUTHERN ENVIRONMENT

1. The sixth series of assumptions relates primarily to the conditioning factors within the South itself, which explain the situation, and by the same token, make change more difficult but also more obligating. Such factors comprehend the cumulative heritage of liabilities of the South and the basic facets of its powerful culture heritage. Relevant, too, will be the theory of Southern efforts to reconstruct the Southern economy and culture.

2. From the cumulative heritage of the South, there has grown up a powerful backlog of both liabilities and hazards and of limited assets. The liabilities are primarily of five sorts. One is the unenviable record of injustice, inequalities, and brutality in race relations. Another is the collective mental and moral concept of the Negro as rating something less than human parity in Southern cul-

ture, a powerful cultural construct that not only colors and explains nearly all of the South's deviate behavior in interracial relationships, but sometimes appears as well-nigh indestructible. A third, following as a sort of corollary, assumes that "The South" is the "White South," a usage that ignores the Negro, both by default and by intent. Still a fourth logically follows, and it is the white South's lack of understanding and sympathy with the achievements of the Negro, and his reasonable expectations and demands. Finally, the South's sensitiveness to outside criticism and its resistance to federal direction and to moral directives has continuously been revivified by pressures and propaganda.

3. The main resistance of the South to change, as is true of any major culture, is found in the power of its cultural tradition and folk society. The elementary sources of this powerful folk society are reflected in a fourfold heritage. There was the growing struggle with nature and the Indian, plus the earlier folk culture which was of the vintage of Virginia and the planter aristocracy. Then, for a time, nearly all of the South consisted of the rural folk with their rugged individualism and their struggle with land and climate—with the victory or defeat of harvest time in their blood. And there were the remnants of frontier folk, symbolic of mountain culture, or flatwood frustration, or swamp and bayou levels of living in the out-of-way places throughout the South. And finally, there was the powerful folk society of the Negroes themselves, as both apart from and a part of the dominant white folks.

4. The first fruits of this heritage were easily discernible in four levels of folk culture which clearly accounted for the institutions and behavior of all the Southern people in their considerable diversity, yet in such essential unity as to be characterized as the South. More accurately, the Southern society was a variegated fabric made from a fourfold pattern: the upper levels of plantation aristocracy; the upper levels of the middle white South; the lower levels of the disadvantaged whites; and the Negro folk society, itself reflecting three sub-levels: (1) the folk society of the slave level, distinguished in any story of universal culture, and exerting a powerful influence upon the institutions and behavior of the white South; (2) the white-Negro folk society after freedom, a dual culture that always distinguished the South from the rest of the country and symbolized folk beliefs for

which men were willing to die; and (3) the new Negro folk society, separate from and within the dominant society of the white South.

5. A knowledge of all this, in the South even more than in most cultures, is basic to the promise and prospect of regional reconstruction. For these are not only identifiable patterns, but they are so organically imbedded in the total structure of Southern society that the problem of general social change and of specific cultural changes is quite different from the ordinary problems of change that flow merely from time, technology, and material progress. Thus, if there is slower change or less change in this setting, it is easily explainable and significant, both for what it is and for the study of cultural change in process.

6. In the South, therefore, more than in other regions, there are two main levels of change. One is the ordinary changes that come from the processes of succession, progress, economic and technological changes, through which the landscape of all culture inevitably undergoes modifications that are easily measurable by statistics. The other is the more stubborn pattern of cultural change, in which the very cultural personality and value systems of the Southern society are at stake and reflect an integrity of religion, loyalties, patriotism, and conformity to the major institutions which are the core of value systems.

SEVENTH SERIES OF ASSUMPTIONS: SOUTHERN AND AMERICAN CREDOS

1. The seventh series of assumptions relates to the more specific facets of the main obstacles to change. They include the Southern and national credos about the Negro and the agelong cumulative assumptions and practices with reference to race differences. In this sense, too, are inferred the technical details of state and local legislation.

2. Perhaps the nearest basic assumption concerning the inherited Southern attitude toward the Negro is the credo that "the Negro, is a Negro, and nothing more." It is difficult for many Southern leaders to agree that this is the central theme of the Southern folkways of race. Yet, the measure of this appraisal appears everywhere to be abundant. And because this, together with the power of caste, is at the bottom of the Southern culture-complex and explains so easily what has happened, it is of the utmost importance that South-

erners face the plain assumption that they do not appraise the Negro as the same sort of human being as they themselves are.

3. The statement of this credo is so vivid that it would be, perhaps, surprising to Southerners and, therefore, might go a long way toward explaining why the other regions of the nation have rediscovered an aspect of their own national life, with which they are either not acquainted or which they have forgotten. The credo is in such complete contradistinction to the urgings and demands that are being made on the South, in the name of war, freedom, and Americanism, that the resulting tensions and conflict are easily explainable. It must be repeated often that an understanding of the realistic folkways of the South is necessary to explain the reaction of people from other regions to what seems to them arbitrary, unreasonable, and entirely unfair attitudes and practices in the South, with reference to the simplest, most common, everyday, reasonable expectations of the Negro for life, liberty, and the pursuit of happiness.

4. This credo, together with the comparative national "dilemma," characterized by Myrdal as the moral conflict between the American credo and actual practices, is perhaps the most impressive evidence that the basic facts of cultural relations and interaction processes constitute the hard core of resistance to the abandonment of segregation and the revolutionary readjustment to a new unsegregated culture-economy in the South. Here, perhaps, the most crucial task, essential to the understanding of the situation and preliminary to the cataloguing and interpretation of what happened, is to sense the realistic, living credo of the South with reference to the Negro, and its relation to what might be called a symbolic credo of the rest of the nation at large.

5. The understanding of a folk psychology, *committed to the defense of this credo at any cost,* by the same token, is a first essential. For, against this well-nigh universal Southern credo arise assumptions and demands from outside that appear to the South to be about as near the complete opposite of its beliefs as it would be possible to find. In substance, here is a sudden demand for the white man, long conditioned in the Negro complex and Southern loyalties, bottomed in the long heritage of race prejudice and cultural evolution, to change its whole structure of race relations overnight. And, equally vividly, the outside regions see reflected what seems an unreason-

ableness of the South in not being willing to conform to the larger American credo of democracy and the American dream of equality.

6. The assumption that the nation, as a whole, has had from the beginning some attitudes toward the Negro similar to those of the South, is not only an inference by the white South. Negro leadership, itself, has stated the basis upon which the national credo is discriminating against the Negro. Thus, the composite verdict of the latest accusation which the Negro has made of the nation is that, "There is in America a belief on the part of great groups of people, in every stratum of social, political, and business life, that the Negro must not be permitted to share as a citizen on an equality with other citizens." And again, "The result has been a deeply planted conviction that the Negro American is a person apart, that he does not deserve, and must not be given, the treatment accorded other Americans."

7. This is of the utmost importance, not only in explaining this transitional crisis, but in looking to the future development of all regions of the nation. Thus, it is of considerable importance that the credo of the nation outside of the South needs to be portrayed in two major divisions. One is a sincere belief in the importance for every American to proclaim and to legislate equal opportunity for the Negro on all occasions. The other is a personal credo of the actual relationships in conflict in practice with the main credo. Yet, in most aspects of attitude and discrimination, the rest of the nation is more mature, subtle, and less frank about it than the South.

8. In addition to the stubborn traditional prejudices of the South, the assumption is that the general verdict is also grounded in a scientific lineage of respectable heritage. First, there is the universal law of differences, such that no two individuals are alike, thus resulting in a wide variety of personality. There is, then, the agelong differentiation of ethnic groups, commonly assumed to be races, the most liberal characterization of which is that they are the product of cumulative differences over long periods of time in the framework of different environmental conditions and pressures.

9. Still further, there are the assumptions of the old school of biologists that physical heredity is an important factor in all human aggregations, as well as in animal aggregations. And, it has been the common assumption of traditional ideologies that races differ, in terms

of certain measurable traits such as cephalic index, texture of skin and hair, color, and certain other traits used primarily for identification and differentiation. The white South has been accustomed to cite this as scientific sanction for the policy of separation.

10. Moreover there is the assumption that, in the great religions of mankind, class distinctions and ethnic groupings have constituted a part of the basic structure of the cultures of which those religions are the primary index. This, from the Southern viewpoint, was no less true in the great Biblical tradition, both in the Old and New Testaments, in the earlier assumptions of hewers of wood and drawers of water, and the later assumptions of master and servant. This had become one of the major trends in the fabric of Southern folkways and mores with reference to the Negro.

11. There are, then, the more specific traditions of the white South, set in the total framework of slavery, and the abolition of slavery, and the epochal experiment and trial of making the slave a free man under the terms of the Reconstruction. To the other traditions have been added the powerful structure of caste, based on sex and race, and the intensification through discussion, trial and error of certain of the principal Southern folkways and mores incorporating cultural values for which the people would fight.

12. There are, finally, two rationalizations about what had been assumed as "Americanisms." One is the "one-hundred per cent" kind, holding that the white race is the basic American ethnic group, and the other has to do with geographic representation and states' rights. The structure of American democracy derives its form and function through the representation of all the people through the states and majority rule; and the majorities, as well as minorities, have the right to choose how they will be governed. Southerners cite the definite trends, in the national organization of governors in the 1940's and the Republican party in the early 1950's, toward a revaluation of the principles of rights and obligations of the several states.

EIGHTH SERIES OF ASSUMPTIONS: FOUR LEVELS OF CHANGE

1. The eighth, ninth, and tenth series of assumptions are related to changes that have occurred in the South, in the light of the total situation, that offer most relevance to future directions. The eighth

series will focus upon general changes in the region, the ninth on specific changes, and the tenth on fluctuations and contradictions. The general changes, dated at about the mid-century point, may be identified with (1) achievement, (2) the new Negro, (3) the white South, and (4) the revivification of the old "North-South" conflict.

2. With reference to general *standards of achievement* in the South, major changes seem to have been in the following areas: the increase of wealth and income; the rise of the general standard of living, with considerable improvement in rural living standards; urbanization and, therefore, the bringing about of a better balance between country and city; an increased balance between agriculture and industry, and a diversified, balanced agriculture; an increased mechanization of agriculture; an awakening to the meaning of conserving resources; the great strides in technology, such as research, specialization in manufacturing, transportation, and communications; an increase in public works and special public social services; and an increase in public education and public recreation facilities. These achievements, greater in proportion than in the total nation, reflect an extraordinary transformation in the Southern economy and culture.

3. With reference to the *new Negro,* the main changes seem to have been in the following areas: a large migration out of the South, and, therefore, a decreasing ratio of Negro people to the total population of the South; the increasing articulation of the Negro in politics and national affairs, and the consequent backwash of influence upon the Negro in the South; a large migration from the rural South to Southern cities, tending to make the Negro an urban rather than a rural people; a considerable increase in educational opportunities, especially as reflected in high school and college enrollment; a rising standard of living, leading to the rise of the middle—and to some extent an upper—class Negro; changes in the Negro worker, especially the woman worker; the rise of the "new Negro," especially a "new Negro" youth; the development of an extraordinarily able Negro leadership; an increase of feelings of frustration and consequent aggression; and an aggressive attitude toward segregation in particular. Perhaps the simplest way to emphasize the change is to point to the almost complete "newness" of the Negro with the "oldness" of the whites, and to sense the near pity which the new intellectual Negro has for many Southern whites who are called liberal.

4. The third general, current change, namely, the ideologies and attitude of *the white South,* can be understood only in relation to the total configuration of Southern culture and the social pressures from outside. In general, there has been an apparent temporary increase in sectionalism and the recrudescence of the North-South concept; in the light of the improvement in most everyday aspects of Negro life and of great progress by the Negro, a tendency on the part of the white South to insist on having credit for these changes and for the continuing improvement within the framework of segregation; a freer discussion than formerly, but, in reaction, a sharpening of resistance and a reinforcing of opposition to changes in segregation practices; an increase in thought and talk about "racism"; revolt against the Supreme Court decisions, with reference to voting and higher education; more articulate opposition to federal legislation affecting the South; the still solid South, with minor threats of secession from the Democratic party; some progress in Southern organizations for civil rights; a relatively large number of young college students and returned servicemen advocating more liberal practices in race relations; considerable progress in organized labor; strong reaction against radical change by many young people who work on farms, in factories, and who operate trucks and taxis; and some recrudescence of the Ku Klux Klan, but severely dealt with by the courts and public opinion.

5. With reference to the fourth level of regional change, namely, Southern reaction to the accelerated trend of *outside pressure* for complete transformation of the Southern segregation pattern, it will aid the understanding of the situation if we look at these pressures in the light of the South's unchanging attitudes, as cited above and enumerated further below. But it also reminds us that today and tomorrow are not yesterday. The intensity of the South's reaction, seemingly so difficult to interpret to the other regions, is, after all, an inevitable and logical product of the cumulative process, and the product of tradition and interaction with multiple forces. As evidence of interaction stimuli, the extremity of Southern reaction is often matched by the extremity of attack. Yet, with all of its stubborn loyalties to a powerful culture, there is no escape from the verdict that the South is probably the only major regional culture in the world

where the segregation and exploitation of the Negro are considered as a part of virtue in preserving Western civilization.

6. There is also an apparent over-all change on the part of the white South that reflects a new sort of assumption, namely, that the South is really willing to face the facts and that decisions and action on many counts cannot be put off much longer. In particular, the problem of nonsegregation can be, and is, discussed freely and dispassionately on practically all levels of association. Perhaps the most marked general change, relative to goals and objectives, may be reflected in the goals of the earlier race relations groups to secure for the Negro better facilities, better work, more jobs, and generally better opportunities, in contrast with the current motivation to guarantee all rights and privileges as a citizen, rather than as a Negro. The acquiescence of the South in this respect is a fundamental change from the general credo as recorded.

NINTH SERIES OF ASSUMPTIONS: THE OLD AND NEW

1. Many of the specific illustrations of change, within recent years, reflect extraordinary progress from a less desired situation to a more desired one, defined as such by all factions—the white South, the Negro South, and the critical nation. What "could not be done," has been done; common refrains reflect: "I never would have believed it"; "I never thought I would have lived to see the day"; "Well, maybe you are right, I don't know, I don't know"; and "I'll go along with you, if you will just satisfy me in this one respect." Even the hundreds of NAACP members and guests, meeting in the city auditorium of Atlanta in 1952 in unsegregated convention, were astonished at what they called great progress.

2. As evidence of how far the South has come, comparison of the vanguard of Southern so-called liberals with the intellectual liberals of the North reflects an unbelievable advance. Many Southern leaders, and many of the run of mill common folks in leadership positions on this new social front, are far ahead of the distinguished professors and historians of the first quarter of the century. Call the roll of the Harvard and Columbia historians, sociologists, economists, and check with later Southern authors. Even James Truslow Adams, with his *American Dream,* or Albert Bushnell Hart and his *Southern South,* that led to his being burned in effigy in Mississippi, were old-timers,

compared with the young editor of the "Ole Miss" student magazine who addressed the 1952 NAACP meeting in Atlanta, or the winner of the annual gold medal for oratory at Mississippi College, the main theme of both of whom was a bold attack upon segregation. Especially "reactionary" now appear such historians as William A. Dunning, William E. Dodd, Ulrich Phillips, and W. E. Woodward. Liberal fighters against racism and the "Nordic nonsense" such as E. R. A. Seligman, Franklin H. Giddings, and others, while in the vanguard of men like John W. Burgess and Frank W. Goodnow, nevertheless assumed the limited participation of dual culture to be the logical normal situation to be expected.

3. Another way to note the great change is to contrast two pronouncements, one made before the turn of the century and one at mid-century. The first was from Henry W. Grady, hero of both North and South, in the genesis of the first "New South." He said:

The supremacy of the white race of the South must be maintained forever, and the domination of the Negro race resisted at all points and at all hazards, because the white race is the superior race. This is the declaration of no new truth; it has abided forever in the marrow of our bones and shall run forever with the blood that feeds Anglo-Saxon hearts.

The second was the credo of the Southern Regional Council at Atlanta in 1950, which read:

The South of the future, toward which our efforts are directed, is a South freed of stultifying inheritances from the past. It is a South where the measure of a man will be his ability, not his race; where a common citizenship will work in democratic understanding for the common good; where all who labor will be rewarded in proportion to their skill and achievement; where all can feel confident of personal safety and equality before the law; where there will exist no double standard in housing, health, education, or other public services; where segregation will be recognized as a cruel and needless penalty on the human spirit, and will no longer be imposed; where, above all, every individual will enjoy a full share of dignity and self-respect, in recognition of his creation in the image of God.

4. By the 1950's, many examples of change can be cited to indicate advance beyond the expectation of leaders, North and South. These include a vast catalogue: higher education for Negroes up to

the top degree levels in both Southern and Northern universities; economic gains and standards of living; great advance in labor; advance in public health and welfare; advance in political privileges and civil rights; extension of social courtesies and etiquette; extension of jury duty to Negroes, and justice to Negroes by white juries; representation on city councils and boards of education; equality in health and welfare services; the greatly improved status of Negro women; the rise of Negro leadership; the elimination of lynching; and other reforms.

5. These and many other advances have led some commentators to protest the bitter criticism and severe denunciation of the South, on the one hand, and to argue that, given time, the South will voluntarily work out the problem satisfactorily. Gerald W. Johnson makes a vivid challenge:

If you compare the rise of the American Negro since 1865 with the rise of any other dominated race, you will find in the record of the white South a magnanimity, wisdom, and charity, never approached by any other dominant race in the history of mankind. Compared with any similar episode, the treatment of the American Negro is not the disgrace, but the supreme glory of America. It is ironical that the greatest thing we ever did is now used against us because it was not the perfect work of archangels instead of the merely creditable work of men.

6. Why then, if advances are unprecedented and are beyond the expectations of most of the earlier advocates, are they not enough? In general there are two principal explanations. One is that the convulsive changes, which we have recorded, have literally made a new world as compared to an era so recent as fifty years ago. The other is that the chasm of difference between the conventional advances made by the South and the demands of complete elimination of segregation is so great, that none of these other advances even register in the judgment of the norm demanded.

TENTH SERIES OF ASSUMPTIONS: NEW SOUTHS

1. This irreconcilable difference between two basic ideologies reflects the frame of reference for difficulties, contradiction, and hazards inherent in the total evolution. For there is far from consensus in the South on the most advanced changes being achieved and advocated by

the South. And when we try to set up an accurate balance sheet, we run head-on into almost complete paradoxes, contradictions, and dead ends. For example, consider a half dozen inconsistent behavior types. Southern professional organizations and societies, on the state level, have not only been slow in inviting Negroes to become members, but have generally opposed it. Library groups, teachers' groups, medical groups, and many others have appeared not only adamant and stubbornly traditional, but narrowly provincial, in many ways. The main reason for exclusiveness is usually cited as the difficulties involved in eating together. University trustees are opposed to giving honorary degrees to distinguished Negroes because of the hazards of commencement entertainment, among other reasons. University trustees oppose the incorporation of Negro institutions into consolidated patterns with white institutions because of the hazards of having Negro members on the board of trustees, and the consequent indications of social equality at commencement and at trustees' meetings. So far as evidence is available, state legislatures are unanimous in opposing legislation for integration, except the minimum necessary for operation within the national legal framework. Farm and home demonstration work, although making forward strides, does not follow reasonable non-segregation practices.

2. Perhaps one answer to the attempt at definition and diagnosis is found in the fact that most of the factors involved in the final balance sheet have to be entered on both sides of the ledger. For instance, the fact that it is reported everywhere as a great gain that hundreds of thousands of Negroes now vote regularly constitutes powerful evidence that opposition still operates, since other hundreds of thousands cannot vote. The fact that more and more Negro names are included in the jury panel is the powerful exception that proves the rule of his neglect by default as well as intention. The fact that North Carolina and other places have hit the Ku Klux Klan so hard, with real prison sentences in so many instances, is evidence of the still burning backlog of Southern lawlessness. It takes no credit from the South for its increasingly uniform justice to Negroes, through white juries, and in rendering verdicts against whites charged with injustice to Negroes, to point out that all this is still news. It subtracts no credit from the region to note with pride the elimination of lynching, while at the same time to point up the unreasonable record

of brutalities and the phenomenally high rate of homicide in the South.

3. Another conclusion may be that, after all, the crucial test of the situation may be found in the degree to which the South of the 1950's is really a different South. In general, there have been three eras in which the South has been designated "new." The *first* new South was a recovering South, needing the help of the nation. Although in many ways receiving the generous helping hand, it was still exploited as a colonial segment, paying a price and struggling under tremendous handicaps. It was still suffering from the terrific conflict between the questions of moral rights in the North and constitutional rights in the South, as was the *third* new South, to reverse the order. The South of that era was never integrated into the nation as other regions were. Even when the region was celebrated at home and abroad as having achieved notable attainments, it was as if the verdict was always: "Fine! Good! For the South that is a record to be proud of." The rating was still by Southern standards. And the South was still brutal in its post-Civil War heritage of lynchings and murder.

4. The *second* new South, from the turn of the century to the New Deal, was characterized not only by its moderately great economic gains, but by heroic and spasmodic efforts toward what was termed "progressive" and "liberal," as applied to poverty and wealth, education, health, civil rights, labor, and the ever-present economic, social, and moral issue of the Negro's part in Southern culture. Sometimes the South seemed to excel in movements, committees, commissions, and conferences and in the pioneering work of agricultural extension, and profited greatly by cooperative financial assistance from the Federal Government and national foundations, in diagnosing and directing its own policies and adjusting itself to directed advances. But the South never did quite catch up, in either the national structure or as a fully integrated region. Although the South had reduced its lynchings greatly, it was still the old South in that respect.

5. The *third* or current new South, extending back to the 1930's, is something different. In the first place, it is two great regions, the Southeast and the Southwest, each recognized and taking its place as a major region in a powerful nation, which is seeking to integrate its increasingly strong and diversified regions into a pattern of resources and power adequate for both leadership among the world of nations

and for defense in case of attack from a threatening menace subversive to the American way. Although the phenomenal gains being made by the South owe much of their genesis and success to the unprecedented expansions of the national economy, for the first time, the Southern regions reflect not only equal, but possibly priority, ranking in both the national economy and defense.

ELEVENTH SERIES OF ASSUMPTIONS: RESOURCES FOR SUCCESS

1. What are the relevant assumptions with reference to the South's resources and probabilities for readjustment to the new demands? As compared to the first two "new Souths," the current South shows certain inventories that promise basic capacities and prospects. In the first place, there is perhaps for the first time a national consensus that the regional balance of America is more than a mere euphemism. New England, the Far West, the Northwest, the Southeast, and the Southwest, in the structure of the national economy and defense, are now all prime areas for optimum-maximum concentration and integration programs, featuring cooperative procedures that work both ways.

2. On this assumption, the Southeast and the Southwest may be said to have inherited a sort of "share and share alike" economy that obligates a greater degree of cooperation with the nation than heretofore. More than ever before, the sectional concept of separation, self-sufficiency, and "operation opposition" are not the dominating conditioning factors in regional development. By the same token, there is the assumption that the total nation will cooperate more effectively in interregional interactions than ever before, and that there is for the first time, perhaps, a matured and mellowed understanding of the crucial problems involved by all the regions and the Federal Government itself.

3. The assumption here is that the South of this current new era is in many ways scarcely recognizable as being like either of the earlier Souths. Instead of being a relatively dependent section, primarily characterized by deficiencies and a "have not" economy, it has taken its place as not only one of the major economic bulwarks of the nation but, in the pairing of its two constituent regions, as a potential leader, powerfully essential to national integration and strength. For one thing, the South today, far from being a retarded agricultural

economy mostly in a rural setting, has the greatest accelerated rate of urban and industrial development of all the regions; it can catalogue more than twelve thousand concerns employing more than fifty workers each and predicts a gain of at least three thousand major plants in the next ten years.

4. A Study of the South's vast resources, the increasing elimination of its waste of the past, its progress in conservation, and the accelerated trend toward industrialization and economic advance indicates the critical importance to the nation, as well as the South, of so negotiating the reconstruction of economic and cultural relations, with reference to the Negro, as to contribute powerfully to the nation and the Negro's welfare, instead of to threats of secession and confusion. For the Negro—in his rapid rise in all aspects of life and labor, and especially his thousands of teachers, educators, and other professional folk, and the stream of youth flowing into the South's human resources reservoir—constitutes an unprecedented economic and professional potential, needing the best possible development. Along with the South's integration of the Negro into its full culture-economy goes the comparable, perhaps greater, problem of integration of the South into the total national structure, in the framework of a nation that is strong and united because of the integration of its strong and diversified regions.

5. A further assumption is that the South will accept the challenge to go ahead and do well something of its own, voluntarily, rather than something done poorly, under compulsion, and will make the 1950's the beginning of "Operation Equal Opportunity." We have often pointed out, with reference to the monumental task of equalizing facilities for education, that this is a big job challenging not only the will, strength, and capacity of a strong people, but the cooperation, judicial interpretation, and constitutional structure of the nation. The reconstruction of educational facilities, including buildings, equipment, salaries, and administrative features, involves an extraordinary multibillion dollar industry, which, operated at its best, will enrich the South, develop its resources, and raise its standards of work, income, and living. This, done adequately, will not only make the South prosperous beyond previous measure, but will enable it, through increased prosperity, to pay for its new investments and in turn contribute powerfully to the national wealth. But there can be

no doubt of the nation's obligation to share this investment, both because of the federal strategy of equalization of funds and reciprocal cooperation with states and regions and because of the federal origin of the ruling, which makes mandatory the South's rebuilding of its educational structure.

6. The assumption of the positive achievements already presented are primarily inferences of the white South. Yet the Negro South, always assumed to be an integral part of the total South, provides a bulwark of resources to make the total assumptions valid. And here, two major sources of both actual and potential advance, often neglected in inventories of resources, are inherent in the human factors of Negro culture and personality. One is in the expanding body of leadership; the other is in the everyday behaving mass of Negro people adjusting to all sorts of situations.

7. Of the leaders, three segments reflect basic resources for accommodation to whatever strategy the South and the nation may adopt. The first group of top Negro leaders in the total Southern effort, moving especially with white leaders toward advanced policies, constitute what might be termed a composite biography of an era, and they can be named. There is no way of measuring their influence, but it has been powerful. Their lives and their work constitute a major part of the South, too little known outside the South, as well as by the great majority of white people in the South. One way to look at them is to call the roll alphabetically: Mary McLeod Bethune, Horace Mann Bond, M. O. Bousfield, Rufus E. Clement, R. P. Daniel, John W. Davis, Albert W. Dent, W. E. B. DuBois, Gordon B. Hancock, William H. Hastie, Charles H. Houston, Charles S. Johnson, Mordecai W. Johnson, C. C. Spaulding, Charles H. Thompson, H. L. Trigg, Forrester Washington, Robert C. Weaver, Carter Woodson, Monroe N. Work, and P. B. Young.

8. A second, much larger segment of Negro leadership is comprehended in a miniature of the above leaders, multiplied many times in a thousand communities and cities where they work in cooperative endeavors, gain places in public services, and give actual leadership in their own communities. The roll call here is as startling as it is impressive.

9. The third special segment of leadership is that of the Negro teachers. First, the college and university professors whose training

and high motivation set them both apart and inseparable from the total higher education picture in the South. They can and will do what is needed. Then, into the hinterlands and communities, the roll call of school teachers again reflects a startling advance on nearly every level. Check them in the city and county teachers' associations, in the state groups, and in the farm and home demonstration programs.

10. A second segment of the Negro human resources, the behavior of which we catalogue here as "gains" and "advance," is the great body of Negro families that have stood the test of time and crisis. We have often pointed out how the Negro, as a folk society operating within the larger society of the white South, has advanced more rapidly than much of the older farm tenant white South operating as a part of the white culture-economy. The assumption has been that in the cultural struggle the Negro has grown slowly, but surely, into an increasingly higher status, and an increased capacity on all levels. This reflects a rare composite personality, as well as millions of rare individual personalities, taking a powerfully difficult situation in stride. There are so many illustrations of this that it constitutes a special field, which falls in the early priority schedule of research to be undertaken as rapidly as possible. However, even with present knowledge, its is easy to point up here the relevance of this great segment of human resources available for whatever adjustments have to be made in the near future. The assumption is that the great body of Negro families will more than match any reasonable advance and resolving of difficulties which may be made by the white South.

11. The further assumption, here, is that the white South will rise to the occasion of appreciating the extraordinary record of the Negro South and will, by the same token, contribute more abundantly to the richer personality and cultural gains now in process among Negroes. Our assumptions have been that the main liability in the total situation has been the factor of personality and culture as reflected in the South's inherited verdict that the Negro, as a Negro, has not been esteemed as a person on the same level as the white race. By the same token, the personality element has been a universal bottleneck of advance. It has been pointed out that the attack upon the Southern credo, back in the early part of the century and on up through the second "new South," was led by Southern white leaders. Now, the college and university situation is conclusive evidence that the old

credo has been relegated to a dim, but not too distant, past, insofar as articulate verdicts are expressed in terms of educational equaltiy of opportunity. This verdict seems accurate in the face of almost universal exceptions that prove the rule, in that the great majority of Southern white people have never really faced this question as needing an answer. Indications are that they can face it honestly, and will do so, if and when they must.

TWELFTH SERIES OF ASSUMPTIONS: COMPLEXITY OF THE PROBLEM

1. Some of the foregoing assumptions of sure advance may be based upon oversimplification of the complex situations involved. In the catalogue of resources and prospects, liabilities and obstacles must be listed also. Some of these have already been cited in the consideration of contradictions and paradoxes. On the negative side of the ledger are a number of common assumptions prevalent throughout the white South, one of which has to do with advances in the field of labor. The assumption has often been made that FEPC legislation would be militantly resisted, and compulsory employment of Negroes in, let us say, textile mills, would result in violence. At the same time, however, there is already a shortage of labor, which suggests the possible employment of Negroes in the mills. The experience of neither the AF of L nor the CIO can give definitive indexes here. Another assumption, already mentioned in the Southern credo, is that the issue of segregation is not debatable. This couples with the cynical feeling that those who advocate the complete abandonment of segregation in the schools have to be tolerated as a part of the American doctrine of freedom of speech and teaching, but they are hardly to be respected. But now, as never before, people can talk about segregation and be undisturbed.

2. The fact must be faced that there are still common assumptions that the South is the white South, and the Negro is only the Negro. Although it is generously acknowledged that several thousand Negroes attending the Negro Elks convention in Atlanta in 1943 behaved with greater dignity and credit to the American ideal than the similar meeting of white Shriners in the same city, nevertheless, they were Negroes and not the South. There are assumptions by many of the younger Negroes, and by whites as well, that enmity, bitterness, and even hate characterize interaction processes between the races; but such as-

sumptions must face such assertions as those of the great militant Negro leader, Dr. Mary McLeod Bethune, who as late as August, 1953, said, "There is a growing understanding in the South. We Negroes have found there is a great deal of hatred in our hearts that we must get out. We must love, not hate. We must learn to be ready to give rather than simply sit back and try to take."

3. Of special significance are the logical and inevitable limitations of the great body of Negro citizens whose opportunities have been limited or who have had no long-time conditioning by education and nondiscrimination. By the very nature of the situation, they could not make the equalized contributions to an integrating culture that might be expected by those who are not conversant with the situation. There is practically no empirical data on this level. Such is also the case where the Negro culture and personality have been identified primarily with favorable resources; the estimates are based upon observable case examples and general impressions. In all forward specifications, there must be allowed a considerable lag in economic, educational, political, and social handicaps inherent in the Southern heritage.

4. On another level, it is important to examine the differences between common assumptions and what is almost universally asserted about situations on the one hand, and the dynamics of the actual situation on the other. Thus, of course, it is true that the problem of segregation is primarily a Negro problem, but more recently the crucial element has been assumed to be not that of the Negro, but of the *white South,* whose problem it has become. And so for other dichotomies and contradictions: It is not solely a Negro problem, but a Negro problem *and* a white problem. It is not solely a Southern problem, but a Southern *and* a national problem. It is a problem of compulsory segregation, and while its elimination may be accomplished by judicial and legislative processes, it is also a larger problem of fulfillment of cultural potentialities and integration. It is the responsibility of the nation; but, in terms of ecological and demographic situations, it is the supreme problem of the region. Although, as is more and more frequently asserted, it is the problem of the white South, it is the Negro segment that makes it the South's responsibility. It is not a problem of segregation or nonsegregation, but of non-

segregation *and* segregation in the framework of individual and group diversity and freedom of choice.

5. Although the main focus, commonly reflected in the problem of segregation, is one of democratic equality in the elementary school systems, another powerful immediate problem will be one of school administration and community relationships. If, in its main drives and conceptualization, it is essentially a problem of justice, morality, and democracy for Negro leaders and the future members of the race, in its immediate profile it reflects great cumulative handicaps of all the people, black and white, again in cultural and ecological imbalance. The ethnic-cultural-political situation in the United States is in some ways comparable to that in South Africa, but it is also so distinctively American that its solution must be properly identified with American ways.

6. It is a problem of international prestige and interaction processes, but it is even more a problem of achievement at home. Its reverberations in India and Pakistan, in China and Indonesia, are profound; but its ultimate relevancy to world order will stem from America's decisions. At home, it is not only a problem of Negro minority groups, but also of other minorities and of the white majorities. It is an economic and political problem, but also essentially a societal problem of cultural development. It is a dilemma in the framework of the old "states' rights" vintage, but that is essentially technical and incidental. So much is this true, that in the present diagnosis and definition of the Southern and national challenge, the facets commonly identified with "states' rights" are not considered determinant. As a technical and legal aspect, it is not primarily crucial to the main problem, except as it is relevant to the ultimate structures of the democratic state and its guarantees of freedom.

7. On still another level, decisions and judgments must rest upon concrete situations at a given time and under defined conditions, not necessarily applicable to other situations and other times. In the present instance, the issues are found in the difference between compulsory segregation in the elementary schools in the total South and in graduate and professional institutions of higher learning which are more susceptible to national conformities. In cases already projected for Supreme Court decisions, suits demanding the elimination of

compulsory segregation have argued that rules handed down for higher education "cannot be peculiar to any level of public education. Public elementary and high school education is no less a governmental function than graduate and professional education in state universities." The latter part of the assumption is true, but assumptions that there can be no difference between the two involves several factors, in addition to the matter of governmental functions. One is the total cultural configuration of the South. Another is the problem of educational administration and standards of teaching, rather than just a problem of right or wrong. Another is the relation of the community and family to the school. Still another is the very heart of family freedom, involving the intimate side of parents and children. Thus, elementary education, *as the function of the state,* is not the exclusive nor, in fact, the crucial issue.

8. Among other issues in the elementary and secondary schools, that are not involved in higher education, are those of double or triple compulsory behaviors. That is, there are not only the local school districting regulation and state compulsory school attendance laws, but federal compulsory attendance upon a mixed school, radically different from accepted practices, and where there are no alternatives for voluntaristic choice. Thus, all parents are subject to penalties if children do not attend school. But this is not true of attendance in universities and professional schools, or in the use of transportation facilities. Attendance at institutions of higher learning is optional for both white and Negro. As a matter of fact, a very small proportion of all youth goes through the universities. White students are not compelled to attend universities, and if they were, they undoubtedly would not have to attend any given state institution. Again, decisions about higher education are made by adults, or near-adults, so that there is no issue of the intimate life of the family where mothers interpret the first years of the child's school life as being inseparable from his family and social experience. Involved also are religious and other ideologies, race prejudice, and a sort of panicky terror of something about to happen beyond the realm of reality.

9. The question, now, is whether the courts are authorized to create and interpret rules for which the legislative referendum of the people has set no mandates. There is also the question as to whether the court's function is to rule on school administration and pedagogi-

cal principles, which are clearly crucial issues. Other issues might reside in the relative degree of freedom and opportunity involved, let us say, in compulsory school attendance upon religious schools.

10. So, too, the oversimplification of the approach as one of "either-or"—as moral directive or ideal type—does little justice to the complex needs of the situation. The assumption that reconstruction in the South is merely a matter of growing with technological change, economic development, and moral or governmental directives, may not be any more relevant than a similar assumption relative to India and Pakistan or Israel or a thousand island cultures which may not respond to the "Voice of America" on the partisan basis of equalizing economic and cultural forces through superimposed American specialization. The passage by Israel's Knesset of a bill in 1953, that no Jew may marry a gentile may be no more symbolic of the conflict between culture and technology than the requirement that the American woman married to a Jewish husband and migrating to Israel must abide by the ancient customs of shaving her head and having the children re-circumcised, while overhead jet planes celebrate the ceremony.

11. In the case of crucial decisions, with reference to critical situations in a problem setting, the relevance of sweeping generalizations and intellectual directives will be determined more through identification with special problems, oriented to national economy, ecological and regional situations, and balanced structures, than in their universal application to all social systems in a total society. This may be illustrated in many instances where the United States is perennially attacked by foreign critics. The nation hewed its own form and pattern, contrary to the criticisms and advices of the mother country or of the Nazis, of numerous diagnoses based upon certain truths not relevant to the main task of American development. To illustrate specifically, the dictum of a professor of French at Yale University that, "An American who cannot or does not read a foreign language newspaper or magazine is today a pitiful cripple," may be true for a specific objective—bottomed in a very special value system, limited to a relatively small number of people, and oriented in the culture pattern prevailing in France; but, it is scarcely relevant to the crisis of the United States leadership in economy and world fellow-

ship through resource development and conservation in relation to population policy.

THIRTEENTH SERIES OF ASSUMPTIONS: QUESTIONS AND ANSWERS

1. The complexity of the situation may be further inferred from many questions that are difficult to answer, but which must be asked in order to clarify and understand the situation. Questions which are relevant are of several sorts. The first type of query will ask simply whether that can be done, which, allegedly cannot be done. And if it is done, what will happen? If it is not done, what will happen? What are the legal ramifications involved? What are the means of resistance in the South? What are the avenues of federal enforcement? What alternative procedures are avaliable? Can the South justify its present system of biracial education any longer? Does the South's discrimination retard Southern regional advance? Does the South have any choice in the matter?

2. From the over-all viewpoint, is the immediate enforcement of nonsegregation reasonable? Is it constitutional, in the framework of states' rights and the doctrine of majority rule in local jurisdictions? Is it commensurate with the risk of resistance, and with what such resistance may do in supporting communistic propaganda against the United States? Do the people of both races want it?

3. What will be the effect upon the great strides made by Negro institutions of higher learning, and the preparatory and professional opportunity for Negro teachers? Would the majority of the Negro masses vote for the elimination of separate Negro schools? Would the trustees, administrators, and faculties of Negro colleges and universities prefer no separate Negro institutions? Is there a structural and an operational difference between the promise of the ultimate disappearance of segregated schools and the prospect of immediate federal enforcement of nonsegregation? Is "gradualism" already outmoded?

4. Granting the need for "action and action now," how, actually, will the school systems be administered under the new regime? How balance the rights of minority individuals transcending the institutional sanction of the majority group? How identify the rights of the majority with the rights and justice demands of the minority? How evaluate, for action programs, the role of moral principles over against

the essential requisites of effective administration and educational standards? How reconcile, in action programs, the conflicting claims that the issue involves, literally and compositely for both races, "life, liberty, and the pursuit of happiness," but in diametrically opposite directions?

5. If there is apparently no single, immediate "solution" possible, in the framework of all or none, now or never, right or wrong, good or bad, white or Negro, is it possible that there may be several "solutions?" Are the main inferences of decisions necessarily to be "either-*or*" so much as "both-*and*?" If it is possible to construct reasonable and attainable programs and objectives, what will it take to bridge the distance between what we have and what is wanted? And what is the best way of going about getting what is needed? What will it actually cost in financing—as well as in the "tragedies of progress?" And who will pay the costs? Is a part of that obligation upon the Federal Government, whose compulsion sets the incidence for the change?

6. Finally, what can be learned from the experiences of the past? Is it likely to be true, as is often held by both Northern and Southern leaders, that the liberal South, white and Negro, will really come up with the best answers? Is it true that inferences, that anything can now be done, may be drawn from the South's great advance? Are the minority of liberal white Southern youth representative of what will be a majority shortly? Are the current reports, that the majority of white college students in many institutions vote for nonsegregation, an important index of what to expect? On the other hand, in the light of violent opposition to the most advanced action patterns, is the conclusion justified that nothing radical or revolutionary can now be successfully undertaken? Concerning those Southern leaders, who are militantly advocating elimination of segregation on the total front, are they to be identified with the majority or "responsible" South?

FOURTEENTH SERIES OF ASSUMPTIONS: ALWAYS DILEMMA

1. Final assumptions must rest upon continuing exploration, education, testing grounds for federal and state programs, and for a working balance between voluntaristic and coercive action. For, from special studies, general observations, and recorded experiences, it must be clear that all our exhibits of evidence appear as a sort of tug

of war, now moving this way, now that. The real definition of the situation comes back again and again to inferences about issues, cultural values that are characteristic of the region, and to exploration and survey, projection of trends and predictions, and potentials that can be identified with alternatives. In this dilemma it would seem that never have the old classical, "On the one hand and on the other," and "but also," appeared to carry such a multitude of dichotomies, paired contradictions, major premises assumed, "ands," "ors," and "buts," in the loom of interaction processes. And rarely ever have we run across so many generalizations based upon so little basic research or tested observations. All of this is relevant not only to the elemental cataloguing of facts and the appraisal of causal factors, but to the orientation of value judgments and strategy priorities.

2. Although our final diagnosis and definition must be derived from cumulative evidence and be identified with the historical and cultural analyses of the regions and their total institutional structure, they must equally be oriented to the specific problem involved in the present concrete dilemma of the nation and its minimal obligations. If adequate diagnosis must be bottomed in sound theory, as we assume, the obligation is to construct sound social theory so as to discover fundamental assumptions that will be useful in meeting stated needs through practical application to this particular problem. This means the analysis of the situation must reveal the special and distinctive—new and exclusive factors that will be determinant and crucially relevant for this particular problem, at this particular time—as opposed to some general problem, or this particular problem at some other time and in some other setting.

3. One assumption of definitive change of great importance seems to be that, on the conceptual and methodological level at this particular time, "gradualism" is out. This is true for two reasons. One is that the term itself has outlived its traditional connotations. The other is that modern technics have so accelerated the rate of change as to make a new world. For, whatever ultimate decisions and procedures may be adopted, the rate of change has already been so accelerated as to constitute a new tempo, and the objectives so restated and constructed as to require radically new orientation. Now the prevailing inquiries revolve around the *how* and *when* of process and strategy, rather than the *what* and *whether* of argumentation. This means.

then, that conclusions based entirely upon precedents and previous experiences are not likely to be valid, and that whole segments of truths and arguments may not be relevant to some crucial decisions.

4. It follows that the most important assumptions now need to be identified with next steps. Some of the most important needs are for a more realistic interpretation of the situation and for mature action programs that are no respecters of race or region. Yet, for both the Southern regions and the nation, next steps must be identified with a multipatterned composite and comprehensive program. In conformity with the complexity of the total situation and the cumulative nature of diagnosis and definition, the approach to readjustments and "solutions" is logically a many-sided one. Although the core of the problem is primarily one of action, rather than conceptualization, nevertheless, our premises assume the validity and availability of research and the tools of the behavioral sciences to point directions, both in the present diagnosis and in future planning. By the same token, it is assumed that action programs in particular cases cannot wait on research and educational programs, but that enduring adjustments must be based on adequate information and the maturing of methods and processes commensurate with the best that America has produced, and will continue to achieve, in the realm of statesmanship and the democratic process.

5. In a very short history, the United States has developed a very long road of destiny. Its past record, in the light of the total configurations of cultural development and of comparative eras, may be said to be distinguished. Yet, its future could be greatly enhanced by avoiding mistakes of the past and by utilizing the gains of learning and common sense as working symbols of science and technology. And perhaps the first requisite here, at least in the crisis of ethnic and regional balance and equality, is a problem of intelligent focus and sustained attention commensurate with the sheer necessity at hand. The assumption seems justified that such attention has not yet been manifest.

6. More specifically, perhaps, the manifest destiny of the South, in the dynamics of regional integration and integrity, may appear as a supreme challenge. The regional approach constitutes, in reality, an appeal for the creative South to work out its own positive practical adjustment to today's crisis, rather than to be driven, coerced, and

politically patronized into a negative defense to meet the letter of constitutional decisions.

7. The appeal is for scientific and statesmanlike ways of achieving a powerful and enduring reconversion program, within the framework of a stable culture, a sound economy, a just morality, a changing folk psychology, a workable political democracy—and all set in the framework of an America of sanely balanced regions. This is an extraordinarily difficult task, worthy of any people, and worthy of the challenge of world dilemma in which survival and welfare are at stake. Yet, the challenge for the creative South to achieve such mastery is more specific. Here, it is the hope not only for positive and noble attainments, but also for the emergence of an articulate South that will substitute for much of its fears and frustration a new faith in itself.

FIFTEENTH SERIES OF ASSUMPTIONS: NEXT STEPS

1. The final series of assumptions relates to next steps. It seems clear that the way on from the present can be clearly identified with a fivefold program. The *first* segment infers "action and action now," in all instances where decisions and operations can proceed in full relevancy to each individual situation. This means, there is to be no continued delay in instances where the evidence is clear and procedures are available for the forthright guarantee of justice, equality of opportunity, and full civil rights. This means further, that the South, in addition to fulfilling its optimum obligations to the best of its ability and in return for a national cooperative reasonableness, will abide by all Supreme Court decisions, undertake revised state and local legislation and ordinances, and focus its energies upon positive operations rather than resistance. The particulars of such action programs are now in the process of being determined and will be further processed in due logical order.

2. The *second* segment infers a minimal research program, projected on the premises of as comprehensive and scientific research attainments as is commensurate with the best of the current American skills, and in the spirit of the American tradition. It is a strange anomaly that in an area so comprehensive and pressing, everywhere accepted as one of the most crucial problems, not only here and now, but of all time and places, that practically no basic research has been

done by any of the behavioral sciences. This deficiency stands in glaring contrast to the richness of the field and the abundance of opportunities for research in anthropology, psychology, sociology, education, politics, biology, and the medical and public health fields.

3. The *third* segment infers an educational program to function more powerfully and comprehensively in the adult field than has been heretofore envisaged and undertaken. Included in this prospect are new reaches in a leadership, more articulate than has yet been even approximated. The two prime segments of this educational endeavor are, first, getting the attention of the people through the presentation of challenges to face facts and to react reasonably in conformity to their norms of fairness, democracy, and Christianity, and in striving to put themselves in the place of the other group. Then, secondly, to present facts and perspectives as a basis for action.

4. The *fourth* segment requires the immediate organization and strengthening of regional and national commissions or councils, in the setting of which may be provided state and local groups operating cooperatively. Such councils, committees, and commissions would be of two sorts, voluntary and governmental. These, in turn, may require an effective dichotomy of regional and national. The Southern Regional Council, expanded and made more articulate, is an example of the regional type of voluntary agency. Involved in the federal types might be new national legislation or administrative directives, calling for congressional committees or president's commissions to negotiate procedures and to act as a buffer between the South and federal authorities. The states in turn could make provisions for state and local councils.

5. The *fifth* segment, then, follows cumulatively from the others and provides for the logical next steps in legislation, decisions, and long-time planning commensurate with advances in American leadership and strategy. The assumption, here, is that for such dynamics as the readjustment to a crisis of such propensities, it seems self-evident that the same maximum effort and planning should go into the reconversion on this interaction level as into reconversion from peace to war and again back from war to peace. Now, since this is a major problem of American democracy, the failure to meet which might very well destroy the soul of the South and cripple a great nation, it manifestly deserves the best that social science and political strategy

can achieve. The same sort of basic inquiry, which was undertaken in the statesmanship such as was made articulate by the founding fathers, is required, rather than relegating the problem to a simple moral or a complex emotional issue, or leaving it to vested frustration, political demagoguery, or intellectual exhibitionism. It would be unbelievable, if it were not true, that the South and the nation, facing their greatest domestic dilemma of the century, would not set up the means and procedures for the same statesmanlike inquiries as are assumed in other major problem areas.

PART TWO

The Region and Regionalism

A region is a reserve of energy whose origin lies in nature but whose development depends upon man. It is man who, by moulding the land to his own purposes, brings out its individuality. He establishes a connection between its separate features. He substitutes for the incoherent effect of local circumstances a systematic concourse of forces. It is thus that a region defines and differentiates itself and becomes, as it were, a medal struck off in the effigy of people.

Paul Vidal de la Blache

INTRODUCTORY NOTE

Throughout much of his life Odum worked on the analysis of his native region; the development of a theory of regionalism came later in his career. The South, it is clear, was Odum's case—the phenomena as given which he was to analyze. Just as other sociologists were to choose urban or rural society as specialties, Odum started with an attempt to understand his own region. His work on race, in regional theory, even his folk sociology can be seen to have this point of origin.

Moreover, the South was both a case for analysis and a cause for social action insofar as a sociologist he allowed himself to pursue a cause. While Odum was never bleakly factual in exploring phenomena, except possibly in *Southern Regions,* he remained always objective and critical in interpretation, so that his work rarely reads as though tinged with southern partisanship. The South, however, required more than description; its ills also called for prescription. To grasp its full implication, the reader needs to see Odum's work as it must have appeared to his contemporaries, that is, to bring to the excerpts a sense of history—a realization of time and place. This is obvious enough in his account of the Dayton "monkey trial" which he attended in company with H. L. Mencken.

Odum's work on the region and regionalism falls naturally into three parts: (1) portraiture and analysis of the South, (2) the meaning and theory of regionalism, and (3) cultural and literary regionalism. From the large variety at hand we have made seven selections.

An early piece on the place of the intellectual in southern life—rather his lack of place—virtually announced Odum's program. "A Southern Promise" written in 1920 as introduction to a volume on southern leaders remains one of his most readable essays. The theme is continued in "A Duel to the Death." Here, seeing the intelligentsia set in conflict over against the folk at Dayton, Odum resisted the temptation to join the metropolitan press in "lambasting the yokels." Again he saw a failure in leadership, the failure of the intellectuals to get over to the folk what was happening in science.

With *Southern Regions,* a study of the South as an underdeveloped area, Odum shifted to economic and social science analysis regarded as preliminary to social planning. Here the South was viewed as potentially rich in the primary bases of wealth—natural and human resources, but poor in the derivative sources of wealth—capital wealth, technological resources, and institutional resources. It has not proved feasible to publish selections representative of this large monograph, but the content of Odum's particular doctrines is presented in several selections. In an introduction to a study done by Harriet L. Herring, Odum gave cogent statement to the necessary role of industry in regional development. This is interesting as both scientific and popular justification of the cause beloved of the local chambers of commerce.

If Odum's doctrine of the trend from sectionalism to regionalism and regional-national integration represents his major achievement, as is sometimes said, it must be sought in his books. Rather than resort to inadequate articles from the journals, we have violated our rule about using work done with others and have reprinted the first two chapters of *American Regionalism* written with Harry Estill Moore. While the book was in every sense a collaboration, Professor Moore has encouraged us by saying that these two chapters were the major responsibility of the senior author. Here we leave the more facile style of Odum writing for a general audience and follow the work of a professional. Chapter I is extended enough to present the concept of regionalism and the various facets of regional analysis as related to different disciplines. Chapter II shows Odum's appreciation of Frederick Jackson Turner's work and argues for the trend from sectionalism to regional-national integration.

Our last section shows Odum writing as a humanist, concerned with cultural and literary regionalism in the United States. Among the major papers he contributed to the *Saturday Review of Literature,* Odum's "American Blend" was selected as best representing his interpretation of regional diversity and national unity in our literature. In addition to its other qualities, "Literature in the South" shows Odum at his polemic best in a controversy with Donald Davidson—often an adversary—as well as his appreciation of William Faulkner. Odum was widely read in contemporary literature, and other selections could well have been presented.

R. B. V.

1. The Problematic South

A Southern Promise [1925]*

L eaders of the first order in the Nation have come out of the South. The South has now much of the same admixture of blood and social heritage that produced George Washington, Thomas Jefferson, Robert E. Lee, Andrew Jackson, Woodrow Wilson, Walter Hines Page, and other men of distinction. Moreover, the South has an excellent physical environment for the development of strong personalities. Why, then, are the Southern States so barren of individual leaders who represent the highest achievement in their fields? In politics, in education, in literature, in art, in industry, in religion, in any aspect of human endeavor, where are there to be found in the South leaders occupying the foremost place in their respective groups? Or how many even are there who have attained more than mediocre rank?

I

At the outset, however, let it be remembered that the shortage of leadership is being lamented generally throughout the states and elsewhere. One need only call the roll of the great and near-great in the national political parties or in congress or in the realm of international community. If one feels inclined to complain that certain of the Southern States are "the worst led states" in the Union, he may also catalogue the strife and bickerings or reactionary inertia of other states. If he grieves over the fact that there are almost twice as many persons of distinction born in a certain Southern State as now reside within its borders, he need only look for comparison to certain other states, Ohio, Indiana, Iowa, Pennsylvania, Maine, New

* From *Southern Pioneers in Social Interpretation* (ed.) (Chapel Hill: The University of North Carolina Press, 1925), pp. 3-27.

Hampshire, even Wisconsin, for similar conditions. Other states there are whose roll of distinction is not long. No, the South is not alone in its present dearth of distinctive leadership if it be compared with individual states in other regional divisions of the Union.

There is another point of emphasis which the South shares with the rest of the country, and with much of the rest of the world. It is the changing basis upon which leadership is now developed and made effective. There are many aspects of this transfer of emphasis, and many grounds, therefore, for crudeness and poverty in the transitional stages. Of course it has long since been recognized that leadership has been transferred from kings to people and that we no longer educate for royalty. But what has become of the leader with "authority," whether in government, in church, in industry or elsewhere in which the bigness of the leader is measured by the subjection of his followers? What has become of the dominant leadership of the church? Is there being transferred from capital to labor much of the important leadership of the future? Has there been a transfer of leadership from country life and agricultural groups to city and industrial folk? Is the dominance of lawyer and politician being taken over by farmer and worker? Has the one-man superdomination epoch given way to the crowd, and if so how much mob and how much democracy? Has the family surrendered its leadership to other agencies? What will be the effect of woman's enlarging leadership? Is the leadership of youth encroaching upon that of maturity? Is Mr. Babbitt taking the place of the former man of professional distinction?

Whatever changes there are, the leaders of the future will approximate an antithesis of the old leaders of the political, military, or religious type. They will be leaders who represent movements and their leadership will draw its strength from the cause represented rather than from the overpowering individual. Alexander and Napoleon, indicted on many counts and sentenced to much labor, would scarcely be respectable in the modern community. So would the great men of yesterday be shorn of their glory by the social codes of today. However perfected in type and technique the old leaders were, the world will know them no more forever. In their stead will be a diffused leadership, of the untapped potential resources of which the world yet knows little. The task of developing this leadership is the task of the present. The verdict of the future may well agree with Joseph K. Hart that "a democracy cannot survive unless all the people, or the greater part of them, possess the quality of potential leadership and the actual leaders possess a deep sense of social responsibility and quality of potential loyalty to other leaders." Many of our deficiencies in present-day leadership are due to the failure so far to make quick adjustments to social change and to the shortness of time for the evolution of new types. The South is far from being an exception to the rule.

II

If this failure to make adjustments to social and economic change in the aspects of transfer of leadership already mentioned be charged against the Southern States in general, as a first count, the second deficiency may be said to grow out of the first. It is that the South lacks experience and training for the newer leadership. By this I do not mean merely the normal deficiencies of after-war desolation, real and tragic as they have been. I mean rather the specific situation in which the leaders of the present South have had neither experience nor training for leadership outside the atmosphere of political strife, economic limitations, educational and social deficiencies, and general mediocrity in many aspects of life. How, then, could they lead with distinction or govern well? Or how attain an equal place in the last half century of rapid development? Who were the old Southern leaders, the lawyers, the mayors, the judges, the statesmen? Consider today the same communities, towns, cities, states in which they held forth; how many of their children now occupy the same positions of leadership as did their fathers? If their children have not come into the succession, others have. Who are they but the chance representatives of the diffused leadership previously referred to, but whose potential abilities have in no wise been brought out or tested? Some there are of the same heritage as the old leaders; more there are of the common folk, mixed here and there and everywhere in a varied composite of the land. Now whatever else may be said of the old Southern leaders; whatever their shortcomings in democratic standards, in attitudes toward the Negro and the working man, there can be no doubt that they stood forth in their leadership as examples of distinction, charm, order, force, character. They led. And while the younger leaders, of mottled mien, do have many ideas in advance of their predecessors, and may have in them the making of another generation of distinction, they do not stand out as did the leaders of the Old South. This does not mean that the present status is a final criterion any more than the first efforts of women in politics will prove to be the permanent mode or index of ability. It means simply that here is a new generation with limited experience, limited training and limited leisure but with the abundance of energy, enthusiasm, and small-town adolescent zest for participating in politico-social activities and for enacting righteousness.

As a rule too much significance is attached to temporary results that come from lack of experience and education. There is a vast amount of difference between judgments based upon limited experience and education and those arising from low intelligence or potential intelligence for future generations. Witness the foolish things which any previous generation of folk have done. The distinguished father of a future leading progressive thanks the Lord for the lowly fly, mankind's faithful scavenger! The parents of a leader in hygiene education are mortally afraid of night air! The embittered Virginian in his last will and testament bequeaths to his children and grandchildren and their descendants "throughout all generations, that bitter hatred and everlasting malignity of my heart and soul against the Yankees, including all the people north of the Mason and Dixon's line—to instill in the hearts of their children and grandchildren, and all future descendants, from childhood, this bitter hatred and those malignant feelings against the aforesaid people and their descendants throughout all future time and generations." If nearly all of his children marry above the Mason and Dixon's line and become generous lovers of a generous people, is it therefore a matter of intelligence or mellowed time and experience? Is progress of scientific son over enthusiastic father a matter of more intelligence, or is dogmatic limitation of father a permanent handicap to the distinguished son to be? Or what man of distinction does not blush to think of youthful statements made, or early convictions for which he has proclaimed himself willing to make the great sacrifice, or make a fool of himself generally? Is he now, in the glow of his prestige and honor, the more intelligent or merely more learned and experienced? If one be inclined to consider these merely academic questions, unrelated to his severe judgments upon the folk, let him inquire into the history of peoples and let him look forward to the future of the governing groups in the grand old empire of Britain, in the coming government of women, and in the newer aspirations of race and common man. The measure of experience today ought not to be the fruit of to-morrow.

Finally, this poverty of the South in experience and training is not found alone in the field of politics and general leadership. "Blessed are the poor in spirit," but the Southern people have not been poor in spirit. Rather they have been poor in almost every other way. And theirs has not been the kingdom of achievement or leadership or Heaven or anything else save perhaps the kingdom of the proud spirit and the glory that was old! In education, in wealth, in public health and public welfare, in the development of the people and homes and farms of the countryside, in literature, in art and in many other fine things we lack the opportunity and experience for leadership and distinction. Even in religion and morality, for which we claim so much, we have been poor in the fruits of social righteous-ness, justice, and the essence of Christianity. The religion that boasts much, complains continuously, seeks motes in other people's eyes, klans together for persecution, mobs the weak, has little respect for truth, is selfishly self-centered, is emotionally and lazily inclined toward the easiest way, would hardly be expected to produce dis-tinguished creative contributions in any field. So long as the majority of leaders and the great group of followers are rich in that spirit of self-righteousness, of sensitive antagonism toward things not our own or of our way of thinking, so long will the South be thrice not blessed.

III

The third count against us is that we have lacked universities. "Tommy" Wilson at home becomes Woodrow Wilson at Prince-ton. The mediocre lawyer at Atlanta, from Southern fields becomes Woodrow Wilson, the political scientist, teacher, university presi-dent, governor, President of the United States. Walter Hines Page, restless youth, hunting for himself, critical of his surround-ings, from Johns Hopkins finds the promise of a great leader.

Scores of men today in places of distinction began their careers of achievement, ambition, redirected purpose from the larger universities of this country, many of them remained permanently away from the South. Other scores, of the same blood and heritage and potential ability, but without this opportunity, have never developed. Count the men from the South—there are hundreds—who have achieved distinction, whether inside or outside, and see how many have had their pushing force from the outside. In fact we measure our professional folk by the extent to which they hold degrees from Northern and Western universities, albeit often complaining of the bad influence of those universities upon us. What right have we, in all fairness and justice to the South, to pass judgment upon Southern capacity to produce distinction when, by our own and by all estimates, we withhold the means and stimulus for distinguished effort and service?

Perhaps the worst part of the situation is the fact that the great majority of our Southern group, including many colleges and universities, do not think in terms of university. And by this I do not mean merely the physical plant or the student body which goes to make a university, but the spirit of the university, such as that implied in President Chase's recently stated obligation of giving the student a chance to find and love the truth. We have had in the South a few examples of campaigns being made to build great universities, but too often when anything approaching university standards is suggested a halt is called. Much of the propaganda for finance is too often based on the demagogic appeal to religious or local stubbornness or pride, all of which instead of giving us the universities for which we set out, will delay that much longer the coming of real universities. Consider, for instance, a Southern denominational leader proclaiming in his campaign for financial support for "the South's greatest University" that the South "must endow and equip its own institutions of learning, and then by the most watchful care keep them clear of liberalism and liberalists. This is a high and holy obligation which the South owes the great Republic of which it is so important a part." Contrast this then with the estimate of that other Southerner, former president of Princeton and at the time of this utterance at the University of Paris, President of the United States. "University spirit," he said, "is intolerant of all things that put the human mind under restraint. It is intolerant of everything that seeks to retard the advancement of ideals, the acceptance of truth, the purification of life." Contrast it also with the dream of President G. Stanley Hall of universities of the future as the shrine and power house of the research spirit that shall permeate the whole field of inquiry into human knowledge and human welfare. His "University Invisible" would be "composed of all those everywhere who are smitten with the passion of adding something to the sum of the world's knowledge."

Not all of our limitations in college and university are due to ignorance of university standards or lack of university experience and training. Lack of resources, the poverty of material things already referred to, of course is responsible for much. I have before me now an earnest request from one of the more progressive smaller institutions for women asking for a teacher whose classes will include family case work, child welfare, community organization, social pathology, labor problems, economic theory, economic history, and of course some social theory. And the head of the department, holding his doctorate from one of the largest universities of the land, ought to know better. Other illustrations are legion. Thus much of the teaching and claims of the smaller institutions become superficial. Many of the smaller institutions in both state and church are clearly hypocritical in claiming what they manifestly do not have. This claim and this atmosphere, as well as the limitations themselves, tend to lower standards and certainly do not provide the educational leadership needed. There are other defects that hold back even the best of beginnings. One of these is the prevailing tendency for trustees of colleges and universities, in both state and denominational schools, to assume both the legislative and administrative functions of the institution, meddling with minute details of internal administration, and limiting faculty, administration and even students in their normal performance of duty. There are, of course, notable exceptions to such a general state, both among the smaller schools and the larger ones. And the fact that a Southern university has recently been admitted into membership of the Association of American Universities, and is now president of this body, is evidence both of the exception and also of the South's ability to develop and maintain universities. It is also evidence that in the past the South has not had such universities, there being only one other Southern university member of this group—a charter member from the beginning.

IV

The South has lacked an atmosphere conducive to achievement and distinction. We have already said that the South has an excellent physical environment for the development of strong personalities. There are fewer more absurd assumptions than that which attributes the South's lack of achievement to climate or southern physical conditions of soil, topography, or other geographical and physical conditions. On the contrary, it will be shown in time that the South's charm of climate, variety of situations, richness of physical setting, coupled with newer social and educational attainments, will prove a superior land for the nurture of leaders and for the promotion of the finer things of life. What we mean in this statement is that there has been no suitable social, cultural, and spiritual atmosphere in which leadership could develop or distinction survive. Besides the limitations of experience and universities already referred to there has been conflict between races, between classes, between denominations, between visible and invisible government, between dominant demagogues and their following. With conflict has come protest. For years now the dominant note has been negative and the South has been sensitive and "against" the things that are progressive and the things that are not her own. And within her borders she has built up faction and clique, the one against the other, all against outsiders. One can scarcely believe that this querulous pessimistic South is the same South of the heroic fighters of the war between the states, or the earlier cheerful optimists, or that of the epic struggle to rebuild her devastated estate. Furthermore, the South is afraid, not of Negro domination, but of itself, of each other, afraid to speak the truth or act justly because of what the folks will say; and as Gerald Johnson says, afraid of its eighty million northern critics. A South so depressing in atmosphere cannot achieve; and to remain so, in the face of all her natural resources and her ethnic and social inheritance, would prove one of the most abortive epochs in recent history.

There are, however, heavy tasks ahead if this cumulative atmosphere is to be changed before it alters the whole structure of the

South. We have pointed out before the fact that we are ignorant. How could we be otherwise in the face of past experience? But even so, with the handicap of poverty and struggle now happily past, we are not learning enough of the great truths of science or attaining knowledge of social facts and social righteousness. We are afraid of the truth and have few leaders to guide us in its paths. We have pointed out before how little we read and how we fall short of the rest of the country and of our reasonable expectations. And much of the limited reading is of the inbred sort of provincial passing type. We have pointed out the fact that we rank low in creative effort, in writing worthwhile literature, and that we are not willing to pay the price for an achievement which many reliable critics believe lies within the grasp of Southern talent. And in other fields, in the beautifying of our country homes and farms, in the planning of towns, in the building of school houses, and in many other aspects of material achievement the South has come to reflect itself in terms of second rate standards and as not willing to sink individual opinion and financial cost into the common good.

In its sensitiveness the South is still hot-headed, emotional, unthinking in its attitude toward many questions and toward those who do not agree with its opinions or traditions, or those who do not approve of its conduct. This is especially true of matters relating to race, religion, industry, and outside criticism. On the other hand, the South is boastful and superficial with reference to its achievements. Of course it has so long been considered backward that its defense mechanisms would naturally develop something of this sort; and of course the statements made about it have often been hard to bear. Further, it would seem to deserve recognition for what it is achieving, for like Lincoln's gingerbread, no one ever liked it more or had less of it. Nevertheless, it is in grave danger, as has been proved in certain sections, of crippling its future achievement through the constant backward look or the prideful boast of mediocrities. Blessed are the meek, but the South has not been meek nor has it thereby inherited much of the earth. The South is too proud of its nonprogressive fundamentalism and enjoys an easy-going rationalism which places entirely too much responsibility for its shortcomings upon the Lord. The South, claiming to be preëminently Christian, is yet in many instances in danger of breeding a gross spirit of boastful materialism with ecclesiastical dogmatism and of joining political demagoguery in unholy alliance with religious fervor, thus producing a mongrel barrenness, the despair of classification. Such an atmosphere coupled with ignorance and intolerance will scarcely produce leaders of distinction.

The South has not accorded due recognition to merit within its own borders. By this I do not mean merely the "prophet without honor" habit, which after all is one of the social order's best mechanisms for the development of its fledglings. Nor do I mean simply that recurrence of the South's failure to recognize such men as Walter Hines Page or Woodrow Wilson; for, as Professor Connor points out, much of this was their own fault. Nor even do I mean only the failure of the South ever to recognize or follow them except to further its own plans or to please its vanity. It need not be replied that the South takes great pride in its distinguished sons who, having departed from its midst, return to receive acclaim. The South has not yet shown that this enthusiasm is more than a glorification of southern achievement. We mean more than all these; we mean a recognition that includes position, financial reward, esteem and an atmosphere for work, and the privilege of free speech and unhampered proper personal pursuit of achievement.

The factor of inadequate financial support is an element of the situation, not a censure of past performance. But as a fact it is a most powerful and determining element and one which must be reckoned with in the future. And the future is what counts. It is but natural that in the past a region characterized by the limitations already mentioned, should not only be unable to meet the financial terms of more prosperous and experienced sections, but also that it should develop an atmosphere unfriendly to larger rewards. There is, however, less reason for a critical and jealous state of mind on the part of professional or common folk which tends to discourage adequate salaries or suitable pay for professional work. In particular, there is no excuse for the attitude of many of the approximating richer folk which holds, to all intents and purposes, that teachers, professors in colleges and universities, or literary folk, ought to be thankful for whatever salaries or financial rewards may be apportioned to them by their generous boards. They are in it simply for the money anyway and should be employed if they are of the faith and can be had cheap enough. Such an attitude adds immensely to the attractiveness of better positions and higher salaries in other places. It is, of course, often the lack of appreciation as measured by small salaries, rather than the limited salaries themselves, which constitute the turning point.

If to the absence of a sympathetic atmosphere or of appreciation of progressive social, economic or political effort, or of creative work, be added denial of freedom of speech or opportunity to produce, how much surplus energy, ability or power must one put forth to achieve even an average? And of that average what chance is there for objective measurement or visible recognition? This, again, is no mere academic question, for there are many who make no pretense of speaking or writing freely. Then there is that great number who, surrendering little by little, gradually benumbed through easy-going rationalization from the promise of great things to static acquiescence, who do not know that they do not know. How many manuscripts there are unpublished, how many positive impulses unobeyed, or how many progressive steps there remain untaken because of the surety of vanishing position and influence, no one of course knows. But I do know of many. Nor is the prevailing forbidden fruit limited to radical doctrines in politics, economics, education, religion or sociology, but restrictions encompass the simple, sincere, courageous telling of the truth about the South, its people, its history, its tasks. Indeed, the atmosphere of fear is not limited to Herrin, or to the common folk of the South. It permeates the whole body politic.

And of what sort is the merit which we do recognize within and without the South? There could be named, of the older group still living, fivescore individuals now in the South whose abilities, personalities and achievements, in a fair field of opportunity and support, would easily rank among the first order in any larger company. And of the younger group I should gladly undertake to find another outstanding one hundred with promise as great or greater than these. Of course they are held in high esteem in the home state in smaller ways, but who follows them? What recognition do they have? What time, means, opportunity and irresistible impulses have they had since the first days of their promise? Who outside of local groups ever knows of their abilities or benefits from their work? Or what larger promise have they for the future? Who are they, on the other hand, by whose reputations the South is known and whose leadership the South follows and esteems? Are they not far too frequently the demagogues and the dogmatists in politics and religion?

And here is a peculiar thing, a sort of *paradoxum paradoxorum*. With all of our agitated protest against outside suggestion or interference and all our enacted "home boy" and "home talent" appointments to the great majority of positions, nevertheless when we have distinction or honor to confer, advice to publish, money to pay for services, forthwith we hasten to find someone from afar off upon whom to bestow honor, in return for which we expect kind words, high praise, and local commendation for having brought the great of earth to our small town. Indeed the chief service rendered by our distinguished visitors is usually our own verdict that we have got the best of talent for fortuitous display. If there be home folks within the domain of the Southern States let them consider it high honor to pay their own expenses and attend conferences, universities, but let them not presume to know more than the local folks or expect financial reward or appreciation. If there be those from afar, let them know forsooth that we have the willingness and ability to pay whatever is necessary, and the more the honorarium the more we neglect the rest of the program. It is commonly assumed in the South that nothing which might be produced there can possibly be of more than local interest. If something is done well in the South it must be forsooth southern. It is true that we talk about its being time something of national importance should be produced from the South, but we either expect such an effort to fail or we are surprised that it does not, and to ask southerner to take counsel of southerner is presumptuous indeed. If we have a large fund to pay for a series of lectures or a survey or for expert work, we find someone outside of the South who agrees to take special time, pains, energy, and very commendably and successfully gives us a good piece of work. It seems never to occur to us that if money were available, if time and leisure and resources were afforded, the type of efforts which our own folk put forth would be far different from the hurried, unappreciated results which are obtained whenever there is free service and emergency task. It is a commonplace to affirm that creative work of quality must be produced in workable atmosphere and with workable tools.

VI

Much more ought to be said. Other factors ought to be discussed. These that have been presented ought to be qualified. It must be remembered of course that the term "the South" is not accurate. There are vast differences between the states and in many instances the differences are growing. But most of all we should hasten to say that not one of these counts against the South need in any sense be a permanent fundamental part of our structural civilization and promise. And the statement of these glaring deficiencies ought to give particular emphasis to the startling assertion that in the face of the limitations that now exist it is entirely possible that the South has within its being much of the supreme quality and potential which the nation needs above all things else at this time. To give evidence that this is true and to set in motion forces which will turn the southern potential into national power will constitute the supreme task of the next few generations.

The usual rebuttal that most of the shortcomings which may be charged to the South are also in some degree found in other states and in other sections amounts to nothing. What we are concerned with is the actual fact of what the South is doing and can do. The only criterion will be results. We are tired, eternally tired, of limitations. Tired of wrong impressions, tired of the defense complex and mechanism, tired of unending ridicule, tired of taking second and third and fourth rate places in achievement, tired of undeveloped potential, tired of lack of opportunity, tired of complacency, ignorance, poverty, and all the paradoxes that now flower out of a soil which can produce better. Anyone can add up the five counts which we have enumerated and see the impossibility of ever hoping for distinguished achievement and service so long as these conditions last. A full expectation under these circumstances is ridiculous and immoral. The wonder is that the South has done as much as it has. And the story of its achievement both in its regional rebuilding and in its contribution of outstanding individuals in the nation is the greatest possible evidence of its possibilities and of the critical need for a spiritual revolution throughout the Southland.

We have not mentioned some of the commonly discussed handicaps. We have not referred to the old tendency to render judgment upon individual and creative effort only in relation to family standing. We have not discussed the misunderstanding of one class by another, and other specific factors. We have referred only indirectly to the handicap of race. We have not taken into consideration the economic history of the South and many factors of mediocrity which were already appearing even before the war between the states. These we believe are well on the road to their place in the historical record of the South of other days. Nor have we enumerated under each of the general deficiencies discussed the outstanding beginnings looking already in the direction of new days. There is ample evidence to show that the South can evolve its situation. Certain it is that the South can be brought to make adjustments to meet the need of social and economic change. Certain it is that the South can gain experience and training. The South has already shown that it can produce and maintain universities and leaders if it will. It would be absurd to say that because the South in the past had not produced an atmosphere conducive to creative effort and social progress it therefore would always be so limited. And to affirm that the South will not in the future give adequate reward and recognition to its leaders would be at once for the South to set upon itself the seal of inferiority. And the South has no inclination to do this.

After all, however, is it possible that the South has something to offer besides its determination and its ability to eliminate the common deficiencies which all Southerners must agree now exist, and its will to develop its resources, human and physical? This itself is, of course, a rich offering and one that will require heroic efforts to bring forth. Nevertheless I do not believe that any fair student of the South, adding up and analyzing his accurate data on the subject, can come to any other conclusion than that it can be done. Looking forward, then, to the time when the southern civilization, freed from its self-imposed impassable barriers, shall have created favorable situations, what else is there which the South may offer to the nation at large in addition to the development of its own potential? What is there in its groups from mountain crag to shores of sand which might contribute to a recreating epos? Is there in the spiritual mode, religious zeal, demagogic appeal, stubborn individualism, ethnic unity, heroic pride, adolescent combativeness, imaginative romance, something which exists in abundance in the rough, which the South and the Nation need to mine and refine? There is much evidence to show that there is. The Nation needs some sort of renaissance of intellectual conviction, spiritual rejuvenation and stable morality that does not rattle with superficial verbiage. Shorn of the glory of its introverted social personality and its objective material limitation, what may the South not offer in its newer day? To turn this southern potential into national power is a southern promise, the spirit of which is foretold in the stories of southern pioneers.

The Duel to the Death [1925]*

What is the meaning to the social scientist, the educator, and the social worker of this echoing phrase "duel to the death" but recently hurled across the hills of Dayton to one group by another group far more distantly separated than is realized by most of those who study in halls of learning, or work in fields of professional effort? What is the meannig of the "fight to the finish" challenge being relayed by certain organized groups? For they have a very definite meaning and challenge which can be ignored only with disastrous results. What I found at Dayton [Tennessee] was more pathos than joke, more futility than fighting, more tragedy than comedy, more inexperience and ignorance, including visiting seekers after truth or sensation, than lack of intelligence. While mediocre leaders may be indulging in what President Glenn Frank calls an indecent scuffle, it is not so with great cross sections of the American people. Here, representing scores of American communities and millions of American folk were earnestness, sincerity, simplicity, frankness, stubbornness, and the honest fruits of generations of nature and nurture. Years of institutional and physical environment have produced a full grown fruit now being gathered and marketed by self-centered leaders who feel that they have found perfect weather in this new incidence and mass response. What other results can be possible?

MORE SEARCHING INQUIRY

Satire, ridicule and jest thrown back by critics across the hills seem to me only to rebound to mock a great host of scientists and students

* Editorial in *Social Forces,* IV (September 1925), 189-94.

of the environmental basis of society who are honestly surprised, discouraged and disgusted with the present situation. Bitterness and pessimism, on the one hand, or mere cheerfulness and optimism, on the other, are superficial and unsatisfactory makeshifts for hard scientific inquiry, earnest efforts toward wise social policy, and a frank facing of the facts. Are the "progressive" leaders of society, then, no more farseeing than the leaders of reaction? Are they, as has been claimed by many critics, leaders of less courage than those who lead the fanaticism of the day? Do the educators and the social scientists, however intelligent and learned, manifest no more intelligence in their methods and technique, or is their thinking any less subjective and dormant, than the other group? In terms of diagnosis and cure, what is the meaning of this duel to the death in this day when peace is prized above war? What is the meaning of this fight against science in the evening and morning of the first day when social science begins to find itself, and to see that it is good? What is the meaning of this new panic among leaders and believers in democracy on the eve of its first great test? Why a new proposed fatalism reaching all the way from *laissez faire* satisfaction to the recent gains in social direction and telesis? Why bitter accusations and limited judgments unsupported by due process of thinking and the necessary accompanying scientific inquiry and poise?

POSSIBLE MEANINGS

Suppose we pass over the usual meanings ascribed to the present situation. There are undoubtedly great principles involved in the current statements of alarm and danger. There may very well be danger to science. There may be danger to religion and to social morality. There may be great danger to the churches and Christianity. Dangers there may be to the whole public education system, to standards of scholarship and higher education. The issue of freedom of speech and thought and of teaching may very well be involved. The whole question of the trend of the churches to dominate politics and government and thus violate great American principles is a most important one. What is to become of scientific research, of the social sciences, of the search after truth, if this sort of thing goes on, sanctioned by majorities, unstemmed by minorities? Where is the courage and unified action of the more highly educated groups? And there are many other meanings: a broken old man, champion of lost causes, pathetic again in his mischoice of an issue; unscrupulous use of demagogic methods by thousands of leaders of the fray; the farcical mixing of law, the courts, the abstractions; the pitiful commercialization of the whole episode and process, and the sight of myriad intelligent folk, if not following, allowing themselves to be led by the mentally and spiritually deficient. The pathetic eagerness and provincialism of all America's reading public to find something satisfying, and the epochal farce being enacted may also be registered as factors. These and other aspects may be of considerable importance and have had a great variety of treatment. They are a part of the total situation, from which other meanings may be sought. In these editorial notes, however, we wish to raise the question as to what the situation means to the social scientist in terms of its magnitude and application, in terms of a possible verdict that the situation is neither understood nor under control by those best prepared to lead, and in terms of a research situation.

THE SIZE OF IT

Pounding away on varied types of interpretation and description of the present situation have been some 2,310 daily newspapers in this country, some 13,267 weeklies, about 3,613 monthlies, no less than 392 quarterlies, with perhaps another five hundred including bi-monthlies and semi-monthlies, tri-weeklies and odd types. It profits little to deplore the over-emphasis or the exaggerated reports and the sensational methods. The fact remains that the newspapers alone have printed, on a fair estimate made from actual counts of typical samples, words in the aggregate amounting to three thousand volumes of three hundred ordinary pages each. And this within a short period of time, thus concentrating attention and energies upon a single subject. And the circulation of these papers has been enormous, reaching millions of folks who do not read books. Added to this have been scores of articles and editorials in the learned journals. I have found no periodical of any sort, agricultural or trade as well, which has ignored the subject. Nor have I found a weekly or denominational paper which has not presented the matter in some form although of course the actual examination of these has been very limited. In going to and fro in the out-places and country-side

I have yet to find a single white person who is not willing to talk about the subject, who does not know something of it, or who does not have ready-made opinions. Some of the best things I have heard have been from the natural wisdom of such individuals. I need scarcely proceed with the other enumerations to show the quantitative appeal which the present situation must have to all students of society and social progress. What about the 237,945 churches with their 219,876 ministers and a membership of 48,224,014? How many of these churches have left the matter alone? What of platform and chautauqua and everyday discussion and smoking car? What of the almost thousand universities and the 276,881 schools with enrollment approximating twenty-five million folk? As a matter of fact, however, these last have been perhaps the least in the discussion and presentation of the subject, leaving to the billion-worded newspapers and conversation, religious argumentation and the like. To these factors should be added the almost 800 books published last year on religious subjects and the number now climbing, exclusive of the scores of cheap pamphlets, circulars, with their dogmatism, vulgarity, and intolerance. Can any student of the times ignore such a quantitative situation, regardless of the respective merits of its several phases? Whatever the type of educational propaganda put forth, whatever the status of those who read, here is challenge to the student to open his eyes and see what is going on about him. To continue to hide from the truth may leave a verdict against him not creditable to judgment or intelligence.

THE OPPOSING CAMPS

There is another way to measure the size of the situation, and the surprise of it, although it ought to be clear to any student who has made a business of keeping in touch and checking up social situations. This is by examining the two opposing groups, with their clear cut and decisive unity. Mr. Bryan was correct in affirming that he could find in any state, and therefore in all states, a majority of the folk to be fundamentalists. Here is a majority of the American people lined up on one side. Equally clear it is that the great majority of professional folk and of certain clearly defined groups of larger experience and education are unanimously on the other side. Here, then, is the spectacle of colleges, universities, lawyers, many ministers, editors, literary folk, publicists, and the great host of more experienced folk, whether intentionally or not, literally ranked, according to the crude terminology of the duellist, against the great mass of people whom they are to serve. If that situation is not tragic enough, on the one hand, and comic enough on the other, to wake up the academic and cosmopolitan mind, then may we invoke the shades of Sumner, the scientific militant professor. If there are those who doubt the extent or intensity of these opposing attitudes, let them take a count of the millions of trustful folk whose minds have been filled with virus against inquiry and education or of those learned folk whose every-day opinion of the common man is expressed only in terms of negative intelligence.

The difference between the two groups is not intelligence, but vast, yawning distance—distance so great and abysmal that lines from smoky range to fertile valley or mountain crag to shores of sand appear futile symbols. Such distance is not spanned by one group in mental eagerness and anguish hoping to see what lies upon and beyond the purple hills, or another group near-sighted with much study, learning and experience, and seeing nothing save the broad expanse from lofty viewpoint above the hills. One may ascertain the degree to which these distances are not spanned by a study of the misstatements, demagogic appeals, and unfair methods used by Mr. Bryan and many others in their effort to ridicule scholarship and learning and to flatter the masses of people who have had little opportunity or habit of learning better. The measurement of distance comes when he numbers by the thousands those who believed Mr. Bryan and stood ready to fight for him and to accuse all opponents of sinister motives and mean character. On the other hand, what chasm is revealed in the startlingly inaccurate statements and reports, the naïve ignorance of ordinary humanity and social order displayed by the learned ignorati who talk and write about all aspects of the situation. To say, with a simple dismissal of further interest or hope, that the great majority of American people are of inferior mentality, without distinguishing between types, individuals, and concrete causes, or to confuse present status with reference to experience and learning with the social potential to produce intelligent citizens in other generations, is at least to combine ignorance with the unscientific spirit. Now it may be said that such distance has always existed between scientist, scholar and common people; and so it has, except that it has not been a conscious distance of antagonism and battle line. Nor has the scholar and scientist in other generations attempted to extend his science and his scholarship into service and democracy, and therefore made contacts so broad and so directly related to the folk. Nor have the taxpayers been so marshalled by visible and invisible agencies against learning and education. Yes, this distance must be bridged and by the more able leaders.

WHAT TYPE LEADERS?

In attempting to answer the question as to whether those who are best prepared to lead in this country have the situation in hand or understand the situation in any comprehensive way, perhaps the first task would be to find out who is leading. On the other hand, who should lead and who should not? In many of the states and contests it is said freely in private that the best leaders on both sides refuse to be brought into the conflict, while at the same time other leaders contribute greatly to prejudicing the common folks against science, learning and the higher education. The most timely statement I have seen concerning the nature of those who should not lead is that of Professor Ross:

In every society, in times of stress or alarm, there crop up men whose temperament, upbringing, or personal experiences is such that they become wrought up over this and that unlikeness and cry out that the nation or the race is headed for ruin if a certain element be tolerated. Such are the fanatics, bigots, inquisitors, fire-brands, stormy petrels, alarmists, demagogues, for-God's-sake-ers, bunk-shooters, and finders of mare's nests, who spread incendiary lies about the Mormons, the Free Masons, the Catholics, the Negroes, Wall Street, organized labor, the foreign-born, the "reds," the liberal professors of economics, the social workers, the teachers of evolution. Men of breadth and balance should be at all times ready to "go to the mat" with these.

If to leaders of this sort the reins of leadership are given there could be no other result than that the majority of people to whom they appeal would show the normal reactions of combativeness and conservatism.

It does not suffice for the critic to affirm that the intelligent folks will not follow the type of leadership described. Whom else will they follow? What does the more experienced and educated group offer? On the eve and during the recent trial at the entrance to the Rea County courthouse, set over against a huge banner of the Anti-Evolution League, which proclaims one moment Hell as burning reality and another "Hell in the high schools," was the following chief pointer:

> The Kingdom of God
> The sweetheart love of Jesus Christ
> And Paradise Street is at hand
> Do you want to be a sweet angel?
> Forty days of prayer
> Itemizing your sins and iniquities
> For Eternal Life. If you come clean
> God will talk back to you
> In voice

This inscription is signed by Deck Carter, Bible Champion of the World. Compare this with the New York specimen, the A.P.P.P.P.A. of William H. Anderson, who not only claims to lead but does lead great groups of people with the following announcement of

A new Protestant movement
An American Prohibition Protestant Patriotic Protective Alliance
Which, national in scope, will be
A League, Offensive and Defensive
Of Allied Protestant Americans
To Resist Abject Surrender
In the Name of a Bogus Tolerance
Of Everything Vital to True Religion
And a Genuine Patriotism
Foursquare in Defense of American Institutions
And Civil and Religious Liberty
Against Every Secret Conspiracy
And Every Open Attack of Anti-American
Or Anti-Protestant Hate,
Passion, Bigotry, Intolerance
Or Religious Fanaticism

The presentation of the number and extent of this type of movements, activities and organizations would make a valuable object lesson set over against the number of more constructive movements as well as that large body of mediocre, middle-ground propaganda which is all too prevalent. The standard way to bridge distance is not blindly to ignore its existence on the one hand or to demolish the opposing embankments upon which must rest whatever superstructure is to be built. There appears considerable tendency on the part of the intelligentsia to follow the first course and of the militant enthusiasts to follow the latter. It would seem a fair conclusion, from evidences observable from my viewpoint at least, to say that professors and social workers, for instance, understand little of the situation now. They therefore have little of it under control. And what is more they do not know how to go about finding out the truth or influencing the situation in broader ways commensurate with their opportunities. In the old days, while the common man was accustomed to ridicule and satirize the professor, he nevertheless looked upon him with considerable respect, esteem, and often with envy. A few more years of the present tendency wherein the college professor, the general educator, and the social worker continue to fail in social planning, concrete study, and a more effective unity, and the common man will add to his satire and ridicule, hostility and loss of respect. Nor will all of the failure to show intelligence be found on the part of the common man.

We have made some tabulation of the type and methods of demagogic appeal made by emotional agitators in recent months. A study of half truths and false logic used as a common mode of appeal today, together with the bitterness and accusations, will offer a fair challenge to educators to stop and search after facts during a decade of truce in the fighting business. If, as a brilliant writer has said, Mr. Bryan descended to such low depths of demagogy that even many of his followers blushed, is there evidence that the publicists, journalists, the professor, the administrator of national agencies have been careful in presenting only the truth with scientific methods in their campaigns of education? A distinguished scientist and administrator reads from the newspapers a story that a certain German anthropologist had his engagement cancelled by the president of a university who had made the most clearcut and distinguished fight against bigotry perhaps in the history of this movement. He does not stop to investigate, he proclaims in address and in publication this as fact; whereas it had no basis in fact. A representative from a publishing house informs a professor in a mid-western university that the ministerial attack on *The Journal of Social Forces* has cost it the support of the President of the University. The professor does not question the report, but passes it on. The facts are just the opposite, and could have been ascertained. A distinguished editor publishes statistics concerning a state situation. The figures he uses are approximately a thousand times too large. He apologizes, but he has lost the enthusiasm of his constituency. A governor of a state as chairman of a board adopting books for common schools throws out a volume on biology and chooses another, his choice being made on the basis of evolutional doctrine. In hundreds of cases this incident is listed as statewide legislation against evolution in all state supported schools including the university. Literally thousands of similar instances of inaccuracy of fact, of unscientific method, of denunciatory approach may be listed in the columns of those boasting of the new scientific method and direction of society. These deficiencies do not bridge distance.

SOCIAL SCIENCE AND SOCIAL PLANNING

This distance between the two extremes and this futile situation in which the language of one group is in no wise understood by the other is not limited merely to the conflict between religion and science or the new attack on evolution, which happens now to provide a sort of epochal culture in which a number of startlingly interesting and generic processes are developing. Differences almost as great, and certainly in many instances at present as completely unspanned, are found in other contrasts between fundamentalism of various sorts and modernism in its various expressions. In the field of race, in industry, in certain cultural ideals, and territorial groups will soon be appearing, even more than now, urgent needs for bridging distance. If this be the day of the social sciences it must be remembered that "social" implies contacts, relationships, adjustments, and that if the social sciences expect to function in the newer epoch as the physical sciences have in the old, they must at least conform to the scientific standards set for the new social studies and programs. May we not therefore propose a truce from duelling; a peace without victory, a generation of social study and research? Better a decade of research than a cycle of futility.

The Role of Industry in Regional

Development [1940]*

The people of the South and of the Nation are concerned with few themes more than with the role of industry in regional development. Indeed there are few people and perhaps no institutions that are not vitally concerned with such balanced economy as will enable the region to develop and utilize wisely its resources, give employment to its abundance of workers, contribute to the development, education, and welfare of its people, and enrich the culture and well-being of the Nation.

Professor Herring's volume on *Southern Industry and Regional Development* appears peculiarly appropriate at this time. It is not only timely in the total framework of industry and national defense and in the relation of industrial location to national policy, but is especially important in the total framework of permanent defense and prosperity. With reference to the southern regions, it is a distinctive unit in the general framework of "The South at Its Best," interpreted as attainable standards of economy and culture, a theme to which the Institute for Research in Social Science at the University of North Carolina has for many years devoted a major portion of its purposive research. It is, moreover, an important unit in the larger framework of regional-national planning in the new and dynamic sense, in which the nation is seeking its new strength and integration through the

* Foreword in *Southern Industry and Regional Development* by Harriet L. Herring (Chapel Hill: The University of North Carolina Press, 1940), pp. vii-xi.

development and strengthening of its diverse regions. Furthermore, the book presents a vivid challenge to all those who hold that the South constitutes the most important testing ground for American regionalism and a working manual for those who are ready to achieve.

It is important to emphasize not only the importance of this program of optimum development, but also something of its meaning. As Miss Herring points out, *optimum* means the best that can be done in the total framework of the South itself, of the other regions, of the total national and international balance, and in relation to geographic, cultural, population, and time factors. We re-emphasize, therefore, two characteristics: the one in relation to the nation and the other in relation to the southern regions, and in this volume, the Southeastern States as presented in *Southern Regions of the United States*. This first emphasis is that the southern regions of the United States are a component part of a great nation, whose development and well-being depends upon the corresponding development and well-being of all regions integrated and correlated to the best possible degree. The nation has now come to recognize that one way to make the American dream come true is to make it possible for the people in each of the regions of our country to achieve the ends desired. We have come to see that the way to make a strong nation is to create strong regions; the way to make strong regions is to balance people with resources; the way to redistribute wealth is to create the capacity to produce and to use wisely in each region; the way to develop children and youth is to give them opportunity in their own regional setting; and always the balance of men and resources to be achieved through the democratic process.

The second point of emphasis on the nature of the program is that "The South at Its Best" implies no specific panacea, no single-type program, no exclusive values, but always has its assumptions well bottomed in the growth of the region through the work of its people, the development of its resources, and through the cooperative processes of community and government. It must be clear, therefore, that our statement of desirable and attainable ends of southern regional development must be in terms that are flexible, comprehensive, enduring, and commensurate with the cultural, economic, and social framework of our American democracy. Our attainable standards must be stated in terms of capacities of growth, of development of natural resources and people, of the devotion of the people and their wealth to institutional services through which we seek a balance and equilibrium between the people and wealth, between men and technology, between culture and civilization. We do not, therefore, say "The South at Its Best" is a wealthy South, or an industrial South, or an agrarian South; but we say that "The South at Its Best" is a growing South, a developing South, utilizing, developing, and conserving all of its resources in a balanced economy, of, for, and by the people, and of, for, and by all of the institutions. Its specific objectives and its specific needs will then be worked out in relation to each diversified phase of life, each changing situation, and in the combined and cooperative work of all acting together. Our statement, therefore, of what the South needs to be at its best is not something very specific in the field of education or industry or labor or capital, but it is the development of all of its people and capacities.

By indicating the relation of industry, as presented in this study, to the total southern regional development, we may point up perhaps in an oversimplified way the strategic importance of this subject. We may recall that in an inventory of the southern regions, it has been estimated that the South excels in two of the basic sources of wealth that go into the making of an enduring economy and lags in three. That is, it has a superabundance of natural resources and of human resources, but lags in the skill, training, and technology necessary to translate its resources into capital wealth. It is, therefore, poor and lags in the support of many of its institutions. The assumption is that if it could train its people, develop skills, science, and education, through which it would then develop and conserve its resources, it would immediately excel in all five of the types of wealth, namely, natural wealth, technological wealth, capital wealth, human wealth, and institutional wealth.

It must be clear that the goals to be sought focus clearly upon the wise use of the two sources of wealth in which we excel, namely, natural wealth and human wealth. In so far as the South is not utilizing its resources through planning, conservation, and new reaches in manufacturing, industry, and agriculture, it cannot give employment to its superabundance of people, without which in turn it is not possible for the region to share that common American heritage of prosperity and welfare.

We may indicate further the role of industry in this program by recalling some of the immediate elementary tasks that await the South if it is to seek these attainable standards of culture and economy which will vouchsafe the South its leading part in the new American scene.

First is the problem of educating the new generation of the South to sense the meaning of natural wealth and its relation to the living realities of the people and their welfare; this includes a sensing of the value of work and high standards of achievement. Second is the problem of widening the range of occupational opportunity, through new developements, to the end that the superabundance of southern youth may have a chance to work, and thus to develop and use our resources. The third task is, then, actually to train and equip these youth so that they may function adequately and in competition with workers everywhere.

Manifestly, more capital wealth is necessary for the undertaking of these tasks. This wealth must come from several sources: from the South's own economic gains in line with the extraordinary progress that has been made in the last few years; from the investment of wealth owned by southerners who are joining in the new frontiers of southern development; from investments of those who live outside the region, but who see in it an opportunity for regional and national development; from national foundations whose monies in research and experimentation can give leverage to regional support; and from the Federal Government in equalization programs—agriculture, roads, health, education, public safety, and the like.

It is evident that our youth at the present time do not have a sense of the real meaning of natural wealth, of standards of work, of achievement. It has not been fashionable either for boys or girls to be interested in soil erosion, natural resources, conservation, waste of men, and waste of soil, or in social problems. One of the most pathetic spectacles of our whole situation is that of the most attractive youth in the world literally hanging around drugstores and way places, wondering what it is all about and what to do next.

With reference to the widening range of occupational opportunity, it must be clear now that scarcely more than half of our southern youth can hope to have equal opportunity in the old sense of the American dream—opportunity to work, to create, to have families, and to find security. There must be new avenues through increasing industry and the balance between industry and agriculture and increased opportunity for trained leaders.

It must be clear also with reference to the third need that at the present time our southern youth are not trained to do anything very well. In an age of scarcity and need for work, for engineering, for skills, for farming, for dairying, it is not possible to find personnel equipped to do the jobs that must be done and in reality jobs that the youth themselves would want to do if they knew about them and were so equipped.

It must be clear, therefore, why these tasks are part and parcel of the whole southern program—the schools, the universities, the towns, the cities, rural communities, the national and local governments, the national and local civic organizations and chambers of commerce. It must be clear that this is literally a program of, for, and by all the people and all the institutions, and that there is no one throughout the broad reaches of the region who should not have a portion in the development of this part of the American dream of opportunity. Thus, it is no longer tenable to say that the development of industry belongs to this or that group or is limited to this or that function of economy.

Immediately, it is argued, of course, that this task is a difficult task. It is. There are problems of interregional relations and problems of conflict in economic interest. There are problems of labor and problems of capital to be readjusted. There are problems of untrained people and the cumulative handicaps of a region. But by and large these are standard problems and are all involved in the attainment of the objectives which have been suggested. Thus, our academic queries become matters of very practical concern when we ask:

How many and what sort of new and old industries
Will give occupation to how many people
Who in turn will create purchasing power
To enable how many more people to remain on the farm
To produce commodities of what sort
In turn to provide raw materials for what other industries
Which in turn will employ how many more workers
Who in turn will become skilled
Who in turn will continue the cycle

Seeking to approximate the better balanced region
Of attainable standards of culture and economy?

Now in the past most discussions of this problem have been very general; most efforts fortuitous or at least scarcely well planned. In contrast, here is a volume giving many facts about the 352 types of manufacturing in the Nation; more specific facts about those that are more related to the South and its potentialities; all set in the framework of indices which can be utilized in southern regional development. This has not been done before; it has long been needed. Here is in reality the making of an actual working manual which should be in the hands of all students and statesmen and of all industrialists, planning groups, councils of governors, chambers of commerce, boards of trade and all that great host of others who seek the ends of the best possible southern regional development.

It is a far cry from the abstract discussions of the agrarians, of the industrialists, the professors, and the idealists to this challenge to test and try out these formulae, for, as Professor Herring points out, "The solution will not just grow. It will take something more positive to create in the South a healthy balance within itself and allow it to make its greatest contribution to the national well-being." But "with a broad philosophy that is fundamentally sound it should be possible to work toward details that will be equally sound, even down to specific industries for specific states."

So, too, it is pointed out that there is a negative side, namely, that "along with planning for optimum production must go firm, if gradual, planning to correct production of a kind that is unsound and unhealthy."

Finally, here are two types of challenging statements that ought to be tested. One is that such an examination of the situation as is presented in this book "will reveal the directions in which the Southeast has pushed its industrial development far enough, and the directions in which it could wisely plan for, and encourage expansion." And another is that "the reasons for the lack of skills in the Southeast boil down to lack of manufacturing in which to learn and practice skills."

2. The Theory and Promise of Regionalism

The Implications and Meanings of
Regionalism [1938]*

The theme of American regionalism is, after all, essentially that of a great American Nation, the land and the people, in whose continuity and unity of development, through a fine equilibrium of geographic, cultural, and historical factors, must be found not only the testing grounds of American democracy but, according to many observers, the hope of Western civilization. How the new regionalism may be the key to a better understanding of the past and the richer development of the future, to the theoretical study of our society, and to the practical planning of its new frontiers, constitutes the more specific theme of this volume.

Basic to all this is, of course, the new science of the region, a science descripitve of how all societies grow, fundamental to realistic planning, and important in the interrelation and co-ordination of the social sciences and the new co-operation between the physical and the social sciences. The implications and meanings of such regionalism are manifold. From the American viewpoint, it interprets the living society of the historical nation and the quest for political, cultural, and spiritual autonomy. In the generic sense, it magnifies the meaning of the local group in relation to the whole and features the folk-regional society as basic to the growth of cultures. It emphasizes the new realism of the people as the scientific as well as symbolic basic element in modern civilization. From a more practical view-

* Chapter I, pp. 1-34, of *American Regionalism: A Cultural-Historical Approach to National Integration,* with Harry Estill Moore (New York: Henry Holt and Company, 1938). Reprinted by permission of Holt, Rinehart, and Winston.

point, namely, that of the inventory and planning of modern society, regionalism emerges as an equally definitive economy of balance and equilibrium between conflicting forces. It goes further; it offers a medium and technique of decentralization and redistribution in an age now being characterized as moving toward over-centralization, urbanism, and totalitarianism.

When we come to define the concept of "regionalism," there is the twofold dilemma of interpreting the many concepts and of focusing upon an adequate meaning which is both authentic and realistic. First of all, of course, we assume certain broad societal implications of regionalism such as that it implies "the regional framework of civilization," "the pluralism of America," the natural origins and quality of all folk-life and culture. In this general sense we recall that regionalism is a symbol of America's geographic as opposed to occupational representation; of popular as opposed to class control. It is, therefore, a fact, both product and process, and not something new, arbitrarily fabricated as a panacea. Regionalism, in this general sense, is envisaged for what it is rather than for what it does.

These general meanings are of the greatest importance to the public. "Is there a regional history of America?" asks one group of students. The historians answer that there is. "Is there a regional psychology?" asks another. The literary and governmental folks have found out that there is. "Is there an average America?" asks still another group. Our foreign visitors and the statisticians tell us that there is not. "Is the answer to this question of bigness and technology in relation to the problem of freedom and opportunity in any way bound up in the implications of regionalism?" The regionalist answers that it may be.

Yet we need to go further than this. We need to test the validity of the term "the new science of the region," by which we have in mind a considerable and growing body of knowledge about the region gathered through tested methods of research and study. We have, therefore, presented samplings from the geographers, the anthropologists, the ecologists, the economists, the historians, the political scientists, and the sociologists. On this assumption, then, regionalism through the co-operation and co-ordination of the efforts and techniques of the several sciences and social sciences may actually approximate a methodological approach. Implied in this science of the region is the universal twofold motivation of all science, namely, to discover truth and to attain mastery, both of which are inherent in the new regionalism which, perhaps more than anything else, explains the nation, and may be now utilized in its further planning. This twofold objective of science is implied throughout the book in the dichotomous arrangement—first, the historical and theoretical, and then the illustrations and application through which implementation is assumed. It is in this area that the efforts and techniques of the different sciences may be examined and co-ordinated.

The significance of regionalism as the key to equilibrium is reflected in an extraordinarily wide range of situations, such as the conflict between nationalism and internationalism, between sectionalism and federalism, and the imbalance between agrarian and urban life, between agriculture and industry, between individuation and socialization in governmental trends, between a quantity civilization of standardizing forces and a quality world, between machines and men. The significance of regionalism as a technique of decentralization and redistribution is reflected in an equally wide range of examples. Some of these are basic to the decentralization and redistribution of population, of industry, of wealth and capital, of culture, of social pathology, and of bigness, complexity, and technology in general. In all these aspects of regionalism, it is important to note that, whether in the historical explanation of society, in the broader meaning of economy, or in the more specialized meaning of technique, *regionalism assumes no all-inclusive or single exclusive force or panacea; rather, as a comprehensive tool, it assumes approximation and direction in the sum total of achievements of which it is itself a part.*

More immediate and vivid, however, than the science of the region is the reality of actual American regionalism in the United States. Regionalism is no longer merely an academic subject. The theoretical and historical aspects, therefore, become essentially phases of practical importance. For the nation has already been divided into numerous regions for many and varying purposes. There are regions of earlier historical significance. There are regions of newer administrative functions. There are regions of convenience and of necessity. There are regions of government and regions of commerce. There are regions of literary achievement and regions of agricultural adjustment. There are regions of land and of water, of forests and of minerals, of flora and of crops. There are regions of educational institutions and football arrangements; regions of whole-sale trade and of Rotary and Kiwanis. There are regions within regions, subregions and districts. Within and among all these and many other manifestations, regionalism becomes a realistic frame of reference for research and study and a practical framework for planning and for adjustment in such areas as population development and policy, standards of living and work, the increase of wealth and well-being, the changing status of race and minority groups, the equalization of opportunity, the development and mastery of new "social frontiers."

Much of the realism of this "American" emphasis upon regional-ism flows naturally from the historical backgrounds of the nation which must constitute a chief thread throughout the volume. Rupert B. Vance sees arising from such background "great hordes of America's regions, the number and variety of which are limited only by the frames of reference chosen. On the frontier emerged zones of ex-ploration, of military control, of missionary activity, of the 'long hunter,' fur trapper, Indian trader and squatter. Spanish frontier, French frontier, Indian frontier, Puritan and Tidewater, Fall Line and Appalachians, Old West and Old Northwest, Southwest and Middle Border, California and Oregon Country, these are the regions the pio-neer process carved out of a virgin continent. Natural areas change into cultural-made areas, drainage basins become hydroelectric power zones, biotic areas become types of farming areas, harbor indentations become the zones of port authorities and the list continues *ad infin-itum*. Today one may take his choice of physiographic areas, trade areas, types of farming areas, census areas, railroad nets, superpower zones, army corps areas, Federal Reserve Districts, newspaper circu-lation areas, voting maps, or any of the multitudinous indices gathered by statistical agencies to delimit his regions."[1] Now comes the author of *The Great Plains* challenging America to relegislate so as to adjust its economy to what he calls "the North, the South, and the West. Each will be shown to have a history of its own, a distinct way of life determined by the character both of its inhabitants and of its physical environment, and a fundamental economic structure, which the political, economic, and financial expansion of this country has tended to accentuate."[2]

1. Rupert B. Vance, in E. W. Burgess and Herbert Blumer, Editors, *Human Side of Social Planning,* pp. 91-92.
2. Walter Prescott Webb, *Divided We Stand,* p. 4.

So abundant are the evidences, so wide the range of application, so far-reaching the implications, so varied and diverse the meanings and discussions of this new cultural economy called regionalism that it makes little difference from which angle we approach its general treatment. Perhaps the best approach will be through some current illustrations and through certain rather broad assumptions, prefatory to later characterization and definition. Closely paralleling such illustrations and assumptions will be the organic relationship which regionalism shows to the continuing evolution of man and culture. They will be followed with abundant evidence of the vitality and realism of American regionalism as found in a very large and growing body of literature, in important national, regional, and state developments, and in the increasing importance of regionalism as tool and technic in social planning. Frequent recapitulation will emphasize, alongside current developments and implications, the historical and theoretical foundations with their extraordinarily wide range of documentation basic to the understanding of present postulates and movements.

Perhaps we may best begin with current examples of popular interest and practical implications. Thus our assumption that regionalism is in reality a national economy may be illustrated by William Allen White's characterization of the Supreme Court issue, national of all national issues, as essentially one of regional elements. Pointing out that the United States has more conflicting interests and claims than any other nation, he continues: "First of all, they are questions of region. From the beginning, regional differences have required a compromise." And, again, pointing up certain areal problems of the North, the South, the West, the pioneer frontiers, he continues: "These regions are not merely colored places on the map. They present different views of life. Justice for one region is not justice for the other. Yet a rough approximation of justice for each region must be worked out if all these regions are held together in the bonds of a continental commonwealth."[3] A similar illustration may be cited from the many current realistic discussions of the southern regions of the United States, commonly called "The South." Thus, Dorothy Thompson, speaking before the Union League in New York and pointing to the past isolation of the South as well as to its historical, economic, and cultural conditioning since 1865, is "con-

3. William Allen White, "Supreme Court—or 'Rule by Impulses,'" *The New York Times Magazine*, April 25, 1937, p. 3.

vinced that the fate of this vast region is the central problem in our whole national economy."[4] Referring to the historical side, she points out how any policy which leads to the enrichment of one section at the expense of the other, as was the earlier case of the "North" against the "South," must eventually threaten the total economy, and she appeals for national-regional policies to minimize the dangers of a revolting, impoverished mass of people. Pointing to the future, she emphasizes the similar danger of developing these regions, without design, in unwise competition with other regions. So, too, recent filibusters in Congress have accentuated and made vivid the very problem of continuing reintegration of all regions into the changing national fabric. The action of the New York State Legislature turning aside from its own problems to pass the resolution demanding legislation for Florida or Mississippi is sectionalism equally with that of filibustering senators. The revival of sectionalism in the New York mayoralty campaign of 1937 was illustrative of the same problem. It was perhaps with many of these problems in mind that Mr. Justice Brandeis has expressed the thought that in these southern regions may be found our greatest national problem.

Illustrations of the regional-national approach are abundant. One is that of experimental regionalism in which a given area may be set up as a testing field for the nation. The example which has most frequently been cited, as a way of testing such a postulate, is the TVA. Further illustrations of the growing realization of the significance of regions in the total national economy may be found in many of the proposed experiments and policies advocated by the national government. One is found in the advocacy of planning for river valley regions described elsewhere. Another is found in the studies of the Great Plains and the Dust Bowl. Still others are found in the search for satisfactory administrative regions for governmental functions, many examples of which will be cited later. A specific illustration of an unofficial type is that of Secretary Wallace's characterization of the problems of the northeastern agricultural program in the first major agricultural regional conference of his administration. The twelve states of the Northeast, he pointed out, can greatly increase their agricultural efficiency through their own co-operative endeavor. But especially, he pointed out further,

4. Dorothy Thompson, address before the "Ladies Night" dinner of the Union League Club, published in *New York Herald Tribune,* April 26, 1937.

they are dependent upon the purchasing power and co-operation of other regions of the nation. Citing the great increase of shipments from the Northeast to the Southeast of producers' goods, he pointed out how the purchasing power of the southern farmer and the southern textile worker, for instance, affect the prosperity of the northeastern farmer through the increased production and purchasing power of the manufacturers and people of the Northeast who supply the goods to the purchasing region.

In a subsequent characterization of the several regions of the United States, many more examples will appear. These bare samplings are adequate for the present to illustrate, perhaps in oversimplified current terms, the general assumptions of regionalism in the practical affairs of the nation. We proceed then to a still broader assumption with reference to both the practical and theoretical significance of regionalism.

Once in every generation or so, in every new period of development, there arises some new movement or economy or motivation through which next stages of development are evolved or through which impending crises are met. So, too, in the broader fields of scholarship and research, of experimentation and study, new concepts arise or old concepts are expanded and revivified in the effort to construct sound theory upon which to base realistic endeavor. The assumption here is that the new regionalism may provide such an economy, technique, and concept at the present time, granting a new science of the region in general, and in America a new realism of the region. These assumptions may be supported by a number of larger implications of regionalism in the present American scene.

Continuing the assumption that regionalism is a key to balance and equilibrium, it is important to note that these constitute not only the motif of social planning but the basic need for all social reconstruction. Such equilibrium is needed not only between and among the several diversified areas of the nation, but between industry and agriculture, between urban and rural life, and between and among the various groups of people who constitute the democracy, since the aim of that democracy is to offer not only each individual but each demotic group full opportunity and representation. Mumford points this up vividly when he headlines these three problems: "the problem of tempo; the problem of equilibrium; the problem of organic balance; in back of them all the problem of human satisfaction and cultural achievement—these have now become the critical and all-important problems of modern civilization. To face these problems to evolve appropriate social goals and to invent appropriate social and political instruments for an active attack upon them, and finally to carry them into action: here are new outlets for social intelligence, social energy, social good will."[5]

In the search for this equilibrium, regionalism represents both a philosophy and a technique of opportunity and representation. The geographic and areal, the local, the racial, the civic representation in an enduring democracy must be somehow co-ordinate with individual representation. Democracy assumes opportunity and representation for the individual, but it is too often overlooked that the same guarantee applies to the group or state or race or region. This is especially significant in the problem of the distribution of wealth, in which regional capacities and regional needs are of the greatest importance.

In this connection there may be mentioned the rigorous demand for rural representation and agricultural parity in the new national planning. The conscious desire for representation of the rural regions was well illustrated in an incident which occurred soon after the passage of the Wagner Labor Act. An enthusiastic and distinguished speaker over the radio was eloquently congratulating the nation upon the fact that now at last capital and labor, employer and employee, would move arm in arm down the halls of time dictating America's new destiny. To which the leader of one of the great farm organizations replied: "The heck you will; agriculture must certainly have something to say, won't it?" Thus is set in new perspective rural regionalism over against urban and metropolitan regionalism. The principle of equalization of opportunity, wherever found, is always valid in the democratic process.

Regionalism, again, to point up motivations of the past, represents the philosophy and technique of self-help, self-development, and initiative in which each areal unit is not only aided, but is committed to the full development of its own resources and capacities. This, on the one hand, is in contrast to dependency by any region upon the nation or to submarginality as compared with other regions; and, on the other hand, to exploitation from any sources from without. It assumes that the key to the redistribution of wealth and the

5. Lewis Mumford, *Technics and Civilization*, pp. 430-33.

equalization of opportunity will be found in the capacity of each region to create wealth and, through new reaches of consumption of commodities, maintain that capacity and retain that wealth in well-balanced production and consumption programs.

Regionalism is thus essentially an economy not of scarcity but of abundance, to the end that all the people may have access to adequate food, clothing, housing, tools, occupational opportunity—an accomplishment to be made possible through regional techniques of use as well as production. Special adaptation to resources and people will be the key to both production and consumption. Furthermore, regionalism represents an economy of specialized industry as well as decentralized industry, an economy offering an opportunity for the several regions not only to realize upon their own peculiar resources, but also to do so with minimum competition with other regions. Thus, if the Southwest can grow cotton and tung trees and can evolve new industries for developing its resources and increasing its wealth without competing with the great states north of it in cattle and corn and hogs, the benefits are apparent. If the Southeastern states can create millions of dollars of new wealth through hundreds of processing plants to make starch from sweet potatoes, paper pulp from pines, and other products now imported or representing scarcity, then regionalism becomes a very realistic and practical national economy.

Another broad assumption is that decentralization is inherent in regionalism. If this is true, one implication of regionalism may well be the opposite of the present tendency toward urbanism, centralization, and concentration of power and wealth. Regionalism as the natural mode of decentralization rests upon the logic of earlier evolutionary processes. Cultures grow from beginnings outward. The margins of bigness are the occasion for redistribution. An economy of decentralized industry is usually cited as the most common example of decentralization. Here regionalism offers what many students consider the best "way on" in so large and complex a nation as the United States. It is not merely decentralization as found in metropolitan regionalism. It comprehends also the foundation of small industries—industries adapted to village and town—and, through farm chemurgic and other inventive aids, it promotes a wide distribution over the nation. It comprehends part-time industry and planning. It is not merely the regional mercantilism of Professor Gras and others; it is not merely Stuart Chase's solution of "rich land, poor land," through economic regionalism, or Lewis Mumford's economic regionalism in *Technics and Civilization.* It is all of these and more, a totality in which all past historical experience—including such lessons as are provided by French, German, and Polish regionalism—is utilized in the projection of regional planning of the future.

Of great significance is the culture economy of regionalism through which the decentralization of people, of culture, and of pathology, may be attained in the new frontiers of American life. Here are involved the dilemmas of megapolitan culture emphasized by Geddes and Spengler and the more immediate crises of unemployment and relief in great cities. Yet, again, such decentralization does not apply only to the metropolitan regions or the planned towns and communities 'round about the great cities. It takes into account the whole phenomenon of the new mobility of people, the migrations to and from cities. It comprehends movements to and from farms, providing technical ways for the reintegration of agrarian culture in American life. It points to the development of new frontiers of American culture, which may provide new centers of health and recreation, of opportunity for urban decentralization where surplus wealth may be expended or normal cultures develop in the new Southwest or the changing Northwest with their great water resources, or the great playgrounds of New England and the Southeast, or in the multitudinous parks and playgrounds and public domains of a great nation. Regionalism is, therefore, the essential symbol of the new American physical and cultural frontier.

Again, regionalism provides an economy for the decentralization of political power and administrative procedure in government and business. As such, it transcends the older "pure" states' rights and safeguards the people from federal over-centralization. In administrative procedure it provides for economy and efficiency in governmental and social services as well as representative opportunity for production and distribution of goods. Thus, Burdett G. Lewis says, "Regionalism strikes an effective and natural medium between uncontrolled individualism among the states and complete centralization of administration at Washington." Regionalism represents also an economy of essential flexibility so fundamental in an American democracy.

From the historical and cultural viewpoint regionalism is reflected in Sir William Beveridge's verdict concerning the United States. Said he: "If I had to sum up my impressions, I should think in terms of drama; I should choose a parody from Pirandello: 'Six Americas in search of a faith.' " Our six great regions, he decided, are characterized by "profound divisions of race and history, with opposed economic interests, with different ways of life and thought." So, regionalism represents an essential minimum tool for planning, through which not only administrative balance and efficiency may be attained but the contributions of science, of engineering, of chemurgy, and of all the new evolving social techniques may be tested in living, areal, cultural laboratories.

Finally, a study of historical developments and of the universal patterns of societal evolution will show the supreme practical validity of regionalism. This does not mean only that in America the nation has grown and grown from expanding domain and has evolved from earlier local and sectional patterns to current regional and national design. It means this and more. It means also that all cultures and civilizations have evolved logically from regional beginnings. The local regional group represents the elemental unit in all societies whether that of the oriental city, the medieval city, or the empire. Cultures and peoples, nations and empires grow from regional sustentation areas out into expanded entities. It is not possible, therefore, to understand or to direct society except through the regional approach. Somewhere within the realistic bounds of regional science and arrangement will be found both the elements and tools of any great totality and unity of national development.

The broad assumptions of this theory—and it should be reaffirmed that the most practical thing in the world is dependable theory—may be supported by studies made in wide and varied fields. We may mention, as evidence of the distinguished heritage of the concept of regionalism in both the natural and the social sciences, the organic and functional regions of the geographers, the structural and functional regions of the ecologists, the cultural regions of the anthropologists, the cultural determinism of the sociologists, the mercantile regionalism of the economists, the administrative regionalism of the political scientists, the aesthetic and literary regionalism of the arts, in addition to that large cataloguing of composite world regions and peoples symbolic of man's long, hard, historical road up to now.

We have presented enough of this broad sweeping picture of the range and implications of regionalism to indicate something of its organic nature and significance and to show that *regionalism is in reality the opposite of its most common interpretation, namely, localism, sectionalism, or provincialism.* We have yet to approach more specific and authentic definitions of regionalism, first through the cataloguing of its general attributes; second, through illustrative definitions of the many types of regionalism; and, third, through the cataloguing of the many concepts which are *not regionalism.* First, then, we continue the further characterization of regionalism by pointing out certain attributes of the region, regionalism being defined here generally as the science of the region or the culture economy of which the region is the basic unit.

Beginning, then, with the elemental factor of space, the region is, of course, first of all an area, a geographic unit with limits and bounds. Regionalism is, therefore, an areal or spatial generalization. This is true, whether it be the geographer's region, the geologist's region, the ecologist's region, the anthropologist's region, or any other. This attribute may be illustrated by a large number and variety of definitions from authentic sources, samplings of which will be presented subsequently. Yet, in the second place, the region differs from the mere locality or pure geographic area in that it is characterized not so much by boundary lines and actual limits as it is by flexibility of limits, by extension from a center, and by fringe or border margins which separate one area from another. Climatic zones, the range of rainfall, the gradually changing types of soil and configuration of land, and the diversity of natural resources are examples showing how relative and flexible regional delimitation is. So, too, in the economic, political, and cultural life of a nation, the region finds its boundaries overlapping state lines or rivers and valleys in accordance with the nature of the common indices basic to the regional homogeneity in question. R. D. McKenzie points out that a region "may or may not conform to the boundaries of a natural unit. The base of the region becomes tenuous and changeable with variations in influence from the center."[6] The third attribute of the region is some degree of homogeneity in a number of selected characteristics. This is true of the geographic region, which is characterized by closely related surface features and is contrasted in these respects with neighboring areas, or which shows essential uniformity "in dominant physical conditions and consequently in dominant life responses."[7] Likewise

6. R. D. McKenzie, in National Resources Committee's *Regional Factors in National Planning and Development,* December 1935, p. 147.
7. Cf. Radhakamal Mukerjee, *Regional Sociology, passim.*

the cultural, economic, administrative, or other region is one which exhibits homogeneity in a clustering of selected units of measurement or aspects of its life. Even the simplest of spatial regions must be characterized by some limiting quality or qualities.

The definitive nature of the region and the aspects of its homogeneity will be determined by the fourth attribute of the region, namely, some structural functional aspect or aspects through which the region is to be denominated. Sometimes the "function" or purposive nature of the region seems little more than a "class" of similarities. Yet the geographer's region may be delimited not only by homogeneity in climate or rainfall, but by land use or by research objectives in which the region serves as a workable unit of inquiry. The economic region may be characterized not only by resources but by accessibility, transportation, power. There may therefore be, generally speaking, as many regions as there are purposes or functions available.

Yet there must be a limit to the multiplicity of regions, so that in general a fifth attribute must be found in the relative, composite homogeneity of the largest number of factors for the largest number of purposes in view, to the end that the region may be a practical, workable unit susceptible of both definition and utilization. This is manifestly of the greatest importance and may be illustrated in the case of, let us say, the geographic regions of the world or the administrative regions of a great nation which must have a reasonable limit as parts of a whole, regardless of the possibility of academic delineation through manifest homogeneity of a very few characteristics. It is possible to catalogue seven or eight hundred soil regions in the United States, yet for all practical composite purposes such a classification is not practicable.

This brings us to the two final and key attributes of the region. The geographic area, characterized by a large degree of homogeneity in selected traits, does not in itself constitute a region in the more comprehensive and scientific sense. The geographic area, on the one hand, may find its chief characteristic one of isolation and separateness, and, on the other hand, it may be a specialized area devoid of the joint indices of geography and culture or the frame of reference for societal study or planning. A key attribute of the region is, therefore, that it must be a *constituent unit in an aggregate whole or totality.* Inherent in the region as opposed to the mere locality or the isolated section is the essence of unity of which it can exist only as a part. Thus, "the regionalist sees the region as a unit, a microcosm of society, a set of factors combining to form a regional pattern; and believes that these elements can be understood only when conceived as a part of the whole."[8] In this more vital sense urbanism or metropolitanism is not regionalism in so far as urban centers seek their own ends regardless of relationship to other great centers or in opposition to national or rural ends. In agreement with this view, Lewis Mumford points out that "regionalism is the antithesis of false cosmopolitanism." This point is manifestly of the greatest importance. If some of the social scientists posit the thesis that progress consists in the urbanization of the nation, and if others protest concentration and urbanism, it must be clear that there is conflict worthy of more study than we yet have. Here regionalism will have considerable significance in the interrelation of the sciences in such research. Regionalism is also important in the realistic breaking away from the old sectionalism in American life—a radical departure necessary to the attainment of equilibrium and unity in the national culture on what are often called the social frontiers.

The final key attribute is found in the organic nature of the region. A region has organic unity not only in its natural landscape, but in that cultural evolution in which the age-long quartette of elements are at work—namely, the land and the people, culturally conditioned through time and spatial relationships. Thus, Professor Aronovici defines regionalism as "the study of the relation of man to geographic areas, and the potentialities which this relation represents in terms of human welfare and progress. The history of tribes, nations, and races is one long record of regional realism, in terms of security and productivity, sought through expansion and contraction of regional boundaries."[9] So, too, Clark Wissler writes that "one cannot read anthropological discussions without becoming aware that the procedure is based on a belief in regional differences in social behavior and that social evolution itself is regional."[10] From such an organic

8. Cf. Harry E. Moore, *What Is Regionalism?*
9. Carol Aronovici, "Regionalism: A New National Economy," *Columbia University Quarterly,* December 1936, p. 268.
10. Clark Wissler, "The Culture Area Concept in Social Anthropology," *American Journal of Sociology,* XXXII, p. 882.

implication it seems possible to characterize regionalism as a cultural *Gestalt,* in which are balanced all the constituent factors of culture in the making.[11]

Before turning to the further support of these assumptions and implications, attributes and illustrations, with authentic definitions from other sources, it is important to emphasize the great diversity of usage and meaning of the concept of regionalism in recent literature both in professional journals and in popular discussions. Although these will be discussed at length in the several respective chapters, it may be well to call attention here to three or four of the most common examples. The multiplicity of conflicting meanings and their varied application give emphasis to the need for as clear a presentation of the subject as possible.

A common usage is the very general one of making metropolitan regionalism synonymous with the total comprehensive, organic regionalism which has evolved so rapidly within recent years into a new national economy. This is illustrated in perhaps more than half of the articles dealing with regionalism and regional planning listed in current bibliographies, including some of those current in 1937. This is pointed out well by Carol Aronovici, who says: "It is unfortunate that in this country the terms region and regional planning have been loosely used, so that metropolitan planning has become interchangeable with regional planning. Metropolitanism and metropolitan planning apply only to the relation between a given center of population and its outlying areas, while regionalism and regional planning should embrace the study and development of all geographic entities. . . ."[12]

A second type of usage has been that which assumes that regionalism and sectionalism are synonymous and that the essence of regionalism and regional planning is to be found in the objectives of local and provincial study or in the practical ends of local development, or at most in a sort of regional mercantilism. Professor Turner's pioneer work on sectionalism is often cited as the record of American regionalism. Manifestly, as will be shown in Chapter II, this is an unfortunate confusion of meanings. This distinction between regionalism and sectionalism is of the greatest importance at the present time. By regionalism we mean a new American social economy and societal determinism, as opposed to the early American sectionalism

11. Cf. Harry E. Moore, *op. cit.*
12. Aronovici, *op. cit.,* p. 271.

and geographic, economic determinism. Such regionalism is also opposed to the traditional literary localism. Indeed, perhaps the first distinction between the new realistic regionalism and the older sectionalism is that regionalism assumes first, last, and always a totality composed of the several areal and cultural units, a great national unity and integrated culture in which each region exists as a region solely as a component unit in the whole. Sectionalism, on the other hand, always assumes isolated, segregated areal divisions with potential completeness in themselves and looked upon as separate entities. This was the magnificent picture of Frederick Jackson Turner's sectionalism in American life. This was James Truslow Adams' *America's Tragedy*.

A third popular usage is that found almost universally in the discussions of literary regionalism, which usually connotes location and provincialism. . . . Manifestly, such regionalism is in reality a sort of sentimental romanticism for the local area or for the historical period. No matter how much there is of this sort of thing or how real or how productive of certain results, it is not scientific regionalism. A notable exception to this has been the constant reiteration of William Allen White that, for instance, the great American novel, as a representative of the great American totality, must logically be a regional product. Here it is clear that the significance of the local area or culture in regionalism is found in its contribution through delimitable phenomena and interrelated study to the larger study of society and cultures. Regionalism involves the local; but much more. It involves the past, but not merely the past. The local becomes a medium for the understanding and characterization of the universal. The past becomes material for the study of the present and the future.

We have already implied that another basis of confusion has grown up through the various conceptions of geographic and cultural areas as symbols of geographic determinism or economic determinism, whereas genuine regionalism is in reality a larger societal determinism in which all the factors of life are balanced in harmony with the natural heritage. As such, it affords new living laboratories for the study of culture and for the development of peoples.

Professor Franz Boas gives a clear critique of this phase of regionalism when he writes: "Political theories have also been built upon the assumption that single forces determine the course of cultural history. Most important among these are the theories of geographical and economic determinism. Geographical determinism means that geographical environment controls the development of culture; economic determinism that the economic conditions of life shape all the manifestations of early culture and of complex civilization. It is easy to show that both theories ascribe an exaggerated importance to factors that do play an important part in the life of man, but that are each only one of many determinant elements. The study of the cultural history of any particular area shows clearly that geographical conditions by themselves have no creative force and are certainly no absolute determinants of culture."[13]

We come now to our next task of presenting further representative and authentic concepts and definitions of the region and regionalism in support of our previous assumptions and characterizations. We select only a few under each general division. First, the geographic area comes nearest to epitomizing the physical region. That is, it is an area in which natural features constitute the determining criteria within spatial limits.

Thus, Joerg defines the natural region simply as "any portion of the earth's surface whose physical conditions are homogeneous."[14] So Herbertson characterizes the region as "a complex of land, water, air, plant, animal, and man regarded in their spatial relationship as together constituting a definite portion of the earth's surface."[15] Fenneman's region is "an area characterized throughout by similar or closely related surface features, and which is contrasted in these respects with neighboring areas."[16] Another good definition is one from Professor Aronovici, which combines the areal and homogeneity indices. The term regionalism, he says, used in its broadest implications, refers to "a geographic area or areas which a given civilization-standard of a people seems to require for the fulfillment of its aspirations through material resources."[17] Two others are selected

13. Franz Boas, *Anthropology and Modern Life*, p. 229.
14. Wolfgang L. G. Joerg, "The Subdivision of North America into Natural Regions," *Annals of the Association of American Geographers*, IV, 56-57.
15. A. J. Herbertson, "The Major Natural Regions: An Essay in Systematic Geography," *Geographical Journal*, XXV, 300.
16. Nevin M. Fenneman, "Physiographic Boundaries within the United States," *Annals of the Association of American Geographers*, IV, 86.
17. Aronovici, *op. cit.*, p. 268.

from the many excellent characterizations of the geographic region by Isaiah Bowman. In the first example he points out that "most branches of knowledge have to deal with *area.* From this simple fact and its multiplied bearings flows one of the most important values of geography in studies that deal with mankind. In going from the abstraction, *area,* to specific regions, geography provides: (1) a framework of physical facts region by region, the world around; (2) unifying explanations of physical phenomena in terms of laws evolved through experimental methods or by the elaborate testing of hypotheses following both inductive and deductive methods; (3) an identification of regional characteristics, physical and human, through detailed statistical methods and by field notation; (4) a comparison of regions with the object of widening the generalities of physiography and human experience that have their bases in local and detailed observation."[18]

The geographers have long set up the region as a divisional means for study. A second quotation from President Bowman reinforces the relational significance of the geographic region to the study of culture. "We generalize real men and real places," he writes, "by grouping them according to likenesses of function or location. To think of groups is at once to be aware of the relationships between groups. A given group has, like any one of its members, a limited and particular set of conditions to face. These conditions are spread over an area or region. It is the purpose of the geographer to study limiting or significant environmental conditions in their regional association, basing his understanding upon physical examinations on the one hand and upon human reactions or relationships on the other."[19] This concept leads to the twofold objective of seeking knowledge of both land and men, of areas and cultures.

An excellent characterization of this interpretation may be found in V. B. Stanbery's studies of regional planning. In one of these he distinguishes between the geo-physical and the organic region, defining each as follows: "Geo-physical regions may be described as areas bounded by definite physical conformations or areas having similar physical characteristics, such as rainfall, temperature, climate. Physical regions, like organic regions, are of many different kinds and may be classified by their individual characteristics such as geologic,

18. Isaiah Bowman, *Geography in Relation to the Social Sciences,* pp. 145-46.
19. *Ibid.,* p. 24.

geographic, climatic, or ecologic." On the other hand, "organic regions may be defined roughly as areas within which a higher degree of mutual dependency exists than in relationships outside that area." "An organic area," he says further, "may thus be described as an area whose people are bound together by mutual dependencies arising from common interests. In its inherent nature, and in the common meaning of the word, a region is a territory of indefinite extent. Its boundaries cannot be sharply delineated; nor its essence captured by categorical definition. Human activity is not confined to any one area, and, hence an organic region cannot be entirely self-contained."[20]

Next, a few definitions of the functional character of the region will indicate both the nature of regions and the methods of their delimitation. This functional characterization may be based upon research or administrative factors or upon economic character or purposes or upon as many functions and characteristics as may be desired. Thus, McKenzie considers "a region to be a geographic (areal) unit in which the economic and social activities of the population are integrated around a focal economic and administrative center."[21] Two statements from the findings of the American Society of Planning Officials will point out other functional aspects of regionalsim. Thus, "Regionalism, as a *motif* for planning, seems to offer manifold promises, the road to which involves several definite steps: (a) identifying the regionalism which is present; (b) demarking the area which encompasses it; (c) determining the needs of this area; (d) making a plan and fitting it to the area in question; (e) implementing the plan in terms of state and federal sovereignties." Again, ". . . our main concern is to identify the fundamental regionalism which is the core or nucleus of the area. Similarly, our major objective becomes that of preserving the area's essential unity and homogeneity as a frame for program formulation and for the execution of those programs. Thus the paramount emphasis is placed upon the problem area and not the states, although the sovereignty of the latter is not impaired."[22]

Further discussion of the structural and functional nature of the region will be found in the several chapters dealing with metropolitan

20. V. B. Stanbery, *An Approach to Regional Planning,* pp. 6, 7, 4, 3.
21. R. D. McKenzie, in National Resources Committee's *Regional Factors in National Planning and Development,* December 1935, p. 146.
22. *Planning for City, State, Region and Nation.* Proceedings of the Joint Conference on Planning, 1936, pp. 108, 110.

regionalism, administrative regionalism, river valley regions, the economist's region, the ecologist's region, the political scientist's region, and others. So, too, the functional nature of the region appears in our catalogue of types of regional planning on the functional level, such as land planning, water planning, conservation planning, economic planning, cultural planning, in each of which the regional implications and variations constitute a fundamental part. Still further illustrations of the unity, compositeness and organic nature of the region may serve also to recapitulate the various characterizations and definitions of the region already given. B. A. Botkin, searching for the total background of regionalism upon which to base a general literary regionalism gives the following summary: "A 'region' is the geographer's term for an 'environmental type' in which 'the geographic elements are combined in certain definite and constant relations.' From the concept of the natural region—physiographic, geological, climatic, biotic, etc.—the human geographer, correlating social with organic and inorganic factors, has developed the concept of the cultural landscape and the human use region. From human geography, in turn, the sociologist and the ethnologist have derived the concepts of the sociological region and the culture area. In the natural, social, and engineering sciences, 'regionalism' as a discipline has not only opened up new research leads but supplied the technique of regional planning."[23]

Marshall E. Dimock, in his studies of the regional factors in national planning and development, characterizes regionalism as "a clustering of environmental, economic, social and governmental factors to such an extent that a distinct consciousness of separate identity within the whole, a need for autonomous planning, a manifestation of cultural peculiarities, and a desire for administrative freedom, are theoretically recognized and actually put into effect. Regionalism is something which remains to be realized and further developed, as well as a phenomenon which has already appeared and taken form. In one sense, and perhaps the best one, regionalism is a way of life; it is a self-conscious process."[24] In another contribution, he points out that "political boundaries, sectional loyalties, climates of opinion are just as real (although admittedly more complicated and less predictable) as water, land and vegetation. . . . Regional factors are in

23. B. A. Botkin, "Regionalism: Cult or Culture?" *The English Journal*, XXV, No. 3, p. 181.

24. National Resources Committee, *Regional Factors in National Planning and Development*, December 1935, p. 138.

part measurable and predictable; in part they are traditional, contrived and emotional. Whether regionalism results from the growth of a sense of community, in turn dependent upon common traditions, interests and aspirations, or whether it results from man's rational analysis of economic and governmental problems needing solution, it is none the less regionalism."[25]

So Lucien Brocard points out that, "To an even greater extent than the nation as a whole, the regional economy depends for its complete development upon continuous contact with other regions, so that, by co-operating with them, it may facilitate the movement of commodities and men. It is necessary to combine with the complex economic development already discussed a certain geographical specialization of industry, by means of which the various communities may accentuate the prosperity of one another and of the whole nation."[26] Still two other types of characterization are those of Lewis Mumford on artistic regionalism and R. K. Gooch on French regionalism. Mumford features "a soundly bottomed regionalism [which] can achieve cosmopolitan breadth without losing its integrity or virtue; it is only a sick and puling regionalism that must continually gaze with enamored eyes upon its own face, praising its warts and pimples as beauty marks. For a genuine regional tradition lives by two principles. One is, *cultivate whatever you have*, no matter how poor it is; *it is at least your own*. The other is, *seek elsewhere for what you do not posssess;* absorb whatever is good wherever you may find it; make it your own."[27] Gooch's regionalism of France "stands somewhere between administrative decentralization and federalism. It touches on both; and if a more rigid logic envisages three schools of thought and three movements, a basic similarity none the less exists and a common principle underlies all three. In this perspective, French Regionalism, which has been called *un fédéralisme très atténué,* is only a special, though a very important, manifestation of world federalism."[28]

It yet remains to point up two other aspects of regionalism basic to the general picture. The one is the rise of American regionalism through the chronological and evolutionary development of the nation

25. Marshall E. Dimock, unpublished manuscript.
26. Lucien Brocard, "Regional Economy and Economic Regionalism," *Annals of the American Academy of Political and Social Science,* CLXII, 84-85.
27. Lewis Mumford, "Orozco in New England," *The New Republic,* LXXX, 235.
28. R. K. Gooch, *Regionalism in France,* p. 17.

from area to area, from frontier to frontier, and ultimately from section to region. The other is to focus upon American regionalism as a tool and area of planning, especially as it has been featured by the National Resources Committee in *Regional Factors in National Planning* and in the analysis of regional factors involved in much of the federal program within recent years. Since both of these aspects will be treated adequately elsewhere a few illustrations will suffice to present the case.

We may begin with the historical development of the nation in which its Atlantic seaboard states early tended to divide themselves into North and South while the great diversity of the land made regional entities a natural product. Thus, James Truslow Adams points out: "The Northeast of rolling hills and low mountains, wholly covered with forest and dotted with a thousand gem-like lakes, had nothing in common with the waterless cactus-spotted deserts of the Southwest; nor had the Southeast of low-lying sandy pine barrens, humid swamps, and slow-moving mud-brown rivers with the Northwest of bright cascades, snow-capped mountains, and highlands reaching down to the blue Pacific. There was equally striking contrast between the wide horizons of the ocean-like plains and the endless complexity of the barren and forbidding western mountains. The climate was also of infinite variety, from the tropical and moist heat of the low-lying gulf coasts to the dry air of the high western plateaus or the long cold of the Maine winters and the blizzard-swept plains of the northern central valley."[29] So New England "is the geographical region east of the Hudson valley. It is the historical region of the Yankee. It is the ethical region of the New England conscience and of Puritanism. It is an industrial region separate from all other industrial regions, a recreational region of rugged coast, tumbled mountains, crystal clear streams and lakes, sloping orchards, and white-pine forests."[30] Again, Lewis Mumford has pointed out the natural evolution of regional units in the nation. He says: "Before the Civil War there had grown up in the United States a number of differentiated regions, each of which had its characteristic polity and art and way of life. New England, Virginia, South Carolina, Louisiana, had distinct and special traditions, and in New England and New York particularly the poetic cycle of regionalism had begun: Hawthorne, Thoreau, Emerson, were New Englanders first; and Americans by the grace of certain political connections which they neither repudiated altogether

29. James Truslow Adams, *The Epic of America*, p. 5.
30. W. R. Greely, "Regional and City Planning in New England," in James Truslow Adams, *et al., New England's Prospect*, p. 408.

nor over-valued; and although Whitman and Melville were in their conscious political philosophies identified with 'these states' as a unity, one sees in their work the local influence of the brisk cosmopolitan part of New York, adventuring out to other parts of the world, or, on shore, welcoming each new cargo of men and goods."[31] Finally, to select one other example, A. B. Hulbert continues the picture of the ever westward movement of regional frontiers: "The story of the American Republic, territorially speaking, has been the story of the planting of one 'West' after another, from the Atlantic to the Pacific; and, in a measure the political history of our Republic has been the story of reactions of 'Wests' on 'Easts,' or vice versa, with reference to almost every problem of national life. Therefore what was 'West' and what was 'East' was almost always, and is yet, a matter of personal viewpoint. To many a typical 'Down Easterner' anything beyond the Hudson is the 'West' today; to the sons of the Middle Border nothing is really 'West' until the Great Plains are reached; while a friend of mine, hailing from Bellingham, Washington, remarked to me within the year: 'When I cross the Rockies and get off the train at Denver I can tell where I am by my nose—it just *smells* East.' "[32]

The classical story of American sectional development is, of course, found in Frederick Jackson Turner's contributions on the influence of both the frontier and of sections in American life. Since a separate chapter [see the following paper, "From Sectionalism to Regionalism"] will be devoted to the general theme of sections and regions, it is necessary here only to point up Professor Turner's portraiture of the nation as a series of sections to the end that the historical picture may be clear and that the fundamental difference between sectionalism and regionalism may be emphasized.

"The frontier and the section are two of the most fundamental factors in American history," wrote Professor Turner. "The frontier is a moving section, or rather a form of society, determined by the reactions between the wilderness and the edge of expanding settlement; the section is the outcome of the deeper-seated geographical conditions interacting with the stock which settled the region. Sections are more important than states in shaping the underlying forces of American history. . . . The West was a migrating region, a stage of

31. Lewis Mumford, "The Theory and Practice of Regionalism," *Sociological Review*, Vol. 20, p. 137.

32. A. B. Hulbert, *Frontiers, the Genius of American Nationality*, pp. 127-28.

society rather than a place. Each region reached in the process of expansion from the coast had its frontier experience, was for a time 'the West,' and when the frontier passed on to new regions, it left behind, in the older areas, memories, traditions; an inherited attitude toward life that persisted long after the frontier had passed by. But while the influence of the frontier permeated East as well as West, by survival of the pioneer psychology and by the reaction of the Western ideals and life upon the East, it was in the newer regions, in the area called the West at any given time, that frontier traits and conceptions were most in evidence. This 'West' was more than 'the frontier' of popular speech. It included also the more populous transitional zone adjacent, which was still influenced by pioneer traditions and where economic society had more in common with the newer than with the older regions." And again: "We must remember that each of the sections of this continental nation—New England, the Middle States, the Southeast, the Southwest, the Middle West, the Great Plains, the Mountain States, the Pacific Coast—has its own special geographical qualities, its own resources and economic capacities, and its own rival interest, partly determined in the days when the geological foundations were laid down." Once again, "We in America are in reality a federation of sections rather than of states." Yet, "American sectionalism has been very inadequately dealt with by our historians. Impressed by the artificial political boundary lines of states, they have almost entirely given their attention either to national or to state history, or to the broad division of North and South, overlooking the fact that there are several natural, economic and social sections that are fundamental in American historical development. As population extended itself, it flowed into various physiographic provinces, some of them comparable in size and resources, not only to the greater nations of Europe, but even to some of the great empires that have from time to time been formed by combinations of these nations. The American physical map may be regarded as a map of potential nations and empires, each to be conquered and colonized, each to rise through stages of development, each to achieve a certain social and industrial unity, each to possess certain fundamental assumptions, certain psychological traits, and each to interact with the others, and in combination to form that United States. . . ."[33]

It may be pointed out here, too, that sectionalism in the nation is analogous to nationalism in the world at large, each signifying isola-

33. Frederick Jackson Turner, *The Significance of Sections in American History,* p. 183.

tion and self-sufficiency as opposed to co-operative participation and unity. Thus, Professor Hayes' characterization of the evils of nationalism might well apply to sectionalism. The attributes which he ascribes to nationalism include an intolerant attitude and behavior; belief in the imperial mission of one's own nationality; carrying a chip on the shoulders; dwelling on the memory of past wars; a willingness to be led by self-styled patriots; a diffidence about thinking differently from others; a spirit of exclusiveness; ignorance of others; and gross pride.[34]

The significance of the new trend from sectionalism to regionalism is reflected also in the growing recognition of the reality of the region in all national planning. Thus, regionalism and regional planning often become synonymous, so that through the concept and techniques of regional planning we may recapitulate again various aspects of American regionalism. Frankfurter and Landis emphasize the factor of equilibrium and balance between the states and the federal power: "The overwhelming difficulties confronting modern society must not be at the mercy of the false antithesis embodied in the shibboleths 'States' Rights' and 'National Supremacy'.... Our regions are realities. Political thinking must respond to those realities. Instead of leading to parochialism, it will bring a fresh ferment of political thought whereby national aims may be achieved through various forms of political adjustment."[35]

John Orchard in *Regional Factors in National Planning and Development* describes the region for planning purposes: "As I see the problem, the optimum region for social and economic planning should possess certain characteristics: (1) There should be some unifying core (problem or interest); (2) its area should include all the territory tributary to the core; (3) there should be an absence of serious conflicting interests within the areas; (4) the region should not be so diversified that it will place too great a burden upon the ability and training of the planners. It seems that the geographic region most nearly includes the above characteristics."[36] Benton Mackaye characterizes regional planning in terms of the composite region: "Regional planning ... consists in the attempt at discovering

34. Carlton J. H. Hayes, *Essays on Nationalism,* p. 275; see also his *The Historical Evolution of Modern Nationalism.*
35. Felix Frankfurter and J. M. Landis, "The Compact Clause of the Constitution," *Yale Law Journal,* XXXIV, 729.
36. John Orchard, in National Resources Committee's *Regional Factors in National Planning and Development,* December 1935, p. 148.

the plans of Nature for the attainment of man's ends upon the earth; it visualizes industry as the servant of culture; and its chief concern is the guidance within a region of 'the flow of civilization.' . . . This flow may consist of electric fluid, of lumber, of wheat, of beef, or dairy products." It may consist of the "flow of population, . . . of housing and living facilities."[37] Another characterization from *Regional Factors in National Planning and Development* points out that: "It is patent . . . that the whole meaning of regional planning is to devise a cultural pattern which will fit a large areal unit, and that the qualities inherent in the area not only dictate in large part the features of that plan, but also its territorial extent."[38] The region for national planning should represent organic relationship as well as organic unity in such fields as transport, land use, recreation, power, use of water, redevelopment of forests, conservation of mineral resources, etc. Finally, two popular passages from Lewis Mumford give varied interpretations of regional planning: "Regional planning asks not how wide an area can be brought under the aegis of the metropolis, but how the population and civic facilities can be distributed so as to promote and stimulate a vivid, creative life throughout a whole region —a region being any geographic area that possesses a certain unity of climate, soil, vegetation, industry and culture. The regionalist attempts to plan such an area so that all its sites and resources, from forest to city, from highland to water level, may be soundly developed, and so that population will be distributed so as to utilize, rather than to nullify or destroy, its natural advantages. It sees people, industry and the land as a single unit. In sum, regional planning does not mean the planning of big cities beyond their present areas; it means the reinvigoration and rehabilitation of whole regions so that the products of culture and civilization, instead of being confined to a prosperous minority in the congested centers, shall be available to everyone at every point in a region where the physical basis for a cultivated life can be laid down."[39]

All these and other aspects of regionalism will be discussed and illustrated elsewhere. It remains to emphasize at this point the importance and difficulty of delineating the major composite regions of the United States through which the greatest degree

37. Benton Mackaye, "Regional Planning," *Sociological Review,* XX, No. 4, pp. 298-99.
38. National Resources Committee, *Regional Factors in National Planning and Development,* December 1935, p. 20.
39. Lewis Mumford, "Regions to Live In," *Survey,* Vol. 54, No. 3, pp. 151-52.

and homogeneity for the largest possible purposes may be attained. These regions, flexible and susceptible to adjustment, may then constitute the basis for uniform study and planning and for the vivid portraiture of the nation both for scientific and practical purposes and for creating popular interest and for giving a satisfying sympathetic understanding of the nation's dilemma and progress.

Since the term region has been used in such a variety of ways, it is necessary to note these meanings and to interpret them in relation to the relatively specific usage in the present work. Exclusive of the popular usage which denotes any sort of areal subdivision and of such specialized natural regions as those of the plant and animal ecologists, the geographers, and the soil classificationists, there have been five general types of regions commonly discussed in the United States. From these we develop one which may well be defined as the major composite societal region, as opposed to the limited specialized region. Such a region is selected as embodying the fewest contradictions, the greatest flexibility, and the largest degree of homogeneity for all purposes of study and planning. Within the framework of such a region there must also be provision for overlapping, flexibility, and the inclusion of other areal units, such as subregions, districts, specialized areas and zones. These five types of regions are: *first,* the natural region, such as mountain range, river valley, great plains; *second,* the metropolitian region, where the city is the center and focus of the radiating territory adjacent; *third,* a general loosely used designation which implies the section or provincial locality from which loyalties, patriotism, folkways radiate; *fourth,* the region for convenience, such as administrative divisions of natural organizations or governmental departments; and *fifth,* the group-of-states region, which, if state lines be primarily the arbitrary margins of measurement, may comprehend in varying degrees most of the other types.

Each of these types of region has a distinguished heritage in historical development or authentic usage. Thus, the *river valley region,* brought so much to the forefront by the National Resources Committee and President Roosevelt's proposed seven regional planning agencies, has long-standing advocates in the persons of the geographers. Perhaps the first of distinction was Vidal de la Blache, who envisaged an economy in which societies would be organized around river valleys. Burgess, the political scientist and founder of Columbia's graduate school, thought state lines should be determined by mountains and not rivers. More recently the TVA, the Mississippi River Valley, and the Ohio River Valley Committees and many illuminating studies of water problems and planning have given precedence to river valley regions. So, too, the "Dust Bowl," the Great Plains, the Belt of Drought areas have all featured the natural region as the unit for planning. The *metropolitan region,* perhaps in America the "Dean of Regions," has been featured notably through such major reports as those dealing with New York and its environs, the St. Louis region, the Washington-Baltimore region, and others. Likewise, the metropolitan region has been emphasized in the regional arrangements suggested by the National Resources Committee for Federal Administration, whereby such major region finds its genesis and definition in the urban center. So, too, the proposals of Charles E. Merriam and others for the city-state and urbanism studies of the Chicago human ecologists inquiring into territorial aspects of the city have given considerable distinction to the concept. The *section,* of course, finds its most distinguished heritage in Frederick Jackson Turner but it has been given great emphasis also by James Truslow Adams, William E. Dodd, Charles A. Beard and others. *Literary and aesthetic regionalism,* symbol of local color and culture, has had a long and distingushed record. *Administrative regionalism* finds ample documentation and usage in the hundred and more administrative divisions of the Federal Government, and similar divisional arrangements of educational, religious, and commercial organizations. *The group-of-states region* is found as a technical tool in most of the administrative units of government and as an attempt at co-operative effort across state lines in such recent experiments as the New England Planning Board, the Northeast Planning Board, certain interstate compacts, and in many voluntary organizations. To some extent also the TVA has consistently catalogued the seven contiguous states as areal boundaries of its experimental and co-operative concern.

"Region" in this volume means the *composite societal region* combining a relatively large degree of homogeneity measured by a relatively large number of indices available for a relatively large number of purposes or classifications. This means it must comprehend both the natural factors and the societal factors which must, of course, include the American states and prevailing historic, economic, and culture traits. The region may be, therefore, a "major" region not because of its geographical size but because of the number and importance of classifications of functional or cultural units. The Northeast is such an area, having the smallest area of any of the six major regions of the nation, yet having the largest and most complex population and industry, the largest ratio of wealth, and the largest number of national agencies and organizations. Yet the size of the area is an important factor in determining practical limitations within the measures of homogeneity. In some such way as the astronomer's region is the space that can be explored with existing telescopes, so our region must assume reasonable maximum distances for travel, organization, study, administration. This is illustrated again by Lewis Mumford's dictum that for a region "it is necessary to take an area large enough to embrace a sufficient range of interests, and small enough to keep these interests in focus and to make them a subject of direct collective concern."[40]

Composite societal regions are of two sorts: *the major region* and *the minor region,* which we designate as the *subregion.* Both of these are clearly differentiated from single-purpose, isolated, specialized areas, such as organizational or administrative units including districts, provinces, centers, zones, and the like. Within this frame of reference, both major regions and minor regions may be of two sorts, namely, the *natural* or *physiographic region* and the *societal* or *cultural region,* and, of course, in the exceptional case they may approximate both.

The nature and importance of the *subregion* may well be illustrated in the case where both the physiographic and the societal region are combined. Such instances may be found in the classifications of J. Russell Smith in his arrangements of regions jointly characterized by "men and resources." Thus he says: "This point of organizing by regions is made clear if we think of the State of Minnesota. Northeastern Minnesota is a sparsely peopled land of forest and swamp, nearly all too rough and rocky for good farms. This part of the state had long been called the *Upper Lake Region.* Western Minnesota is a grassland now famed for its farms. It is one of the levelest, smoothest, softest lands in the world. Its smooth levelness makes it the perfect land for the operation of large-scale agricultural machinery. It has long been known as part of the *Spring Wheat Region.* Very few things can be said about both of these two sharply different sections of Minnesota. But there are many

40. Lewis Mumford, *The Culture of Cities.* Quoted by permission from proof sheets.

things that can be said about the *Spring Wheat Region* and the *Upper Lake Region* because each area has a unity that enables us to tell things about the whole of it. Now, it so happens that this Spring Wheat Region extends into South Dakota and North Dakota and into Canada where it stretches across the three prairie provinces of Manitoba, Saskatchewan, and Alberta. How foolish it would be to describe the Spring Wheat Region three times for each of the three American states and three more times for each of the three Canadian provinces. And how clear other wheat-growing regions of the world become if you think of them as regions similar in climate and soil to western Minnesota."[41]

The "American" Region, further, as used in the present work is the *composite group-of-states major societal region.* For those composite areas or minor regions in which it is necessary to cut across state lines the term *subregion* is used. For the societal subregion which must ignore state boundaries but which manifestly must have arbitrary boundary lines for measurement, the counties and smaller civil units assume the same sort of role as the states in the major region. For group-of-county subdivisions within states or for mere administrative areas, *district* rather than region is the characterization which is used. For still more specific delimitation of functional or administrative areas defined by legislative fiat, the term *zone* is available. These do not preclude the specialized usages which are in general synonymous with the district, namely, such terms as division, area, station, branch, center, field office, section, territory. The term *district,* however, is adequate for all of these, and *zone* is a very specialized term, so that the threefold delineation of *region, subregion,* and *district* is quite ample for all purposes.

In substantiation of this classificatory arrangement certain further considerations are timely. One is in contrasting the group-of-states region with the natural region, in which certain contradictions might appear to exist. Thus, the great Appalachian Mountain natural region, extending from near the Lower South up almost into Canada, might be a *larger* area than, let us say, the Southeastern States. Yet its classification units for the purposes of societal study or planning are so much fewer than for the group-of-states region that it becomes a minor or subregional area. If it is a natural subregion it will be appraised in units of topography, situation, soil, rivers, and mountains. If it is a societal subregion it will be appraised as was the case in the

41. J. Russell Smith, *Men and Resources,* Introduction, pp. vi-vii.

survey of Gray and his associates, in county units with such special subregional concentrations as may be devised. For, because of its great heterogeneity of temperature and of topographical relationship to the society of the nation, it must be broken up into numerous subregions. The same is true of the Mississippi River Valley Region which is far larger, let us say, than the group-of-states region designated as the Middle States, yet because of the limited and specialized classification purposes and its great heterogeneity in so many natural, economic, and cultural indices, it cannot qualify for the composite major societal region. On the other hand, within the group-of-states region may be incorporated numerous subregional arrangements to provide for both natural advantages and for cutting across state lines. The socio-economic-natural subregion may again be illustrated in the case of areas in which there is a clustering of a large number of socio-economic traits which are no respecters of state lines, such as the Cotton Belt, the Black Belt, the Dairy Region, the Winter Wheat Subregion, and the like.

All of these considerations and others lead to the conclusion, therefore, that the group-of-states major region will qualify best as the composite region which approximates the largest number and variety of indices available for the largest number of purposes or classifications. In the projection of American culture into the next frontier developments, it seems clear, too, that it is the societal region with which the nation and its changing civilization is primarily concerned. By the same token, then, it would seem that the natural region, no matter what specialized advantages it offers, cannot qualify as the key major region not only because it cannot be made to coincide with the societal or cultural region, but because it is not practically realistic. Range of climate, topography, historical and cultural diversity militate against its use as a composite culture region. Such regions do not, therefore, approximate adequacy without ignoring the legal, sovereign, cultural foundations of the nation. More important, however, as the irreducible criterion of reality is the historical, constitutional, and organizational status of the 48 states, which are the very warp and woof of the national fabric. Natural regions can be utilized for new political and sovereign arrangements only by changing the American form and spirit of government and by ignoring the sweep of technology. Furthermore, to urge the formation of new regional states, based on natural regions, is to repeat the imperfect arrangements of the present states, or to set up too many new states, or to leave out of the picture innumerable border areas not comprehended in natural regions of approximate homogeneity. The natural region, therefore, as found in the United States, cannot qualify as the major societal region in the present American scene. On the other hand, this accentuates the importance of the natural region as one of the key subregional tools for every desired specialized concern and especially for interstate co-operative efforts and for co-operative arrangements between the nation at large and the states and regions.

Applying this test of the composite group-of-states region and keeping in mind also the greatest possible flexibility for future trends as well as adaptation to as large a number of natural subregions as possible, we have set up for exploratory purposes and for a comprehensive frame of reference for research and planning, a sixfold regional America to comprehend the *Northeast* and the *Southeast,* the *Northwest* and the *Southwest,* the *Middle States* and the *Far West.* These are realistic extensions of the earlier historical "sections." They represent two "Souths," two "Norths," and two "Wests." Still more historically literal, they represent one "East," one "South," and four "Wests." These are *major* regions approximating a greater degree of homogeneity measured by a larger number of indices for a larger number of purposes and classifications than any other regional framework that has been utilized or than any other that, on the basis of our data and premises, would appear possible.

From Sectionalism to Regionalism [1938]*

In the preceding paper on "The Implications and Meanings of Regionalism," we have pointed out the tendency in the past to confuse sectionalism with regionalism, and we have called attention to considerable usage which still assumes sectionalism and regionalism to be synonymous. To the extent to which such usage has become common, it is necessary to trace the development of sectionalism as basic to the evolution of regionalism rather than coinciding with it. The way will then be open to point up fundamental differences in meaning and implications.

That which was Frederick Jackson Turner's magnificent sectionalism and James Truslow Adams' *America's Tragedy* had its rise and incidence in the historical and geographical development and expansion of a great frontier nation. The great range and variety of the physical resources and topography of America constituted the basis for a many-regioned nation. America became, in reality, a nation of varied *sections* due to the incidence and vicissitudes of economic development and cultural conflict. The story of the nation is in one sense essentially the story of this sectional development. The thesis of this volume is that the promise and prospect of the nation in the future is, in another sense, to be found in the substitution of a realistic and comprehensive regionalism for the older historical sectionalism.

* Chapter II, pp. 35-51, of *American Regionalism: A Cultural-Historical Approach to National Integration,* with Harry Estill Moore (New York: Henry Holt and Company, 1938). Reprinted by permission of Holt, Rinehart, and Winston.

The story of sectionalism in American life is a fascinating one and may be glimpsed through several avenues of approach. First, there are many authentic concepts and definitions of sectionalism; second, there is the story of its rise and incidence through the naturally expanding domain in which geographic regions become articulate sections because of economic incidence and cultural conflict. Next we may examine some of the fundamental distinctions between sectionalism and regionalism. And, finally, we may explore the possibilities which inhere in the implementation of this transfer from sectionalism to regionalism through this emerging economy of regionalism.

Frederick Jackson Turner has made the most significant contribution to the understanding of sectionalism in American life, and his premise is adequately supported by most of the works dealing with the historical development of the United States. In the preceding paper we have already cited examples of the ever-expanding nation and of its earlier sectional divisions. Professor Turner's premise was that "the economic, political, and social life of the United States, even its literature, psychology, and its religious organizations, must be described by sections, . . . In spite of similarity of traits and institutions throughout the nation, it is also a congeries of sections." Professor Turner points out further that "arising from the facts of physical geography and the regional settlement of different peoples and types of society on the Atlantic Coast, there was a sectionalism from the beginning." So, again, contrasting the East with the West, he points out that "from the beginning East and West have shown a sectional attitude."[1] Evidences of this were numerous: the condescension of the East toward the upland folk; the disrespect in which the West was held by the East and the East by the West; the story of the grangers, populists, anti-monopolists, progressives, farmers' bloc, and others. This was illustrated by movements so to fix the number of representatives from the Atlantic States that the eastern quota would always be greater than the number from the West.

This comprehensiveness of American sectionalism is fundamental both to the understanding of the nature of American institutions and dilemmas and to the further ordering of the nation in the next period of development. "Sectionalism in American history," wrote Pro-

1. Frederick Jackson Turner, *The Significance of Sections in American History,* pp. 183, 22, 25.

fessor Turner, "has been so commonly conceived by historians as the struggle between North and South over slavery, that the much more complicated sectionalism, involving all the various geographic provinces of the United States . . . has been neglected."[2]

Evidence that the South and the Civil War constituted only a part of the issue of American sectionalism is supplemented richly, not only by Turner, but by Charles A. Beard, James Truslow Adams, William E. Dodd, Arthur Schlesinger, and many other historians. The Civil War, as Turner pointed out, "was only the most drastic and most tragic of sectional manifestations, and in no small degree the form it took depended upon the fact that rival societies, free and slave, were marching side by side into the unoccupied lands of the West, . . ."[3] So, too, the physical divergence between the East and the West was accepted as evidence of potential separateness. "Nature," said Rufus King, "has severed the two countries by a vast chain of mountains, interest and convenience will keep them separate, and the feeble policy of our disjointed government will not be able to unite them." Even if the West should become a part of the nation, "the Western States, multiplied in numbers and augmented in population will control the interests of the whole."[4] It was inevitable that the West, resenting both the conceptions of the East and the attitudes manifested would, as Turner points out, take "the attitude of a section itself." Thus quickly, in undesigned and rapid growth, grew three great sections, the East, the South, the West, so that Turner concludes that "throughout our history, then, there has been this sectionalism of West and East and this eastern conception of the West as recruiting ground merely for the rival Atlantic Coast sections."[5]

Yet this East-West-South sectionalism did not stop with the earlier history, or with the earlier struggle for priority in lands and canals and railways. William E. Dodd points out the gigantic sectional struggle which followed the Civil War between certain factions of East and West, and which constituted a continuing or a revivification of sectionalism. "Here were two powerful sections of the nation, the South and the West, which had formerly supported each other in national affairs. They each had grievances. If the South were readmitted to the Union, southern and western men would inevitably unite their strength and arrange a national policy which would serve

2. *Ibid.*, p. 193.
3. *Ibid.*, pp. 26-27.
4. Quoted from *ibid.*, pp. 28, 29.
5. *Ibid.*, pp. 30, 33.

their interests. Andrew Johnson, in spite of his loud talk during the early months of his presidency, represented the promise and guarantee of such a combination. Hence the bitter struggle to impeach him. Industrial men succeeded by a campaign of hatred both in defeating Johnson and in holding the South out of the Union for a decade. Meanwhile, industrialism made its position secure."[6]

Dodd pictures vividly the place of industry and economic development in the forming of sections seeking their own interests. "From Boston to Minneapolis stretched this vast industrial domain," in which, he points out, "railroads tied the mines and the farms of the rest of the country to the nerve centers of this busy, smoke-blackened region. National, state, and private banks fed the industries, the railroads, and the other ancillary businesses with the necessary capital which was borrowed from Europe or from the savings of the country. Real estate rose in value beyond the wildest dreams of its owners because industry brought millions of tenants; bank and industrial stocks doubled and quadrupled both in volume and in price because vast populations gathered in the cities increased the consumption of goods. Rich men grew to be millionaires and millionaires became masters of hundreds of millions of wealth." To the economic factors were added sectional patterns in politics in three decades of powerful development. Thus Dodd points out that: "From 1866 to 1896, the process went on almost without interruption. The opposition, led in the beginning by members of Congress from the Middle West, called itself the Democratic party. It consisted in a solid South voting against the East whether in good or ill repute and the provincial West. The provincials of America could not see that it was a blessing to cover the earth with great plants and wide-flung mill settlements so long as cotton, corn, tobacco, and all other products of their lands declined in value. Their sons ran away to the cities to swell the enormous tide of newcomers from Europe, both of which masses of men added to the representation of the industrial districts in Congress and made the more difficult the election of any leader of the farming groups to the presidency. Every year the country regions not touched by industry became less attractive. Houses took on a tumbledown appearance. The South became a waste. Planters became farmers; farmers became tenants; and tenants took places as day laborers or emigrated to the city. There was no help for it. Old America that lived upon the land and talked of liberty and equality was vanishing."[7]

6. William A. Dunning in William E. Dodd, *Woodrow Wilson and His Work*, p. 61.

7. William E. Dodd, *Woodrow Wilson and His Work*, pp. 62-64.

So came the powerful forces which were to contrast the earlier rural regions of America with a great urbanism which was to constitute a new and powerful "sectionalism" in the sense that urban and industrial regions, in conflict with rural interests, were bent on self-interest more than national development. And what could the rural regions, the Southeast, the Southwest, the Wests, do except to fall in line and set the pace for a new nation. Says Dodd, "Country merchants far and near endeavored to have their names on the books of these elect of the world; little bankers in every town and city scraped together as much money as possible in order to maintain big balances in Wall Street; clergymen learned the law from real masters rather than from musty books said to come from a certain mountain in ancient Palestine; and universities were very loth to fall into ill favor with the only men of power in the country. What else could men do? They were caught in a system, as the people of the old South had been caught in the slavery system."[8]

Returning now to our examination of the basic factors of sectionalism, we may cite Turner's statement that, unlike France and Germany, "the United States has the problem of the clash of economic interests closely associated with regional geography on a large scale." On this basis he predicted the certainty of sectional clash of interests in which "sectionalism will hereafter be shaped by such new forces. We have become a nation comparable to all Europe in area, with settled geographic provinces which equal great European nations. We are in this sense an empire, a federation of sections, a union of potential nations."[9]

Herein lies the essential quality of sectionalism; inherent in it is the idea of separatism and isolation; of separate units with separate interests. It must be clear that, since the very definition of regionalism implies a unifying function, it must be different from sectionalism as everywhere defined by the historians. Here the distinctions are clear between the divisive power of self-seeking *sections* and the integrating power of co-ordinate *regions* fabricated into a united whole. The premise of the new regionalism goes further and assumes that the United States must not, either because of its bigness and complexity or because of conflicting interests, become a federation of

8. *Ibid.,* p. 68.
9. Turner, *op. cit.,* pp. 36, 37.

conflicting sections but a homogeneity of varying regions. Professor Turner, warning of the likelihood of an increase of sectionalism and pointing up multiple bases for this trend rather than the tendency toward a wholesome regionalism, points out "the danger that the province or section shall think of itself naïvely as the nation; that New England shall think that America is merely New England writ large or the Middle West shall think that America is really the Middle West writ large and then proceed to denounce the sections that do not perceive the accuracy of this view as wicked or ignorant or un-American. This kind of nationalism is a sectional mirage."[10]

The Turner warning, of course, was logical. So, too, Professor Turner's nearest approach to the ideal of national unity, though a projection of a possible regionalism through homogeneities of states and resources, now appears to be one of the most important trends in American life. In this approach he recognized the cultural significance of regions when he pointed out the fallacy of generalizations which may ascribe to a single geographic or economic or other interest alone the compelling explanation of sectionalism. "There are," he wrote, "also the factors of ideals and psychology, the inherited intellectual habits, derived from the stock from which the voters sprang. Some of these ideals carry the voters into lines that contradict their own interests. But as a rule there has been such a connection of the stock, the geographic conditions, the economic interests, and the conceptions of right and wrong, that all have played upon each other to the same end."[11] This is transition from sectionalism to regionalism, in which the nation will avoid "the insistence upon the particular interests and ideals of the section in which we live, without sympathetic comprehension of the ideals, the interests and the rights of other sections. We must shape our national action to the fact of a vast and varied union of unlike sections."[12] This substitution of regional units is the basis for regional planning in the nation. This is the challenge which comes also from James Truslow Adams' dictum: "Sectionalism, whether of the North and the South, that of the East and West, or others, is still a living force molding our destiny."[13]

Others warn of the continuing danger of sectionalism. Thus, H. G. Roach writes in the *American Political Science Review:* "Sectionalism is a fundamental and persistent factor in American politics.

10. Turner, *op.cit.,* pp. 45-46.
11. *Ibid.,* pp. 48-49.
12. *Ibid.,* p. 51.
13. James Truslow Adams, *America's Tragedy,* preface, p. v.

In the shaping of Congressional legislation and even in the foundation of the platforms of our national parties, the influence of conflicting sectional interests is of prime importance. . . . A study of the period from the early 1870's to 1890 shows that sectionalism at that time was in large measure the product of the interaction of two movements in our national development,—the rapid expansion of Western settlement, particularly the trans-Mississippi Middle West (the West North Central States) and the Mountain region, and the marked intensification of industrialism in the older sections of the country, especially in the North Atlantic States."[14]

Perhaps we need give only a few other characterizations of sectionalism before we contrast it further with the current emerging regionalism. The spirit and motivation of the old sectionalism has been well described by Waldo Frank. "Each part," he points out, "believed itself whole. Kindred or adjacent parts joined loosely to create a Section. And now America was a crazy-quilt of sections. There was the section of Puritan New England, the section of more conservative New York and New Jersey, the feudal section of the South, the dissident section of the southern mountains, the section of Jacksonian Mississippi. Each section created a sectionalism of its very own: a rabid rationalization of its specific interests; and the idea of each was a sprawling makeshift pieced from splintered Europe. Within the section, there was no harmony. The religious and rationalist fanatics of Boston dwelt askance together. Farmers and town mechanics in New York spoke no concordant words. There was only a minimum of accommodation; only the fulsome rhetoric of the politician to make them at least drunk together. Between the great sectionalisms—the North, the South, the Wests—there was the hostility that turned to bloodshed."[15]

The most clearly stated measures of sectionalism, however, are still those of Professor Turner's criteria. Thus he says: "I shall recognize as tests of sectionalism all of those methods by which a given area resists national uniformity, whether by mere opposition in public opinion on the part of a considerable area, or by formal protest, or by combining its votes in Congress and in presidential elections, and also those manifestations of economic and social separateness involved

14. H. G. Roach, "Sectionalism in Congress, 1870 to 1890," *American Political Science Review,* Vol. 19, No. 3, p. 500.
15. Waldo Frank, "Rediscovery of America," *The New Republic,* LIII, 345-46.

in the existence in a given region of a set of fundamental assumptions, a mental and emotional attitude which segregates the section from other sections or from the nation as a whole. Sooner or later such sectional influences find expression in politics and legislation, and they are even potential bases for forcible resistance."[16]

Professor Turner's political sectionalism finds some sanction also in Stuart Chase's distinction between regionalism and sectionalism. Says Chase: "A *region* may be defined as an area where nature acts in a roughly uniform manner, . . . The Old South is a section, but the land is cut into several natural regions . . . a region provides a major basis for economic planning, a section a basis for political uproar."[17] Turner's political sectionalism was delineated in four ways: First, in a group of states contending with other groups or with the nation; second, in a congeries of congressional districts mapped by homogeneity of congressional votes; third, by approximation of areas delimited by presidential and state elections; and, fourth, by sectional homogeneity denoted by the mapping of election precincts.

We have now traced something of the rise and significance of sectionalism and pointed out enough of its characteristics to enable us, on the background of the preceding paper, to contrast sectionalism with regionalism. We have already pointed out the analogy between sectionalism in the nation and economic nationalism in the world at large. We have pointed out certain conflicting factors between metropolitan regionalism and the more comprehensive national regionalism now emerging, and later we shall contrast the interests of urban and rural areas as possible bases for "sectional" conflict. We may now turn to the further examination of five important distinctions between sectionalism and regionalism which we have previously discussed.

In the first place, we have pointed out, regionalism envisages the nation first, making the national culture and welfare the final arbiter. It is, therefore, essentially a co-operative concern. On the other hand, sectionalism sees the region first and the nation afterwards. It is, therefore, essentially a competitive emphasis. In the second place, sectionalism emphasizes the autonomy inherent in political boundaries and state sovereignties. It confuses the state as a unity in the regional or national whole with the state as a separate entity. It emphasizes

16. Turner, *op. cit.*, p. 288.
17. Stuart Chase, *Rich Land, Poor Land*, pp. 10-11.

technical legislation, provincial interests, local loyalties. Over against the co-operating group-of-states region it sets up a confederation of states "with common interests, menaced by federal action." Where sectionalism features separateness, regionalism connotes component and constituent parts of the larger national culture. Another way to look at sectionalism is to liken it to cultural inbreeding, whereas regionalism is line-breeding. The most common illustration of this terminology is probably found in the criticism of educational institutions for too much "inbreeding," that is, utilizing their own graduates almost exclusively.

Inherent in the new concept and practice, by the very nature of its regional, interregional, and national co-operative processes, in the fourth place, is the implication of more of the designed and planned society in regionalism than in sectionalism, which is the group correspondent to individualism. Finally, one of the most critical aspects of sectionalism is the fact that it must have its counterpart in a potential and, in the full flowering of its development, an inevitable coercive federalism, which is contrary to the state ideals of American democracy.

Some such comprehensive distinction between the two is well stated by Hedwig Hintze: "Regionalism must be distinguished from nationalism in that it recognizes a higher national unity and superior national interests transcending the attachment to the local region. It must be distinguished also from mere sectionalism in that it is not based exclusively on regional economic or class interests, but involves certain ethnic factors, such as cultural, traditional or linguistic peculiarities, which provide a basis for what is often termed a sub-nationality."[18]

The assumptions of this volume are that these distinctions, so far from being merely academic, are realistically fundamental in theory and practice. Regionalism is organic, basic to the evolution of all culture. Sectionalism is mechanical and is basic to specialized and temporary ends. We may, however, at this time examine Donald Davidson's alternative characterization in which he thinks that on matters of general culture, traditions, and perhaps economics, regionalism may be a reality; but that when tested by political arrangements it is still sectionalism. Davidson is quite willing to help work out the reality of regionalism if it can be done, but he feels that the historical and structural sectionalism is so firmly ingrained that we

18. Hedwig Hintze, "Regionalism," *Encyclopaedia of the Social Sciences*, XIII, 209.

shall have to keep it. Thus he writes: "The sectional peculiarities of the major divisions are now thoroughly intrenched in differences of climate, population, specialized economy, and cultural tradition. In older sections like the South the differences go so deep as to seem practically ineradicable, and they beget loyalties that cannot be over-ridden without damage to the human spirit. To enlist these loyalties rather than to over-ride them would seem to be among the pressing obligations of the new regionalism; for without loyalty no nation, however perfectly planned in theory, can endure. To persuade and guide sectional loyalties is a task that regionalists have not yet under-taken. But it must finally be undertaken; and the practical name of such persuasion is politics."[19] This viewpoint would seem to corre-spond to Turner's political sectionalism and is, therefore, still "his-torical."

Davidson seems to sense this point. He continues: "It is evidently becoming necessary—for the political scientist, if not for the soci-ologist and economist—to work out a kind of Federalism which will officially acknowledge the existence of sections and discover the means of adapting the national policy to permit their healthy functioning within it. We have never had that kind of Federalism. The Federal-ism of the constitution makers, who were intent upon building a na-tion out of bodies that claimed separate sovereignty, took only the states into legal regard. Partly because of that too limited regard the old Federalism came finally into trouble, since it was difficult to frame a sectional reciprocity that would be both legal and satisfactory under a governmental instrument that did not recognize sections. The post-bellum Federalism crystallized an old error and allowed the East to dominate West and South. It was a false Federalism and is perishing before our eyes. What kind of Federalism will emerge from the New Deal remains to be seen. If it is a centralization more drastic than we have yet known, which will be heedless of sectional differentiations, it will not be the right kind of Federalism and will bear the seeds of its own failure. In advocating respect for sectional-ism, I should not be understood as having any disrespect for region-alism, but rather the complete contrary. If the regionalist in action often turns out to be a sectionalist, the reverse is equally true: the sectionalist, in analyzing the problems of his section, inevitably turns regionalist. My intention has been to show a necessary relation be-tween sectionalism and regionalism and to correct a prevailing im-

19. Donald Davidson, "Where Regionalism and Sectionalism Meet," *Social Forces,* Vol. 13, p. 30.

pression that there is something dangerous and vindictive about sectionalism, and that regionalism, by contrast, is safe, orderly, and affectionate. Both are 'isms,' both are natural and reasonable, both have vices and explosive possibilities as all human phenomena must have."[20]

Davidson argues that sectionalism has as many conservative as destructive tendencies. On the one hand, it is conservative in the Jeffersonian sense, providing an automatic check against over-centralization. Furthermore, he thinks the existence of sections diminishes the possibility of violent revolution and guarantees that changes in the social order must adapt themselves to democratic institutions. On the other hand, in sectionalism is the possibility of realizing the values which come from regional study and of the great system of regional study now being planned. The sectional units, he thinks, may be the tools for regional enrichment.

Appraising further the fivefold distinction between sectionalism and regionalism, which we have presented, he resumes: "Although I should not agree with every detail of this description of differences, I should say that the general lines of this distinction are correct. The distinction must be granted so long as regionalism operates only as a technique of social study. But when regionalism goes into action and becomes not only a study but a working force, or even a doctrine, the distinction tends to break down. In the field of action the two terms are far from being opposed. They are complementary aspects of the same thing. Sectionalism is the political approach, and regionalism is the economic and cultural approach to an identical set of facts. Under a democratic government, regionalism will hardly avoid developing sectional features as soon as the conclusions drawn from its studies begin to be applied. When regionalists declare against sectionalism, they mean that they want to escape the embarrassment of dealing in the old sort of politics. For the desire they are not to be blamed. But where there is democratic government there must be politics. We cannot shut up large-scale social experiments in a vacuum and expect Americans not to exercise their suffrage pro and con; or if not their suffrage their age-old habits of jockeying and manipulating, in blocs and lobbies. Or, if by some extraordinary means politics is ruled out of regionalsim, we shall then have to abandon our present political society and substitute for it the scientific society. As matters now stand, we cannot escape the political implications of

20. *Ibid.* See also Davidson's volume, *The Attack on Leviathan: Regionalism and Nationalism in the United States.*

our actions by invoking the spirit of science, by insisting on the name of regionalism, or by talking of the general good of society. The hope of the regionalist should be for his studies to achieve the kind of political instrumentation that will realize their latent possibilities. That kind of politics will mean sectionalism, though not the kind of sectionalism which tyrannizes over other sections, like the old sectionalism of the North; or the warlike, seceding sectionalism which was the answer to it. Experience teaches us that it is fatal to ignore the existence of sections and sectional interests in a nation so large and diverse as ours is. If we again ignore them, we will once more invite disaster, and the wholesome purposes of the New Regionalism will stand in danger of defeat before they have had a fair trial."[21]

What Davidson appears to overlook is the fact that regionalism connotes unity in a total national composition, while sectionalism with its separatism is inherently different. This is true even more in a federation of states. He overlooks the fact that administrative regionalism is a very small part of the total construct of regionalism. It is important to note also that the habits of a people do change with relative rapidity and that, as the nation is knit more closely into a unit by economic interdependence and the efficiency of communication facilities, there arises a new situation which in and of itself demands new modes of action and at the same time brings an acute awareness of this need to the public consciousness. Equally, the separatism of sectionalism retards the expansion and growth of the units involved and the broader services of the nation to these units. Lewis Mumford's interpretation describes most effectively the situation and the problem.

The re-animation and re-building of regions, as deliberate works of collective art, is the grand task of politics for the opening generation. It raises anew, in a form that now has fuller human significance, the fundamental questions of human interrelationship across the ethnic, ideological, and cultural boundaries that have been carried over from the past. And as the new tasks of region-building imply shifts in the population, migration into more favored areas, and the building up or reconstruction of a multitude of new urban complexes, the politics of regional development become of critical importance. Not merely must we define and express the region: we must work out, by deliberate experiment, the areas for interregional co-operation

21. Donald Davidson, "Where Regionalism and Sectionalism Meet," *Social Forces,* Vol. 13, pp. 24-25.

and for super-regional authority. . . . What we have to conceive and work out is a federal system of government which shall be based upon a progressive integration of region with region, of province with province, of continent with continent: each part loose enough and flexible enough to adjust to the continuing changes in local and transregional life. Once such a structure has been outlined, it will tend to make effective that concentric regrouping of political, economic, and cultural functions, whose absence is today a severe handicap to co-operative effort. . . . Political consolidation, in indifference to regional realities, has met with unexpected obstacles: under the even whitewash of "national unity" the colors of the underlying geographic, economic, and cultural realities are beginning to show through. Not the least important sign of this new regime is the recognition accorded under Lenin in Soviet Russia to the principle of cultural autonomy. The fact is that real communities and real regions do not fit into the frontiers and the ideological pattern of the national state. The state is usually too big to define a single region, with its political, economic, and social elements in symmetrical relationships, and it is too small to include a whole society, like that of Western Europe or the North American Continent, which must ultimately become the sphere of a larger system of co-operative administration. The limits of functional authority, such as is involved in the organization of a continental railroad system or the steel industry, cannot rest effectively within the fortuitous boundaries of the state: the larger relationships need a larger framework of authority, and the more intimate relationships require a narrower field of effort. This is no less true of art and science and religion, which are by nature part of the common stock, not of a region, a province, or a state, but of a whole society. There is no way short of tyrannical repression in which the interests of a scholar, a man of letters, or a member of the Catholic Church can be kept within the boundaries of the national state.[22]

In his *Roads to Social Peace,* Professor E. A. Ross featured "The Avoidance of Sectionalism" in a separate chapter.[23] While "the new regionalism" had not emerged at the time he was writing, his emphasis upon realistic ways and means of avoiding social conflict within the nation may well serve to interpret from another angle the fundamental importance of changing from the old order of sectional conflict to national co-ordination through regional integration. We may

22. Lewis Mumford, *The Culture of Cities.* Quoted, by permission, from proof sheets.
23. E. A. Ross, *Roads to Social Peace,* Chap. I.

debate the question whether the difference between sectionalism and regionalism is an academic matter, but the realities remain that the difference in ideals and objectives is so great that, academic or not, the old sectionalism must be transcended by the new regionalism if the nation is to avoid the old mistakes. Just as there is need for decentralization through regional divisions, there is also need for minimizing the narrow, local, state dominance through enlargement into regional homogeneities. These will be the buffer between the state and the federal power.

Illustrations of the national-regional and regional-national approach, as opposed to the sectional, are abundant. One type of illustration is that of federal grants and equalization funds for the use of states, the nature and amount often being determined by the regional nature of the need and problem. Land grant colleges represent the joint efforts of federal and local agencies working together on a unified basis. Through this sort of co-operation a new era in American education and agricultural development may be ushered in. Federal public health services, road building, vocational education, and social security represent other federal-regional techniques of co-operation.

Many of the more recent federal-co-operative arrangements represent the national-regional ideal, although a few have appeared to focus so much on federal control as to endanger genuine regionalism by fomenting sectional antagonisms. However, there are ample illustrations of the positive sort. . . . Of the federal illustrations, the TVA is an excellent sample. Manifestly, it promotes the regional well-being through the development and enrichment of both physical and human resources. It does not, however, limit itself to southern employees or southern ideas, neither does it reject southern people or southern ideas. Manifestly it overlaps state boundaries, but in no sense assumes to take over or dictate the ways and rights of the seven states involved in the river valley region. Manifestly, it is national in so far as it sets up an experiment which might be helpful to other similar regions of the nation. Manifestly, it would run contrary to soundly bottomed regionalism if and when it should transcend the rights and freedom of the people within the region either by manifestly intentional organization or by subterfuge.

So, too, many of the agricultural adjustment policies are based upon the realities of regionalism. Obviously, the adjustment acts which take cognizance of wheat and cotton and corn and hogs and tobacco get their specifications from the regional needs and settings. So, too, it is possible to project a federal equalization fund in education with a view to balance and equilibrium between and among the regions and with a view to equalizing opportunity for rural and urban or for whites and Negroes. Again, some of the great dams which provide irrigation and power are of the greatest importance in enriching regional cultures where they are and adding to the national total, rather than attempting to starve them out or move the people from the areas involved.

These are adequate to illustrate the case in general. We may cite a more specific example utilized in the study of the southern regions. One of the best illustrations may be found in the problem of race development and relations in the South. The evidence all indicates that it is not possible to make adjustments or work out solutions on any purely "southern," section basis, which logically would have in mind primarily the interests of the white South. On the other hand, in view of the dominance of folkways over stateways, of the actualities already existent, and of the cultural and historical backgrounds of the several regions and of the American principles of government, it is not possible to effect immediate readjustments through complete federal coercion and control, which would be analogous in many ways to the extreme sectional viewpoint. What is needed is a comprehensive approach looking to the facts and welfare of the nation, of the North and the South, of white and Negro, all according to the regional-national approach inseparably bound together both in ultimate ends and in methods of attainment. There are fundamental differences involving both cultural and technical difficulties based upon sound historical and philosophical grounds.

"A specific illustration of a real regional-national approach as opposed to the earlier narrow sectional [viewpoint] may be found in the upbuilding of Negro institutions of higher learning in the South, in which southern institutions are being developed through inter-regional co-operation and aid, approximating mutual satisfaction to the South, the North, the Negroes, and the whites, as nearly as is possible under the circumstances. Thus the most eminent Negro men of science and letters in the nation have come to southern Negro colleges to develop a new era. This new educational statesmanship is a maturer development than the earlier limitations set by the South, in which it sought little education for the Negro, on the one hand, and the missionary spirit of the philanthropists from the North, on the other. It also represents the best thought and effort of the Negro race, whose personnel, skill, and training are being brought more and more to bear upon the problems in hand. A similar illustration might be cited in the case of public and elementary education in many of the southern states, in which such out of the region funds as Rosenwald, Slater, and Jeanes have contributed to a richer regional culture and a broader interregional contact."[24]

The other side of the question, apart from the advantage to the area involved through its richer development and better national integration, reflects important advantages for the nation as a whole. As its regions are in wealth and welfare, on the one hand, or in poverty and conflict, on the other, so will the nation reap or lose. If the Southeastern Region sends its millions of people into all parts of the nation, there will be enrichment in proportion as these people are well educated and equipped. In times of stress and depression these assets and liabilities are especially demonstrable as also in time of war the national unity must be geared with the national wealth. So, too, other phases of the national-regional aspects are apparent in the development and conservation of natural resources. We shall, therefore, examine next something of the regionalism involved in the natural regions of the nation.

This problem of natural resources and their development will prove one of the most important corollaries to regional concepts and practices. One of the most important of the new implications of regionalism in the nation reflects a trend contrary to what has often been predicted and finds a sort of counterpart in the increasing tendency toward economic nationalism. This is the basis for new difficulties and obligations in the way of the new regionalism. It had been freely predicted that modern communication, technology, and standardization processes would tend to minimize regional and national differences. There is, however, the important fact that certain economic aspects of both regionalism and nationalism have been accentuated by modern technology. Communication, transportation, and invention bring regions and nations closer together, but they may also solidify groups and standardize production. In the older days, for instance, the manufacture of finer fabrics, cloths, and paper was centered in northern and eastern regions of the United States. The progress of science and invention later made it possible for the South to compete on more favorable terms. Continued development easily

24. Howard W. Odum, *Southern Regions of the United States,* p. 255.

leads to competitive rivalries which accentuate regional or sectional interests. The same sort of thing is likely to apply in other regions and to other commodities, setting, for instance, the Middle States and the Southeast in regional rivalry in furniture-making and the dairy industry, or the Southwest and the Far West in citrus fruits, or the Southwest and the Southeast in cotton growing and manufacture. It applies also to other nations—the production of cotton and cotton goods, of oil, of many things originally imported or exported; so that a new type of economic planning will be necessary to gear together interregional and international programs. The assumption is that science has broken down the old division between manufacturing countries and raw material countries and is reducing the number of raw materials which come primarily from nature. The further assumption is that general cultural factors, science, ideas, literature, travel, recreation, should be international, but that goods, finance, economic processes, should be primarily national. The same presumptions are applicable to regions within the nation, changing many of the earlier assumptions.[25]

Finally, an important distinction between regionalism and sectionalism is found in the recent rapid rise of regionalism in America. The very urgency of river valley and other natural regions for planning and development, through which the national whole is envisaged as being better promoted by regional rather than state action, implies a definite meaning of the region quite different from the section. No one uses the term river valley sections, or natural grass sections, or winter wheat sections, or soil sections.[26]

25. Adapted from *ibid.,* pp. 248-49.

26. Few themes are more abundantly supported in the best of the popular and authentic historical writings than this sectional-regional development of the American republic. In addition to Turner's *The Significance of Sections in American History* and *The United States, 1830-1850,* a wealth of materials and interpretation is found in Beard's *Rise of American Civilization;* Adams' *Epic of America, America's Tragedy,* and especially in his *Provincial Society* and his *History of American Life Series;* Schlesinger and Fox's edited series of volumes on *A History of American Life;* Morison and Commager's *The Growth of the American Republic;* and Buck's *The Road to Reunion.* Some of the evidences from these historical interpretations will appear elsewhere and especially in papers dealing with the six major regions of the United States, each of which reflects much of the sectional constituency of the United States.

3. Cultural and Literary Regionalism

The American Blend: Regional Diversity
and National Unity [1949]*

About ten years ago, Constance Lindsay Skinner wrote that "if the average American is less informed about his country than any other national, knows and cares less about its past and about its present in all sections but the one where he resides and does business, it is because the books prepared for his instruction were not written by artists. Few artists have displayed to him the colors and textures of the original stuff of American life; or made him comrades of the folk who came from the crowded civilizations of the old world and entered the vast wilderness of the new by all its shining rivers; or thrust him, as one of them, into the clash of spirit with circumstance under the green arches of beauty, from which emerge the democratic ideal and American individuality."

Somewhat earlier, a Nobel Prize winner of 1939 wrote about eternal yearnings based upon diversity and the quest for unity. As isolation makes for difference, so "difference makes for comparison, comparison gives rise to uneasiness, uneasiness to wonderment, wonderment tends to admiration, and finally admiration turns to a yearning for mutual exchange and unity." But not alone did Thomas Mann write of the power of the regional folk culture of peoples but with his master compatriot of two centuries ago, J. W. von Goethe, and Thorstein Veblen, master critic of a later century, he could predict that a great people, strong in the diversity of their regional folk cultures, would become weak and destroy their nation through technological standardizations and the lust for centralized power. Goethe's formula

* *Saturday Review of Literature,* XXXII (August 6, 1949), 92, 96, 169-72. Reprinted by permission of the *Saturday Review.*

for unity and a vanishing of hatreds was to rise to a plane where "one feels the weal or woe of a neighboring people as intimately as if it were one's own."

Here then is the quest for what Lewis Mumford has recently called the new regionalism as opposed to the old professional localism, or what we have identified as sectionalism after the manner of Frederick Jackson Turner's earlier designations. The first is the quest for the understanding of this perennial puzzle, the unpredictable and immeasurable American culture. The second is the conceptualization of the role of regionalism in the processes of differentiation and integration so essential to the living cultures of the ever-changing "one nation," "one world" society. The third is the increase of knowledge and sympathetic understanding, one folk and region of another, and the clearing up of certain misconceptions about regionalism itself; and the fourth is to weave a construct that will give living physical areal tabernacles for the folk cultures of the world to maintain a quality culture in a quantity world.

There are ways for the asking "to prove this puzzle," not only of the first new world, but the vastly more complicated new world of America at mid-century, 1950 and later. For even Walt Whitman's "vistas of glory incessant and branching," or the dreams of the founding fathers, or the predictions of the frontier scientists and inventors fall immeasurably short of America's attainment in economic wealth, in material power, in technological achievement, in potential world leadership, or even in the extraordinary richness and diversity of regional development and the potentials for integration and unity of the total American configuration of culture and economy. Yet what was so freely predicted as the melting pot waywardly developed a nation of multiplied diversities as well as conflicting ideologies and powerful differences to be resolved. Indeed, where Walt Whitman heard America singing "with open mouths their strong melodious songs," "solitary," striking up for a new world of unity, one can hear America now quarreling and challenging all the strategy of an unbelievably complex America, still "Each singing what belongs to him or her and none else." And all this diversity of folk and region, commonly characterized as the most diverse culture yet recorded in history, has come as the fruit of America's quest for freedom and liberty, for the democracy of equality in all things, for the spiritual

quest for all the freedoms, even as the United Sations sets its goals of
universal freedom.

And we hear again that one asked for something to prove this
new world not only to Americans, now 150 million strong, but to all
those who seek to understand us, coming from the folk cultures of
Europe and Asia and Africa, complaining of our inconsistencies and
contradictions but honestly seeking the answers to their troubled
quests. The answers for both Americans and the others are to be
found in the complexities of a rich American diversity of folk and
region, set in the pattern of the achitecture of universal culture and
made increasingly articulate through communications and the ideologies of one world inter-cultural relations.

But how is it possible to understand so easily and so quickly so
complex a configuration of regional folk and culture? There are
several ways. First, there is the formal study of American civilization
in the university and in the history books. At Yale, at Harvard, at
Cornell, at North Carolina, at Wisconsin, at Oklahoma, at California,
and in many other centers, the study of American culture features
the regional factors. Increasingly also, the standard texts and series
on American history interpret the regional structure of American
society. From all these studies it must be clear that realistic Americanism was grounded in the physiographic measures of the continent
and in the adaptation of the people to the places where they lived.
This was true not only because of the extraordinarily wide range and
kinds of natural phenomena but because of the sheer size of an
America in which all Western Europe, so to speak, could be lost in
her mountain fastnesses or river valleys or great plains. In this happy
convergence of a superabundance of natural wealth and human wealth
was to be found the measures of both the nation's extraordinary
strength and power as well as her growing pains and sectional conflict.

Another way of "proving this puzzle" of American culture, however, is through the study of the literature of regionalism and the folk.
Here, within very recent times, America has provided extraordinarily
rich source materials, including many periodicals and the numerous
regional and folk series of books. *The Saturday Review* itself,
through its editorials, its reviews, and six special regional issues on the

Southwest, the Upper South, the Deep South, the Ohio Valley, New England, and California, has led the way.

Two of the most significant regional series of books, the "Rivers of America" and the "Folkways Series," may well illustrate. The thirty-eighth "River" book has appeared in a series rich in regional portraiture of the total culture. For instance, in the Northeast are the St. Lawrence, the Delaware, the Brandywine, the Hudson, the Kennebec, the Winooski, and the Twin Rivers: the Raritan and the Passaic. In the Southeast are the Lower Mississippi, the Kentucky, the Tennessee, the Arkansas, the Shenandoah, the Suwanee, and the James. In the Middle states are the Illinois, the Chicago, the Upper Mississippi, the Wisconsin, the Sangamon, and the Wabash. In the Southwest are the Santa Fe, the Lower Mississippi. In the Northwest are Powder River, the Red River, the Kaw, the Missouri, and the Colorado. In the Far West are the Sacramento, the Salinas, the Humboldt, the Columbia.

Through the "Folkways Series" it is possible to map much of the total nation in folk-regional units, shading like culture areas into each other in a fascinating fabric with warp and woof of subregional cultures. Here are some of the quilted patterns: "Golden Gate Country," "Town Meeting Country," "North Star Country," "Deep Delta Country," "Far North Country," "Mormon Country," "Palmetto Country," "Desert Country," "Pinon Country," "The Lakes Country," "Short Grass Country," "Ozark Country," "Blue Ridge Country," "High Border Country," "Southern California Country," "Canoe Country," "Snowshoe Country."

In addition to these there are perhaps no less than a baker's dozen of other series, including those on lakes and mountains, cities, states, special culture areas, folklore, architecture, travel. In addition to these, scores of books discuss how the people live, where they live, what they do, what they say, and what they sing.

Here at last is a patterning of American culture into one composite fabric of great richness and beauty. Yet, the most intimate regional literature is, after all, the extraordinary wealth of regional fiction, the catalogue of which would constitute a book of American literature. Even samplings would extend this treatise beyond its authorized limits, although one may quote an enthusiastic reviewer's estimate of Walter Van Tilburg Clark's "The Track of the Cat" as justifying the new American regionalism, provided he will document the even richer contributions of the earlier regionalists, Mary Ellen Chase, William Faulkner, Ellen Glasgow, Gertrude Atherton, Edna Ferber, Sinclair Lewis, as well as a host of new regionalists.

There are still other ways of proving this puzzle of the American culture. The best of these is through first-hand observation by highway routes, by railway travel, and by airways that give sweeping views and symbols not otherwise attainable. This is, of course, a "must." Yet one of the most talked-about recent volumes on America written by observers from abroad asserts that it has no portraiture beyond the Eastern Seaboard and its immediate hinterlands. The limitations here are also apparent. For many observers see only a superficial part of the folk and their culture. They see not what the folk are but what is observed through their own cultural cameras. They marvel at the commonplace, as if it were something new and rare. They see the folk for the first time but do not understand them, sentimentalizing over the simple things and trying to be hardboiled over the general realities of life. Yet there is no substitute for the firsthand picture of America on the three level routes of highways, railways, and the airways. Here, again, amazing vistas are being opened to the millions of interregional visitors who move hither and yon in a new American cavalcade, complaining of poor railroads, bad food, but having a wonderful time and getting acquainted with that great diversity which is America.

Our second and third quests are more important in the world of ideas than our first. For, in contemporaneous society, where area-culture relationships and group intercultural situations constitute the central problem, the conceptualization of regionalism as a structural-functional reference for the analysis of specific cultures, and their relation to each other and to the totality of area-culture situation, becomes increasingly important. Equally important is the definition of the role of regionalism in the reconstruction and balance of conflicting cultures and the clearing up of certain misconceptions about regionalism itself.

In his references to regionalism looking toward the definition of culture, T. S. Eliot complains that "the usual regionalist is concerned solely with the interests of his own region, and thereby suggests to his neighbor across the border what is of interest to one must be to the disadvantage of the other." At the same time he corrects this common misconception of regionalism by pointing out that "the absolute value is that each area should have its characteristic culture, which should also harmonize with, and enrich, the cultures of the neighboring areas." This means we must distinguish between that which concerns the area primarily and that which relates to the area in relation to other areas, or an area's place and/or role in some total structure. In the United States, both historically and functionally today this is a matter of distinguishing between the old sectionalism which features homogeneity in isolation and separatism, and the new regionalism which features differentiation and integration in an ever flexible, complex, and conflicting changing social structure. This is what Justice Brandeis foresaw in 1936, when he called regionalism a "first step in grappling with our most serious problem!"

The literary regionalists, however, are not the only ones who promulgate the fallacy which identifies regionalism with localism or with areal homogeneities due primarily to isolation, either in space through lack of communication and extra-regional relationships, or in time as in the case of primitive peoples. Two American sociologists may be cited specifically. In "Twentieth Century Sociology," published as recently as 1944—and widely used by sociologists—the younger Faris writes: "The mobility and fluidity of the United States population, the diffusions and standardization of culture, and other influences of the sort, are having the effect of reducing the regional basis of differences in American culture. If this trend continues, as it appears likely to do, the interest in regionalism may become a historical subject." This, of course, is an absurd interpretation of both regionalism and the facts of contemporary trends.

Compare, in contrast to this, the point of view reported by another sociologist, Robert C. Angell, of the University of Michigan, who concludes from his many studies "that many believe that the chances of world peace would be greater if we cut off communication between nations altogether." Or, in contrast again, note R. M. MacIver's characterization of modern society in his admirable "The More Perfect Union." Pointing out the multiplication of conflicting groups, he says, "Many historical forces combine to make the relation of group to group the central issue of modern society.... Mankind has made great advances toward the solution of many of its ancient problems. But *this* problem is not only unsolved; it has become greatly aggravated. The aggravation has come in the train of technological and social change. The tendency itself is as old as human nature. . . ."

Or to take another illustration, compare F. S. C. Northrop's notable "The Meeting of East and West," in which he points out how each part of the Orient is coming to impress its existence and values upon the Occident: "This coming can be evil and dastardly as well as it can be benign and beneficent," depending upon "each knowing the other's values and interests as well as its own." Again, "It is literally true that . . . what the one people or culture regards as sound economic and political principles the other views as erroneous, and what the one envisages as good and divine the other condemns as evil or illusory. The time has come when these ideological conflicts must be faced and if possible resolved. Otherwise the social policies, moral ideals, and religious aspirations of men, because of their incompatibility one with another, will continue to generate misunderstanding and war instead of mutual understanding and peace."

The other example of misconception is that of Professor Louis Wirth of the University of Chicago in his paper before the Wisconsin Symposium on American Regionalism in April 1949. Three of his characterizations of regionalism appear almost wholly in contradiction to the widely accepted tenets of the new regionalism. One is identifying it with the long outmoded geographic determinism. Another was to identify it as a cult. A third was to identify it with a "one-factor theory" in contrast to its multiple approach through the integration of all the social sciences, literature, and other tools of study and planning. Regionalism, he wrote, "must be recognized for what it is, namely, a one-factor theory, which taken alone will furnish only a one-sided, and hence distorted picture of social reality." And again, "it would be naive to believe that such simplistic interpretations of the complexities of social life have not obscured other equally significant elements and have led to distorted versions." This is clearly a naive confusion of regionalism with some of the special concepts of geographic factors in society or with some limited literary picture.

Perhaps we should not be surprised at the limitations of those who have not had time or occasion to sense the structural-functional meanings. For it is easy to follow the old fallacy that regionalism is essentially divisive, or is synonymous with separation, is opposed to centralization, and connotes a doctrine opposed to universalism. Here it must be emphasized that it is not regionalism *or,* but regionalism *and,* since the multiplication of divergent groups and interests in the modern world and their discovery through communication render their integration through regional group units an absolute "must" in any construct of "One World" or "One Nation." It is not regionalism *vs.* universalism, regions *vs.* nation, but regionalism *and* universalism, regions *and* nation in such a construct as the United Nations, or the more limited construct of the unity of "The Americas," or even of "One America" envisaged by so many recent writings about the USA.

With reference to the structural-functional definitions of regionalism, it is necessary to reemphasize the fact that the primary objectives of regionalism are found in the end product of integration of regions more than the mere study and development of regions themselves. The regions are studied and planned to the end that they may be more adequate in all aspects of resources and culture; yet regionalism itself is primarily interested in the total integration and balance of these regions. In the case of American society it is not so much a question of centralization of authority in conflict with state rights as it is of developing an adequate federalized central authority capable thereby of achieving realistic decentralization. In other words, it is necessary to have some sort of world-order organization before the world's regions can be integrated and before they may be co-operatively developed to their best. In American society there must be strong national character and organization before the nation can be made strong through the strength and integration of its diverse regions so that regionalism may supplant the older separatism and isolationism of sectional development.

So, too, the global situation with reference to races, minority peoples, and nationalities has made increasingly clear and vivid the organic significance of this regional quality and balance of the people everywhere. The assumptions of regional balance here are both sound theoretically and administratively practical, in so far as our key tasks must be to rediscover and catalogue all the culture groups; to recognize and give full credit to their folk personality or culture; to provide for resolving differences made more articulate by modern technology and communication; to group geographic and culture areas into regional clusterings of practical administrative proportions; to give them representation; and finally, to integrate them in the total order.

The formula for economic justice follows a similar structural-functional arrangement: first, opportunity for all people wherever they are to have access to resources and especially work in the places where they live; second, to have opportunity for access to inter-regional resources and contacts, thus utilizing the modern technology of communication and transportation to equalize opportunity; and third, reasonable opportunity for migration, thus utilizing the universal process of mobility.

This regional quality of culture, behavior, and institutions is, of course, universally applicable to all regions of world society. The recognition of this regional quality of world society, of its imbalance, and of the need for regional arrangements and integration for world organization and peace, while relatively new, is rapidly becoming the basic consideration in nearly all plans for stabilizing world organization.

This discussion has to do primarily with cultural aspects of regionalism. Omitted are considerations of special phases, including regional mercantilism or economic regionalism; political aspects, often conforming to the Turner concept of sectionalism and affording greater difficulties in integrating the whole national organism; geographic aspects, especially economic geography; regional planning; and historical regionalism. Also omitted are measures of the changing regional structure of America, due to the above factors, as well as to the influence of the two great wars, of interregional exchange of students, of tourist travel, and the general awakening of the nation to its greater diversity and power as it enters the second half of the twentieth century. Here are dramatic and sweeping changes in the Pacific Northwest, the Pacific Southwest, the Southeast, and Southwest, where accelerated rates of change challenge the new imagination and integration. All of these are rich fields for sociological study but also afford materials for literary and artistic creative work, as, for instance, "America Surges Westward" again or as there is the revival of the North-South conflict and the Dixiecrats, or as the divergence of Southeast-Southwest culture and economy sets a trend. All these challenge new reaches in description and measurement.

Nevertheless, the framework of structural-functional regionalism which we have presented does comprehend many of the facets of these other aspects. Such a functional regionalism thus becomes a tool for attaining balance and equilibrium between people and resources, men and machines, the State and the folk. It is a tool of the democratic process in that it provides for the redistribution of the good things of life and of the opportunity to work within the framework of every people's geography and of their inherent cultural equipment. It is a tool for democratic world reconstruction, because it is through cooperative regionalism rather than economic nationalism that the society of tomorrow can be organized for human welfare instead of for military achievements. It is a tool for social planning, because it takes into consideration the rights, privileges, resources of people and areas, and stresses self-government and self-development as opposed to coercive centralized power. It is a tool for social planning also because it offers specific technical workable ways of developing and conserving resources for human-use ends. But it wants no self-sufficiency in economy. It wants no isolation and separatism, and it wants no totalitarian tragic imbalance between the folk and the State or between power and the people. What it does want is rich diversity, powerful unity and dynamic integration in the regional balance and equality of society.

On Southern Literature and Southern

Culture [1953]*

EDITOR'S NOTE: *In a recent talk delivered at Mississippi State College, April 21, 1950 on "Why the Modern South Has a Great Literature," Mr. Donald Davidson made the following statement:*

... I turn to sociology and ask whether it can account for the appearance in Mississippi, of all places, of William Faulkner, in the three decades between 1920 and 1950. My question has a corollary which I believe I am entitled to state: Can sociology also explain why William Faulkner, or some novelist of comparative stature, did not appear, during this period, somewhere north of the Ohio—say, in Massachusetts or Wisconsin?

In the opinion of the editors, Mr. Davidson in so doing asked a root question, one which must be thoroughly considered in any serious attempt to understand the modern literature produced by Southerners. Mr. Davidson, the editors felt, was asking the sociologists to account for the seeming paradox that the South, which by so many of the standards of sociological measurement was the most backward, the least "progressive" region in the United States, was also the region in which American literature seemed best to flourish.

Accordingly, the editors agreed to invite two eminent sociologists [Howard W. Odum and John Maclachlan] to comment on the prob-

* From *Southern Renascence: The Literature of the Modern South*, edited by Louis D. Rubin, Jr., and Robert D. Jacobs (Baltimore: The Johns Hopkins Press, 1953), pp. 84-100. Also printed in *The Hopkins Review*, VII (Winter 1953), 60-76. Reprinted by permission.

lem, taking as their theme the paragraph from Mr. Davidson's address
quoted above. [Dr. Odum's] conclusion are herewith presented.

The sources of American ideals, the regional quality of American letters, and the genesis of Southern writing have long constituted major themes for students of American culture and literature. Although it must be clear that it is not possible to oversimplify causal factors or to identify complete characterizations or distinctive qualities of writing as related to either regions or authors, nevertheless few themes appear to be more persistently popular in the search for satisfying answers. In the case of Southern writing there are several factors which accentuate the timeliness of questions that are often asked concerning the sources and nature of Southern literature. In addition to the general assumption that American literature has been pre-eminently regional, the South has itself contributed more than a proportionate share of the nation's literary output during the first half of the 20th century. So, too, since the South has been more thoroughly documented and written about, both by Southern and national authors, than any other region, it has constituted a sort of perennial theme for public appraisal. Then, within more recent years the widespread critical discussions of William Faulkner and Thomas Wolfe, to mention only two, have focused new critical queries as to the genesis and nature of Southern writing.

This paper, by request of the editor, has to do with two aspects of these queries, namely the possible relation of general socio-economic factors and cultural backgrounds to Southern literature and the specific question raised by Donald Davidson and others as to why William Faulkner should be the product of Mississippi and the South rather than of Massachusetts and New England.

Donald Davidson's question as to whether sociology can explain why William Faulkner, or some novelist of comparable stature, did *not* appear, during the first half of the 20th century in the United States somewhere north of the Ohio—say, in Massachusetts or Wisconsin?[1] offers a fair setting for a reasonable discussion of the genesis and development of regional literature. Moreover, his question is a

1. Donald Davidson, "Why the Modern South Has a Great Literature," *Vanderbilt Studies in the Humanities,* I (Nashville: Vanderbilt University Press, 1951), 3.

sort of specific corollary to a broader question as to why the contemporary South has produced great literature when its general socio-
economic culture reflects statistical ratings in the lower quartiles as
compared to the other regions of the United States.

These questions are apparently based on a general misunderstanding of sociology and the facile assumption that the sociologist
would always look for a great literature in an advanced society with
a high index of gadget civilization, advanced achievements in the
arts and sciences, and in the setting of intellectualism and cultural
specialization. Nor would he, by the same token, appraise a great
literature as exclusively the highest achievement of culture. On the
contrary, culture for the sociologist is identified with the sum-total of
all the cumulative processes and products of societal achievement,
rather than any one or two intellectual or technical specializations.

Nevertheless Davidson's specific insistence upon exploring the
reasons why William Faulkner, coming from Mississippi, the lowest
indexed state, should not have been produced in Massachusetts, the
highest indexed state, affords a setting for the answer to his more
relevant general question as to why the South, rather than, let us
say, New England has excelled in its recent general literary writing.
For, during the first fifty years of the twentieth century the South
has contributed no less than five-thousand titles to the full-sized-book
literature of the nation as measured by standard catalogues and major
publishers. Of these approximately one half may be classified as
"literature" in the traditional sense, with 1000 volumes of fiction, 500
biography, 400 poetry and 125 drama. The total "writing" contributions, however, include something like 800 volumes on History,
800 on Negro Life, 400 on Nature and the Folk, more than a hundred
each on Socio-economic Studies, Nature and Resources, Travel and
Description. So far as our inquiries go none of the other regions, the
Northeast, the Middle States, the Northwest, or the Far West approximate this quantitative measurement of achievements.

To limit our inquiry to fiction, in which William Faulkner is
the representative and Nobel Prize winner, and toward which Davidson has directed his inquiry, the qualitative measure of Southern writing is indicated by the fact that there have been no less than eight
Pulitzer Awards to Southern novelists and perhaps one hundred
Southern best sellers, as compiled by the *Publishers' Weekly* ratings

of each year's ten top best selling books. In addition to Pulitzer Awards in fiction, and exclusive of journalistic awards, there have also been three in drama, three in biography and three in poetry.[2] In all the categories, Pulitzer Awards have been made to Southern authors in more than half of the years since the first awards in 1917.

Of the eleven best sellers that have exceeded or approximated a million copies, ten were by Southern authors. An examination of the titles of the Pulitzer Prize winners and best sellers will indicate the closely related themes of most of these volumes to Faulkner's own major contributions, so that the answer to Davidson's specific question about Faulkner and Mississippi will surely throw some light on the more general inquiry about the South's total literature.

Davidson's oversimplified assumptions with reference to the sociologists' analysis of interacting causal factors in societal development may be found in a number of quotations. First, Davidson asks,

Now in the formative period of William Faulkner—and, if you wish, of his contemporaries—what cultural factors, exactly, were at work in the Southern scene?[3]

He then answers,

I am very sorry to have to report to you that during William Faulkner's formative period the cultural factors were extremely forbidding in the State of Mississippi. I can hardly see how Mr. Faulkner survived, much less wrote novels. On the evidence of Mr. Odum's tables, culture was at a very low ebb in Mississippi—so low that, if I had only these tables to depend upon, I would confidently assert, as a devoted follower of sociology, that a William Faulkner in Mississippi would be a theoretical impossibility; and that if he emerged at all, he would have to originate in say, Massachusetts, where the cultural factors were favorable to literary interests.[4]

2. The Pulitzer Awards are: Julia Peterkin's *Scarlet Sister Mary;* Oliver La Farge's *Laughing Boy;* T. S. Stribling's *The Store;* Caroline Miller's *Lamb in His Bosom;* Margaret Mitchell's *Gone With the Wind;* Marjorie Kinnan Rawlings' *The Yearling;* Ellen Glasgow's *In This Our Life;* Robert Penn Warren's *All the King's Men;* Hatcher Hughes' *Hell-Bent for Heaven;* Paul Green's *In Abraham's Bosom;* Marc Connelly's utilization of Roark Bradford's *Ol' Man Adam and His Chillun* in *The Green Pastures;* Marquis James' *The Raven;* Douglas Southall Freeman's *R. E. Lee;* Marquis James' *Andrew Jackson;* Conrad Aiken's *Selected Poems,* George Dillon's *The Flowering Stone* and John Gould Fletcher's *Selected Poems.*

3. Davidson, *op. cit.,* p. 4.

4. *Ibid.*

Davidson continues by asserting that "The cultural factors described by Mr. Odum either had a causal influence on William Faulkner or they did not."[5]

If they did have a causal influence, we must, under the rigorous impulsion of sociology, reach an astonishing conclusion: namely, that the way for a society to produce a William Faulkner is to have him born in a thoroughly backward state like Mississippi, of a chivalrously inclined, feudal-minded, landed Southern family that was ruined by the Civil War and later dipped, not very successfully, into modern business. In other words, a prevalence of rural society, devoted to cotton-growing, afflicted by sharecropping, rather poverty-stricken, conservative in religion and politics, prone to love the past rather than the future, chockful of all the prejudices and customs of the South—that is what it takes to produce a William Faulkner.

Contrarily, a prevalence of material progress, great wealth, modern institutions such as libraries and art museums, factories, industrial gimcracks, liberalism, science, political radicalism—that is the way *not* to produce a William Faulkner. If it were otherwise, Massachusetts and Wisconsin by this time would have produced not one but a couple of dozen William Faulkners.[6]

As a matter of fact, Davidson's assumption that William Faulkner would be an impossibility in any complex cultural setting negates the authentic findings of historical and sociological study, as do his assumptions as to the nature of cultural factors which are "favorable to literary interests." For the sociologist, if he is scientific, like the historian of great literatures and the biographers of great writers must understand and portray the total configuration of culture, with all of its interrelationships and interaction with the heritage and behavior of the individual as well as the interlocking causal factors that have made him what he is. On these assumptions the sociologist would predict a Faulkner from Mississippi rather than look to Massachusetts for some or many expected greats.

More important for the question at hand, Davidson queries the sociologist only in terms of the partial socio-economic measures, not in terms of the folk-regional analysis of a relatively unified and dynamic culture. The socio-economic statistics which Davidson cites do indeed present a partial picture of the South in relation to the

5. Davidson, *op. cit.*, p. 7.
6. Davidson, *op. cit.*, pp. 7-8.

total nation. This relative picture was drawn in order to have realistic, attainable goals for future development, in the normal and traditional American custom of "state of the union" stock-taking.[7] More fundamentally, however, the vigorous development of the Southern people within the last generations has so clearly demonstrated that these attainable goals are an integral part of Southern aspirations, even as defiance toward total conformity is shouted from the platforms of national political conventions. So that any analysis of the regional culture that does not have a place for this dynamic is bound to be progressively tangential.

But even so these technical goals are but frames upon which rest all the other cultural conditioning forces, the backgrounds of causal factors, the present social structure of the South, and the possible facets of future development. For, as I have pointed out often in many places,

the way of the South has been and is the way of the folk, symbolic of what the people feel, think, and do as conditioned by their cultural heritage and the land which Nature has given them. The culture of the South is the culture of the folk often in contradistinction to the civilization at its flood tide of urbanism, technology, intellectualism, and totalitarianism. This folk culture is deeply bottomed in the realities of Nature and the frontier struggle, in the heritage of multiple migrant people, in the rise and fall of the upper-folk aristocracy, and in a later powerful race and regional conflict. This is an elemental reality definitive of most of the South's culture and economy. The folk society of the South is well-nigh all-inclusive and is reflected on many levels of time and class and in the organic nature of the folk-regional society as definitive of how all societies are formed and grow up.

The elementary sources of this powerful folk society are reflected in a fourfold heritage. There are the growing up of the earlier frontier folk in their struggles with Nature and the Indian alongside the earlier folk culture which was of the vintage of Virginia and the planter aristocracy. Then for a time nearly all of the South consisted of the rural folk with their rugged individualism and their struggle with

7. See: Howard W. Odum's *Southern Regions of the United States* (Chapel Hill: The University of North Carolina Press, 1936), *American Regionalism* (New York: Henry Holt and Company, 1938), *The Way of the South* (New York: The Macmillan Company, 1947), and *An American Epoch* (New York: Henry Holt and Company, 1930).

land and climate, with victory or defeat or harvest time in their blood. And there were the remnants of frontier folk symbolic of mountain culture or flatwood frustration or swamp and bayou levels of living in the out-of-way places throughout the Deep South. And finally there was the powerful folk society of the Negroes themselves as both apart from and a part of the dominant white folk.

*   *   *   *   *   *

In reality the vigorous and lusty South that was growing up in the way of Nature and the frontier, of race and the folk, could be understood only through a knowledge of the way of all culture as it develops from the earlier folk stages on through various maturing levels until it flowers in civilization.[8]

About this South as a nursery for the conditioning and nurturing of writers and for stimulating them, we have pointed out something of the conflicts, frustrations and intellectual and emotional tensions which were basic to any creative contributions that Southerners would be making.

So came the challenge to critics, North and South, in America and Europe, who saw the South capable of contributing powerfully to the greater American epoch of the twentieth century. Whatever contributions the South had made, whatever forms and patterns had evolved in the past, had grown out of realities, now springing from soil rich in romance and large undertaking, now from poverty and hardships, now sinking back into the sources from which they came. These sources remained in perpetuity and awaited the full development of a well-balanced civilization. To the pictures of the Old South and the New South of 1930, therefore, must be added still other pictures of the South of a New American Epoch built upon the Old. And whatever the distance backward or forward, the measures of resurrection or resurgence or of new trail-blazing were to be found in the vigor of the common-place, in the power of new biological and cultural combinations, in the social potentiality of these four generations of Southerners, and in the happy blending of these elements with the other essential elements of the nation and of the times.[9]

8. Howard W. Odum, *The Way of the South* (New York: The Macmillan Company, 1947), pp. 61-62; also Chapter V, "The Way of Culture and History"; *In Search of the Regional Balance of America* (Chapel Hill: The University of North Carolina Press, 1945), p. 25; "The American Blend," *The Saturday Review of Literature*, Aug. 6, 1949.

9. Howard W. Odum, *An American Epoch* (New York: Henry Holt and Company, 1930), p. 333.

There was no doubt about the power of the old tradition in conflict with the new, nor the struggles for survival alongside the stubborn allegiance to the departed glory.

An era had ended. An era had begun. Old golden pages of history, shining parchment records of culture, then yellow and faded, scorched and seared with years of embattled conflict, and epic struggle . . . Gallant figures on black horses and white . . . and crude, simple folk, sore with the footfall of time, passing across an epoch which was to be destroyed by physical and cultural conflagration and to rise up again in another American Epoch strangely different and vivid and powerful. Cultures in the making, social processes at work, portraiture descriptive of how civilizations grow. All the South's yesterdays, with their brilliant episodes and with their sordid pictures receding, giving way to the South's tomorrows, through a sweeping American development of universal culture.

Both the old and the new culture abounded in sharp contrasts and logical paradoxes. There were many Souths yet *the* South. It was preëminently national in backgrounds, yet provincial in its processes. There were remnants of European culture framed in intolerant Americanism. There were romance, beauty, glamor, gayety, comedy, gentleness, and there were sordidness, ugliness, dullness, sorrow, tragedy, cruelty. There were wealth, culture, education, generosity, chivalry, manners, courage, nobility, and there were poverty, crudeness, ignorance, narrowness, brutality, cowardice, depravity. The South was American and un-American, righteous and wicked, Christian and barbaric. It was a South getting better, a South getting worse. It was strong and it was weak, it was white and it was black, it was rich and it was poor. There were great white mansions on hilltops among the trees, and there were unpainted houses perched on pillars along hillside gullies or lowland marshes. From high estate came low attainment, and from the dark places came flashing gleams of noble personality. There were strong men and women vibrant with the spontaneity of living, and there were pale, tired folk, full of the dullness of life. There were crusaders resplendent with some perpetual equivalent of war, and there were lovers of peace in the market place. There were freshness and vivacity as of a rippling green-white rivulet, and there were depth and hidden power as of gleaming dark water beneath an arched bridge.[10]

Now it is exactly in this framework of the folk-regional society of the South that the sociologist finds his testing ground for understanding and exploring much of the behavior and achievements of

10. *Ibid.*, pp. 330-31.

the Southern people. For it is his assumption, based upon adequate source materials, documented by students of many disciplines, and reinforced by his own historical and empirical studies, that all societies grow up and mature in a continuum from the folk culture of the state civilization, the one coinciding with growth, development and creativeness and the other with maturity, standardization and decay. The Massachusetts and New York of Mr. Davidson's premises reflect the most advanced state of civilization that has yet appeared on this earth and is in somewhat opposite polarity from the main folk culture pattern of Mississippi and the old and recent South. The sociologist, in this case, points out that

This complex society of the world we live in may best be characterized by the term *state civilization,* as comprehending the total traits of the most advanced technological and organizational society in a continuum which has its genesis and constant growth and survival processes in the contrasting folk culture, symbol also of the close knit societal integration of all growing civilizations. The state civilization, symbolizing the secularization of the folk culture, is fabricated of five main threads so thoroughly interwoven in warp and woof as to make a clearly defined and powerful pattern of human relationships. The first is *science, invention, and technology.* The second is *industrialization and urbanization.* The third is *intellectualism and cultural specialization.* The fourth is *centralization and power.* The fifth is *totalitarianism and the super-state society.* Each of these is fabricated of still other weavings of multiple minor designs.

Interwoven with science, invention and technology are unprecedented achievement, with speed, technics, standardization. Interwoven with industry and urbanism are the machine economy, the assembly line, stratification, a new way of community living, an extraordinarily high standard of living, and great concentrations of art, drama, and wealth. Interwoven with intellectualism and cultural specialization are scientific humanism, the concept that the intellect is the supreme guide for living, the standard of living as a chief index of social values, and undreamed of contributions in creative art and literature, science for science's sake. Interwoven with centralization and power are bigness, concentration, corpocracy, organization, limitless production, efficiency like a miracle. Interwoven with totalitarianism and the superstate are coercion, regulation and secularization with ruthless power more relevant than human liberty and with force as a living ideal. Needless to say, all these are inseparably related in an indescribably rich fabric of human achievement beyond the dreams of men and constituting a continuum of interaction processes in the loom of societal development.

The *state civilization* is sequel to and an extension of the universal *folk culture,* the two constituting the main currents and levels of cultural development in the universal societal continuum from early folk society to late state society. The folk culture is also fabricated of a number of threads with their multiple qualities of interaction between the folk and nature, between the folk and their own cultural environment, and between the folk of one culture and of other cultures. First, the folk culture is identified with nature with reference to natural laws, time, climate, geographic environment, close to the soil. Folk culture is further characterized by primary relationships and institutions, kith and kin in ethnic relationships, and primary occupations. The folk culture conforms essentially to rural and religious institutional character reflecting primarily the solidarity of a moral order. It is essentially institutional, deriving its social character from societies that are small, isolated, reflecting love of liberty, loyalties, homogeneities of structure. The folk culture is closely knit, cohesive, nonorganizational, with behavior primarily spontaneous, personal, traditional, yet strongly integrated through its community of growth and moral order. The folk society is thus essentially in contrast to the state society, the one geared to nature and to ethnic and moral structure and the other to technology and to civil organization and specialized structure.

*   *   *   *   *   *

Such a state civilization, flowering into its complex attainment of technology, industrialization, urbanization, intellectualism, cultural specialization, organization, centralization and power, tends to assume the nature of a *technological order* rather than a *human society* or a *moral order* such as has been assumed as the universal constant in all growing human societies. Inherent in such a technological order could be not only such complexity as to accelerate antagonisms, conflict, derangement, breakdown and disintegration, but the capacity to weaken or destroy human society, through decay from non-use of cultural processes, from the exhausting and destructive power of science and technology, and from the literal capacity of atomic science to destroy; or from the assumption by the totalitarian state of the functions of all the other institutions which are the creators and creatures of the total healthy social system.[11]

11. See also Odum's *Understanding Society* (New York: The Macmillan Company, 1947), Chapters, 5, 7, 11, 12, 14, 15, 19, 20, 29, 35.

So much for the general reference to the sociologists' conceptualization of cultural development as it might be utilized to explain
Faulkner's Southern origin and achievement. Logically this would
place him in a favorable position on two counts. In the first place
he has been contemporaneous with the growth stage of a folk-regional
culture. In the second place in identifying him with the folk culture
of the South we identify him with struggle and travail, in conflict with
race, nation, and powerful tradition, fighting for survival for itself
and its people. This might very well be illustrated by a sort of analogy
between William Faulkner's contribution to the stream of American
literature and that of the Elder Dumas to France. For I have pointed
out how

This Southern picture was, for instance, in many ways reminiscent
of the century-old picture of an incredible, bushy-headed, country
bumpkin come to Paris, destined to usher in a new romanticism and
to divert 'the stream of French letters from its narrow channel into a
wide and rushing river.' In the development of his career and the
reshaping of a literature were present to a remarkable degree the
elementary forces whose blending creates new cultures and challenges
human vitality, tested in a social crucible white hot with the stirrings
of physical power, emotional conflict, and intellectual striving. There
was a heritage, on the one side, of maturity, experience, prestige,
glory, and aristocracy; and, on the other, of primitive folk-stock and
fresh blood, rough hewn pillars and strong foundation fabric for some
noble superstructure. There were youth and strength and temper.
There were ability, temperament, and genius. There were trial and
error, successes and failures; and again failures and successes. There
were time and unforeseen resistless incidence. There were social conflict and revolution, fire and sword, death and exile. There were old
and new epochs witnessing the rise and fall of new leaders and followers. And there was the flowing stream of social process, now
suddenly shallow and sluggish, now bursting forth in full volume and
power.[12]

Or, it might not be amiss to refer to an abundance of illustrations
from Davidson's beloved classical literature to indicate that "a native
theme central in the shaping of ancient fiction was the desire to defend
and perpetuate cultural values which were in danger of being lost."[13]

12. Odum, *An American Epoch*, p. 328.
13. Moses Hadas, "Cultural Survival and the Origin of Fiction," *The
South Atlantic Quarterly*, LI (April 1952), 253.

Certainly the analogy would not be inappropriate to the Davidson query as to why Tennessee, with its low socio-economic cultural index, produced the Agrarians and the Fugitive group of poets reflecting "the expressions of a minority's will to cultural survival" and so eloquently striving to glorify a Southern tradition and echoing the sentiment that "a subject people can have no glories but departed ones." But, to return to Hadas' citations relevant to cultural survival:

> In Asia Minor the conquest of the Persians made Ionian Greeks look back wistfully upon their past glories and their departed heroes. . . . A subject people can have no glories but departed ones, and when epic is dangerous or ludicrous, prose chronicles take its place. Herodotus . . . states specifically that the object of his book is to keep alive the memory of the great deeds of the Greeks and non-Greeks. . . . among the ancient peoples on the eastern periphery of the Greek world the break with the past was catastrophic, and here we have evidence of a remarkable proliferation of books which dealt somehow with national traditions and glorified ancient national heroes. . . . In all the books of this class the vanished grandeur, military and social, of depressed minorities was glorified. . . . Of all such literary efforts calculated to insure the cultural survival of depressed minorities in the Hellenistic world we have most extensive remains and are best informed concerning those produced by the Jews especially by the Jewish community of Alexandria. From the time of Ptolemy Philadelphus onwards, Alexandrian Jews devoted themselves to producing a body of apologetic literature . . . calculated to demonstrate the antiquity and high merits of the Jewish tradition.[14]

Returning now to Faulkner's own writings and whatever of his works may reflect the power of Southern creativeness we note that Malcolm Cowley has estimated that three major themes have dominated Faulkner's work. The first of these is "The Southern Tradition," meaning the South's historic cause. The second is "The Contemporary Chaos" which is Faulkner's "anatomy of the present world, its nihilism, violence, and horror." The third is "Man's Future" in which "man's hope lies in the reversion to a simpler life with its concomitant virtues of stoicism, simplicity, and decency."[15]

14. *Ibid.*, pp. 254-56.
15. Malcolm Cowley, "The Portable Faulkner," *William Faulkner: Two Decades of Criticism*, eds. Frederick J. Hoffman and Olga W. Vickery (East Lansing: Michigan State College Press, 1951), p. 63. See also Harry Modean Campbell and Ruel E. Foster, *William Faulkner:*

In the light of our present inquiry we need to add to these at least three corollaries, if not major themes. One of these is the power of the historic evolutionary past of mankind so often implied in Faulkner's themes of contemporary chaos and man's future. One aspect of this is the powerful sensing of the merging of the early past in America and its European heritage with the frontier and its ruthlessness, the rich details reflecting the transfer of culture from aristocracy, pseudo-aristocracy and power, from the coastal states to new southern and western frontiers. This is, of course, a main pattern in the expansion, south and west, of the Southern States that later came to be "aristocratic," and subsequently a basic pattern of the Southern way of life defended by the Agrarians and others. This is essentially also, on the upper levels, the same pattern that made Mark Twain "descended from a miscellany including rifle-toting trail-blazers, pious Quakers, and hard-working Southern yeoman, with haughty but dubious claims to aristocratic ancestry in England and Virginia."[16]

Perhaps the most powerful of these corollaries is Faulkner's sensing of the deep stream of consciousness in the human mind evolving and struggling for survival and salvation as well as his mastery of many of the newer psychological and psychopathological techniques. Perhaps no one has succeeded so well in running the gamut of the human mind between and among the facets of brilliance in waking hours, dreams in sleeping tempo and near-derangement in mental pathology, of the stream of consciousness that pervades every mentality sometime, somewhere, somehow; or in merging in some sort of continuity the awakening processes of youth with vigor, physical power, and limitless aspiration; or mental degradation with the revivification of the creative mind and body in maturity and old age. Certainly no one has succeeded so powerfully in portraying the irresistible tropism of woman, in the lower and higher brackets, toward doing what she aims to do and what she is driven to do, as reflected in the multiple folk conflicts of a South in travail.

A third corollary must surely be found in the major theme of the Negro with his tragic evolutionary background, his stranger-than-

---

A Critical Appraisal (Norman: University of Oklahoma Press, 1951), p. 12.

16. Walter Blair, "Last of the Jongeurs," *The Saturday Review of Literature* (August 30, 1952), p. 9.

fiction Southern story, and his modern unprecedented quick entrance into the total consciousness of a nation. One cannot imagine a Massachusetts author with so compelling and frustrating environmental pressure as an upsurging source of power as is reflected in a Faulkner page-after-page long sentence reflecting a powerful sympathy, a bitter satire upon the South and the white man, and an eloquent and logical defense of the Southern doctrine, rationalized for the good of the Negro. Yet this, stewed in an inchoate mass of Southern mixtry, inseparable from subliminal psychology and sex, in perpetual conflict with unfathomable subconsciousness, provides a powerful genesis for mastery in literature, scarcely found anywhere else.

Finally there is another unequaled combination of blending what is usually called an "imaginary locale" with a powerful reality of situation. For, I myself have known Yoknapatawpha and it is no purely imaginary fantasy. Once when a son of the first and noblest families of "Jefferson," weakened by frustration and conflict between aspiration and reality, had gone off the deep end, I remember riding an unbroken colt from Toccopola to Pontotoc, to Tupelo to New Albany in and out across swollen streams and backwoods and pine hills, often reflecting physical reality stranger than fiction. I have been close enough to Faulkner's quicksands to sense something of their terrors and have often imagined, behind the cedars and columned houses, that anything could happen there. Faulkner's Yoknapatawpha was symbol of frontier, a frontier echoing both primitive and civilized heritage; of Mowrer's three men of civilization, one savage and ruthless, one soft and civilized, and one hoped for, balancing the qualities of the folk and civilization.[17] Suppose there *is* a barbaric past, merged with a "flowed and cherished past melting into one desolation, one hopelessness," so what? In the light of these and other overpowering evidences, Donald Davidson's query as to why Massachusetts did not produce one Faulkner or many Faulkners appears to be little more than rhetorical.

But, returning again to possible interacting causal factors responsible for the conditioning of Southern authors and the quality of Southern writings we need to note a number of situations other than the general socio-economic and cultural-historic backgrounds.

17. Edgar Ansel Mowrer, "The Third Man," *The Saturday Review of Literature,* (July 5, 1952), pp. 6-8.

First of all we must emphasize the futility of attempting to isolate a single "cause and effect" relationship. Rather we must undertake to analyze the total configuration of complex environmental factors playing within the framework of universals, and especially of the changing structure of society and its institutions in relation to the conditioning of the individual and the psychological aspects of his behavior. Here, as may be seen from our previous diagnoses, the South has proved to be rich soil for the growing of varied cultural crops, sometimes thin and sparse on eroded lands, sometimes rank and luxurious and often untilled fields of mixtures of weeds and grain with now and then rare specimens to be selected, replanted and multiplied.

Another fundamental causal factor, the most important of all, is the individual, with his inherited endowment even though he is inseparable from the society which produced him. In the South, no less than anywhere else, the natural answer to oversimplified questions of environmental factors would be to ask why, if Faulkner was produced exclusively by Mississippi, there was only one Faulkner or why would Stark Young, born and raised in the same town of Oxford, turn out to produce such distinctively different literature as reflected in *So Red the Rose* and in his many years of literary criticism. At the time Faulkner was growing up in Oxford and before the University of Mississippi had its chance at him, why would the influence of the University at Oxford reflect such different conditioning on the three new instructors that came to the university at that time, namely Stark Young, Dudley Howe Miles, Howard W. Odum, respectively nurtured in Mississippi, Texas, and Georgia? Or, more profoundly, did the endowment of the individual have the definitive answer as to why there was one Ellen Glasgow in Virginia, one William Hines Page in North Carolina, one Julia Peterkin in South Carolina, one Margaret Mitchell in Georgia, one Marjorie Rawlings in Florida, one Robert Penn Warren in Kentucky and Louisiana? Or again, why only one Emerson or one Walt Whitman, or Mark Twain? Why would the same environment produce one William James the psychologist and one Henry James the novelist? Or was it the environment mainly that produced an Amy Lowell or Gertrude Stein?

In addition, however, to these fundamental factors of environmental conditioning, individual heritage, and the complex setting of universal humanity and cultural struggle, there have been at least two major external factors responsible for much of the flowering of Southern writing. The first of these was the extraordinarily prolific writing of, for, by, and about the South at the turn of the century and during the first quarter of the 20th century. Illustrative would be the greater part of such a body of writing as found in the national magazines: the *American Mercury, Atlantic Monthly, Century, North American Review, Harpers, Review of Reviews, Scribners,* and *World's Work.*[18] For instance, we have catalogued a varied exhibit of titles ranging all the way from specialized literary criticism and writing to specialized research and social interpretation. In the *American Mercury,* samplings of no less than 25 articles; in the *Atlantic Monthly,* 32; *Century,* 23; *Harpers,* 18; *North American Review,* 26; *Review of Reviews,* 42; *Scribners,* 25; and *World's Work,* 54.

The other major influence, stemming partly from this featuring of the South by national magazines and others, was the specific influence and cooperation of many national publishers, national foundations, and distinguished literary leaders, especially H. L. Mencken, who was both symbol and reality of outside goading and encouragement of Southern writers. Referring again to similar influences which molded Dumas in France, we have pointed out that there were

. . . five friendly influences which were to span the distance between bumptious youth and brilliant Frenchman. These influences were four friends and a notable company, the arsenal. One friend was forever impressing upon the youth the shame of his abysmal ignorance. Another was ever opening the doors of living literature. A third relentlessly spurred him on to constant achievement. A fourth assured him resources, time, and leisure. And a fifth provided him with a finishing school for his artistry. And in the final picture the backgrounds and forces were transcended by form and line and pattern and brilliance.[19]

H. L. Mencken, the bad boy of Baltimore, not only did "The Sahara of the Bozart" but went out of his way to stimulate, to encourage, and to give special priorities to Southern writers. And there were others, none like him, but in the same category of favoring the South and of soon discovering that it was a very profitable business, even at that. A single publisher such as Alfred Knopf, Bobbs-Merrill, Double-

18. Odum, *An American Epoch,* pp. 346-56.
19. *Ibid.,* p. 329.

day, Page and the others were very real decisive factors in the bringing to light and rewarding the creative work of Southern writers. Many of the national foundations and awards were constantly underwriting and endowing situations from which a new generation of the South, even as Dumas, were assured resources, time and leisure.

Among the criticisms that have been leveled at Faulkner was that he has not had the benefit of association with the literary elite and the constant fellowship of those who excelled in the literary techniques of fiction writing and new forms. Three considerations perhaps here are relevant. The first is that even the critics sometimes admitted that Faulkner may have profited from his isolation and concentration over and above the benefits he might have received from the technicians. Next, we may well note that of the 446 U. S. members of P.E.N., the supreme international organization for authors, all but 42 are from the Northeast, while New York has 296 of the total and Mississippi has just one member. On the basis of technical advantages would New York be expected to produce many equivalents of Faulkner? The third consideration may be found in the reference to the literary refugees of the United States who "escaped" America in the 1920's to concentrate for great production in the setting of fellowship and leisure abroad but who, as pointed out by Malcolm Cowley, not only lost their own feelings, beliefs and integrity but found no substitute for them and created little as the price of their sojourn. And many promising authors who migrated from the hinterlands from which they gave such promise to urban centers where they were expected to excel, found more intellectual and literary fellowship, more autograph parties, more cocktail parties and talk but less writing. And even the "great ones" could not "come back," loosed from the moorings of the cumulative incentives and power of their cultural milieu.

William Faulkner is a "natural" from Mississippi and not Massachusetts, yes?

PART THREE

The Folk and Folk Sociology

To know the soul of the people and to find the source from which flows the expression of thought is to comprehend in large measure the capabilities of that people. To explain the truest expression of the folk-mind and feeling is to reveal much of the inner consciousness of the race.

Howard W. Odum

INTRODUCTORY NOTE

There were two organizing concepts in Howard Odum's lifelong preoccupation with understanding society. There was the concept of the folk, or the folk culture, as the "universal societal constant in a world of historical variables." And there was the concept of the modern state civilization—a social order significantly different from any that had gone before. The difference, a matter of kind and of the speed of social change, was the focus of his thought. Odum's work is distinguished not only by his characterization of these two modes of social life; but especially by his unremitting insistence that mature social analysis requires that a connection between the two be established in the realistic setting of an on-going society.

The origin of his fully developed concept of the folk is found in his first published work, in the first sentence: "To know the soul of a people and to find the source from which flows the expression of folk-thought is to comprehend in a large measure the capabilities of that people." The work was a study of Negro folk songs in two deep southern communities, as these songs might reflect to him the nature of the Negro and his culture. The experience of this study had a powerful, seminal effect on Odum's thought over the following years. In the Negro culture he saw, and never afterward blinked at the sight, the irreducible minimum of human social life—like a flower growing out of a rock, the Negro culture had appeared in the hardest of circumstances: informal, sustaining, adaptive, powerfully conditioning. Here was cultural identity and social structure achieved in spite of established society and held in the minds and acts of the people. The process by which this was done remained for Odum the very core process of social life, both antecedent and survivor. The folk culture was the root of society; all else the flowering and the fruit.

Odum was no folklorist. His primary interest was in modern society, just as his interest was in the present, not the Old South. Thus his major effort was given to understanding the nature of what, in contrast to folk culture, he called state civilization. "State civilization" he considered to be characterized by science and technology; by industrialization and urbanization; by intellectualism and cultural specialization; by centralization and power; and by totalitarianism and the superstate society. The contrast with the folk culture is clear enough, but Odum had a special way of illuminating the difference. In the folk culture, the Sumnerian folkways, growing slowly from unknown origins, were the dominant mode of social process and change. Out of the slow process by which folkways were formed there appeared mores, institutions, a moral order, and law. In the state civilization, however, what Odum called the technicways are the dominant mode. Technicways are habits and customs that grow up quickly, from known origins, in adjustment to change demanded by state civilization, notably by the innovations of science and technology. Technicways rapidly override existing folkways and morality, change institutions, and require massive changes in the law.

In Odum's view the state civilization, if it is to survive, requires strengthening in the direction of the folk culture: toward greater emphasis upon individuality, upon primary groups and processes, and upon balanced regional development as an antidote for centralization. He did not suggest that the clock be turned backward. He did not propose all the answers, but, in his last published major work, thought, "It may well be, however, that the social technic-ways, in the form of social planning, will be the answer to accelerate development and to harmonize conflicting forces."

In our selections we have presented major phases of the folk sociology as it developed. By the time of his election to the presidency of the American Sociological Association, Odum was prepared to present his view of the folk as the definitive comparative society through whose study changing cultures can be analyzed. In his presidential address in 1930, Odum used the modes of regional and racial conflict to point out these folk processes which, extra-organiza-tional, extra-technological, and transitional as they are, nevertheless pervade modern society. Later he wrote of the South: "To attempt . . . to reconstruct its agriculture and economy without coming to grips with its folk culture and attitudes would be quite futile."

Unable to shape up his folk sociology in a book-length treatment, in the latter part of the 1940's, Odum incorporated his theory in *Understanding Society* (1947), the most original part of the book. Since this work is no longer in print, certain chapters are here pre-sented in their entirety. Those who wish to know Odum's use of such terms as folk culture and folk society, the folkways, the stateways, and the technicways, and the use he meant to make of the technicways in modern society will do well to peruse these chapters.

Finally, in a long bibliographical article, featured in *Social Forces* (1953), Odum made an assessment of the resources to be found in sociology basic to folk sociology. Here will be found his final attempt to outline the field, to estimate where its development might lead, and to show its usefulness for social action.

G. L. S.

1. The Folk Society

Folk Culture and Folk Society [1947]*

The folk society is the definitive human society. We have pointed out that the folkways and the mores go a long way toward comprehending the whole range of elemental factors and socializing forces which make up early culture, exclusive of what is often called "material culture." Subsequently, we have pointed out how the social institutions, which are products of folk-socializing forces, represent perhaps more than anything else the universal societal arrangement for order and control. We anticipate the further explanation of these assumptions by pointing out that the sum total of all the elemental processes and products of culture, which have been studied in Part III, constitute the folk culture which is the definitive, basic culture from which all advanced cultures and civilizations grow. This folk culture, as the supreme product of the folk society, reemphasizes the folk society as the basis from which all societies develop.

We must recall here the distinction between "society" and "culture." The terms are used coordinately but not synonymously. Society is the over-all frame-work within which culture grows. The people *plus* the natural environment are the physical basis of a society which comprehends, *then,* the total of associational processes, organizations, and relations. Culture is the cumulative processes and products of the societal achievement and denotes the quality of a society. Thus, finally: the folk culture is the achievement of the folk society, just as the state civilization is the cultural achievement of the Technological State Society. And the *folk* is the constant element for bridging the distance between the two. And we recall that the folk quality coexists in all societies with the cultures of cities

* Chapter 14 in *Understanding Society: The Principles of Dynamic Sociology* (New York: The Macmillan Company, 1947).

and technology. Sometimes it is the folk society within the state society; sometimes it is the folk quality in the heritage of the people.

So elemental and organic, and at the same time so comprehensive, is folk culture that we have suggested a more liberal use of the term *folk* as a substitute for *race* wherever the word is so generally misused, and so variable and indefinite in specific applications. Many traits ascribed to race are attributes of the folk. Some societies labeled as races are more nearly folk societies, naturally and logically so conditioned by their setting in geography and time. A notable example of the folk society commonly confused with race is the culture of the Jews. Another notorious example of a powerful folk society is the German people who, especially under Nazism, claimed to be a superrace.

The nature of the folk. We have characterized the folk as a universal constant in a world of variables. This means that the folk survive as basic elements of new cultures; remnants of old. There is no record anywhere of human society perishing from the earth. When old civilizations, such as that of Greece and Rome, pass away new cultures arise from the folk. This means that the folk reflect a natural product of the interaction of people and environment and of the interaction of people with people. The folk represent not just the people, not just population, but the people who, integrated through various units within a regional culture are inseparable from the regional environment which has produced them. In complex modern society, the folk represent the dominating pattern of the behavior and culture of any particular society in question. The folk may be said to approximate the homogeneity of traits and the unity of behavior which would result in strong attitudes and loyalties, pronounced opinions, or mass action, in the setting of the primary institutions and natural ideologies.

The folk society as natural in contrast to civilization as technical. In order to give contrast of meaning, we again re-emphasize the basic distinction between the folk society and the state society, between the folkways and the stateways, between the folk society and culture, on the one hand, and the state society and civilization, on the other. This means that the differences between culture and civilization are fundamental. Culture and civilization are not synonymous, although civilization is always a part of culture, approximating the most advanced stage of culture, representing the maximum achievements of industry, the state, centralization and power; the city, technology and intellectualism. To continue our procedure of pointing up the relation of each of our subjects to nature, we may point out that culture is essentially natural in contradistinction to civilization, which is artificial in terms of definite meanings which we shall use. Culture as a product and a part of the folk is as natural as the physical environment and the regional habitat in which each folk-regional society evolves. Culture is natural in the sense that no society has ever developed without its distinctive folk culture, as a product of the relationship between the folk and the physical environment. Culture is again natural in the sense that it is a distinctive and universal trait of all human society. Once again, the folk culture is natural in the sense that race is natural and in the sense that "human nature" is natural.

The folk are natural. We say that the people in isolated areas are natural and free. We speak of them as behaving naturally. We think of them as close to nature. We think of them as learning from nature and communing with nature. We follow their religion, magic, and superstitions, fabricated out of nature and the search for truth. We think of the folk as one integrated, relatively homogeneous society as contrasted to the heterogeneity of people in the cities or under superorganization of totalitarian civilization. We think of the folk as having a quality of inner consistency and unity, of spiritual and religious motivation, in contrast to the more individualistic behavior of individuals in the larger cities, on the one hand, or of their regimented behavior in the case of the most advanced totalitarian countries. The contrasts between folk culture and civilization, between the natural and the technical, are further illustrated in the several institutions, such as family life, religion, education, industry, and the community, in contrast to a single dominating institution, the state.

Civilization and state society. If we seek to understand the culture of the folk in contrast to the civilization of the states as synonymous with the most advanced culture, there are a number of distinguishing traits. In the first place, civilization is the essence of the state. As Giddings pointed out long ago, civilization begins where political organization transcends the ethnic of folk integration. *Civis,* the civic, became the cornerstone of what was later to be civilization.

Indeed, if we seek to characterize civilization in a single term comparable to the folk society, it is the state society. How organically true this is may be sensed from the spectacle of a world in which civilization is threatening to destroy society itself. This was civilization. This is civilization. This is the essence of the superstate, a totalitarian machine transcending the folk culture and enslaving the folk. We shall see later that this concept of civilization applies more or less to the final stages of the seven great cultures or civilizations of the ancient world.

Civilization is urban. In the next place, as contrasted with folk culture, civilization is synonymous with urbanism and with the universal trend toward megalopolitan culture. The city represents the constituent society seeking specific ends not related to the natural functions of the folk and their institutions or to the reproduction of the race. The city represents the specialized, technological, artificial functions of economic co-operation, of defense, of art, of leisure, of science, of concentration of wealth, of people. The city represents the secondary occupations as opposed to the primary occupations dealing with nature and making a living directly from nature's resources. The people in the cities are "civilized" and the ones in the rural districts are not "civilized." Comfort, convenience, the art of eating, drinking, and playing; commerce and industry, transportation and rapid communication, all distinguish civilization from the earlier natural folk cultures. No implication of evaluating the inferior or superior attributes of civilization or culture is intended here, but merely their characterizations in terms of societal development.

Civilization is technological. In the third place, civilization may be interpreted as synonymous with technology. Technology is all-comprehensive in the modern day. It comprehends science and invention, which, through the use of invested capital, has brought such comfort, convenience, leisure, and happiness to people of the modern world as to characterize them as enjoying the advantages of civilization. Technology includes not only science and invention but centralized power and the accelerated tempo of the modern world. Technology includes organization, management, propaganda, communications, and as part of the technological world modern industry with its scientific research and its machines, including mechanized agriculture, it assumes a leading role in civilization. Symbols of technology in terms of behavior and societal processes are the technicways of modern civilization in contrast to the folkways and mores of folk society.

Civilization is intellectual. In the fourth place, the folk society may be characterized as being nearly the opposite of formal intellectualism which seeks progress through overspecialized technical means. Civilization is essentially scientific and intellectual in that science tends to be the chief means of attaining specialized ends in a framework set up by intellectual leaders. This often results in the intellectual, which is only a part of the human, tending to become the whole. It ignores the total Gestalt, or all-sided, culture of nature, the emotions, and the intellect, which alone can develop the realistic individually-socially equipped personality necessary to the enduring society. That is, man neither lives nor survives by intellect or mind alone but by the full exercise of the whole man. The state society as synonymous with civilization is essentially specialized and stems from the intellectual. That is, the state society in contradistinction to the folk society is that society which is primarily organizational and, in the modern world, technological in the sense in which we have characterized technology.

Civilization is concentration and power. In the fifth place, a chief trait of all civilizations has been concentration and power. How this was true of earlier civilizations will be illustrated presently. In the modern world one of the most powerful of all trends has been toward centralization and the resulting political, economic and social phenomena of power. The two main aspects of this trend are clearly in the fields of government and economics. On the one hand there is the trend toward totalitarianism which we have already described and on the other, the trend toward large scale economic production and organization and the consequent corporation products. Even in such socialistic economies as that of Russia, there is the admitted sanction of the use of technology and large scale production under the dictation of the state. These trends inevitably point toward a major dilemma of civilization which will be reflected in the struggle between government and business. All of this is in contrast to the folk society.

Civilization is artificial. Finally, in order to make the meaning of the folk society a little clearer, we may continue to contrast it with the state society by elaborating on the distinction between the folk society as the natural society and the state society as the artificial society. Here again we must boldly assume our postulates in the face of the oft-repeated assertions that it is difficult to identify the marginal lines between the natural and the artificial. It is possible, however, to give quite satisfactory preliminary definitions which are sufficient for further examination of the postulates. Thus, the primary occupations—agriculture, hunting, fishing, lumbering, mining—are "natural" occupations in contrast to the fields of commerce, industry, transportation, communications, and the professions, which have given rise to several hundred new ways of earning a living. Or in the development of agriculture and mining, the animate power of man and beast represents the "natural" primary occupation as opposed to the machine mass processes of later development. The subsistence farm stands in contrast to commercial farming. So, too, the rural is primary and natural as compared to the urban, which is secondary and technical, if the latter is measured in terms of societal evolution from the first stages of the metal and industrial ages.

What is natural? It is possible to posit as natural certain elemental factors that are everywhere constant in early societies. Some of these processes center around sex, food, struggle, conflict, work, children, women; or the list might be limited to such completely elemental classifications as Wissler's nine culture traits; or the Sumner-Keller fundamentals of food, sex, magic, ornamentation; or to such analogies as the Sumner-Keller postulate that the study of custom is for a science of society what the study of a cell is to biology, in which case custom is the natural as opposed to the formal institutions and stateways. Conception is a natural process. When technical methods of fertilization are used, as in artificial insemination in livestock-breeding, or if and when science should discover ways of creating life in the test tube, then this would be the artificial as opposed to the natural, and would modify the whole realm of human behavior and human values. Or, again, a society in which the women of child-bearing age regularly have children, such that it reproduces itself, is a natural society; those groups which do not reproduce are not "natural." There are already many trends growing up in the field of sex relations which illustrate this distinction and which already are influencing the processes and rate of cultural change.

The "natural" sciences, the "technical" sciences. As indicative of the methodology which will be needed to explore these premises further, we may find another illustration in the sciences. What are called the basic sciences—astronomy, mathematics, physics, chemistry, and biology—may readily be termed *natural,* while the thirty or more derivative and applied sciences may be termed the *technical,* as may many applications of technology and the social sciences. That is to say simply that there is a distinction between the basic and the applied sciences. The applied sciences constitute the basis for the artificial and technological. So, too, the social sciences can be contrasted to the natural sciences.

Theoretical analogies. If we seek illustrative definitions from the social theorists, we need go no further than Herbert Spencer's formula "from the homogeneity and indefiniteness of non-organization to the heterogeneity and definiteness of organization," which is the perfect analogy for contrasting early ethnic society with current technological society. So, too, Franklin H. Giddings' "consciousness of kind" as natural, is opposed to "mutual aid" or co-operation as derivative development. So, too, his postulate was that democracy, or the integrated orderly rule of the people, must vary directly as the natural homogeneity of the people, whereas strong organizational and authoritarian society is necessary for the very heterogeneous society which must have state technicways superimposed from above if order is to be achieved. If we seek further support from Giddings' postulates, there are his "component societies" over against his "constituent societies," a very fine and clear distinction; his "genetic" societies over against his "special" societies; his kinship groups over and against his civil societies; his regional sustentation area and circumstantial pressure over and against his social pressure.

Informal culture in contrast to organizational society. There are the earlier kinship, tribe, clan, and political groupings as contrasted with the many forms of the modern state—democracy, fascism, communism, socialism. There are the folkways of freedom and the later stateways of civil liberty, religious liberty, political liberty, individual liberty. There are magic and nature worship and there are the later "churches" and formal religion—natural worship transcended by ecclesiastical ritual, church laws, and disciplinary regulations. There is the early communal education and the later formal educational system. There are the frontier cultures and the later developed civilizations.

There is, of course, the original burden of Comte's major objective "to discover the natural causes and natural laws of society," still an important aim of social study. There is Ludwig Gumplowicz's postulate, that conflict, amalgamation, and assimilation among heterogeneous ethnic groups constitute the elemental natural forces. There is Gabriel Tarde's concept of imitation as the natural transmission of impulse, feeling, and the idea from individual to individual, from group to group, from generation to generation, in distinction to the great mass technicways of radio communication.

There is much of politico-philosophical theory. Jeremy Bentham's natural society over and against his political society is an example. The finely wrought theories of the state by such scholars as M. J. A. de Condorcet are capable of answering such questions as "When is society the state and when is it not? which are basic to the distinction between the folkways and the stateways.

Natural rights and natural law have a distinguished heritage. Then there is the great body of speculation concerning natural law, natural rights, naturalism, in which alone can be found an excellent rationalization of the concepts of natural *versus* artificial, folk *versus* state. Thus the doctrine of natural rights, so solidly rooted in human experience, posited the natural as the universal, the "golden mean" as opposed to the particular, the accidental, the excessive. Natural law was grounded "in the innermost nature of man or of society, independent of convention, legislation or other institutional devices." Again, as used in the sciences, "natural" is the normal contrasted with the pathological, or "the spontaneous and unconscious flow of life as opposed to that which is artificial." So, too, Rousseau's natural man is set over against the artifical man of civilization. There is, finally, the folk psychology of Wilhelm Wundt, a social psychology capable of forming a complete framework for the study of folk sociology. Wundt's folk psychology comprehends a long catalogue of backgrounds and composite "community" mental and social products not demonstrable in the laboratory or accessible to quick experimental methods. And there is, of course, the great body of data from cultural anthropology such as the folk societies contrasted with civilization by A. L. Kroeber, Clark Wissler, Ruth Benedict, and others; or the primitive societies described by Bronislaw Malinowski, Margaret

Mead, Robert Redfield, Richard Thurnwald, and other anthropologists.

Folk society and folk sociology. These illustrations are sufficient both to indicate the meaning of the term *folk society* and *natural society* and to emphasize the importance of folk sociology as a major field in which new inquiries must be made. They are enough to emphasize the fact that the unit of study is not the *socius,* or the socially behaving individual, but the folk group, the folk mass, the folk-regional society, which also involves a new science of the region as an illustration of cultural determinism. These, of course, are always posited in contradistinction to the organizational, technological stages of societal development.

Folk sociology also is the study of transitional society as the natural definitive society, whether this transition is of the older, slow-moving sort or whether it is being accelerated by technology. Thus, folk societies may abound in any stage of culture or civilization whenever the major conditioning factors are extraorganizational or when a synergy of conflicting forces and processes results in an integrated transitional society; the transition is marked by the change from one state of culture to another, from individual and primary group development to social organization, or from the "paths of individual development" to "the process of cultural evolution." How practical such theory is in its application to modern society can be seen in the current dilemma of the masses paradoxically struggling against the forces of modern technology and the apparently equally critical forces of bigness and speed. Society has apparently been able neither to explain the powerful mass revolt of people with their nonrational and nonlogical actions nor to cope with it through government, in local and world crises.

FOLK CULTURES AND PAST CIVILIZATIONS

Whatever great diversities were found in the great cultures and civilizations of the past, there was almost universal uniformity in the final stages of these civilizations. That is, they were characterized by some form of the state society exercising its dominance through political and military power. This power, even as in the modern world, was approximately synonymous with each civilization at its most advanced stage. In exploring these civilizations, in addition to substantiating the general premise of the meaning of civilization versus folk culture, we note an even more impressive evidence—the vitality of the people in the earlier days of a culture.

The cultures commonly designated as the great civilizations of the past include the Egyptian, the Babylonian-Assyrian, the Persian, the classical Greek and the Hellenistic, the Roman, and the less well-known but brilliant Minoan, Aegean, and Sumerian, together with still other minor civilizations, commonly designated as the Hittite, the Philistine, and the Lydian. A study of all these reveals an extraordinarily consistent similarity in the rise, climax, and decline of each nation from its folk culture to its civilization. The pattern of the rise and fall of these civilizations may be characterized in three ways in order to point up the contrast between the folk society and the state society. The first of these characterizations is that of Oswald Spengler, a part of the thesis of his prophetic *Decline of the West,* yet in nowise satisfactory as a scientific explanation of the rise or the decay of cultures or civilizations. The second characterization is found through general historical inquiry into the cultures of these civilizations to see what elements are constant in all. The third characterization may be stated in terms of certain sociological axioms, having to do with the capacity of the folk and their institutions and of the conflict of folkways and stateways.

The Spengler natural cycle of culture. Spengler's prophetic diagnosis of modern civilization is first of all one of the distinguished cycle theories of culture and civilization. All cultures, he wrote, go through analogical stages of nature's seasons. There is a springtime culture, a summer of development, an autumn of reaping, and a winter of decline. Moreover, cultures conform to another organic analogy of nature. First, there is childhood and youth, then middle age, then maturity, then old age and decline. Again symbolic of this cyclical rise and fall, each great civilization progresses through the rural and agricultural, through village and industrial, to urban and technological. In all of these stages, the contrast between the earlier stages of culture and the later stages of civilization is consistent: machines take the place of men, the state takes the place of the folk, the city takes the place of the country, money takes the place of value, and power takes the place of popular sovereignty. The comparisons between the older civilizations and modern civilization, Spengler points out, are all too clear, since the modern world has already reached the advanced stages of civilization—urbanism, technology, power. Spengler's use of the word *contemporary* made the comparison striking. To Spengler, New York as the most advanced stage of American civilization is contemporary with Rome at its height, or with Athens in the heyday of its glory. Paris is contemporary with Babylon; Vienna with Nineveh. On these premises the decay of modern civilization is already well under way. Since Spengler published *The Decline of the West* in the early twenties, the movement of events in Europe has accelerated the rate of his prediction until much of it now appears as fulfilled prophecy.

A uniform trend from the folk culture to civilization. The sociologist does not need to accept Spengler's analogies as accurate, comprehensive, or scientific, in order to sense the realistic nature of his analogy and the historical accuracy of his analysis. An examination of the great civilizations, based upon secondary sources of the authentic historians, indicates certain uniform and constant elements or characteristics which were present in each. In the first place, each great civilization had its beginning in a strong virile folk society, closely integrated and loosely organized in relation to the geographic regions from which it sprang. From this folk society each civilization expanded its dominion, widened its horizon, flourished, reached its zenith, and then passed from the scene. The fact that the length of the period of decay and disintegration varied gives a broader basis upon which to test the hypotheses.

Passing over the gradual evolution of the folk society and the folk culture into a widening civilization, always culminating in the dominance of power accelerated by the state through political and economic extremes, two universal sources of decay are uniform, one internal and the other pressure and conquest from external forces. Perhaps there were a half-dozen character traits of internal weakness—overexpansions; the incorporation of too many subject peoples; internal dissension and civil war; the widening of the chasm between the rich and the poor; superorganization, crystallization, and the loss of purpose and motivation; and finally, the exhaustion of both spiritual and physical vitality. External conquest was relatively easy when attacking people, whether barbaric hordes or more civilized peoples had the superior strength to overcome a weakened civilization. Let us examine some of these sources of decline because of their basic significance to an understanding of society. These explanations are assumptions of historians and must be considered as partial explanations only and as premises for study of the theory of marginal survival from folk culture to state civilization.

CAUSES OF DECLINE OF FOLK SOCIETIES

Overexpansion. Imperialism offers many attractions to a growing civilization, but an outstanding cause of decline is overexpansion. We find this true of ancient Egypt; it was true of imperial Rome. There are historians who feel that the sending of the Athenian fleet to Sicily so crippled the Athenian Empire that she could not regain her former strength; in this can be found the explanation that no Greek city-state was sufficiently strong to withstand the advances of Philip and Alexander. In other words, the desire for new lands, new adventures, and new power so weakens the resources of a civilization that, when external danger threatens, she is often helpless to defend herself.

Heterogeneity of cultures. So closely allied with overexpansion as to be almost a corollary is the matter of subject peoples. For one thing, in overexpansion there is danger that the quality of the culture will be diluted. People of different, widely varying cultures are brought within the circle too rapidly to assimilate the civilization of the conquerors. Politically, subject peoples are always liable to revolt at the most critical time. Even when they are prosperous, subject peoples cannot be trusted, and they have proved a menace to the security of their conquerors. Subject peoples particularly brought about the downfall of Assyrian supremacy, and, in a different way, that of Rome, for undoubtedly at the time of the fall, Roman civilization had already been barbarized from within. The fantastic sweep of Hitler's world empire early drowned the German folk society that might have surprised the world by its strength had it been kept within bounds.

Civil war. But, even more than subject peoples, civil wars tend to undermine civilizations. The best example in ancient history of the harm that internal dissensions can do is, of course, the Greek city-states. Continual wars among themselves eventually proved their doom. To a lesser extent, civil wars played their part in the decadence of Egyptian, Persian and Roman civilizations. Civil war also is an index of the lack of homogeneity and unity which sometimes come from the integration of diverse elements.

Exploitation and civilization. Somehow, too, as the past nations and empires extended their boundaries and developed industrially and commercially, the chasm between the rich and the poor widened. And this appears to have been a tendency in every civilization whose histroy has been traced. As early as 2700 B.C. we read of Urukinga endeavoring to introduce reforms in order to rescue the various classes and thus save the state—but the reforms came too late. The same cry is heard in third-century Rome. Unquestionably a state is more healthy and a culture more creative when too wide a gulf does not exist between the rich and the poor. Inevitably, such separation leads to the dominance of one class or group. In Egypt it was the priestly class, in Rome the aristocratic. The result was the same: the upper class became arrogant and the lower subservient; and neither attitude is conducive to cultural development, or the building of a great empire.

What happens when there is no new folk blood? The word crystallization is used to denote that period in the history of a people when, for some reason—nobody seems to know just why—all creative ability is exhausted. This creative ability applies to the birth rate of the upper brackets of society as well as to stereotyped hedonism. Art then becomes stereotyped. Conventionalism takes the place of new ideas. There is a tendency for each man to follow in the footsteps of his progenitors. Opportunity to rise is lacking. Perhaps a caste system rises, or a highly complicated bureaucracy, or perhaps a sterile formalism of the intelligentsia. It is apparent that Egypt passed through this stage before her eventual downfall; but it is not quite so obvious that the same state of affairs existed during the later period of the Roman Empire. And perhaps it is even less known that signs of crystallization can be found in the art of that earlier Greek civilization, the Aegean. Yet Greek culture at its best was based upon the assumptions of folk slavery. For a civilization to remain alive and grow there must be some way for new blood and new ideas to be infused into it.

Another cause which is sometimes listed as exhaustion of vigor and virility, at others as decline of morale, is rather difficult to explain. But perhaps an example will clarify its meaning. In third-century

Rome, there is no evidence to show that the people had deteriorated physically or morally. And, strangely enough, there is not even evidence that material prosperity had declined. It is true that her wealth was very unevenly divided and some of her population were dependent upon charity for a livelihood, but her resources had not even been tapped. Yet a feeling of futility had grasped the people, and the old spirit which had caused the ancient Romans to hold back the attack of Hannibal, and for twelve years to endure the presence of a foreign foe on their soil, and had given them the courage to turn defeat into victory again and again was gone. Somewhere, somehow, Rome had lost her nerve. Call it artificiality, if you will, but it is undoubtedly true that when a people have lost confidence in themselves and their future, their days are numbered. Egypt, it has been said, became a body without a soul ere the end of her civilization came. Fustel de Coulanges in *The Ancient City* calls it spiritual decline and says that is the explanation of the fall of Rome. Certainly, he is partly right. And the same could be said for the rest of the civilizations which have passed.

External conquest and internal weakness. Turning from internal causes of the decline of nations and civilizations, we discover that there is not a civilization which has passed from history but that can produce an external explanation for her extinction. Barbarian hordes from the north brought an end to the Aegean civilization; the same was true for the Sumerian. Assyrians, Babylonians, Persians, Philistines, and Hittites all had their share in the downfall of Egypt. Babylonian-Assyrian culture fell before the advance of Persia; and Persia could not withstand the advance of the Macedonian phalanx, and neither could the Greek city-states; the rise of Rome brought an end to the Hellenistic period and the advance of the Teutonic hordes spelled the doom of Rome. In spite of all this, historians agree that internal decadence, in every great civilization, has preceded external aggressions. And, they point out, each of the civilizations in the days of its greatness and glory could have withstood the foe who brought about the end.

Axioms of survival value. It seems probable that the sociologist may find a much better explanation of this cyclical rise and fall of cultures and civilizations than Spengler's theories in an axiom which may be stated as a sound premise upon which continued evidence may be sought to prove or disprove. If in the disintegration of these great civilizations there is a single constant law or axiom, it might be stated somewhat as follows: whenever the demands of an artifical society or of supertechnology exceed the capacity of the folk and their institutions or of an organism of any sort to adapt, adjust, or absorb, there is tension, strain, weakness, disintegration, and, if reinforcements are not brought into the societal development, decay and disintegration. In the advanced cultures, the comprehensive demands of civilization inevitably exceeded the capacity of the folk, so that, as in the story of the goose and the golden egg, civilization itself used up the basic reserves of its own powers to survive. The notable modern example is that of Hitler's Germany and its overweening demands.

FOLK SOCIETY IN THE UNITED STATES

When we turn to the culture and civilization of the United States, there is little need to recapitulate or to do more than to point out the nature of the folk society of earlier America and the rapidly advancing civilization of America today. Since the contemporary scene will be appraised in our discussion of problems and trends, it is necessary here only to anticipate. We may do this simply in two ways, first, with reference to the American Indian. His folk society was symbolic of the evolution of primitive culture in many ways and recapitulated those early societal forces which contributed to the development of earlier human societies. In the second place, with reference to the Indian society, we need only recall the popular and universal explanation that the Indian culture could not stand up under the test of modern civilization. This was true for two reasons. One was that the too rapid acceleration of the evolution of primitive society into what was commonly called the civilization of the white man was too great a strain on the Indian folk culture and the folk society, and it perished more quickly than the older cultures and without going through the complete cycle of maturity, urbanism, and civilization. In still another way the American Indian's culture could not survive civilization because of the ruthless exploitation and destruction by the civilization of the white man, in the ever quickening tempo and powerful drive of American civilization to reach special ends of achievement in the development of wealth, science, technology, comfort, conquest. Here is an instance in which civilization wiped out most of a primitive culture before it could develop into a more mature stage as has been the case with many primitive peoples and with the American Negro. In the later American policy there is increasing survival and acculturation in the attainment of a better balance between "Indian" culture and "American" civilization.

We may also characterize the early American folk society by repeating what Americans themselves have sometimes asserted, that Europe was civilized and frontier America was not. That is, in one sense of the word, according to the interpretation of civilization as European culture, America was still a frontier folk culture composed of a young, virile, struggling people working through a rapidly growing folk society in the frontier regions. This characterization of early American culture has already been used and will be again in relation to the search for balance between culture and civilization in the new era. The sociologist points out that the survival power of American folk society lies in utilizing wisely its still enormous resources and keeping open the streams of new blood and the avenues of freedom, in balance between the folk and the state, and between culture and civilization.

Folk and Regional Conflict as a Field of

Sociological Study [1930]*

In an earlier period of the development of this modern society of the United States, there lived a family of ten children and a widowed mother, the first two of the children and the last two being boys, so that when the two oldest, Albert and Andrew, were nineteen and seventeen years of age and mighty sons of valor, wrestlers, and runners, challenging all comers, the two youngest, Floyd and Walker, were little fellows tramping the last long mile to the country schoolhouse. Now it so happened that there lived in the same community a big black boy of the cubits of a giant and the bearing of an African prince, but whose conditioned behavior was of great complexity. This big fellow was wont to pelt the two small boys with varied sizes and sorts of rocks as they wended their way to or from school, morning or afternoon, the motive whereof, whether mischief or meanness, not appearing to the older boys. So they lay in wait for him and caught him, Albert holding his head and arms down, Andrew sitting on his legs, meanwhile exhorting Floyd and Walker to pelt him with stones to their heart's content. The records had it that this pelting was considerable, so that the big black boy ere long mumbled from swollen lips and bruised features, looking up as at four against one, "Look here, boys, look here, we better quit befo' we kills one 'nuther, we might kill one 'nuther." And the boys did quit, with perhaps some whooping

* Presidential address read before the American Sociological Society, December 1930. *Publication of the American Sociological Society*, XXV (May 1931), 1-17.

sense of humor, and there was pleasant peace thereafter for many moons.

The father of these white boys was killed in a war of brothers peculiarly bitter, stranger than fiction, one product of which was to free the father of the colored boy from a superimposed slavery, which also reflected earlier conflicts of various sorts, and in freeing the slaves,

> They took the Old Marster, Lord,
> And fed him on pepper and gall.

And the conflict ramifications went on and on until in time a descendant of the black boy was mobbed by descendants of the white boys, but other descendants of the black boy went far beyond some descendants of the white boys in culture achievement, and there were created still other areas and types of conflict.[1]

Another aftermath of this war was the development of a folk society for both races transcending state and national forms and reflecting frustration and defeat, conflict and pathology, far beyond the usual comprehension of scholar or publicist, and reflecting, besides, all the basic elements that go into the making of a modern society, transition and change, new forms for old.[2] Here was and is conflict not conforming to the generalized theories of the sociologists. For the explanations of Gumplowicz, Ratzenhofer, Ward, Tarde, Giddings, Cooley, Ross, the "culture conflict" theorists, and the others are not enough.[3] What was it that brought that conflict to full power. . . .

> . . . It wasn't slavery
>
> .   .   .   .
>
> Nor even states rights, at least not solely,
> But something so dim it must be holy,
> A voice, a fragrance, a taste of wine,
> A face half-seen in old candleshine,

1. Cf. the author's *An American Epoch,* p. 11.
2. *Ibid.,* chap. xxi; also William Graham Sumner, *Folkways,* p. 90.
3. I.e., the Gumplowicz process did not apply. The North conquered the South—it did not destroy the conquered people, it did not assimilate them, it did not make them slaves. The conflict was a folk cultural one, which, however, could easily have been analyzed and for the most part predicted.

A yellow river, a blowing dust,
Something beyond you that you must trust,
Something so shrouded it must be great,
The dead men building the living state. . . .[4]

However this may be, the absence of any adequate social analysis of that particular example of war and conflict, with their cultural processes and products, may be considered as only one example in a very large list, such as the World War and its aftermath, or the multiplying processes of social conflict in the modern world, which might be offered in favor of the late Russell G. Smith's assertion that "social conflict is sociologically an unexplored field. . . . In short, the sociology of conflict has yet to be written."[5] Whether, because this is true, or whether, because of the significance and character of conflict processes in modern technological society, or in the breaking-up of old cultures in the new world, it would seem quite important for sociology to attack the problem as one peculiarly within its own domain; for instance, the Cooley concept of sociology as a means of interpreting life situations,[6] or Ogburn's adaptive culture in social change,[7] or Giddings' equilibrium between folk society and state society.[8] Yet the problem of social conflict in a modern world of technology is different from that in an old world of primary conflict, and the developments of social science have been considerable, outgrowing, to some extent, old theories, so that it becomes necessary to attack the problem from various new approaches. One of these is through the study of folk and regional conflict, new in so far as these concepts acquire new meanings and applications, and in so far as it offers new materials and new methods and new media for study.

The meanings of the terms *folk, regional,* and *conflict,* must naturally indicate the definitive nature of such a hypothesis for sociological study. For instance, the concept of *folk* as used in this discussion does not accord with Wundt's assumption of the reality of

4. *John Brown's Body,* p. 77.
5. From unpublished MS, "Sociological Theories of Conflict."
6. Cf. Arthur Evans Wood, "Charles Horton Cooley: An Appreciation," *American Journal of Sociology* (March 1930).
7. W. F. Ogburn, *Social Change,* pp. 203 ff.
8. Cf. "An Intensive Sociology: A Project," *American Journal of Sociology* (July 1930).

collective minds[9] nor Sumner's mass-developed instincts. It is opposed to Sumner's concept that folkways take on the character of a
social force when they become regulative for succeeding generations
in that it assumes a folk process and folk society which regulate current generations more powerfully than formally organized society.[10]
The term as used here is in nowise limited to ethnological or primitive characterization but on the other hand might apply equally well
to the synergy of social forces and processes in New York City;[11]
and it is so far contrary to the Keller-Sumner thesis that contemporary social phenomena are not valid for the scientific study of
society that it assumes they are among the most valid.[12] It may be
distinguished again by contrasting the Sumner concept in folkways
which "arise no one knows whence or why," "all origin lost in mystery,"[13] with the present assumption of a folk society which develops
and evolves as a natural society through normal constant societal
processes which may be known and classified; or Sumner's folkways
as belonging to a "superorganic system of relations," that is, not
organic or material, or Freud's "cultural superego,"[14] compared with
a folk society essentially organic and natural;[15] or Sumner's folkways
as made unconsciously, compared with a folk society essentially a
directive process between different stages of society.

The folk society is, however, of course, an extension of the Sumner folkways as dominating societal life and of the mores as "a phenomenon of society and not of the state."[16] Or, again, folk process

9. Wilhelm M. Wundt, *Elements of Folk Psychology.* See especially
pages 2-10 and chap. iv, Part 3.

10. See William G. Sumner, *op. cit.,* pp. iii-iv.

11. Cf. Edward Sapir's comment on the future of a sociology in which
primitive peoples will constitute a far smaller emphasis than at present. It
will be current society that is important because "civilized" and "primitive" peoples will be increasingly nearer together. Address at annual
dinner of the American Sociological Society, December 31, 1930.

12. Sumner and Keller, *The Science of Society,* especially Vol. I.

13. *Op. cit.,* pp. 3, 5, 7, 8, 45, 71, 76.

14. Sigmund Freud, *Civilization and Its Discontents,* chap. viii.

15. By "natural" we do not mean analogous to the "natural" sciences
but rather what Giddings describes as "a human conduct part of the
normal order of nature.... Explainable ... in terms of 'natural' causa-
tion."

16. Stuart Rice, *Methods in Social Science,* pp. 157-58. Cf. Professor
Park's discussion of the Sumner concepts.

as here used includes not only the usual definitive concepts, so well put in Redfield's "general type of change, whereby primitive man becomes civilized man, the rustic becomes the urbanite,"[17] but also a constant process which gains power in the form of the gradual development of conditioned, comparative society, evolving from one stage to another, merging now into formal or organized society, now gradually being transformed, as old cultures break up, into another folk society which again transcends organized social control. The folk concept here also includes Redfield's excellent characterization of "ways largely unwritten and unremarked"; of groups which have folk lore and folk songs; of "primitive tribes or peasant peoples enclaved within the borders of civilized nations"; of "country peoples"; of "self sufficient folk communities"; of changes in type of culture with common elements in various societies with respect to the "widening influence of modern western industrial civilization"; of the fusion of elements of different cultures. But it goes beyond his concept that "the world of cultivated classes ... is a world apart from that of the folk,"[18] holding rather that folk society may abound in any stage of culture or civilization whenever the major conditioning factors are extra-organizational or when a synergy of conflicting forces and processes results in an integrated transitional society, the transition featuring change from one stage of culture to another; from individual and primary group development to social organization; or from the "paths of individual development" to "the processes of cultural evolution."

The folk concept may be stated in other ways. Folk lore and folk song are commonly defined as elemental processes and carriers of culture growing out of a common stock of tradition but unwritten and unrecorded. On the other hand folk society arises from those social processes and products which, created and developed by what Wundt calls a communtiy of human life, are extraorganizational and extratechnological. Such folk society offers a medium for isolating constant processes in the development of, for instance, the Cooley

17. Robert Redfield, *Tepoztlán: A Mexican Village*, p. 14.

18. *Ibid.*, pp. 1-13. For other current but more popular meanings of "folk," see *Folk-Say: A Regional Miscellany*, edited by B. A. Botkin. Especially Part VII, *Folk Backgrounds and American Folk* by Mary Austin, pp. 287 ff.

concept of culture as the human and social side of society as opposed to the technical.[19] These social processes and products may
relate to conditioning factors which control the individual or the
group, as illustrated, for instance, through the conflict, accommodation, and renewal process of Park; through the interaction of personality and environment of Thomas; or through the stratification
of groups of Burgess, Steiner, and McKenzie; or through institutional and non-instiutional conflict, as studied by Queen, Thrasher,
and others.[20] If the development of the individual coincides largely
with the evolution of culture, the folk society would tend to be united and homogeneous, such as would commonly be called a peaceful
and happy group. If, on the other hand, the paths of individual development were quite divergent from the lines of social evolution,
such as for instance in modern societies created by centralized industry, or in societies with dual biological and social inheritance, or
in powerful backward nations in conflict with modern technology,
there would tend to be heterogeneity and conflict. The stages of
transition between the pioneer society and the co-operative modern
organizations which exceed the power and intelligence of the individual,[21] or between the various stages of adaptive culture in biracial
civilizations, would constitute a folk society in which elemental folk
processes of conflict and cultural transition could be observed ad-
mirably. Indeed, for sociology to neglect so great an opportunity for
basic study of transitional society in the modern world is unthink-
able.

Again, folk society, as the hypothesis for such special study,
while including what Professor Giddings terms minor societies, is
itself an integrated comparative society; and folk sociology is more
than his comparative study of societies. The folk society comprehends, not only his minor societies as units, but also the definite constant social processes of his major or natural society conceived as a
phenomenon of evolution. And folk sociology becomes rather the
study of comparative society, in which comparative societies are

19. See his presidential address in 1918, "A Primary Culture for
Democracy," *Papers and Proceedings of the American Sociological
Society*, XIII (March 1919), 1-10.
20. See *Social Attitudes*, edited by Kimball Young.
21. Compare Dewey's hypotheses in *Individualism Old and New*.

natural units of study just as primitive societies and ethnic groups
are natural units in the study of social evolution. Thus folk sociology as the study of comparative society naturally includes the comparative study of societies. And just as Professor Giddings[22] has
called the equilibrium which is worked out and maintained between
folk society and the state "seemingly the definitive trait of normal society," the hypothesis here is that the folk society, the normal transitional, extra-organizational, and non-technological social
process is the definitive, comparative society itself.

Illustrations of such folk society, properly described, analyzed,
and studied, would constitute a great mass of materials of sociology
which in turn must utilize them for the scientific study of society.
The scientist, of course, would know enough to distinguish between
the materials of science and the science itself, the various usages
that might be made of the materials, or the potentiality of various
data.[23] Illustrations of the folk society would seem abundant. Professor Giddings enumerates many modern minor folk societies, such
as the folkway family, religious institutions, schools, cults, agita-
tions, and parties, and points out their power as witnessed by the
Reformation, the Renaissance, Puritanism, the anti-slavery movement, communism, and others. Many more might be added, ranging
from the folk processes centering around current prohibition enforcement to Stuart Chase's "No" men of old New England and
"Yes" men of present New York.[24] Also included would be the
primitive societies of the ethnologists, or the folk—following of a
"scrawny native clad only in loin cloth," defying a British empire,

22. "An Intensive Sociology," *American Journal of Sociology* (July
1930), pp. 10-11.
23. E.g., The criticism has been made that in *An American Epoch*,
the chapters, "Folk-Music Survivals of the White South" and "Hymns and
Religious Songs" were included either for literary effect or because of
their interest to the author, whereas the author's hypothesis is that these
songs, their singing, and the resultant emotional conditioning are perhaps
the most powerful single folk force responsible for much of the culture
pattern of the region. The fact that analyses and interpretations are
reserved for more formal scientific study or that the superficial student
does not recognize the meaning of the data in no way affects the scientific
validity of the materials.
24. Stuart Chase, "The Luxury of Integrity," *Harper's* (August 1930),
pp. 336-44.

or the long-evolving Russian folk society in transition, or the various subethnological cultures in the United States today. Or, again, there was the folk society of Roman Africa producing a St. Augustine or a Terence, quite different masters from what would have risen out of an African Rome. For Roman Africa was Roman in name and government and in the designation of its major deities and eminent folks, but most of those who "dwelt in the houses and trod the streets" were conditioned by a Punic folk society which lasted for several centuries.[25]

Or to return to our first example of the war between the states, the after-war society of the South was pre-eminently folk society in that this region, although conquered and outwardly controlled by organized stateways and state force to the nth degree, had its culture and its future primarily conditioned by a folk society which was organic, natural, and material, such that its mastery was almost complete. It was the state society which was superimposed. Likewise, Negro society in the United States today, both South and North, both low and high, is so extraordinarily representative of folk society as transitional and extrawhiteman-organizational that it comprehends two societies differing so radically that great masses of people do not know of the existence of one or the other. Yet under scrutiny it must be clear that the folk society is the all powerful and realistic one for the Negro, as would be inevitable when a race has such a dual biological and social inheritance. It is again the definitive society in the evolutional long run.[26]

Or, again, keeping to modern cultures, there are the episodes arising from religious development and conflict. All religious conflicts throughout the world reflect folkways which transcend stateways. There was the transformation of formal Christianity through folk processes developed by humanistic tendencies, which were quite extra-Christian. And there are the nation-wide prayers for rain in the United States alongside the primitive and ancient prayers for fruitful crops; or the invocations of the savage going into battle compared with the modern allies and central powers "God on our side," mass faith and folk process completely tran-

25. Giovanni Papini, *Saint Augustine*, translated by Mary Prichard Agnetti, pp. 3-12.
26. See Sumner, *op. cit.*, pp. 77, 90.

scending all technological and reasonable considerations. Or, in the current culture of the United States, the religious folk process may reflect opposite manifestations: the one, among some rural and regional areas, reflects religious feeling as the chief reality, more powerful than all stateways or formal church ways, while the other, among those of larger social experience and learning, reflects form and ritual and conformity to unbelieved dogma as dominant, although quite outside the world of reality.

The concept of *region*,[27] as used in this discussion like that of *folk*, is somewhat different from that most commonly used in discussions of regionalism. The region as the hypothesis for special study is at once an extension and a subdivision of the folk society, characterized by the joint indexes of geography and culture and deriving its definitive traits through action and behavior processes rather than through technological functions or areas.[28] Perhaps most of the regions commonly so designated are primarily areas of technological boundaries or of social incidence. And while they constitute essential units for measuring and delimiting social study, they are not regions in the sociological sense.[29] Thus one thinks of certain types of industrial regionalism in Germany, of political regionalism in France,[30] of economic regionalism in America, or suburban regions of metropolitan America, or ecological divisions of cities. Other technological areas would include regions of agriculture, soil, of physiographic character; or, again, geological, eth-

27. For the purpose of this discussion "region" is not an entirely separate concept but an extension and an attribute to the "folk." As contrasting it with the technological region it cannot be separated from the main discussion.

28. E.g., "the South" as a "section" would comprise the technical, geographic, and political "Confederate States of America"; as a region it would vary, with subdivisions according to the fusion of culture and geography—the Piedmont mountain folk, the Piedmont mill folk, Saint Helena Island, the Black Belt, the Southwest, etc.

29. Victor Branford's stimulating discussion of the regional survey tended toward the analogy to the field naturalist, on the one hand, and to conceptualism on the other—place, work, folk, city, region, etc. Cf. "Science and Sanctity," *Sociological Review*, XIX, 341-42.

30. Cf. Mildred Hartsough, "The Concept of Regionalism as Applies to Western Germany," and Niles Carpenter, "The Nature and Origins of the French Regionalist Movement," *Studies in Quantitative and Cultural Sociology* (May 1930).

nological, topographical, or general ecological areas. Or, again, regions have been defined as life zones, activity areas, organization areas, sentimental areas, or city areas, or as fixed limitation, enlarged units of control, or merely as social groupings. Or, finally, the region is a different sort of technological area for the entomologist, the botanist, the general biologist, the taxonomist, the ecologist, the geographer, the banker, the student of labor or of wages.[31] These technological areas change and vary more easily because of changed techniques and scientific progress, whereas the folk region takes much longer or may even retain its power as the definitive society, sometimes weathering several technological cycles, and finding itself more harmoniously in accord with later technologies than with those it resisted. Or the folk society may reflect a dominant, rather than a recessive, adaptive culture. Such a cultural dominance or survival reveals a variation of Ogburn's cultural lag.[32] An illustration might be found in an agrarian culture resisting the urban-industrial technology and later adapting itself to newer cultural trends, or in the power of the Negro to adapt certain language and religious forms so completely as to make them his own, or in the case of a conquered people dominating the culture of the conquerors. Thus, in spite of all the modern technological standardization, there are evidences of increased rather than decreased folk regionalism in some instances. The region is smaller than but definitive of society. It is different from the state, section, or division, and it affords a larger medium for the study of the minor folk societies and a smaller unit for delimiting special studies of the larger folk society.[33]

A regional unit might afford isolation and concentration of study within a special area, or it might make available cultural materials unified over a period of time as well as within a limited range and thus combine the folk and regional approach.[34] Or it might, through

31. See *Conference on Regional Phenomenon,* issued by Division of Anthropology and Psychology, National Research Council, 1930.

32. See *Social Change,* especially Part IV.

33. The region as specially adapted to social research is urged in chapter v, 81-89, and in the last part of chapters vii-xviii, and xix, and xxiv of Odum and Jocher's *An Introduction to Social Research.*

34. See Margaret Mead, *Coming of Age in Samoa and Growing Up in New Guinea;* T. J. Woofter, *Black Yeomanry;* Guy B. Johnson, *Folk Culture of St. Helena Island;* N. N. Puckett, *Folk Beliefs of the Southern Negro*—to mention only a sampling of recent examples.

special statistical data and groupings of facts, reveal certain cultural-economic combinations which would transcend any one of the special technological characterizations. Such a supercultural region would be in contrast, let us say, to a technical region of the Federal Reserve banking system. Thus, one might select an eastern region in the United States beginning with Boston and extending down as far as Washington, which would include the chief metropolitan, manufacturing, commercial, and shipping centers, the larger universities and educational institutions, the largest concentration of wealth, philanthropy, and social work, and so attempt to measure certain aspects of American culture, in which education, research, philantropy, and co-operative organization were combining to create new patterns to meet the new technologies.[35] Or these same data might be utilized in the study of what Freud calls the discontents of civilization, attacking the problem from the top.[36]

Or, again, if one wished to illustrate simpler contrasts between regional folk society and states or sections, the southern Piedmont region might afford two examples. The one would be a certain mountain section of Tennessee, Georgia, South Carolina, and North Carolina, in which the grouped areas of the several states would show a far more homogeneous folk society than all the people of any one of the states. The same thing would apply to the Piedmont textile South, extending in a narrow strip from Virginia down through the Carolinas and Georgia, not because of manufacturing concentrated there so much as because of the folk culture being developed around it. Here again are fundamental distinctions between industrial regionalism, measured through technical processes at the top, and folk regionalism with its conflict processes at the bottom. Manifestly the transitional society will be started by the folk conflict and the change will be dominated by the folk society. Thus, since the nature of the folk society is conditioned by regional environment,

35. Compare quite a different viewpoint in Radhakamal Mukerjee, "The Regional Balance of Man," *American Journal of Sociology* (November 1930), for a discussion of the processes by which the balance of the region is maintained or shifted. Cf. his "Totality of the Region's Forces."

36. Besides other data implied, use of spot maps showing ratios of millionaires, income-tax payers, per capita wealth, per capita expenditures, concentration of surplus wealth, functional distribution of expenditures, etc.

the region affords specific media and data for the study of natural origins and processes, or social conditioning as opposed to biological.[37] And especially with reference to social conflict would the regional and folk unit prove effective.

To return now to the modern problem of social conflict and the thesis that the old sociological theories do not appear adequate, Lester F. Ward in the first presidential address twenty-five years ago was no doubt correct in saying that the early sociological theories were not false.[38] Nevertheless, they were not enough. This would appear true for the understanding and directing of folk and regional conflict in limited areas; or race, national, or international conflict in the modern world; or intracultural and culture conflicts; or the new conflicts multiplied by modern technology; or the conflicts of America "all in a ferment about itself"; or especially the behavior conflicts between the individual and his conditioning social environment, a natural and organic conflict, dynamically social but long neglected. The Gumplowicz and Giddings primary and secondary conflict are not enough; nor the Ratzenhofer fulfilment of dual instincts; nor the Tarde external and internal opposition; nor Ward's clash and opposition of social forces; nor Cooley's hostility and conflict; nor the Thomas conflict of attitudes—they do not explain or isolate in relation to the cultural environment the general types of conflict enumerated above, or Professor Ross's baker's dozen specific modes of conflicts,[39] or the ethnologists' and ecologists' conflict of cultures.

Or, to illustrate again with samplings, there is that most powerful social conflict between individual and class and social pattern, the ever-present intellectual and spiritual conflict between woman and the modern folk verdict, which continues to run counterwise to the formal, organizational, and even legislative profession concerning

37. Compare Professor Giddings' presidential address on "The Quality of Civilization," delivered in 1911 (*American Journal of Sociology* (March 1912), pp. 581-89.

38. Cf. his presidential address 1906, "The Establishment of Sociology," *American Journal of Sociology* (March 1907), pp. 581-87.

39. I.e., conflict of institutions, age, sex, race, town, country, class, industry, sects, learned and ignorant, etc. Cf. Part IV, revised edition, *Principles of Sociology*. See also E. A. Ross, *Roads to Social Peace,* one of the best discussions of social conflict extant.

the intellectual, creative, and social status of woman. It need scarcely be emphasized that much of the stimulus for this folk conflict
comes from the highest trained and most scientific men who in formal discourse and ways advocate freedom and equality of intellectual opportunity. We have come a long way from the early presidential address of Sumner in which he discussed the folk appraisal
of woman as "a blessing and a curse, a cheat and a delusion," but not
far enough. From the viewpoint of sheer mass behavior conflict,
this might easily be ranked near the top. And the assumption might
be ventured that there never has been an individual or a group of
women free from the Dewey concept of conflict which hampers creative effort.[40] Although a study of the intellectual conflict of many
hundred women would scarcely attract as much attention as the
study of the sex lives of a few hundred, the challenge of such a study
as a difficult and important work would be as great. And since, of
course, all those who study the physical aspects of sex life do so
purely from scientific motives and viewpoints, it would be just as
easy to secure such a study of conflict once it is shown to be of scientific importance!

Or again there is the larger problem of delinquency, let us say,
among certain groups, the Negro and other ethnic groups, or groups
bordering on poverty and want, or backward regions or organized
groups with unorganized mass folk following,[41] which offers new
fields for the study of folk conflict that is natural and organic. Or
the social pathology of mob action growing out of the development
of unwritten law conflict. And there are the growing conflicts between different regions in the United States and widening distances
between classes, and the powerful folk conflict in China, Russia, and
India, likely to be a mode for many years. But the list would take
another twenty minutes and could range all the way from this intra-
conflict of modern China or foreign missions in Africa or peaceful
resistance in India to James Truslow Adams' "Our Changing Characteristics,"[42] Stuart Chase's *Luxury of Integrity,* Llewellyn's folk

40. John Dewey, *Construction and Criticism,* pp. 21, 25.
41. Cf. Professor Charles E. Merriam's suggestion, at the 1930 twenty-
fifth annual dinner, that sociology study extrastate administration, e.g., of
business, religion, propaganda, as a needed contribution to political
science data.
42. The *Forum* (December 1930), pp. 321-28.

252   *The Folk Society*

law as conflicting with state law,[43] or the growing folk-minded conflicts in religious, moral, humanistic, or literary culture in America.

It must be clear that any study of social conflict through the medium of regional and folk units which would give a more scientific concept of group struggle and behavior conflict would require the maximum number of scientific sociologists as characterized in Professor Ogburn's address a year ago and would tax all the methodologists we could muster. It would test all the technology of any group absolutely sure that the last word in method has been reached. If it is objected that the task is too comprehensive or difficult or general or too intangible or even fantastic, I could wish to fall back on the inevitable favorite story. It would be a "chestnut," and it would radiate around the extraordinarily interesting personality of the Negro common man. This particular one was gazing engagingly at a sixty-pound watermelon which had just been brought to the store. A visiting white man offered to pay for the melon if the Negro would eat it all, else the Negro must pay the bill. To this offer the Negro countered with a request for a few minutes in which to go and make up his mind as to whether he could eat one so big. Presently, however, he returned and agreed to eat the melon, which he did in good style. So the white man paid the bill, but begged leave to ask one question, to wit: "What did you do when you left here to help you make up your mind?" To which the Negro replied: "Well, cap'n, I had one at home jes' 'bout same size as this one and when I went home an et hit, I knowed I could eat this one." I'm sure we can all agree that sociology has "et" some peculiar ones in the past in more ways than one.

In support of this general hypothesis of study certain final considerations may be urged. The first is the simple premise that the study of social conflict through the elemental folk society is a way of studying modern dynamic society—a challenge for sociology to come to grips with actual social phenomena as well as with the records of phenomena; with modern transitional society as well as with early recorded societies. The second is the simple premise that sociology

43. Karl N. Llewellyn, "A Realistic Jurisprudence," *Columbia Law Review* (April 1930). E.g., folk law as "what law is thought to be," or felt to be.

be accorded the matter-of-fact perquisites of any science, namely, to attack a natural and realistic problem through its elemental phases. Such an approach to the modern problems of changing culture need be no more characterized as speculative theory and sociological jargon than the study of a problem in the physical sciences through its technical formulas and hypotheses. Nor does the skepticism of those who have made no effort to look into the matter have any validity in the case. Nor need we re-emphasize the fact that we can but touch in this paper upon a subject which must require many years to develop, nor that such a study presupposes adequate methods of analysis and measurement[44]—the accumulation of data alongside the formulation of hypotheses. Even preliminary documentation and topical analysis would be almost encyclopedic. Such study would provide a considerable increase in the range and scope of scientific materials, emphasizing social change and social process, evaluating alike the primitive, early, and ancient societies and the modern and current as well. It assumes the validity of folk and regional phenomena in the United States as well as in Africa, or Europe, and of small units of study as well as large ones,[45] contrary to the earlier peculiar, academic provincialism which appeared to reflect the judgment that to be scientific a project must be afar off either in time or space and of large proportions. It emphasizes the importance of descriptive science so much needed in the transitional development of sociology today. It assumes the substitution of the study of natural, comparative society for unnatural analogies; and

44. Cf. Professor Ogburn's emphasis upon the differentiation of methods—distinction between the scientific and the philosophical, for instance, or the emphasis upon the statistical. The folk-cultural approach in nowise minimizes the statistical approach as an essential tool for study. It emphasizes a sociological approach entirely in accord with the prophecy that "there will be no professors of statistics": "The Folk-Ways of a Scientific Sociology," *Studies in Quantitative and Cultural Sociology* (May 1930).

45. The nature of the folk society might very well be examined in studies of subregions within states, e.g., northern Florida and southern, northern California and southern, northern Idaho and southern; the rural Georgia in conflict with the city of Atlanta, or the institutional character of various states, considered as historical rather than political units—e.g., Tennessee made from North Carolina, the cultural influence of the South on Indiana or Illinois.

of organic theory for organismic theorizing.[46] These distinctions are fundamental. It assumes further that through the study of organic folk elements sociology may learn much of social capacities and prepotency with some such effectiveness as medicine, through comparative anatomy and the biological sciences, has discovered elements upon which physical capacity, prepotency, and vitality rest.[47] And it is in character with a functional sociology which is telic not merely in the sense of general social guidance, but as underlying that, a functional science which conditions both society and sociology through the nature and extent of its findings.[48] Its telic implication is, therefore, one of values and harmony rather than morals.

There is, then, a final assumption that such a study, in one way or another, will carry on further the work begun by the early masters who achieved eminence in the hard school of American sociology. To pay them tribute and to carry on where they left off is at once a welcome obligation and pleasant task. Here is an injunction in the latest published contribution of the dynamic Giddings:

> In these interactions between folk society and the state and in variations of the normal equilibrium between them (all ultimately measurable) the scientific study of human society is offered an opportunity which it would be unpardonable to neglect and is faced with an obligation which it cannot be permitted to ignore or evade.[49]

Nearly a quarter century ago Sumner in his forward look into the future of sociology said:

> If I were a man forty years old and was beginning to be a professor in one of our American colleges, I should think that the opportunity to take hold of a department of sociology and give it shape and control its tendencies, lay down its outlines, and so on, was really the most important thing a man nowadays could undertake because of the tremendous importance of those social questions that are arising.

46. See the hypothesis of the behavioristic "organismic functional approach" in George A. Lundberg, "Public Opinion from a Behavioristic Viewpoint," *American Journal of Sociology* (November 1930), p. 405.

47. For some detailed discussion of this, see Odum and Jocher, *An Introduction to Social Research*, pp. 409-13.

48. *Ibid.*, pp. 308-10.

49. *Op cit.*, p. 12.

That seems to have been a fair appraisal then and peculiarly true today, with the added implication that the most important thing American sociology could do would be to develop during the next twenty-five years, through the added opportunity of training in social research, through concentration in sociological fields, and through the spirit and patience of the scientist, at least one hundred such capable sociologists, capable alike of understanding modern transitional society and of providing scientific facts and interpretation for its development.

2. *Folkways and Technicways*

The Folkways, the Mores, the

Technicways [1947]*

T*he folkways and mores are symbols of culture.* In our inquiries into culture and race, primitive society, religion, sex, war, work, play, rural life, and folk art, and their relation to the backgrounds of nature and resources, we have gone a long way toward exploring the whole range of elemental factors and socializing forces which have conditioned early society. These are elements in which all cultures have deep roots, and they are more or less universal to all societies. Processes within these elemental areas and their societal products make up what is called culture. Culture, growing naturally and inevitably out of the relation of individuals to their environments, results in another product, William Graham Sumner's classical concept of the folkways. The folkways are still important in any attempt to understand society, both because they are inherent in all cultures and because they are powerfully dynamic in their influence; but in the modern world of technology, the folkways are supplanted largely by the technicways. The folkways and the mores are essential elements in all early cultures, and their power must be understood if the technicways are to be utilized successfully in directing social change.

The folkways are, in general, the habits of the individual and the customs of the group, arising naturally and spontaneously and growing up slowly around the different phases of life. The folkways, not identifiable in terms of the specific time and occasion in which they grow up, are, however, necessary for survival. Thus, there will be as

* Chapter 12 in *Understanding Society: The Principles of Dynamic Sociology* (New York: The Macmillan Company, 1947).

many folkways as there are major activities, and the wisdom of the race, a combination of trial and error and experience, tends to crystallize in the folkways. When these folkways have continued over a period of time and have received the sanction of the group, they become the mores, which have a greater binding and coercive effect upon the group than the folkways. We shall see presently how from the folkways to the mores, through what later became morals, the social institutions developed, and still later expanded into the stateways or folkways of control. We shall also need to study the contrast between the folkways of earlier slow-moving societies and the technicways of later quick-changing civilization.

The Sumner science of folkways and its sequel.   Sumner's pioneering volume, *Folkways,* has for its subtitle: "A Study of the Sociological Importance of Usages, Manners, Customs, Mores, and Morals." His study was based upon the assumption that the first function of life is to live, and that in the struggle for existence the ability to adapt and change is vital. Through trial and error and experimentation, through pain and struggle, through the constant meeting of new needs, society itself has not only survived, but has developed its cultures. In order to understand how powerful these folkways are, we need only to check back and catalogue the folkways within each of the areas of general culture—race, religion, sex, war, work, play, art, and the later institutions and stateways. In some ways we may recapitulate our earlier chapters and note that the sum total of folkways, mores, institutions, stateways, and technicways constitute the culture of a given society. Our chief point here, however, is to establish that the folkways and the mores are elemental, organic, natural, and functional in the development of society, and, therefore, must be studied adequately in order to understand society. Our emphasis upon the folkways does not assume a doctrine of laissez faire; that because the folkways are powerful no change can be expected. On the contrary, if change can be brought about, it can best be done by understanding the folkways and substituting the technicways for them.

Sumner grouped folkways around four societal forces: hunger, love, vanity, and fear. Hunger and love, he maintained, are the natural impulses which are the stimuli for self-maintenance and self-perpetuation. They are universal in all animal life. Vanity and ghost fear, in Sumner's opinion, are specifically products of society.

Giddings' classification of the folkways. Franklin H. Giddings, building upon Sumner's foundation, developed a different classification of folkways. First of all come the folkways of reaction to the external world, of which there are two aspects: one is magic, corresponding to earlier religions, superstitious reactions, and the other is techniques, corresponding to later scientific attitudes. These are the natural folkways. Later on, Giddings elaborated these natural reactions by defining the *sustentation area* and the consequent *circumstantial pressure* developed by natural influences, and the consequent *social pressure* developed by social influences. All of these also are fundamental to the elemental, societal forces enumerated in this book. Giddings' next general class of folkways is that of reaction to strangers, including sympathy and enmity. Following these there are the group's folkways of reaction, including avoidance, warning, violence, praise, and approval. Professor Giddings thought that there are special folkways of reaction to the young, such as admonition, restraint, and punishment. The next classification included the folkways of occasion and routine, for instance, domicile, eating, camping, and entertaining. Also, there were folkways of birth and death, and the folkways of organization, from which two great planes of social organization developed—the tribal or ethnic, and the civil or political. Folk culture evolved from the first of these, civilization from the second.

The folkways start early with nature. That the folkways and mores grew up first around all the natural aspects of life may be seen by a review of the origin and development of religion, science, work, play, sex, race, or any part of the struggle for survival. To catalogue this limitless number of folkways and mores would be to review almost the entire early stages of the development of society, and to record the continuing powerful influence in modern societies of race, religion, and sex, as well as many of the folkways of economic institutions. An understanding of the development of the folkways and mores is fundamental to the understanding of how societies grow from earlier natural folk cultures into later political, technological, and urban civilizations. To understand why society is as it is and why men behave as they do, it is necessary to understand these fundamental backgrounds; but also it is necessary to understand them in order to project the further planning and development of human society.

A hierarchy of folkways and their evolution. In general, the order of development runs somewhat as follows: First are the *folkways,* which grow up gradually without known specific origins. Next, the folkways, mellowed and tested by time, experience, and sanction, develop into the *mores.* The mores, taking form and integration, develop into the equivalent of *morals* and *morality,* which exert general coercive or societal pressure upon behavior. The resultant development of morals and morality, custom, right, wrong, values, and the like, provide the bases for the *institutions,* for the family, religion, education, and government. From informal institutions to formal institutions, it is an easy step to the *stateways,* in which coercion and control become definite and legislative. When the stateways become oppressive they are followed by protesting folkways. The protesting folkways are, in turn, followed by nullifying folkways, which in turn overthrow the stateways. The cycle of folkways then begins over again, at least in the earlier slow-moving cultures.

We may illustrate this process in as many ways as we choose. A good example would be that of sex and marriage and the family. To take a specific development, monogamous marriage; first there were the folkways and folk wisdom which held that the relationship of man and woman as husband and wife was the most effective way to reproduce the race and nurture its young, as well as to serve the economic needs and develop the finer sensibilities of society. This became a practice, or, in Sumner's terms, the habit of the individual and the custom of the group. As societies grew more numerous and complex, the power of taboo and coercion and convention developed through the working of the folkways. Thus, failure to accept the folkways, or behavior apart from custom, resulted in the pressure of the mores on the individual. Ostracism or exclusion from the group was usually effective. Thus, the morality of the family and the sex relationship in marriage were established, and, in turn, the institution of the monogamous marriage.

Nevertheless, this was not an adequate system. As society developed, people became more varied and complex, and the mores were not effective enough. There was needed some form of sovereignty or law whereby the folk wisdom and the institutions of the group might be enforced. Thus arose the stateways which legislated the sex relationship and the family into a compulsory pattern. If and when, however, the stateways work hardships upon individuals, groups, and institutions, and a need for a more flexible arrangement arises, the protest of the folk leads to the nullification of the stateways, as, for instance, in a democratic culture, the divorce laws make marriage under certain conditions less of an iron-bound institution.

The power of the folkways. The power of the folkways is indicated by Giddings' remark that after twenty-five years of careful study of the history of human society, he had failed to find a single case in which, when folkways and stateways conflicted, the folkways had not won out. This is fundamental to the understanding of how societies grow, how revolutions arise, and why conflicts in the modern world—through race, religion, war, economic competition, and a hundred other avenues of human association—result in upheaval and change. But when the folkways and the stateways coincide there is practically no way of resisting the power of a people within the framework of their resources and capacities. In Hitler's Germany, the stateways and the folkways coincided and were reinforced by technology and the technicways; the result was the power to carry on six years of world war.

THE TECHNICWAYS OF CONTEMPORARY SOCIETY

In the modern civilized world, at least in the supertechnological area, the old, slow-growing order of folkways, mores, and stateways no longer operates; in reality, there are no longer any mores or matured folkways, since by definition these can grow up only over long periods of time. Instead, because of such technological achievements in atomic energy, transportation and communication, and many chemical inventions, there are the new *technicways,* which are habits of the individual and the customs of the group arising specifically as to time and occasion to meet the survival needs of a modern technological world. Thorstein Veblen anticipated this trend when he reversed the old proverb which held that "Necessity is the mother of invention." What he said was that, on the contrary, invention has become the mother of necessity.

In general, the order is now likely to become: first, the *folkways;* then *exploratory technicways* of trial and error; then *enduring technic-*

ways; then the stateways followed again by the *protesting technicways* and *nullifying technicways;* from the earlier slow-moving tempo the cycle is shifted into high. In demonstration, we must once again characterize the nature of the technicways and illustrate them in sufficient cases to enable us to understand modern society in terms of this new process of social change. In this particular chapter, we shall reiterate merely the simple characterization of the technicways; in later chapters, there will be further elaboration of the role of technicways in modern civilization and an attempt to define the balance and the margin of survival between the folk society and the state society, between culture and civilization, between machines and men.

The technicways make a new world. The assumption is that in the technicways we have phenomenon even more significant than the old folkways and as subversive of them as some of the later developments of science and history are to some of the Malthusian population theories. The principal assumption is, however, that, in contemporary civilization, the technicways, transcending the folkways and supplanting the mores, tend so to modify human behavior and institutions as to outmode the earlier, natural rate of societal evolution. In particular, the tendency is toward acceleration of the rate of change in behavior patterns as well as in technological processes, and therefore of the rate of cultural evolution also. In contradistinction to the folkways, which arise no one knows where and how, the technicways emerge demonstrably through the incidence of new technics and inventions and their use in social life. Folkways are customs and habits which grow up naturally to meet needs, and they ripen through sanction and time into mores. Not so the technicways, which arise from the pressure of technological procedures and force individual and group to conform to their patterns, regardless of empirical considerations or of mass sanction. Accordingly, the technicways can be set over against Sumner's folkways and mores.

Illustrations of the technicways are plentiful. Thus, "fashions" superimposed through the technique of advertising do not represent the tastes of individuals or groups, nor do they reflect a gradual evolution from one style to another. Such fashions are not folkways to meet needs but technicways to fall in line with gadgets of the market place. Technicways, it should be re-emphasized, are not the ways of technology; they are not techniques. Technicways are the *ways of adjustment to technology* and the resulting behavior. Thus, technicways are not airways and their reduction of time and space, but the behavior of people—a business man vacationing in South America, or visiting his plant in Europe; not the atomic bomb but the decentralization of industry or cities for protection. Moving pictures and all that goes into the cinema industry do not constitute the technicways through which are reflected new behavior in contrast with the earlier folkways and mores. This is reflected in the weekly attendance of eleven million children keeping long and unhealthy hours at moving pictures, 80 per cent of which the theme is crime, sex, or "love." This is contrary to both folkways and mores, yet the attendance increases.

Again, the older folkways assumed that when young people married they would have not only children but many. Indeed, children were the normal expectation, and as they grew up in an agrarian culture, they were wealth-producing units of the family. In a world of technology, the technicways, in order to meet needs of present society, assume that children must come later and be fewer. Other powerful technicways that negate the old folkways are those of a warfare that destroys civilians, cathedrals, and hospitals; and the justification of the use of the atomic bomb and other terror aspects of war.

Technicways affect the individual, too. It is almost needless to say that, in the modern world the technicways affect the individual even as the folkways and the mores affected the individual in earlier cultures, for the habits of the individual are still fundamental to the development of his personality and to group relationships and behavior. The technicways that relate to birth control have a close bearing upon the individual behavior of youth and of men and women in general, just as many other modern technicways have changed the individual's attitudes and values in religion, industry, education, and morality. The technicways of the family in which wife and daughters as well as husband and sons work have a great deal to do with the conditioning of the children who grow up. The technicways have had a tremendous influence upon the nature and range of patriotism and loyalties. When modern technicways become the social technicways of authoritarian society, the role of the individual and his motivation are reflected in entirely different behavior. We shall inquire into these more in detail elsewhere.

Technicways give rise to problems. It is but natural that a large number of societal and social problems must arise in the wake of such a fundamental and an organic change in the cultural process. We have pointed out how invention and social change in the past have affected society and its institutions. We have pointed out how modern communications and the automobile, the moving picture, and other inventions have changed the profile of a great deal of our institutional landscape. The nature of government has been greatly changed by good roads and the automobile; the nature of church worship by the radio. Through the technicways it is possbile to understand something more of the process of change and, therefore, to appraise the social problems involved. These are so numerous that they must be treated in subsequent papers, in which we undertake to focus upon certain tentative conclusions in our total effort to understand society. So, too, we shall discuss more of the technicways and the folkways in papers dealing with research and theory.

Folkways and technicways in American society. The history of the culture of the United States recapitulates the story of this evolution from the earlier folkways and mores to the technicways of civilization. American culture has been rich in the folkways and mores of patriotism, religion, Sabbath observance, morality, family, youth, work, industry, and the capitalist system—a long catalogue of peculiarly American virtues and values. A review of America's "only yesterdays" would help to understand the kaleidoscopic picture of our folkways. There would be the folkways of dress, illuminated by changing fashions in the dress of both men and women and college styles; or the folkways of dress in travel, by automobile or airplane. The folkways of sex and courtship, divorce and remarriage, and of "woman's place in the home," and other examples. On the other hand, American technology has transformed not only the material world but the world of behavior as well. Here, again, we need only point to the range and richness of the evidence of the technicways.

FOLKWAYS AND TECHNICWAYS IN HITLER'S GERMANY

So, too, in the cataclysm of global conflict the technicways of war and totalitarian philosophy have so accelerated the tempo of civilization as to pass over morality in the sense of the mores and of folk wisdom. Hitler's Germany is a good example both difficult and easy to explain. It is difficult to explain because of the complexity of factors but it is also easy because the societal factors are clearly demonstrable. Germany is the monumental example of the potentialities of the technicways to destroy society. Now, how do the folkways help explain what happened in Germany, and how could they have helped to predict what would happen and what will happen in similar cases, if they ever arise again? The assumptions here are several.

First, Hitler's Germany represented the complete coincidence of stateways and folkways in synchronization with the technicways. Under the circumstances, within the range of Germany's resources, nothing could stop that combination. In the next place, Hitler's Germany was the perfect example of artifical society and super-technology exceeding the capacity of the people, their institutions and resources, so that in time failure was inevitable. One of the penalties of the Nazi program was that the Greater Reich came to incorporate so many heterogeneous folk within its borders that ultimately there was no unified folk society to coincide with the state society, and therefore the beginnings of weakness were under way. And, finally, there were the folkways of the rest of the world, combined with the powerful technicways of a war for survival, which soon came to be more powerful than all the folkways and technicways of German society. Before the blitzkrieg, many of Europe's folk societies had been weakened through endless struggles, through conflict between state societies and folk societies, and through the excessive demands of modern civilization. Then they were "softened up" by propaganda and fifth-column activities, thus making for disunity among the folk of Austria or France, for instance, whereas the German folk were unified. In the period of waning German strength, the various resistance movements had reached a point of cohesion and toughness sufficient to lend considerable help to the armed forces of the Allies.

A powerful dynamics of nationalism and war. We need to understand how, in Germany, Hitler had made the folkways of the German people coincide with the stateways and then subsequently had utilized technology, through the technicways of warfare, science, communication, and propaganda to implement the folkways and stateways. These folkways, which had a cumulative influence, may be grouped together into seven categories.

A *first* group were the folkways of a *Blut* ethnic determinism of

German nationalism and the German superstate, and of a superior German "race." A *second* group were the folkways of power, of war and blitzkrieg, might as right. A *third* group were the folkways of frustration-aggression, self-righteousness, self-defense—"Germany surrounded by her enemies." A *fourth* group were the folkways of science, technology, efficiency, and ruthlessness. A *fifth* group were the folkways of occasion, order, and obedience, symbolized by the goose step. A *sixth* group were the folkways of subservience to the state—of work, of woman's place in the home and in compulsory labor, and of the training of youth. And a *seventh* group were the folkways of loyalty, patriotism, morality, the attack upon wickedness in high places, and other common appeals to righteousness.

When Hitler had synchronized all of these seven folkway groups into a powerful unity, supported by military strategy and by innumerable resources within the geographical and regional settings of Germany and the conquered nations, there was no way—for a long time—to resist the power and speed of this combination. Observers have characterized the period of the blitzkrieg as the first "perfect" machine age in the sense that it embodied an exact synchronization of men and machines, backed up by a powerful folk.

German folkways in conflict with world folkways. What are the realities of the situation in the crisis of Hitler's Germany from the viewpoint of sociology? The reasons are clear why Hitler succeeded for so long and came so near to attaining his dreams of a Nazi world, just as are the reasons why he failed. For, in the earlier days of successes, not only were many of the folk cultures weak, but the German people all over the world were driving toward a support for their folkways of world conquest. In the South American republics, these folkways were gaining power, and in the United States, there were many people who were beginning to say that perhaps after all, on "the wave of the future" Germany would ride the crest. Then, however, two things happened.

The first was the inevitable expansion of the artificial Nazi society and German technology beyond any reasonable capacity of the folk, as indicated by the seven groups of folkways.

The second was the massing of the folkways and stateways of the rest of the world, supplemented by their powerful technology, to defeat the stateways of Nazi civilization. First there was Britain and then Soviet Russia, both capable of holding out for a period, and then the United States and all the other United Nations massed in this great folk protest against Nazi Germany.

This protest, backed by the combined strength of an aroused world and its resources, is an example of the power of the folk society in conflict with a single state society.

History will record the unbelievable length and breadth of civilization's destruction of European culture and of the rise of a new folk society through which a new world would be born. All of this can be measured in the statistical count of the dead and the wounded, the strain of living in the conquered countries, the tragedies of civilians and family breakups, the destruction of wealth, the lowered standards of living, the complexity and "mistakes" of the military campaign, and in innumerable other ways.

The folkways ultimately defeat the stateways. It is clear also how the widening range of the superstate's territory, peoples, and power increased the complexity and heterogeneity of the folk society, ensuring two things, namely, increasingly conflicting folkways against the superstate and making the quantitative task of keeping the folk in line practically impossible. This strain was measurable in terms of the population of conquered peoples, the little democracies, and the unconquerable folk groups to the east, and finally in the extraordinary spectacle of part of the United States Navy operating in Germany's Rhine River to defeat the whole Nazi people buttressed within what they assumed to be an impregnable fortress. Increasingly, therefore, in so far as the demands of this superstate exceeded the capacity both of its own power and its constituency, and of the needed resources, it was only a matter of time before collapse was inevitable.

In the meantime, on the other hand, there were, as implementing this process, first in Britain and in the United States, and then in the other allied nations, powerful trends toward the unity and harmony of stateways and folkways which were to be supplemented by the most powerful technology and, therefore, possibly technicways in the history of society. Indeed, if the sociologist is to look for societal gains from such world cataclysm, it would be found in this extraordinary spectacle of a great society, seeking to defend its civilization from destruction or to defend its culture from civilization's destroying power, and reconstructing itself in the ways of the enduring equilibrium and strength of the folk and of universal culture strengthened through democratic institutions.

The Technicways in Modern Society [1947]*

S *ociologists have studied the processes of early society.* We have now studied the evolution of society from the folk society to the most advanced state of culture, which is called civilization. We have discussed some of the main traits of civilization as contrasted with earlier cultures, and we have characterized modern world society as having the prevailing traits of civilization rather than of culture, with always the clear understanding that folk cultures abound in the way places of the world and within the great state societies themselves. In the approach to this assumption we described the mode of development of earlier societies as reflecting their growth through the folkways and the mores, which in turn developed and conditioned the various institutions of the folk, which later came to be stablized in social institutions and the stateways. These folkways and institutions have grown up around the elementary, natural processes of religion, sex, family, occupations, struggle for survival, kinship, race, art, recreation, association, government and others. So far as known, there have been no exceptions to this general rule and no societies which have not conformed to this evolutionary procedure. Sociologists for the most part have based their theories of the processes of interaction and the products of social dynamics upon studies of the earlier stages of societal development. It follows, therefore, that we have emphasized the folkways and the mores especially because they are symbols and measures of historical culture, because they are comprehensive enough to take in most of the standard ideas of the

* Chap. 20 in *Understanding Society: The Principles of Dynamic Sociology* (New York: The Macmillan Company, 1947).

"processes" studied by sociologists who have sought to catalogue the elements of society, and because their meaning has become both popular and classical.

The need for new ways of studying modern society. Now we come to study the modern world whose civilization reflects a tempo so extraordinarily different and a speed and power of social change so sweeping that we are challenged to find traits of this civilization which will serve as definitive and distinctive characterizations that differentiate it from earlier cultures. In this search, sociology seeks something more than abstract generalizations, historical analogies, or deterministic philosophy, presented in such works as Spengler's *Decline of the West,* Freud's *Civilization and Its Discontents,* Lombroso's *Tragedies of Progress,* or Sorokin's *The Crisis of Our Age.* Sociology is faced with the dilemma of studying modern civilization within the framework set by earlier sociology. This may be illustrated by contrasting Sumner's concept of the science of society with the needs of contemporary sociology. Sumner's implication was that the science of society consisted of the study of the folkways and the mores as the elemental traits and social forces. But if the folkways are no longer powerful and if there are no mores, what will constitute the study of society?

Civilization is characterized by technicways, not folkways and mores. We approach the answer to this question through the assumptions of the dynamic sociology of this text that the prevailing behavior of present-day civilization as we have defined it is characterized primarily by the *technicways* in contrast to the folkways and the mores of earlier societies. In contrasting the technicways with the folkways and mores in our chapter on culture we have laid the foundation for an adequate framework for the search for the realistic understanding of the modern world. If the technicways make a new world, they afford practical ways of measuring the society of that world as well as providing the framework for social direction of the future. In the technicways, too, will be found a new challenge to concepts of values and progress. If the study of the folkways and mores constituted, in large measure, the science of early society, the study of the technicways becomes a mode for the science of that part of contemporary world society which is civilization.

This new world has been characterized by trends toward urbanism; toward technology and industrialization, including the mechanization of agriculture; toward a phenomenal sweep of science and invention, and toward centralization of wealth and power tending toward totalitarian governments. As both creator and creature of these trends scientific humanism and intellectual totalitarianism have transcended much of the religious folkways and primary ideals of earlier culture, but they have not bridged the distance between frontier culture and technological civilization. All these have resulted in changed patterns of human behavior, climaxed by the blitzkrieg of global war and the sweeping trends of an atomic age, the mechanisms of which have set the stage and pace for powerful technicways of the state. In so far as the technicways are the mode of totalitarian states, and, therefore, coercive, they tend to control or negate the influence and services of the other major institutions which are the cumulative products of the cultural processes through the folkways, mores, and stateways.

The technicways reflected on the screen of the folkways and mores. The simplest way to define the technicways is in terms of the folkways; this approach affords a good basis for comparison with earlier cultures and also an effective framework upon which to study our rapidly changing society. The folkways, we recall, are the habits of the individual and the customs of the group which arise over long periods of time to meet the needs of human beings for continuing adjustment and survival. They are the folk wisdom of the race. Before formal education, the folkways embodied the cumulative efforts of each generation to transmit to the succeeding generation what it considered the essential learning for adjustment and survival. The folkways were the growing, flexible processes of living and learning. In order to set the stage for the technicways, we emphasize again how, as time went on, the folkways were tested through increasingly more effective trial and error, and those which matured to receive the continuing sanction of the group became mores. The mores took on the nature of societal pressure. They represented the coercion of the public opinion and became the basis for more formal judgments. This body of judgments then tended to crystallize into what later became "morals" and constituted the bases for "morality," "ethics," "good," and "bad." The two chief traits of the mores were the time element necessary to their growth and the binding effect of their total influence. We shall see presently that neither of these traits is valid in the world at large today.

The mores were stabilized in the institutions. Whenever a body of values, form of behavior, or the mores of one or more definite areas of life became formalized, stabilized, and sanctioned, the organization or the symbol of the institution arose. The institution was thus a sanctioned organization providing practical arrangement to conserve and enforce the judgments of the mores as to what was "best," "right," "good," "true," or "wise." Those structures that grew up and were formalized and sanctioned in the major institutions reflected modes of group behavior relative to sex, education, religion, government, work, and association within the community. That is, we have in every society the major institutions of the family, education, religion, government, work, association. In the modern world, these generic values were institutionalized around standards and forms of the *home,* the *school,* the *church,* the *state, industry,* and the *community.* These special *forms* of the institutional values were flexible and represent ways and means of the successful functioning of each institution. Later more specific minor forms of institutional sanctions followed. These were detailed ways of working through the major institutions which paved the way for an increasingly larger influence of the state and of the stateways, or legislated order and procedure. Thus, money and banking are part of the economic institution; or institution of industry and work, as we have called it here; so, also, labor unions are another subinstitutional category. Hospitals, courts, and clinics; agencies and organizations for ameliorating the lot of the deficient are called institutions for the blind, the crippled, the insane, the sick. They have usually been termed the eleemosynary institutions or the institutions of philanthropy. Universities and colleges as a subdivision of education are called institutions of higher learning.

The rise of the stateways. These more specialized institutions are the increasingly formal and legalized agencies for serving particular needs. They are, therefore, planned, reasoned, and practical and generally represent what are called the stateways—those ways which are enforced by laws and legislation. The laws of the states, laws relating to marriage, taxation, labor, education, banking, voting, welfare, and health represent one large branch of the stateways. These are reflected in the states' authority to charter business organizations, to license marriage or building permits, to legislate against trusts. So, also, the encyclicals of the Catholic Church, the "Discipline" of the Methodist Church, the rules of labor unions—these are stateways in that they carry with them the necessary compulsion of enforcement or penalty.

The stateways also reflected the community sovereignty. It is important at this time to re-emphasize the role of the stateways because of their intermediary status between the folkways and the mores, on the one hand, and the later technicways, on the other. For there is consistent trend toward the widening range of governmental services and therefore increasing control. Yet, the institution of the state and government, like all the institutions, grew out of the community first. These communities, of one and another kinship and natural association, sooner or later came to have needs of economic co-operation or division of labor, or defense, or expansion, or exploration, or better order. Hence, the state—following one or another form of sovereignty or organization—arose to meet these needs for greater order and conformity. The state was a community government or agreement with rules and penalties. It became a principal institution of society in later stages of development whenever the gowth of population and the increasing complexities of community life demanded its services and jurisdiction. Thus, laws—stateways—were produced that related to all the other major institutions and their activities, to the end that better order would obtain. Stateways multiplied until they became the definite later stage of development in this order: folkways—mores—stateways. The synchronous and intermediary processes—morality, ethics, institutions—continue their development in the order listed.

Now in so far as the extreme developments of modern world society tend to conform to the totalitarian civilization of the state, then a single institution of the state negates the form and primary services of the other institutions, and thus in these instances the state has become synonymous with society. We recall that Sumner was wont to say that since "the life of society consists in the making of folkways and applying them," the science of society might very well become the study of the folkways. If we oversimplify the analogy, the study of society in totalitarian nations would consist largely of the study of the stateways as they conflict with the folkways and the other institutions.

Stateways, like folkways and mores and institutions, have always developed gradually through trial and error, exploration and survey, and by the gradual but sure increase in the functions of the state society. They have usually represented the will of the people and have been planned to meet the essential needs for better order and services to society. And the stateways often, but not always, have incorporated the "best" of the folkways and mores and tend to reflect the tradition and authority of the elders in both range and judicial enforcement.

The technicways have no tradition. Now comes our civilization of the middle 1900's, moving too fast for the formation of mores and folkways and setting up a rate of social change which negates both the folkways, the mores, and the orderly stateways. In the light of actualities and trends of science, technology, with the corresponding speed of change, it seems very doubtful if mores are possible. This is made clear if we contrast the meaning and power of the technicways with the folkways. To do this we need only repeat again some of the traits of the folkways and the mores. According to the Sumner concept, the young always learned the folkways by tradition, imitation, and authority. The technicways which predominate in present-day society are by their very definition so new that they have no tradition or authority and cannot be learned by imitation. They arise quickly from specific, definite, observable pressures and needs, and their survival or success depends upon their quick adoption and usage. So, again, if the folkways and the mores arose through ritual, it seems clear that no such introduction to the new technicways could be possible. If the folkways were powerful because "our ancestors have always done so," the technicways are powerful primarily because our ancestors *never did so.* Manifestly this has powerful meaning in so far as the whole process of child training and home conditioning affect the character and behavior of the new generation.

The technicways make a new world. This new world which the technicways make, therefore, is one that manifestly is developing quite differently from the earlier cultures. In general, the newness of this world can be defined from two points of view: First, it is literally new in the sense that science, invention, technology, speed, and change have wrought so effectively that the world today is essentially different from the world of yesterday. Technology has not only changed the face of nature, but of the ways of living. Second, this world of ours is new in the sense in which it is characterized as a uniform, universal, advanced stage of civilization similar to the advanced stages of other civilizations as they have become top-heavy, artificial, and as they tend toward decay. Now if we understand most common explanations of how modern society has come to such a position, and if it is possible to account for our present dilemmas in concrete and measurable terms, it will be possible to study society concretely and objectively. The assumption should be repeated, therefore, that *in the technicways, which transcend the folkways and supplant the mores,* and accelerate the tempo of societal evolution, what is happening is visible and can be understood.

Explanation of our troubled civilization. We have already summarized . . . the powerful effects of science and technology on the present world, and we have emphasized the fact that they have concentrated their most powerful influence in the two still further disturbing forces of global war and totalitarian government. Now, turning to the second phase of the new world, namely, the predominance of dilemma, confusion, and chaos, there are many verdicts on civilization and its tragedies and costs.

Pitirim Sorokin in a series of encyclopedic volumes which have been followed by popular interpretations, predicts that the present sensate culture, the product of civilization, together with man himself, will drift to self-destruction. In his plaintive prophecy of doom, he says, "Not only have we begun the disintegration of a great super-system of sensate culture but values, including man himself, will be made still more debased, sensual and material, stripped of anything divine, sacred, and absolute." The elements of destructive forces constitute a long catalogue. The House of Western Man will collapse. Everything will contribute to destruction. Here are items: rude force —cynical fraud—might—brutality rampant—bombs instead of bread —death instead of freedom—the family a tool of cohabitation—the home a parking place—atomistic and hedonistic devices—egotistic expedience—bigotry—fraud—atrocious concoctions of fragments of science, shreds of philosophy, stewed in the inchoate mass of magical beliefs—liberties gone—security and happiness turned into a myth—

man's dignity, his value, trampled pitilessly—the previously built magnificent sensate house crumbling—destruction rampant everywhere—cites and kingdoms erased—human blood saturating the good earth—all sensate values blown to pieces and all sensate dreams vanished.

Sorokin's implication is that there is nothing that can be done about it, and that, having thrown off the sensate culture, some bright morning humanity will wake up blossomed into perfect ideational culture led by some new prophets—which would mean, of course, an era of dictatorship. Surely this is not the way human society grows nor is this the goal of human effort.

There are many other explanations of the crisis of civilization. There is Spengler's verdict that all human culture passes through the normal cycles of nature: seasonal as of springtime, summer, autumn, winter; or human as of childhood, youth, middle age, old age; or societal, as rural-agrarian, urban-technological culture-civilization. There is Freud's application of the psychology of the social organism with the resulting conclusions pointing towards disaster. An oversimplification of his formula would be: since all progress is made through the order of natural processes, and since the processes of modern civilization are unnatural, therefore no progress is possible; on the contrary, decay and deterioration must result until such time as mankind restores natural order.

There are also the explanations of the modern crisis in terms of morality. Hitler used this motif in molding the German folk to his superstate, by appealing for moral support for his fight against corruption in high places and for the rights of the folk and of youth. In America, corruption in high places has been ascribed as the cause of the breakdown of society. The "wages of sin is death" applies to society as well as to individuals. Those who undertake to explain the present chaos on the religious or moral basis point out that it is a punishment brought upon the world because of the sins of the nations. Many scriptural explanations are offered: ... for all they that take the sword, shall perish with the sword; the wicked shall be turned into hell, and all the nations that forget God; the wicked rule, the people perish—and a thousand prophecies of the Isaiahs and Jeremiahs, old and new. Then there are those who, attempting to answer the question why God would permit so much suffering, go further and say that it is a part of the divine order which gives man, created in the image of God, the eternal right of choice and of self-determination. Man has chosen, they say, and must still choose between great conflicting philosophies, and it is only through this constant struggle and choice that mankind can evolve into its fullest possibilities.

Finally, there are the more moderate and scientific explanations of what has happened and is happening in civilization. In general, the various theories of social change and of cultural lag are set forth to show how maladjustment and confusion arise with their resulting problems. There are far too many of these even to list them, but samplings will illustrate. For instance, there are the multiple theories of determinism—economic determinism, racial determinism, geographic determinism, technological determinism, and the others—along with the distinguished heritage of philosophical, educational, humanistic, and aesthetic explanations of human values. There are many theories of progress and catalogues of the stages and ages of mankind and his culture.

Now the sociologist in looking at modern civilization finds himself obligated not only to know about all of these explanations, to estimate the relative merits of their multiple assumptions, and to recognize the very existence of so many attempts to understand society, but he must also go further and in so far as is possible check up on as many of the premises as is possible. And, in so far as possible, he must undertake to give a more realistic understanding of what has happened.

How the technicways explain the changed world. It seems clear that what we have called the technicways clearly explain much that has changed the world we live in and also indicate how the changes came about. In the field of sex and the family, or religion and morality, of rural life and urban, for instance, the technicways offer the clearest explanation of what has happened and why. Our task here is relatively simple, namely, to point up differences between the old and the new and to indicate how the technicways have made the new world. We may begin with one of the most universal of illustrations.

The technicways of parenthood. In earlier days and even as late as the first part of the twentieth century, whenever a young couple married it was generally assumed by them and by others that they would not only have children in the early, regular order of married life, but that they would have several children. This was not only an acceptance of the way of nature, but the churches had placed mother-hood and parenthood high in the order of values; some religious bodies have only sanctioned the sex relation for reproduction purposes. In the folkways and the mores of the people, extending all the way up from early times, values were fixed to the point where marriage and large families represented "the way" for rich living and for the development of the race. However, it may be said that now young people who marry do not anticipate large families, nor do they expect to have children until their income reaches a point where a child can be born, brought up, and educated in accordance with the prevailing ideas. This is especially true of youth on the level of higher education and industrial competition. From a rule of procedure in which every married couple was expected to have children, and many of them, we come to a rule where married couples do not expect to have children immediately or large families even when children are planned.

Now the technicways are defined as habits of the individual and customs of the group for meeting needs and survival values in the modern technological world. The development of industry has furnished opportunities for women to work, and large numbers of young women, in order to support themselves or assist in supporting their families, must work a while before starting a family. Many young men out of college with a feeling of lack of security and with various types of opportunities express the conclusion that they cannot support a family, and, with an uncertain economic future, they feel they would be doing an injustice to the wife and children. For a young man of today to set up a home in expectation of rearing four, six, or eight children would be cause for great joking, so unrealistic does it appear.

There are other elements that have entered the question of parent-hood. Science has developed ways of contraception, movements are on foot for the orderly planning of parenthood, and birth control has become a major consideration in population policies. Although birth control has been opposed by a number of the churches, and is contrary to the folkways and the mores of many people, the movement has very clearly developed as a technicway because it is opposed to the folkways and the mores. There is no inclination here to pass on the merits or morality of large families or small families; of having children or not having children; of birth control or no birth control.

The point is that our behavior is that of the technicways which have been developed to meet needs or adjustment in a new world in which technology has made the conditions which have set up new standards of need and survival for the individual.

Technicways of the man-woman relationship. Concerning man and woman, there are contrasting folkways and technicways. In the folkways, marriage was the joining together of two lives in a permanent union, sacred and indestructible; and the relation of husband to wife was often more that of patriarch or master to servant. In the modern technicways, marriage is more of a mutual relationship of emotional and sexual appeasement, social and economic sharing, and sometimes separate careers; with divorce as the way out in a world where women are no longer "dependent" economically, and where divorce is not a disgrace. In the older days, woman's place was in the home, love and marriage were woman's career, and her associations were her family, the church, and with other women. In the modern world, the woman is assumed to be an individual: she can marry or not as she prefers; she may have a career with or without marriage; and she has increasingly broader associations with men and with women.

The old mores and taboos of sex were strongly fixed, with courtship under close supervision, with women in seclusion, with women's fashions, both in the home and in such public activities as gymnastics or mild athletic games such as to obscure the body. In the modern world, courtship is much less formal and is carried on with relative freedom, and there is an increasingly larger freedom of sex relationships.

In earlier days, "nice" women did not smoke and drink, since both habits were taboo, while today it is estimated that women smoke more than men and the number of women alcoholics is increasing. Books on etiquette treat such subjects as good form in drinking and how to handle a drunk date. Popular magazine articles present subjects such as "How to smoke with abandon and kiss with restraint." Superficially, the sophisticated woman of urban civilization bears little resemblance to the frontier woman. Again, in the earlier time there were many false ideas concerning menstruation, with the result that women's activities were limited, whereas in the modern world, owing to increased medical knowledge of gynecology and personal hygiene, menstruation is considered a normal function which does not isolate a healthy woman from normal activity. Where once it was considered "immoral" for a girl or a woman to work in an office with a man, now there are several million such women and many more millions working in other fields than the home and the school. We are not at this time interested in which is the better world, the new or the old. What we do know is that the society today, in regard to women, is different—and we know why.

Technicways of rural and of urban life. The new world made by the technicways can be illustrated by contrasting the earlier rural agricultural economy with the modern urban industrial economy. For whatever else may be true, an urban world is a different world from the rural. Some of the differences may be mentioned to indicate the radical nature of changing needs. Thus, in the early republic, there were relatively few people, of great homogeneity and similar interests, sparsely settled in rural areas, a mutually self-reliant and neighborly people, who worked in the simple, primary occupations and who had little money, the wealth being primarily in private fortunes and land, and in stores and other small enterprises. Over against this is the concentration of millions of people in dense areas, of great heterogeneity and diverse interests, engaged in hundreds of secondary occupations; and wealth is in large individual fortunes and corporate investments.

Whatever else may have been true, the people originally lived close to nature and the land, moved through primary institutions and simple self-sufficing living, worked with animate labor of men and animals, whereas in the new world they know little about nature, have fewer children and fewer community associations, become impersonal "yes men" in the urban-industrial world, move on artifical levels of life, change standards and values. It is a new world which affects all the main ways of behaving and the technicways of urban-industrial society arise to meet its needs.

Folkdrama as an illustration. To illustrate a contrast in behavior between the old rural and the new urban society, we may take the case of what may be called the folk drama. In the old days, amusement was either home- or community-produced; and there was participation by a part of the community in the give and take of cooperative effort, the devising of ways and means of staging, and the final community enjoyment of the presentation. This is in contrast with, let us say, the folk dramas of Walt Disney, as they have been called, which involve hundreds of production devices and mechanical details; twenty-four pictures are produced for each second of the audience's watching time; 8,000 instruments, musical and otherwise, are required, and 1,100 colors can be used. There is a representation of nature and animals presented as no nature and no animals ever were on land or sea; and, translated into many languages, millions of people all over the world find them a happy release from workaday lives. What has happened is that all this has been attained through the artistry of the intellectuals, involving high salaries for many people and the gadgets of technology. What has happened further is that the new folk drama is more for the spectator than the participator and it has been transferred to the moving picture rather than to the little theater, which, while still important, is largely the work of small groups of intellectual folk.

The technicways of war. Again, whatever else may be true, there is a new world of war and war fear on a scale never approached in the history of the human race. New inventions have changed the nature of the problem of survival. The technicways have made a new world of blitzkrieg. Bombing of cities, with their concentrations of industry and people, their hospitals, schools and churches, makes war more terrifying and speeds its tempo. The killing in mass slaughter of women and children becomes the new technicways of survival. And the nations, in order to survive, but against all the folkways and the mores of society's best values, not only devise, but use whatever new weapons of destruction, may be available. In the atomic bomb may be symbolized the whole range of terror technicways which have literally made a new world, not only of work, but of organization and government.

How the technicways grow. Perhaps the simplest and most effective way to study the rise of the technicways would be to catalogue the folkways of the several institutions, then to note what science and technology have done, and then to catalogue the resulting technicways. Thus, in the home and family, what were the folkways and mores of women's place in the home, of children and their nurture, of marriage and divorce? Then what happened in the way of new economic opportunity, of science and discovery in biology and medicine, of new inventions and new educations and new education for women? Then what were the new ways of women outside the home and in?

In religion, what were the beliefs, the ways of worship, the ways of Sabbath observance and the general "morals" that are associated with religion? Then what new knowledge of biology and anthropology changed the profile of faith? What necessities changed the Sunday laws and what did the automobile do to church going?

In the everyday world of modern civilization the résumé of the new technicways requires a continuous cataloguing. In industry, for instance, what were the folkways of the primary occupations of personal relations between employer and employee? Then, what happened in the way of big business, corporations, and what were the technicways of absentee ownership, corporations, labor organizations, strikes and picket lines?

And so for the great body of technicways that have transcended the folkways in the prevailing modes of life; there are folkways and technicways of advertising and propaganda; of urban life and customs; of children and old people; of the old private philanthropy and the new public welfare; of old moral exhortations and the new expediencies. . . .

3. *State Civilization*

The Nature of Civilization [1947]*

W*hat is the relation of civilization to culture?* We come now to inquire into the nature of civilization as an advanced stage and a specialized technical level of culture. As society grows more complex, evolving from the earlier culture grounded in the natural-folk-regional environment, into the more advanced stages of civilization, its understanding becomes more difficult. But the study of contemporary society must be primarily the study of such civilization. In so far as the study of civilization is a continuation and extension of the study of culture as the essence of human society, it becomes a study of the most advanced and most technical level of culture. To that extent, civilization is a specialized development of society distinctive from either the earlier folk cultures or the totality of all cultures. Civilization is culture, but not all culture is civilization. Nor is civilization, as the supreme technical societal product of cultural evolution, comprehensive enough to provide for all the elements necessary for culture to reproduce itself. Culture, therefore, is the supreme generic value, perennial, growing, and maturing, in contrast to the flowering and decay of the technical aspects of civilized society. From these premises and on the basis of the assumption that modern society has too much civilization and not enough culture, or that civilization as an end in itself destroys society, one of the chief objectives of the sociologist's efforts to understand society may well be the attainment of a better balance between culture and civilization. In terms of the previous assumptions concerning culture and the folk society, the most enduring of all societies would be that in which the folkways coincide or are in balance with the stateways, and in which both are reinforced

* Chap. 15 in *Understanding Society: The Principles of Dynamic Sociology* (New York: The Macmillan Company, 1947).

by the technicways of modern civilization. In modern society we seek balance between the co-existing elements of folk culture and state civilization.

Civilization needs new analysis. In order to explore these assumptions further, two tasks must be accomplished. One is to define civilization as definitely as possible, and the other is to contrast civilization with culture in such general ways as will contribute to our understanding of both. In the preceding chapter some of the meanings of civilization have been anticipated in order to emphasize certain meanings of culture. Yet it is important to recall that civilization and culture are generally utilized as interchangeable terms, and civilization has been visualized as not only in contrast with barbarism and primitive society, but as the highest goal to which mankind aspires. European civilization was long idealized as the richest flowering of Western culture. Then, in the thirties, Hitler's Germany was characterized as barbarism in an age of civilized man. Beginning in 1939, a good part of the civilized world swept into such combat that Germany not only was destroyed but also other European and Asiatic peoples wherever they came into the paths of civilized war. Manifestly, therefore, there are new needs and new opportunities for defining civilization as it comes to grips with the society of the future which seeks peace, survival, and continued progress in the place of war, destruction, and regression.

The folk society in contrast with the state society. Earlier we found that the folk society as distinctive from the state society or civilization, is, in a world of variables, the natural societal constant through which the survival, development, and growth of all societies have been attained. The folk society, then, is the norm, the mode, the point, on the one hand, from which we can search back into the origins and development of societal factors, forces, and processes, and, on the other, from which we may be able to find a meeting place between modern technological civilization and the surviving folk society. In this meeting place the marginal values or measures of societal survival would be found.

The distinction between folk culture and civilization is especially conducive to continuing the usual procedure of this volume of presenting some of the natural aspects of the theme. In the present case, the folk culture is posited as the natural culture, growing inevitably out of the struggle for harmony between men and land, and between conflicting forces of nature or of other human aggregates. We have called culture as "natural" as are the laws of nature since it always grows up and out of the natural environment. Thus, every unit of cultural development, every stage in the widening range of folk culture, every societal problem, has what may be called a natural history which must be understood in order to comprehend the meaning of the problem. This is the basis upon which the *folk culture* has been characterized as natural, as opposed to *civilization,* which has been characterized as technical, scientific, or mechanical, and, to that extent, artificial. The folk culture is natural, too, in another sense: it is capable of reproducing itself in contrast to the technological civilization which is a composite of artificial achievements functioning as ends in themselves. That these ends are often in fundamental conflict with many of society's natural needs could be illustrated, for instance, by the megalopolitan civilization in which the specifications for technical excellence in art and architecture, and the concentration of population, business, and transportation, sometimes preclude meeting the requirements for population reproduction, or enjoying the experiences of primary groups or the realistic rapport with nature.

Dictionary definitions. As with most words, the meanings of the term *civilization* have been largely derived from popular usage, although scholars also follow such usage in loosely applied analogies. Thus, if we fall back upon the conventional definitions, as given in Webster's New International Dictionary, one meaning of civilization is "advancement in social culture." Or, it is "a state of social culture characterized by relative progress in the arts, science, and statecraft."

Again, civilization has been defined "as the culture characteristics of modern Europe." Or still again, it has been "the relative advancement of a primitive people." A common summary of these concepts is that "civilization applies to human society and designates an advanced state of material and social welfare." Now in each of these meanings, civilization always represents, from the functional viewpoint, a specialized type of society seeking special ends in themselves rather than the over-all, comprehensive function of society to reproduce, enrich, and strengthen itself through a normal process of action and interaction. So, too, in everyday life, civilization has been synonymous with refinements, comfort, convenience, luxuries, leisure, with the development of organization and institutions as ends in themselves. So much has this been true that the great mass of common men everywhere have been characterized as uncivilized, whereas the cosmopolitan, urban intellectuals have represented civilization. Thus, for instance, many of the literati and intelligentsia of the last generation were accustomed to speak of people as being civilized in proportion as they had refinement in the drinking of liquors, of the cooking and eating of food, in the avoiding of the dung heaps of work close to nature, and in their capacity to attain personalized ends through exploitation of nature and the folk. This was well illustrated by the sayings of the notoriously popular Count Keyserling in his visits to America and his extraordinary selection of Virginia and New Orleans as the two types of civilized living, the one for its artistry in drinking and the other for its foods. Then, too, the brilliant H. L. Mencken contrasted the civilized manners of the "Old South" with the crudeness of the "New South." Oscar Cargill, in his *Intellectual America: Ideas on the March* referred to "that supercilious attitude toward the struggling masses of mankind which denies to their efforts any importance."

These concepts were accurate reflections. Now, it must be clear both from the reading of literature and from an understanding of the aims and ideals of education and the humanities that these characterizations have been accurate. Europe *was* civilized and America was *not.* The urban society *was* civilized and the rural *not.* The educated *were* civilized and the uneducated were *not.* New York and Washington of the 1940's were civilized, but America in the early days of the founding fathers and of frontier development was not civilized. Paris was civilized, but William Allen White's Emporia, Kansas, was not. Or, in terms of American personages, the Astors, the Vanderbilts, the Goulds were civilized, but Walt Whitman was not. Or again, in Europe a Rousseau or Froebel or Pestalozzi was not. Vienna represented the romance and magnificence of an old civilization, but the villages of Denmark and Holland only the folk culture. The blitzkrieg was a product of modern civilization, fabricated of science, invention, technology, power, totalitarianism. The co-operatives of the small democracies were only cultures of the folk.

A fivefold characterization of civilization. The elements and attributes of modern civilization may well be studied through a five-fold classification which reflects both the time levels and the achievements of contemporary society. First, there is *urbanism* and *urbanization* in the societal sense of a great process of specialization, concentration, and achievement. Next there is *technology,* including industrialism, that approaches technological determinism, in which science, machines, organization, set the pace and the quality of modern life. There is, then, *intellectualism* in the sense of cultural specialization and scientific humanism as supreme measures of value. Powerful alongside these are the trends toward *centralization* and *power.* And finally, this centralization and power, reinforced by technology and specialization, flowers into the *totalitarian state.* Then we have characterized civilization in a general way as being *artificial* in the sense in which technology and machines transcend the primary ways of living.

Now manifestly, the achievements of such civilization have been phenomenal. In these ends men have attained what they have sought. They have sought civilization and they have found it. In the light of powerful premises being supported more and more by scientific research, by conclusions of scholars and publicists and pointing more and more to the next steps for societal reconstruction, this civilization without the balance and leavening processes of folk culture destroys society. On the basis of such premises we must explore more and more the question as to whether the civilization which mankind has been seeking is the goal which, with a wider knowledge and a more mature understanding of society, mankind wants after all.

Contrasts between civilization and culture. In order that we may inquire more critically into these assumptions, it is important to continue a little further with the contrast between civilization and culture in terms of a functional sociology, which seeks not only an understanding of how societies grow, but also the way of survival for advanced culture in human society. We have already emphasized that folk culture is natural in the sense that it represents a capacity for optimum or successful achievement for each organism within the framework of its physical environment and its inherent endowment. On this assumption, the folk culture as compared to civilization is always self-perpetuating and enduring, having within its own power the capacity not only to reproduce, but to evolve into different stages of development. Culture, then, is of the folk, while civilization is of the state. Culture is what Giddings called the composite society, capable of reproducing itself, while civilization is the constituent society, seeking arbitrary, specialized ends of a limited nature. Culture is the supreme means for the development of society, while civilization represents an end in itself rather than a means to an end.

Culture a cumulative heritage; civilization a cross section of societal achievement. Culture represents a fundamental social process and societal means, whereas civilization connotes social products and material technical ends. Again following the analogy of nature, culture represents growth, development, evolution, survival, whereas civilization represents material progress, achievement, revolution, and decline. Culture represents the people, democracy, human striving and personal and individual opportunity, whereas civilization connotes more of the machine, the mass, and the class. Culture is youthful, ideological, informal, realistic, and is of the essence of the spirit and soul of mankind, whereas civilization tends toward the intellectual, the organized, the technological, the utopian, the mechanical. Culture grows from the bottom up, whereas civilization is superimposed. Culture represents the broader, societal determinism, whereas civilization reflects the technical determinism. In terms of the areal society and of the time levels, culture represents the community, the rural and agrarian basic background, the primary groups, as opposed to civilization, which focuses upon urban attainments, the industrial order, secondary groups and megalopolitan patterns of the nation and of the empire. In still other comparative terms, culture is organic, reproductive, reinforcing as compared to civilization, which is functional, stressing production and exhaustion. Culture represents the optimum quality value as compared to civilization, which reflects the maximum in quantity and money and in power. Culture if measured in the time levels and culture stages, tends to be moral, purposive, highly motivated, whereas civilization is scientifically technical, specialized, highly stimulated. Finally, in general, culture is a cumulative heritage, applicable to all stages of societal evolution, whereas civilization represents a cross section of advanced progress.

Sociologists and writers characterize civilization. How most of these characterizations of civilization may be found in the work of earlier sociologists and later writers may be seen from an examination of *Special and General Readings* in *The Library and Workshop*. However, we shall illustrate some of the characterizations of civilization by a few samplings. We begin with the last, first, namely, the artificial character of civilization. Lester F. Ward, for instance, observes that what we call civilization "is due almost exclusively to the increased proportion of the artificial over the natural objects in contact with man." Indeed, he makes this proportion of the artificial over the natural a measure of civilization, which he defines as "the artificial adjustment of natural objects in such a manner that the natural forces will thereby produce results advantageous to man." Ward went so far as to imply that the artificial is superior to the natural. William Graham Sumner points out that the adjustment of society, which we call civilization, is a much more complex aggregation than the culture that went before. With reference to the influence of civilization upon earlier cultures, he calls attention to the fact that the virtues and arts of civilization are almost as disastrous to the uncivilized as are the vices of civilization. He thinks it is really a great tragedy of civilization that the contact of the lower with the higher is disastrous to the lower. We have already pointed out how this was true in the case of the American Indian, and the record of civilization in its impact upon primitive peoples has been consistently so. There are other characterizations of civilization as artificial. Clive Bell says: "Civilization is artificial. Civilized man is made, not born: he is artificial; he is unnatural." In much the same way, George A. Dorsey in *Man's Own Show: Civilization* speaks of civilization as "an extranatural super-organic, artificial burden."

Civilization is urban. Perhaps the most common characterization of civilization is that of maturity in urbanism. In Chapter I on the rise of the city, the urban character of modern civilization is discussed in more detail. At this point only a few contributions to the vast body of opinion on urban living are necessary. Howard B. Woolston in *Metropolis* calls attention to the fact that cities are the focal points of our civilization, in which are concentrated the forces that control modern life. Carol Aronovici, who has specialized in the study of the modern city, points out that "Civilization is inseparable from urban living. Without cities civilization is inconceivable." So much is this true that he goes so far as to insist that only when the whole of this country becomes entirely urban shall we have achieved full civilization. Earl E. Muntz, in *Urban Sociology,* senses the trend of modern civilization when he points out that the crowding of human beings into a limited space calls for new mores and customs in response "to the need of this more highly artificialized environment of which the modern city is the extreme type," which is similar to Spengler's noted dictum that in the place of a world there is a city which is enriched while the rest dries up. Muntz remarks that "in the civilized world of today culture is constantly becoming more and more city-dominated." Adna Ferrin Weber, in his monumental study of *The Growth of Cities in the Nineteenth Century,* points out that all the social forces which go to make up civilization are the phenomena of the great cities like Memphis, Thebes, Nineveh, and Babylon: "Indeed, in classic antiquity, the identification of city and civilization becomes complete." He calls attention to the fact that both *civilization* and *city* originate from the Latin word *civis.* Frederic C. Howe, in *The Modern City and Its Problems,* concludes that the city has always been the center of civilization. "Civilization does not exist among a nomad people," he writes.

Civilization is state society. An interesting appraisal of civilization centering around the state is that of John Storck in *Man and Civilization:* "Civilization is a form of culture characterized by a sedentary population grouped around the state as the central institution." At the present time, he thinks Western civilization could be designated by seven main characteristics, namely, natural science, mechanical invention, the national state, the historical attitude, mass education, democracy, and individualism. Another similar viewpoint is that of Carl J. Warden, who says, in *The Emergence of Human Culture,* that a civilization supposes the existence of a centralized political state. Franklin H. Giddings, as mentioned [earlier], pointed out how the first stages of civilization are reflected in the term *civis,* and said that the rise of civilization began with the transition from the ethnic to the civil at the point where the functions of sovereignty, commerce, labor, defense, and organization transcend those of folk society. The distinctions between civilization and culture are vividly emphasized by Spengler, who held that every culture has its own civilization, the civilization being the inevitable destiny of the culture; this conception is in line with the previous appraisal of culture as reproductive, growing, living, and dynamic as opposed to civilization as artificial. Spengler points out that when once the aim of culture, whether a specific culture or a general culture, has been attained, the culture suddenly hardens; it mortifies, dies, and becomes civilization.

Civilization is technological. We have already called attention to the fact that the technicways characterize modern civilization more than the folkways and the mores, which is another way of saying that civilization is technological. This technology comprises not only machines, science, invention, but also organization, administration, management. This technology, therefore, includes social technology as involved in the products and organizations which have grown up through the Industrial Revolution. The new reach of science and technology as measured in their application to modern society through the use of invested capital is practically synonymous with civilization itself. [This can be tested] further by examining the impact of such technology upon the individual and his institutions and by an analysis of the social problems which arise from technological progress.

The individual and civilization. [Later] the relation of the individual to all of society is discussed. It is sufficient to say here that the role of the individual is distinctively different in the modern urban, technological civilization from what it is in early evolving cultures. Contrary to what is sometimes assumed, the role of the individual in the modern world is more important, not less important, than formerly, and in many ways an individual, through means of minority control, communication, and technology, may exert a greater influence on total society than ever before. Perhaps sociology has not given enough study to this important phase of understanding society.

Civilization is intellectual. . . . Perhaps the most dynamic of all the aristocracies is that of the intellectuals, who sometimes become so specialized in their own limited fields and so far removed from reality and the people that intellectualism in this sense may well be said to be the most potent of all the attributes of civilization. This appears to be an amazing conclusion and it calls for definite evidence. Another way of stating the case is, by way of analogy, to say that some of the most active of all the elements of civilization are specialization and intensification of interests and of the scientific and humanistic culture that tend toward what may be called, in an exaggerated sense, intellectual totalitarianism. The quality of the mind that pushes toward perfection, toward higher standards of living, when overconcentrated on a single objective or isolated ways and means of attaining an end, contributes toward intellectualism.

In the case of individual intellectualism or perhaps scientific humanism the situation is similar to that described by William James concerning the institutions. Most institutions, he thought, by the nature of their technical and professional administration, end by becoming obstacles to the purposes for which they were founded. An individual may use his wealth to endow institutions of public welfare but, when profits become an end, through ruthless exploitation of resources and men, the situation develops into the opposite of service to humanity. So, an individual may seek election because he feels he has something to contribute to democratic government, but, when elected, if his lust for power becomes supreme, his usefulness to society is ended. So also, when an exclusive cult of scientific human-ism or of technocracy tends to impose upon society an artificial measure of science or mechanized standard of living or the "rule of the gadgets" of the super-technological society, civilization is again symbolized in terms of artificial demands that become superficial as well.

AMERICAN AND EUROPEAN CIVILIZATION

The sociologist is not interested here in the question of which type of artificial demand may be more modern, aesthetic, comfortable, "civilized"—or even which is "better" or "worse" as a mode of advanced personal living. He is interested primarily in the societal values which are measured in terms of the surviving, growing society. There are innumerable illustrations of what is meant by these attri-butes of civilization. Samplings may well be selected from American culture, from the culture of pre-Hitler and Hitler Germany, or from the culture of Paris or Vienna, or the way places of specialized culture. There was, for instance, a notable company of American literati who, so tired of the life of the United States and so impatient of its crude folk culture as not only to sell it down the river but to discard it for their own society on the banks of a beautiful river in Europe. Now in terms of culture and civilization, the main question is one which asks what they contributed to society, either to the French culture or as a disillusioned company slipping back to an American culture whose new meaning was already being foreshadowed long before World War II, as something much more dynamic and vital than a decayed European culture. Franz Alexander in *Our Age of Unreason* diagnoses much of American society's maladjustment as resulting from the conflict between early frontier society and the new rationalizations. Oliver L. Reiser in *The Promise of Scientific Humanism* discusses the credo of a faith in the exclusive potentiality of man's intelligence. This is in contrast to the assumptions that man cannot live by intellect alone, as reflected in the earlier American classical writers—Whitman, Whittier, Emerson.

So, too, a society whose leaders at the Capital of the nation frankly and openly ridicule the institutions and ways of the people under the guise of liberalism reflects a new individualism as marked as the early American rugged individualism. So long as the great mass of people swear allegiance to their institutions of the family and church and work, such leaders typify a leadership destructive of that society. These illustrations are not examples of moral issues as to the right or wrong of individual behavior or what for the individual may be most aesthetic, advanced, or "emancipated," but they are measures of what happens to society when certain things are done. They are preview questions concerning what civilization does to human society.

Intellectualism and scientific humanism characterized. The premises of what may be called intellectual determinism are well documented in the United States. There are two main viewpoints: one in which humanism or pure intellectualism is seen as the best way on in modern society, and the other in which the limitations of pure intellectualism are appraised as one of the chief hazards of civilization. Representative of the first is the verdict of John U. Nef in *The United States and Civilization* who features "trained authority" as a key value. This "can be obtained only by giving the wisest, the best endowed, the best trained, and the most disinterested philosophers, theologians, writers and artists a prestige and power of leadership that our American civilization would now make it difficult for such persons to obtain even if they existed." In the same vein was the urgent appeal of one of America's foremost humanists in the 1920's to the president of a great university. What this humanist begged was that this particular university stand as the bulwark against the encroachment upon its curriculum of the social sciences and of coeducation which was so detrimental to the higher cultures and education as reflected in that university. Representative of the critical school of thought is the verdict of Oscar Cargill that the intelligentsia have been "contemptuous of the struggling, troubled democracy." His verdict was that "the intelligentsia—all types and kinds—lived too much out of the world to instruct the world in much of anything. Just as German scholarship did nothing to save Germany, so our intelligentsia have done nothing for us." So, too, Ralph Turner in *America in Civilization* gives a challenging warning against the "intellectual aristocracy" who hold that only the "intelligent" should be allowed to vote. Others point out the fallacy of these premises as demonstrated in Greece, in Rome, in Spain, in Germany, and in France.

Hitler's Germany was reaping the whirlwind of science and intellectualism. Destruction of European culture cannot be attributed entirely to softness and corruption, as is often argued, but also to a high peak of artificial, technological civilization. For consider the German science and intellectual philosophy which increasingly concentrated on the ruthlessness of science and nature and the moral quality of Hitler's translation of all this into a new civilization which was clearly the product of science, technology, and superrace humanism. The intellectuals who paved the way for the Hitlers and Himmlers, the scholars who dried up the classics, the industrial leaders and financiers who threw in their vast resources, the scientists who prostituted science for specialized political ends, the philosophers who destroyed the folk spirit, the geopoliticians whose planning would have exploited world resources, and the Junkers who made use of all of these—all were the forerunners of the Nazi civilization that destroyed German society.

American and European civilization again. Once again, when we undertake to test the premises of the rise of a folk culture and its expansion into civilization, the American society as found in the history of the United States provides an excellent laboratory. For, as we have pointed out many times, the frontier culture from its beginnings in the seaboard states through its ramifications into the Northwest, the Southwest, and the Far West, affords case study for the transition from culture to civilization. In this society, which began with the culture of the American Indian and continued through the extension of the frontier, and, in the last part of the nineteenth century, the development of cities and industries and great individual fortunes, together with a phenomenal increase in science, education, and art, may well be found an excellent field for the understanding of human society.

4. Folk Sociology as a Subject Field

Folk Sociology as a Field for the
Study of Society [1953]*

Folk sociology undertakes to provide a basic subject field[1][†] for the historical study of total human society in process and for the empirical study of group behavior in interaction.[2] It is primarily a general sociology on the level of a social theory constructed in the framework of societal continuum with a body of propositions and a series of concepts adequate for scientific inquiry into the interacting causal factors of cultural evolution and the cumulative products of social change.[3]

The conceptualization of folk sociology as theory finds its genesis and development resting solidly upon real situations and continuing needs.[4] For, manifestly, some of the essential needs of sound sociological theory, now inseparably interrelated with scientific research,[5] may clearly be identified with a number of needs of contemporary science and society. These needs are reflected in trends and problems both in the development and integration of the behavioral sciences and in the demand for expanding knowledge for understanding contemporary society and for resolving the critical ideological problems of modern civilization.

THE NEEDS OF SOCIAL SCIENCE AND SOCIAL THEORY

With reference to the social science situation, one need is for the definition, identification, acceptance, and clarification of funda-

* "Folk Sociology as a Subject Field for the Historical Study of Total Human Society and the Empirical Study of Group Behavior," *Social Forces,* 31 (March 1953), pp. 193-223.

† Notes and references start on page 346.

mental interconnected concepts and conceptual schemes,[6] adequate for the construction and application of sound social theory. This is basic both to the minimization of conflict and confusion among individual scholars and the several interrelated disciplines that make up the group of behavioral sciences, and to the approximation of a more unified theory and methodology susceptible to interdisciplinary effectiveness without sacrificing the fundamentals of each discipline. This means that the scheme of concepts and their interrelations will provide basic premises and working formulae for testing hypotheses and for insuring continuing observations. A special aspect of this need is somehow to equate in perspective the data of historical and descriptive sociology with those of controlled observation in concrete situations. This may be, on the one hand, a problem of systematizing the powerful classical contributions in the framework of hypotheses to be tested, or on the other, of utilizing and integrating the works of history, literature, philosophy, law, into the total fabric of behavior study. This involves the utilization, with equal effectiveness, of the facts of relationship and the facts of item.[7] This may well involve the problem of identification of theories of fact and normative theories; or it might involve a problem of fact versus a problem of value.[8] A corollary would be the assurance that the tools and techniques used are matured and fully tested and that objectivity is not merely subjectively determined by agreement among teams of researchers upon unproved postulates or tools or methods that may be so specialized as to be isolated from the total situation.

An over-all need therefore is to construct special social theory which will discover fundamental assumptions about the data and methods of studying total society that will be useful in meeting the stated needs through application on several levels. Of these levels, one of the first is to insure adequate analyses of the changing structure of human society in process and in transitional periods in contrast to the common assumptions and analogical applications of traditional concepts of natural evolution or the oversimplified linear theories of universal progress.[9] This implies the discovery and identification of societal variables, such as technological and cultural factors, alongside the societal constants, such as the folk culture, inherent in the concept of human behavior as an entity. This means that mankind is the crucial societal constant in society, even as the natural environment and biological heritage of human beings are relatively constant basic factors.[10] Conant accepts the premise in his twofold minimal commitment for the practical student, namely "a sharp cleavage between animal behavior and human conduct," in "relation to some large pattern of events."[11] This does not mean that other sciences are not to continue in their unprecedented discovery of new facts and relationships in non-human situations, but that for sociology, the study of man and his society *now* is the supreme scientific task at hand.

On another level, but closely connected in sequence, the need for understanding contemporary society and human behavior better than we have ever done is more urgent for the very reason that the traditional social and moral order is now in competition with the expanding technological order. This task of coming to grips with the world of advanced civilization implies a major objective of understanding the cumulative achievements which have their fruition in the most advanced civilizations and of clarifying the resulting numerous and complex societal problems of adjustment, crisis, and survival in the framework of accelerating social change.[12] Here again, an essential corollary is the task of achieving continuous orientation in transitional society through the study of social groups and comparative societies in such areal and special situations as may mature the ecological and regional approach to the understanding and adjustment of a changing societal structure unprecedented in both speed and extent.

All this implies a more realistic science of society and more basic subject fields accurately delimited but comprehensively integrated. Building upon these needs, upon some of the earlier sociological theories, and upon the more recent contributions of interdisciplinary studies in sociology, anthropology, psychology, and other behavioral sciences,[13] folk sociology assumes certain new directions and concepts that may supplant those which, applied to earlier societies and historical successions, have proved inadequate for understanding total society and for guiding civilization in the current and future world situations in which complex interactions between human society and technological order multiply so rapidly.

FOLK SOCIOLOGY AS A SERIES OF INTERCONNECTED CONCEPTS

Manifestly, although such a folk sociology will necessarily have many facets in order to be consistent with the promise of sociological theory and scientific method and with the identification and integration of interrelated fields, the first task will be to delimit and test its unifying principles if the subject field is to qualify as basic. And we approach this task in the frame of reference of closely interconnected major and minor concepts basic to the conceptualization of the subject field.[14] For the role of concepts in folk sociology will be little different from that in general science which Conant has recently defined as "an interconnected series of concepts and conceptual schemes that have developed as a result of experimentation and observation and are fruitful of further experimentation and observation."[15] For folk sociology, our interconnected series of concepts and conceptual schemes have grown out of both long study of the historical process and social theory and more recent limited empirical observations of group behavior. These concepts, however, give promise of being fruitful of further observation and testing.

With reference to the concepts basic to folk sociology, our need is to define and identify them in such ways as to comprehend both major premises and smaller units of interrelated testing fields, rather than to construct over-specialized individual concepts, not integrated with the total field of inquiry. To this end many of these concepts lend themselves best to definition and identification in closely interrelated pairs, as for instance, culture and civilization, folk and state, the moral order and the technological society.[16] Sometimes the concepts are approximately coordinate, as in the case of science and technology; sometimes they appear as opposing dichotomies, as in the case of folkways and technicways, but always in mutual interdependence of definition and illustration in somewhat the same way in which a major concept is often defined or identified in terms of other concepts, themselves closely interrelated as elementary factors in a cumulative formula. Some of the concepts appear as new in terminology and some relatively new in arrangement but all are assumed to be soundly bottomed in authenticated premises from basic sources.[17]

Assuming a general definition of sociology itself as the scientific study of human society to be the first essential for the framework of folk sociology and its special concepts,[18] logically the first pair of major concepts would be the objectives of sociological study, namely *society and human society,* and the second would be the more particularized facets, *group and group behavior.* Others follow: *social interaction and social process;*[19] *culture and civilization;*[20] *folk and mass; status and role; folk culture and state civilization,*[21] *technicways and the technological order; institutions and the moral order; the regional structure of society,*[22] *social change and social progress; social values and social survival; cultural lag and achievement lag.* Inherent in all of these, the *social situation* is crucial to both the generalization and particularization of such mixed concepts as *social systems.*[23]

Of the minor concepts, many are component interacting factors so closely related to major concepts, that they are clearly an integral part of the total definition. Such is the case, for instance, with *science and invention, urbanism and industrialization, intellectualism and cultural specialization, centralization and power,* all of which are clearly component conditioning factors in the concept, *state civilization.*[24] The *state civilization* and *folk culture,* as paired together, are the main contrasting polarities in the basic *societal continuum* which comprehends also *uniformities, universals, successions, cycles, rhythm and flow of societal evolution.* The *folkways* and *mores* are basic foundations for *morals* and *morality,* while *technology* is basic to the revolutionary *technicways* of modern man. The *stateways* are inseparably related to both the genesis and development of the *power structure* climaxed by *state civilization* and *totalitarian social control.* In the cumulative societal continuum, *mechanization* and *secularization* assume[25] an increasingly powerful and well nigh universal role in the interconnected concept of *social change.*

DEFINITIONS AND IDENTIFICATIONS OF CONCEPTS

Now we define as many of our concepts as clearly as we can and we identify others with interacting situations and interrelated concepts. We recall that so little is known scientifically about human behavior and social process that we do well to approximate, as a first step, even as many of the greatest discoveries in science have had their genesis in trial and error, with approximation and hypotheses to be greatly revised. We recall that in many of the most revolutionary scientific hypotheses and in the learned expositions presenting them, the common approach was "it seems likely that," "it is probable that," "it seems reasonably certain," "in some way which is not yet clear." So, too, definitions of major concepts must often be in terms of minor or closely related concepts. For instance, Sumner never defined "folk" except in terms of folkways and mores, but he set the incidence for later anthropologists such as Murdock and Lowie to give new empirical meanings to *social organization* and *social structure*. For practical purposes, therefore, the *identification of concepts with other related concepts and special situations sometimes proves to be more effective than attempting abstract definitions.*[26] So, too, most definitions require an elementary dichotomy of an over-all generic or abstract meaning and a particularized identification with actual reality or specific situation. To the extent that many key constructs, such as are assumed in folk sociology, can be defined best, or only defined, in terms of the cumulative development of the theme in hand or through the testing of postulates and premises inherent in the problem, no quick, oversimplified definitions are effective. In such concepts for instance, as folk culture and state civilization, conceptual definitions emerge through the examination of attributes, through illustrations from actuality, through identification by contrast or with situations or processes, and through testing back to the first premises. Such was the case in the classical treatises of Sumner's folkways and mores, Tylor's and Wissler's culture traits, Darwin's evolution, Freud's psychoanalysis, and the cumulative definitions of culture being integrated by the anthropologists, sociologists, and psychologists.[27]

THE CONCEPT OF GENERAL SOCIOLOGY

We identify folk sociology as a subject field for the study of human society within the larger concepts of sociology as the science of society. We must, therefore, come to terms with the concept of sociology as a social science, since for the sociologist "science" *is* the science of society.

Sociology itself has had many definitions and illustrates well the dichotomy of a general over-all definition and a special particularized identification. Thus, following the general pattern of a hundred earlier definitions selected from conventional texts, sociology is almost universally accorded the general abstract definition of "the science of society"[28] or "the scientific study of human society," in which immediately the concept of "society" must be defined. But sociology is also the study of societies or of comparative society, or the study of human groups, or the study of social relations as the product of interaction. Immediately then, the component concepts of group, social relations, association, and social interaction must be identified as constituent parts of the definition. The more recent definitions of sociology as the study of how men live together in groups illustrate how *society* is the composite abstract concept and the *group* is the particularized constituent unit concept. Or, if sociology be defined as the science of institutions,[29] institutions must be defined; then, if institutions be defined as organized and unified patterns of folkways and mores,[30] folkways and mores become the key elementary concepts to be defined and identified.

The difficulties in the way of attaining accurate satisfactory general definitions of sociology, however, need not deter us from accurate limited definitions or identifications any more than is the case of the distinguished heritage of countless definitions of "science" itself. The fact that it requires a ten-volume encyclopedia to catalogue the technical terms and definitions of one branch of chemistry and its applications does not negate the necessity for a general definition of chemistry; nor need the fact that the newer specialisms of ecology include oceanography and meteorology confuse the main definition. Kroeber and Kluckhohn itemize 164 definitions of culture and refer to perhaps 150 more in fragmentary notes.[31] The usages reflected in these 300 or more concepts of culture do not preclude the usefulness of the authors' "central idea of culture now formulated by most social scientists."[32]

THE CONCEPT OF SOCIETY

Even more clearly than the term "sociology," the major concept of "society" illustrates the essential dichotomy of general and particular with interrelated facets of conceptual definition basic to social theory. For the term "society," in its general and abstract meaning, is broad enough to comprehend the whole of human association and social organization in total spatial and temporal sequences and the whole historical continuum of social systems and sub-systems. Yet it is particularized enough as "societies" to comprehend the associational relationships of thousands of groups of primitive man, early and late; of thousands of contemporary race and ethnic groups; and the sixty nationals that make up the fabric of the 1952 United Nations, connoting equally the extremes of the U.S.S.R., with an area of 8,598,679 square miles, and a population of nearly two hundred million people, and Luxembourg with an area of only 99.8 square miles and less than three hundred thousand people.

The concept "society" is particularized enough to apply alike to the folk society and the mass society, the one in which the individual is closer to his group and where there are more approximations to solidarity and cohesiveness, uniformities, and cultural values, loyalties and face to face association, and the other reflecting the isolation of the individual from his institutional moorings. Yet for folk sociology, civilization itself is a key concept in the identification of culture as not synonymous with civilization or as the antithesis of civilization, as Redfield puts it. More concretely civilization is a specialized technological development of culture. Again the general concept of society as being the total over-all framework of association within which cultures are created and developed illustrates the need for the clarification of the three general concepts often inaccurately used interchangeably—namely, society, culture, and civilization. The assumptions of a main distinction between culture and society are clearly inferred in the conclusion of Kroeber and Kluckhohn that cultures vary in different societies; that we have no "theory of culture," but only concepts, the variation of which is of crucial value; but that we do have theories of society on the associational level.

THE CONCEPT OF CULTURE

Once again, the concept of culture lends itself easily to a dichotomous definition as general and particular in two ways. First, culture is the sum total of the cumulative processes and products of societal achievement. The majority of scholars include the cumulative factors, while process is the core of Alfred Weber's and product of von Wiese's culture concepts. Civilization is a particularized form of culture denoting a cross-section of the most advanced and specialized technological and material achievement of human society. Society in turn is the constant medium in which cultures germinate and grow. On the other hand, culture is more particularly identified with special qualitative attainments of the group including "explicit and implicit patterns of behavior transmitted by symbols." It is also identified with values and the equipment of the individual in which the process of learning is inherent, with the essential core being traditional or historically derived. Hence the relatively new concept of *personality and culture* becomes inseparably related to the fundamental processes of *social interaction,* another key concept in folk sociology, closely interconnected with *status and role.*

SOCIAL PROCESS AND SOCIAL INTERACTION

For folk sociology, perhaps, first of all, provides a group construct in the frame of reference of social process, social interaction, and social change. The study of social processes and social interaction therefore is essentially a major inquiry into practical knowledge of social reality. Here again the definitions of social process conform to the dichotomy of a general process "summarizing the interaction of the elements of the situation" and the special processes of interaction through which social relationships mature. The first comprehends also the universal processes of nature reflected in the orderly ways of development in physical growth, in cycles of seasons, in time-space relationships, in the natural laws of physics, chemistry, biology, and other sciences. So, too, the general meaning of process is identified with the "historical process" and the evolutionary process. On the other hand, the concept of social interaction comprehends many special processes, as for instance the process of communication or the process of cultural adjustment to technology. Not only numbers of individuals interact with each other in such ways as affect their development and behavior, but, social groups have utilized the same processes under different situations to give rise to different problems of adjustment and institutions, and consequently different patterns of culture as equivalent products of the same general human process.[33] For, the total social interaction includes that between individual man and nature; human groups in interaction with the total natural environment; interaction of the individual with the group; interaction of cultures with other cultures; interaction between groups and their total cultural environment; and especially between folk cultures and technological forces and mass configuration.[34]

Social change in its broadest sense assumes the continuities and uniformities of time spans and successions and of constants and variables in a continuum from earlier folk cultures to later state civilizations comprehending the most advanced stages of cultural achievement. In its study of social change, folk sociology distinguishes between those universal changes that reflect the logical and constant processes of what is usually termed natural evolution and those specific variables of extraordinary revolutionary technological and other environmental factors which so reshape man's institutions and behavior as to constitute "a new world." Folk sociology therefore does not confuse cultural evolution with organic evolution as some "generalized magic force that does the work of the concrete individual factors that shape the course of history."[35] Yet cultural evolution and organic evolution are inseparable interacting and parallel processes in two main ways. First, in so far as the formula of heredity's interaction through variation, adaptation, and selection applies to the biological and psycho-physical aspects of man, cultural evolution needs no repeal of "natural laws." In the second place, cultural evolution manifestly needs no repeal of the laws of nature as embodied in science and the scientific process which applies to whatever is involved in cultural evolution as orderly processes of change.

SOCIAL CHANGE AND SOCIAL PROGRESS

Folk sociology assumes the interaction of many causal factors rather than a few independent causes. It differentiates between the logical interactions of organic evolution in process and the variables of external changes. As relating to the over-all study of social change and civilization, it assumes the constants of folk culture in interaction with the variables of technology. As related to the empirical study of comparative societies and of acculturation processes in the impact of technology on folk cultures, it assumes the constants of technology in interaction with the variables of folk cultures. As related to the general process of social change and social progress, it assumes a continuum from the folk culture to the state civilization, with relatively stable balance in the interaction between the two in transitional stages of development, as fundamental to adjustment, growth, survival and progress, rather than cyclical inevitability or linear processes of universal progress. Patterns of decline and decay commonly assumed to be universal and inevitable have been the products of lack of balance and failure to adjust to the variables of social change. These can be tested through the study of individuals, families, communities, small groups, and also in composite larger cultures and civilizations.

For folk sociology the concepts of social change and social progress involve factors on at least two levels to be added to traditional definitions. In the first place, due to the revolutionary discoveries of science and the unprecedented sweep of technology, a new core is inherent in social change in the identification of that which is new or different from all the folk cultures that have gone into this architecture of modern civilization. In the second place, due to the alternatives which face man either to change and/or adjust to these revolutionary changes or to change himself and his society, the whole concept of progress must be re-examined.[36]

HOW DIFFERENT IS CONTEMPORARY CIVILIZATION?

First, with reference to what might be termed irreversible changes, the answer to the question, how new is the world? at any given stage of cultural development or different periods of time and civilization, implies more realistically, how different is this contemporary society from what has gone before? How different from earlier periods of the same civilization or culture? How different from other cultures that are contemporary? Or, again, how does the most advanced stage of cultural development, which in the twentieth century we call state civilization, differ from all the constituent epochs and cultures that have been woven into its fabric? Insofar as advanced state civilization is different, how did the difference come about? Was change itself the genesis of the differences and are the differences such as to change the main traits and structure of the new world?

Or still again, how does civilized, technological society differ from early, simple, rural folk society? Or, how different is the contemporary Western society of the second half of the twentieth century from the general civilization called Western culture of a century or two ago? Or, again, how different is the American society of the United States from that European society which was called "Western culture?" Or, how different is American culture from what it was in its earlier formative stages of development and as late as a century ago? How different is the society of the United States from that which produced the earliest American Indian cultures in more than a thousand folk regional cultural areas on the continent? How different are the societies of the South American republics from their earlier and contemporary folk forebears or from the Spanish civilization of the early conquerors? Or, how different is western civilization from the classical and Hebrew cultures, and how did they differ from the early ethnic folk society that went into the moulding of those cultures? How different is western culture from the great oriental cultures of the historic past and the living present?

NEW MEASURES OF CHANGE

The answers to these questions, as reflected in actual measurements and universal consensus, clearly indicate that both the accelerated process and the astronomical quantitative measures of social change are such as to challenge the classical concepts of progress and to require new and continuous orientation to the needs of modern civilization. By the same token most of the earlier political and philosophical explanations of social change as a phenomenon of slow moving cultures evolving slowly over long periods of time are not effective or definitive in cases of quick change or mass breakaway from traditional powerful norms; nor do they afford realistic bases for internalizing new directions, for insuring the stability needed for survival, or for renewal processes in postcatastrophic eras. In the literature of the past there have been an extraordinary amount and range of theory, philosophies and "scientific" assumptions of cyclical evolution in historical civilizations and of continuities, uniformities, and universals in cultural development. Until recently, prevailing concepts of social change, on most levels, appear to have been oversimplified assumptions of linear inevitable movements toward universal progress; or abstract formulae of change from "primitive" man to civilized society; or primarily organismic evolution of man and society, analogous to all organic evolution. Manifestly, however, both the urgency of understanding current processes and trends and the accelerated rate of change in a technological civilization, different in tempo and range from the earlier slow moving cultures, require new ways of diagnosing and identifying the nature and the extent of newness and differences in social change. For the earlier theories, except for conceptual background and analogical approaches, are worth almost exactly nothing for understanding and direction in many of the crucial situations of contemporary state civilization.[37]

CONVENTIONAL INFERENCES OF PROGRESS EXPANDED

The concept of social progress again may be defined in the general and specific dichotomy. First, there is the oversimplified etymological inference of simply a general orderly process of moving forward and therefore of measured stages in specified directions. With reference to the oversimplified concept of orderly going forward, there is progress *in time,* which is inevitable in the universal process of succession. *Progress in space* reflects the amazing spectacle of making the world immeasurably bigger through added conquests and the use of air and earth and sea, yet also smaller through transportation, communication, speed, and all the other technologies that eliminate space. *Progress in quantitative achievement* is symbolized in the whole incredible catalogue of scientific discoveries and inventions. By the same token, *progress in the quality of achievement* may be symbolized by a thousand attainments in medicine, transportation, security and safety, and in the upper brackets of human achievements. Yet, for the sociologist it is *progress in the sum total of human achievement and welfare* that is exclusively important.[38]

The particularized concept of progress is identified with the fifth aspect as catalogued above and is crucial in the societal continuum from the folk culture to the state civilization. First, social progress, therefore, is essentially a measure of change in the direction of societal survival and development in which balance and equilibrium between folk culture and the state civilization give continuity and stability to the constant evolution of human society. Social progress implies, therefore, the mastery of forces both natural and societal in the framework of societal arrangements which insure the continuity of human development. The implication of this in contemporary civilization, assuming the characteristics of one-world society, are of the greatest importance in the study and planning of the sort of societal and political arrangements under which an all-world society may be developed. This gives a new interpretation to democracy as a societal arrangement in which all demotic units, including individuals and minority groups, may have freedom in the places where they live and in interchange with other regions and areas where balance of resources and technology may guarantee the widest possible range of freedom and development. More comprehensively, social progress may be defined as the mastery of physical and societal factors and forces and the resulting societal order which insures the continuity of human and societal development through processes and organizations which conserve and develop and give opportunity and representation to each demotic unit in society whether individual or group.[39]

THE HUMAN GROUP

Among the inseparably interrelated concepts which provide equations for both understanding and directing society, three especially require continuous definition and identification. These are, first, the associational field unit, namely, the group;[40] second, the areal and spatial field unit, namely, the region; and third, the cumulatively processive product which we call culture. These again are interrelated to the concept of social systems which again is, of course, identified in varied facets of the larger concept of society. Thus, as the group concept becomes increasingly basic to the definition of sociology as the science of the structure and function of human groups, we need to orient our group concept not only to the interdependence and interaction among members but to the interdependence and interaction of groups themselves in the greater interdependence of world groups that compose the total contemporary society. Such orientation necessitates the identification of special group meanings susceptible to observation and to structural and functional analysis of society.

There are three special identifications of the group, utilized in folk sociology and conforming to the common definitions of the group as an entity in which a number of people function interdependently with each other on the level of association. The three are the primary group with face-to-face contacts and primary institutions; the larger collectivist group such as the mass urban aggregation; and the "small group," categorized because it has been more recently posited as a special technical constituent unit of society most useful as a laboratory for controlled observation and experiment. The primary group is the core of societal genesis and development and is identified with the folk society[41] which is basic to the evolutionary dichotomy of folk culture and state civilization. In the concept of total culture as the cumulative sum total of the processes and products of societal achievements is found the particularized concept of the folk as the creators of culture which sociologists commonly describe as the product of group life.

STATUS AND ROLE IN SOCIAL SYSTEMS

The folk society also reflects the closer identification and the inseparability of the individual with the group and is basic to the more recent emphasis on personality and culture.[42] In contrast to the folk society, civilization brings to focus the frustrations and pathology of individuals isolated from primary associations and from the feeling of belonging to the group. Folk sociology seeks to identify all these phenomena in group observations or in individual case studies, as well as in mass manifestations recorded in the history of many societies. Or we might emphasize the inseparability of the individual from the group by noting the findings of empirical studies to the effect that for most individuals their position and role, their satisfactions, and their welfare constitute the first core of experience and motivation.[43] The powerful sensing of the "I," the "We," the "Me," and the "Us" reflects a revivification of assumed status in folk culture. Millions of mothers with their first born; millions of youth seeking first values; millions of articulate unadjusted peoples of the East and Near East and of a thousand transitional folk cultures of the world, constitute the new and dynamic laboratories for studying personality and culture in relation to folk societies. Inherent in the folk culture and identified by contrast in the state civilization is the relative stability of role, status, and position—concepts that are relatively new in sociology's conceptual schemes but assumed in the structure and function of group interactions which emerge into systems of folk societies.

Although the conceptualization of *status, role, position, class* and *caste,* in relation to the broader concept of *stratification,* is generally considered to be relatively recent in sociological theory, the situations basic to the concepts are so fundamental that they are assumed to be organic and relatively simple in the structure of folk societies. The structural dichotomies of men and women, elders and youth, in- and out-groups, together with kith and kin, familial relations, solidarity, loyalties, and group and individual value concepts are such as to constitute the core or main fabric of culture. Status and role, together with interacting situations which create institutional modes of control and value systems in behavior, are simply natural component units inherent in the total structure and function of the relatively simple community or social system of early societies.

Stratification evolves primarily in two ways. One is in the growth and expansion of a folk culture to a larger complex society with the multiplication of situations, roles, divisions of labor inherent in industrial and urban communities. The other is when one or more folk cultures are introduced into a larger civilization of "melting pot" proportions or when two or more cultures come in conflict by imposition of conquest or the impact of technology upon the folk culture. In both instances stratification is essentially a dynamic process of transitional society, and the concept becomes increasingly important as a measure of change and a medium of analysis. Fundamentally, stratification, therefore, is not so much identified with moralistic-legalistic orientation, as has been so frequently the case in recent sociological conceptualizations, as it is with the problems of differentiation, multiplication, complexity, and integration in mass civilization; or with the dynamics of individuation and socialization in the frame of reference of scientific study of resemblances and differences and of the special psychological study of the behavior of adjustment, frustration, integration, norms and deviations.

THE REGIONAL AND ECOLOGICAL STRUCTURE OF SOCIETY

Yet a part of the essence of the culture of any society is inherent in the areal and spatial delimitation or identification of the group, both in any cross section of contemporary society where groups must have their living space, or in the continuum of societal evolution with all its variables in time and space as reflected in the historical structure of man's total cultural heritage. The folk-regional society, as the culture group within a definitive area, thus becomes the basic ideal type and the smallest unit for the complete study of society, as opposed to the lesser units of the family, the community, or the special small group, all of which may be deficient in the elemental factor of time, total geographic or ecological situation, and complex ethnic structure.

Folk sociology approaches the complex interrelationships between the temporal and areal and the cultural interactions through the special fields of regionalism and ecology. Regionalism, which, as a tool for cultural, spatial analysis, is sometimes identified with world ecology, in the current concept of "one world" society, is defined here as an areal-cultural concept providing a multiple structure approach to special spatial and temporal cultural situations in relation to total cultural configurations.[44] With reference to the functional definitions of regionalism, it is necessary to re-emphasize the fact that the primary objectives of regionalism are found in the end product of integration of regions more than in the mere study and development of regions themselves. Always, regionalism is a two-way concept. The region, yes, but primarily the region as a composite unit of the whole. The regions are studied and planned to the end that they may be more adequate in all aspects of resources and culture; yet regionalism itself is primarily interested in the total integration and balance of these regions. Spatial and cultural generalizations are also correlated with the time element in some such stabilizing processes as are reflected in the ecological adaptation of man to geographical areas. For the dynamics of folk sociology, this definition must also provide concrete regional delineations which take into consideration the organic human-culture regional areas, the geographic factors of situation and climate, the political factors of organization and control, and the more recent technological aspects of communication and atomic potentialities.

Human ecology is identified with the biological concept of ecology as the adjustment of an organism to its environment.[45] The increasing application of ecology to the adaptation of cultures to the human habitat and to the analysis of the role of the natural environment in shaping cultures necessitates a better integration of the two special fields. Both ecology and regionalism are essentially functional in analyzing the structure of society, in the identification of interaction processes, and in the action concept of social planning. This means we must re-examine many of the situations which re-emphasize the importance of the regional equality and balance of man. One is, of course, the world situation of international relations and achievements of science in the modern world. There can no longer be, in the accepted patterns of world order, isolation, separatism, exploitation, with wealth and abundance in some places and poverty and scarcity in others.

For, on the other hand, there has never been a time when the individual and group were so dynamic; when the distinctive folk personalities of the peoples of the world clamored so much for recognition, appreciation, and participation; and when role and status clamored for identification with both the total and particularized situation.

It must be clear that the one undebatable strategy that is needed now is somehow to equalize opportunity and to redistribute resources to the end that we may have a genuine regional equalization and balance of men, instead of the powerful conflict of peoples in nationalistic and economic competition and war. The answers to these situations will be found in some major strategy which provides opportunity for each region to produce wealth and use it wisely within its own domain; yet, at the same time, it provides ample opportunity through technology and communication for the movement of people and resources to and from the region and provides opportunity for achievement outside as well as inside the region.

INSTITUTIONS AND THE MORAL ORDER

For folk sociology the paired major concepts of institutions and the moral order are not only basic to the structuring of any theory of process in a societal continuum but illustrate the interdependence of interacting causal factors in societal development and social change. For, in the first place, social institutions are the logical outgrowth of the mores as matured[46] folkways ripened through folk wisdom and control into morals and morality which then become formalized in what Talcott Parsons calls the institutional structure of a social system[47] which is the "totality of morally sanctioned statuses and roles which regulate the relations of persons one to another." But perhaps even more important, consider a half dozen elemental, constant, causal factors in the shaping of culture and the conditioning of behavior, namely sex, religion, work, learning, control, personal interaction in group relations, as the major social institutions have risen to meet the social needs to these elemental forces through the family, the church, the school, industry, the state and the specialized, composite, voluntaristic agencies and organizations of community. For the primary institutions not only had their genesis and development in primary folk groups, but they reflect areas in which the most revolutionary changes have taken place in the transitional processes from folk culture to state civilization. And both the social changes and interacting roles can be measured and identified in controlled group observations in conceptual schemes to check back to evolutionary principles and processes. Thus, urbanism reflects the changed community; industrialism, the changed forms and function of work or division and role of labor; the complex structure of education and intellectualism reflects the multiplication of interaction processes; the powerful state reflects the extension of power and group control; the modern family with the changed functional man-woman ratio reflects a major deviation from earlier group behavior; and finally, secularization reflects not only a relatively uniform transition from the sacred to the secular but a mechanistic pattern of adaptation to the modern technological order.

The changed social institutions of civilization and the predominance of the technicways (defined later) over the folkways and mores, reflect the accelerated trend toward the new morality of the state civilization as it evolves in the technological order as opposed to the moral order which characterizes all growing group societies. The nature of the new morality will be defined subsequently in the further identification of the several concepts basic to folk sociology as described in this preview. Suffice it to say here that the basic morality in the past has evolved from the folkways and mores in the sense that *social values* accrue through the folk wisdom of the human processes of interaction, as guide to survival. With reference to the moral order,[48] Redfield's main distinction between civilization and pre-civilization is that of the "technical order" and the "moral order," in which he assumes that "all the other forms of union which appear in human societies may be brought together and contrasted with the moral order under the phrase 'the technical order'." Also, "in the technical order men are bound by things, or are things themselves."

SOCIAL VALUES AND SOCIAL ATTITUDES

Closely identified with institutions and the moral order as the core of the folk society and of all developing human societies is the concept of social values. The situation is not so simple as merely to distinguish between a concrete problem of fact and a problem of value. Rather it is a problem of continuing diagnosis of the processes and products of total interaction. Here again we need to define the concept in the dichotomy of a general composite meaning of societal or group norms and a particularized identification with attitudes and action of individuals and groups. The sociologist posits no value judgments in his premises and primary objectives. Values and attitudes are what the group and individuals make of processes, products, and situations, essentially culturally oriented. But the very existence of norms, ideal patterns, institutions, and moral order reflect the general meanings of value as evolving through the maturing processes and products of social interaction. On the positive side there are values inherent in what men want or have to take; on the negative side there is the goal of survival and growth. The folk morality, as the product of the search for values in the fruition of group consensus, has constituted a sustaining background for testing selective processes in which are found the balanced elements of emotion, the width and depth of loyalties, and the rationalization of social change. The core of the concept of social values is found not simply in what the people want or believe but in the roles and relationships which interacting factors and situations play in the total processes of societal survival and development. The selection and articulation of survival values, through group consensus and action, are reinforced by the rich primary personal attitudes, on the one hand, and the primary institutions, on the other. Thus social values are not identified with what is good or less good, what is bad or less bad, in abstract definition, but in terms of situations which affect normative society and continue to challenge survival.

For folk sociology, normative values are defined in terms of processes and achievements whose objectives reflect the results of orderly progress from earlier stages of culture to survival and stabilization in advanced civilization, attained through balanced equilibrium between the folk culture and state civilization.[49] On the other hand, contemporary social attitudes reflect the cumulative processes of interaction with the accelerated changes inherent in the modern technological order, in which the technicways become norms of value in the selective process as reflected in human society's capacity for adjustment and consequently for survival and "progress." This is a normative extension of both the biological and societal concept of survival value as measures of the usefulness of adaptation.

CONTINUING TASKS OF DEFINITION AND IDENTIFICATION

We have now identified enough of the related key concepts basic to understanding the interrelated factors of social change and cultural evolution, on the one hand, and group behavior, on the other, to enable us to proceed further with the remaining tasks of our preview of folk sociology as realistic sociological theory relevant to the understanding and mastery of the contemporary world of human society. Our next task is, then, that of attempting to describe the total contemporary situation which we have identified as the state civilization which is the most advanced cumulative product emerging in the powerful polarity process of changing from that which is primarily folk culture to that which is primarily state civilization. A second task is to define and identify further, in the general evolutionary order of their genesis, the interdependent concepts basic to the main premises of these assumptions. A third task is to identify the societal continuum somewhat further in the framework of its total inferences including the continuity of the future as well as the past. A fourth task is clearly to identify and integrate, in the continuum as social facts, the powerful body of propositions embodied in the great literature and philosophies of the historical process insofar as they describe processes, products, and values which have been relatively constant and powerfully coercive throughout given societies at given times and insofar as they constitute a body of knowledge connoting universal traits and trends. A fifth task for the preview is to identify the abundant sources of both historical and theoretical study and of empirical inquiries, on the one hand as documentation, and on the other, as promising premises for further observation and experimentation in folk sociology. Finally, we need to point up some of the applications of folk sociology to the ongoing of contemporary society and to catalogue some of the special areas and projects of research for the further testing of assumptions.

THE STATE CIVILIZATION

Now we come to identify more fully the concepts of the folk culture and state civilization and the interconnected concepts in somewhat the conceptual order in which they appear in the continuum. We begin with the most advanced complex society of the mid-twentieth century world we live in, which may best be characterized by the concept *state civilization,* as comprehending the total traits of the most advanced technological and organizational society in a continuum which has its genesis and constant growth and survival processes in the contrasting *folk culture,* which in turn is symbol of the close-knit societal integration of all growing societies. The major attributes of state civilization, symbolizing the secularization of the folk culture, appear to be fabricated primarily of five main pairs of interconnected minor concepts, constituting threads so thoroughly interwoven in warp and woof as to make a clearly defined and powerful pattern of human relationships. The first of the pairs is *science and technology.* The second is *industrialization and urbanization.* The third is *intellectualism and cultural specialization.* The fourth is *centralization and power.* The fifth is *totalitarianism and the super-state society.* Each of these is fabricated of still other weavings of many minor designs.

Interwoven with science, instrumentations, and technology are unprecedented achievement, process and product of invention, speed, technics, standardization, mass communication, atomic power, lethal tools of war. Interwoven with industry and urbanism are the machine economy, the assembly line, production and abundance, stratification, a new way of community living, an extraordinarily high standard of living, and great concentrations of people, industry, wealth, and art. Interwoven with intellectualism and cultural specialization are scientific humanism, existentialism, psychological obsolescence, intellectual and moral directives, the concept that the intellect is the supreme guide for living, the popular prostitution of science, the standard of living as a chief index of social values, the idealization of the consumer economy, and undreamed of contributions in creative art and literature, science for science' sake. Interwoven with centralization and power are bigness, concentration, mass organization, the power structure of control, the depersonalization of the individual, limitless production, efficiency like a miracle. Interwoven with totalitarianism and the super-state are collectivization, regulation and secularization, coercion with ruthless power more relevant than human liberty and with force as a living ideal. Needless to say, all these are inseparably related in an indescribably rich fabric of human achievement beyond the earlier dreams of men and constituting a continuum of interaction processes in the loom of societal development.

The *state civilization* is sequel to and an extension of the universal *folk culture,* the two constituting the main currents and levels of cultural development in the universal societal continuum from early folk society to late state society. The folk culture is also fabricated of a number of threads with their multiple qualities of interaction between the folk and nature, between the folk and their own cultural environment, and between the folk of one culture and of other cultures. The concept of "folk," as subsequently defined, is identified with process, on the one hand, and traits or character, on the other. First, the folk culture is identified with nature with reference to natural laws, time, climate, geographic environment, close to the soil. Folk culture is further characterized by primary relationships and institutions, kith and kin in ethnic relationships, and primary occupations. The folk culture conforms essentially to rural and religious institutional character, reflecting primarily the solidarity of a moral order.[50] It is essentially institutional, deriving its social character from unit societies that mature their folkways, mores, and laws into cultures reflecting love of liberty, loyalities, homogeneities of structure with the individual inseparable from the group. The folk culture is closely knit, cohesive, nonorganizational, with behavior primarily spontaneous, personal, traditional, yet strongly integrated through its institutional growth and moral order. The folk society is thus essentially in contrast to the state society, the one geared to nature and to ethnic and moral structure and the other to technology and to civil organization and specialized structure.

In contrast to the folk culture, where behavior is characterized primarily by the folkways and mores and by the solidarity of institutional character and sacred traditions, the state civilization is characterized primarily by the stateways and technicways and the consequent secularization of culture. In the folk culture there is gradualness of change with the usual corollary of cultural lag,[51] in which material progress seems to exceed cultural change, while in the state society ideological conceptualizations greatly accelerate the rate of change with the resultant achievement lag in which the cultural and ideological specifications are in advance of material ways of achieving the specified ends.

Keeping in mind that both folk culture and state civilization are "ideal types"[52] or mental constructs of which no known pure examples can be cited, both of which occur in the social character of every society, we note that society changes from the folk culture to the state civilization when quick moving technological innovations exceed the slow developing traditional culture patterns and when the mode of mass behavior is reflected in the secularization of culture within the framework of stateways and technicways which are in conflict with and subversive to the folkways and mores. Such a state civilization, flowering into its complex attainment of technology, industrialization, urbanization, intellectualism, cultural specialization, organization, centralization and power, tends to assume the nature of a technological order rather than a human society or a moral order such as has been assumed as the universal constant in all growing human societies.

FOLK AND MASS

In our characterization of the folk culture, we have identified the folk with all growing societies. The folk reflects essentially the universal constant human interaction process in a world of societal variables. The folk process in human society is analogous to the universal laws of nature. It is a sort of social denominator of human societal phenomena. In contrast to the mass, this folk symbolizes human society's process in the framework of a given time, areal, natural, and cultural configuration, possessing and conscious of a common heritage and constant traits which result from the incidence of the folkways and mores of group behavior in a universal pattern of human survival and growth. The common heritage and the constant traits are identifiable, both in terms of their structure and function and in contrast to the heterogeneous and changing traits of a mass behavior in the state civilization.

The mass, then, in contrast to the folk, is the composite of multiple societies blended into a total cultural configuration of great heterogeneity, without a common heritage and with rapidly changing traits resulting from the incidence of the stateways and technicways of individual behavior in new and powerful patterns of secularization, mechanization, specialization, power, and coercive societal pressures, and in the framework of universal emergency, achievement lag, and conflict. These traits are identifiable both in terms of structure and function and in contrast to the common heritage and constant traits of the folk.

CULTURE AND CIVILIZATION AS CONTRASTING CONCEPTS

It follows, therefore, that culture and civilization, commonly paired together in earlier concepts are not the same at all. Culture,[53] as the way people live in identified areas, times, and settings, is the sum total of cumulative processes and products of societal achievement. It reflects the social or institutional character of society but is not society itself. Civilization, on the other hand, is an advanced state of culture, representing maximum material, organizational, technological, and artistic achievements. The folk culture grows up naturally within the folk society. The state civilization grows up logically within the framework of the technological, organizational society, dominated by the state society. Both the culture of the folk and the civilization of the state are processes and products of societal achievement, the nature of each being conditioned by the kind of society within which it grows, and by the predominating traits of behavior, which are respectively folkways and mores for the folk society and stateways and technicways for the state society. Insofar as the concept of the folk reflects the interaction of people with nature, with each other, and with other people, the folk become the creators of the folk culture. Insofar as the state and technology reflect the interaction of the people with organization and technology and with each other and world peoples, they are the creators of the state civilization. This was true of the great historical civilizations, as well as of modern contemporaneous society, the difference being in degrees conforming to the specifications of each civilization.

The folk culture stems from the folkways and mores as conditioning social forces. The standard William Graham Sumner concept posits the folkways as the habits of the individual and the customs of the group that have risen over long periods of time largely from non-identifiable sources to meet needs and to survive in normal early societies. The mores, then, are the matured folkways that have been sanctioned through continuous long time process of trial and exploration and have come to assume the nature and power of folk wisdom.

Out of the mores grow the stabilizing morals and morality, precursors of the more formal institutions. From these processes the special sociological meaning of morality or morale may be constructed as a voluntaristic pattern of societal pressure. In terms of time process, therefore, morality can mature only over considerable periods of time. On the basis of this explanation, the decreasing role of morality in contemporary civilization is explained, not in terms of right or wrong, good or bad, but in terms of quick changing customs and behavior which we characterize as technicways, or the ways of a technological civilization and basic to technological culture. This is elemental for both understanding and directing contemporary civilized world society. The technicways, as habits of the individual and customs of the group to meet needs and to survive in the technological secularized society, transcend the folkways and supplant the mores in processes accelerating the rate of societal evolution. Both because science and technology are neutral and nonmoral and because the technicways arise through them quickly from known sources and have no backward or long experience, there is no longer, in the pure technological order, any primarily moral order in the core of state civilization, whose behavior is primarily in terms of technicways.

From morality or morals, which are the co-existent processes and products of the folkways and mores, the next step is the evolution of institutions. Social institutions[54] are agencies and organizations, taking on the nature of more formalized sanction by society than the mores and moral pressure, for the purposes of insuring the specifications of the mores and morality, of achieving order and stability, and for serving as buffer between the individual and social change. Thus each institution grew up to meet composite needs as prescribed by the mores and in the framework of ever increasing social change and complexity. Such social change, then, reflected not only the general process of universal growth and development that occurs everywhere in nature, but also change in social structure that arises because of basic innovations and complexity which evolve through science and technology and the interaction between the people and their ever-changing environment. Social change itself must be posited as a universal constant, setting the frame of reference for continuous adaptation and adjustment.

THE STATE SOCIETY AND POWER STRUCTURE

From morality and social institutions, adequate for voluntaristic control in relatively homogeneous societies, the next need in the social continuum was for some covenant or more formalized and legalized control or sovereignty, created by the folk but vested in a single institution. Thus the *state* grew up as the special cohesive institution to meet special needs for protection, for increasing services to the people, and for enforcing uniformities and stability of desired behavior. The state was thus a means, as clearly as ever were the folkways, mores, and the other institutions.

Hence, next, there grew up the stateways, which have been described as the folkways of the state, but carrying with them inherent power of penalty or coercion. The stateways, however, evolved logically through the folkways and mores and were the instruments of the people as means of control. Nevertheless, in the state and stateways were the beginnings of the phenomenon of *power* which came to denote the capacity and facility of a few to control the many, of the minority to control the majority, of a part to dominate the whole, of the dynamics of artificial control. Thence the natural development was toward centralization which came to denote the concept and practice of substituting large centralized administrative control and management for local government and community priority of participation and representation as reflected in the folk society. When the state, utilizing the authority vested in it by the folk, consolidated power and centralization to coerce the other social institutions and to control the basic activities, behavior, and resources of society, totalitarianism arose and became the power symbol of the state civilization, which embodies and formalizes the cumulative processes, products, and traits of the technological, organizational order, negating the priority of the processes and principles of human freedom.

THE INTERCONNECTED PROCESSES OF CIVILIZATION RE-IDENTIFIED

With the breakaway from the folkways and mores and institutional modes of behavior, the secularization[55] process gains momentum until the secularization of all the institutions themselves becomes a chief mode of social change. By secularization we mean, in somewhat oversimplified terms, the quick and relatively complete adaptation of behavior and institutions to the current demands of contemporary situations in contrast to conformity to the traditional patterns and processes. Here the extension of technicways inevitably leads to the secularization of the family, education, work, worship, government and the community, following the continuum from folk culture to state civilization.

Coordinate causal factors that appear constant in the later development of the continuum from folk culture to state civilization are industrialization and urbanism. Industrialization is identified with the accelerated process of change from the simple, self-sufficient rural culture to the industrial community which is generally identified also as the first and most momentous change as a way of life in human communities. In later successions industrialization came to be identified with the change from agricultural and rural dominance to industrial and urban concentrations in which farmer and laborer were contrasted in a sort of constant polarity. Industrialization, then, was the first elemental causal factor in the rise of urbanism and the process of urbanization which is identified with the concentration of industry, capital, people, the professions, art, and technological advances in civilization and as the beginnings of centralization and power. Coordinate again as elemental causal factors in the acceleration of industrialization and urbanization were mechanization and assembly-line processes, which not only facilitated the flowering of industry and urbanism, but are identified in the radical change of agriculture, rural life and institutional behavior through the mechanization of agriculture and home life through the completely different structure of production through the assembly line, technological specialization, and instrumentation.

INTELLECTUALISM, CULTURAL SPECIALIZATION, AND ACHIEVEMENT LAG

From the search for causal constants in societal process it seems clear that the accelerating intellectualism of man is easily identifiable as both the distinguishing trait of civilization and the genesis of many of the most revolutionary aspects of social change. This refers not primarily to the great minds whose contributions have been called the makers of modern civilization; or to the great intellectuals who have always been synonymous with Greek civilization; or to the power trinity of Marx, Darwin, and Wagner in Western civilization about the time of the industrial revolution.[56] More specifically, intellectualism is identified with the technical products of scientific discoveries and their use as they flow from the work of the best minds in science and the laboratory; the wider and more exclusive uses of intelligence; also the multiplication of ideologies, moral directives, and planning conceptualizations, and the taking over, absorption, and action programs by the mass man who seeks to implement knowledge, skills and ideas in the structuring of civilization. Process and product of all this is cultural specialization approximating the dimensions of the assembly line in the economic and material culture. Tests for the effectiveness of intellectualism and cultural specialism are peculiarly abundant and challenging in the resultant transitional society which emerges as another type of constant wherever there is imbalance between the old and new, the folk culture and state civilization, or where the interaction between diverse cultures and causal factors are changing the structural and functional aspects of a blending societal process. The measures and illustrations of these will again be found in the technicways and achievement lag.

As the extension of power and centralization of the state and the achievements of science, invention, technology, contribute to an ever increasing complexity and bigness of society, with its urbanism and industrialism, its mechanization and assembly lines, and its cultural specialism and technological determinants, the folkways and mores exercise a progressively decreasing role, in comparison with the technicways which are antagonistic to the folkways and mores and subversive of the traditional culture. In transcending the folkways and supplanting the mores, the technicways negate the old order of cultural evolution and accelerate the rate of societal change. As the new modes of behavior in technological civilization, the technicways, subject to control by neither folkways nor stateways, tend to result in quick changes, mass confusion, and what may be termed achievement lag[57] in which the upper levels of culture ideologies outrun the defined specifications for attaining the desired ends and hence the capacity of society to achieve results commensurate with reality. This is well illustrated in what the population scientists call the demographic lag and in the situations in many backward cultures where communications and ideologies have changed the cultural ideals but have left the low economic and living standards in powerful lag. The chasm of distance and bottlenecks between the folk and maximum technological achievement are greater than in cultural lag.

THE SOCIAL TECHNICWAYS AND SOCIAL PLANNING

Here again, it is important to emphasize the fact that in conceptualization of the technicways as determinants of behavior and measures of social change, there is no assumption of moral bias or value judgment of good or bad. The end results may be measured in terms of norms or values but in themselves the technicways have no more nor less moral value than science and technology. If the technicways supplant the folkways and mores, which are no longer adequate for control, and if no stateways have developed, or if the stateways of power usurp the processes of folk culture, then there will be problems of adjustment. It may well be, however, that the social technicways in the form of social planning, will be the answer, to accelerate development and to harmonize conflicting forces. Social planning conforms to the technicways specifications insofar as it is contrariwise to the old folkways of individualism, is subversive of the *laissez faire* traditions, and arises from known needs and technological changes.

CONTINUING INTERRELATIONS OF SCIENCE
AND TECHNOLOGY

Always basic to the great change reflected in the technicways and to the assumption that the most advanced civilization conforms more nearly to a technological order than to a human society are the dynamic forces of science, invention, and technology. Yet after the constant repetitive assumptions about them, even these require definition and identification continuously in the processive formulae of societal developments. Science, in general, is the discovery of truth, including the spirit and methods of inquiry, together with the resulting body of knowledge. Invention, in general, is the discovery of new uses of scientific discoveries as they are applied to devices, processes, or arrangements by means of experimentation, testing, and adaptation to specific ends. Technology is the joining of science and invention in the mechanical and organizational utilization of ways of doing things, including social organization. Technicways, again, then are the resulting modes of behavior in a technological society. Social technicways are the collective concept of social planning inherent in the assumptions of continuity and survival processes of adaptation.

If we anticipate inferences relating to normative science and society these definitions could be illustrated in the case of the atomic bomb. Science was responsible for the discovery of the elements, for the formulation of the theory, and for the processes which were basic to the production of the bomb. Invention was responsible for designing the bomb and for the specifications for its physical form and structure. Technology combined processes of science and invention with achievement through which the bomb was made and put to use. Technicways were responsible for the use of the bomb to destroy men, women, children, animate life and inanimate structure contrary to the beliefs, folkways, mores, and religions of people everywhere. The social technicways would provide strategy and societal arrangements for the banning of the bomb and other master instruments of destruction, thus utilizing dilemma, science, and human relations to reconstruct a new society characterized by a realistic and workable moral order in which atomic energy would be channeled as a very casual factor in the development processes of human society.

THE CONTINUUM AND TRANSITIONAL SOCIETIES

We return now to our first premises and repeated inferences that the series of interconnected concepts and the body of hypothetical propositions basic to the construction of a sound theory of folk sociology may be best systematized in the setting of a continuum adequate to convert the constituent units into a societal "unified whole." This is in conformity with the assumptions of the life sciences that the individuation of parts, supreme as constituent units, nevertheless must be identified as subordinates in the integrated whole.[58] For, just as the total natural environment in which human beings live is not only physical but cultural and the physical factors constitute the "necessary conditions" for understanding, rather than the determinate product of inquiry into culture, so systematic inquiry into social relations and human behavior comprehends first the total society, the full understanding of which, however, can be achieved only through the study of the constituent determinate groups. So, too, the concept of a continuum, featuring the polar extremes of ideal types of folk culture and state civilization, provides equally for the conceptualization of intermediate transitional types and multiple variables of the survival folk process which can be identified and located in the continuum of societal interaction. These transitional types occur constantly on the long road of human heritage and all along the numerous wide excursions into all the cultural hinterlands of time and space, of cyclical, linear or spiral progression, wherever and whenever societies in process of change reflect modification away from the culture with which they have been identified,[59] or toward cumulative acquisitions of their own changing cultures, or radical adaptations to new situations. The concept of transitional society is especially crucial in the current modern world where inevitable modifications are more numerous, more revolutionary, more accelerated, and more universal.

Although the transitional society is essentially an ideal type concept of process, the polar dichotomies such as folk and state, early and late, simple and complex, sacred and secular, rural and urban, *gemeinschaft* and *gesellschaft,* and others, provide a framework for realistic observations and for achieving balance and equilibrium essential to order and adjustment values in survival processes. Identified with balance between the integrity of the individual and the functioning of the group, the bio-social concept posits integration as the "primordial requirement for survival" but in which successful living depends on progressive development in both directions in proper balance.

HISTORICAL STUDY AND EMPIRICAL INQUIRY

Inherent in the concept of the continuum are provisions for the historical study and description of any society of the past when facts susceptible to controlled integration are available and also for the empirical study of any ongoing society in the frame of reference of concepts and methods constant for each selected inquiry. On these premises, inquiry into Japanese personality and attitudes of old or transitional Japan, or Chinese family power through the centuries, or the ethical values or oriental Indian culture, would not be projected in the frame of reference of Western psychological and moral concepts.

Nor would studies of rural mountain groups, wherever found, be projected in the frame of reference of specialized urban sophisticates no matter how advanced and excellent they may be for identifying many of the most relevant situations in megalopolitan civilization. Yet all of the millions of constituent societal units make up the total continuum, the time, spatial and cultural units of which require some such equivalents as the folk-culture constant for identification and integration. The total societal continuum, however, is more relevant for future constituent groups and transitional societies than for those of the past and present in such dichotomies as nationalism and universalism, primary group and mass society, regions and the one world concept, in which the very survival of society will be conditioned by balanced structure and function and by the discovery and utilization of integrating agencies.

THE SEARCH FOR UNIFORMITIES

Yet the urgency for effectual conceptualization for the future does not obscure its relevancy in being identified also with such broad and permissive meanings as to comprehend the total evolutionary processes as inferred in cultural development; the historical process as inferred in the cumulative story of human society; the main social processes of integration as inferred in institutional character and survival values; and in the accelerated technical processes of interaction as inferred in the kaleidoscopic configurations of social change. The very challenge that comes to modern man with the accelerated changes to which he may not be able to adapt himself and still remain in control of his main destiny is accentuating the need for reviewing and diagnosing the most and the best that he has done in the past.[60]

Perhaps no phase of man's unceasing efforts to understand his total society has occupied so large a place as his search for continuities and uniformities in social evolution and cultural development. And, of the special aspects of this search perhaps none has produced so large a body of literature as that of the cyclical, linear, and organismic concepts of the social and historical process. We do not need to undertake an appraisal of the long catalogue of theories and ideologies here to recognize the important place and the powerful influence which such theories have held in the literature of social thought. They constitute a fundamental unit in any undertaking to understand society, both to understand how scholars have tried to explain society and to clear the way for a more scientific understanding of contemporary world civilization viewed from current observation points and from its backgrounds and historical epochs.

FIVE CATEGORIES OF THEORIES AND INQUIRIES

Of the great body of literature seeking to record the history, nature, and destiny of human society, perhaps the greater portion may be studied under five categories: the great folk mythologies; the literature of organic analogies between man and nature; the literature of successions, cycles, and rhythmical repetitions of which Pitirim Sorokin estimated there are four main categories, namely, the cyclical, the creatively rhythmical, the eschatological, and the messianic; the literature of "progress"; and the more scientific attempts to explain social change. All of these then would be set over against the later and current attempts of anthropologists, sociologists, and other students of culture, to inquire into the uniformities and differentiations of cultural evolution as well as the literature of the social historian and philosopher seeking a scientific construct for history and a logic for philosophy and the humanities.

THE NEED FOR NEW THEORETICAL EXPLANATIONS

If the cyclical theories of socio-cultural change, the linear theories of the inevitability of cultural trends are no longer acceptable to any of the varied groups of students of society; and if the analogical theories are, for all practical purposes, completely rejected except as a part of a classical literature of social thought, what is their perspective in folk sociology and their role in the structuring of new social theory? What else besides these theories has been offered as supplementary theory and what as substitutes? What now needs to be gleaned from their magnificent remnants and what framework of continuities may be valid for the search after uniformities and universals? For whatever else may be said of all these attempts to explain the successions of human societies, they reflected serious efforts. They did constitute a rare body of literature so persistent and consistent in their insistence upon laws or trends of uniformity and universality that their conclusions became almost synonymous with social thought about the historical process.

Yet, as early as 1925, F. Stuart Chapin, writing of the collapse of the classical theories of universal stages in social evolution, thought that although the work of Boas, Lowie, Goldenweiser, Wissler, Kroeber, and others, had been of immense value in clearing the ground of obsolete theoretical structure, still "no constructive theory has been advanced to meet the need of a logical explanation of the larger processes of cultural continuity. Historians, archaeologists, sociologists, economists, and anthropologists have all at one time or another mentioned various significant elements of cultural change, but there have been few attempts to organize these elements into sets of related hypotheses which might be combined into preliminary outline of a tentative theoretical explanation."[61] And in 1927 Pitirim Sorokin insisted that "a study of the classical theories of repeated phenomena is, at the present moment, one of the most important tasks of sociology. It must be promoted by all means because it provides many conveniences for solving the most important sociological problems."[62]

This search for a better understanding and integration of the classical theoretical explanations of cultural evolution not only cannot be ignored but needs to be renewed. For such a great body of social theory constitutes not only an important segment of universal learning relevant to man's quest for knowledge of the total continuum of social processes, but a vast catalogue of conceptualizations for both the reviewing of historical theory and the construction of such advanced dynamic theory as will insure a reasonable balance between ideological generalizations and empirical validity. Such knowledge is also crucial to the task of identifying and testing the vast body of both historical and accumulating current concepts in the framework of known facts not only in every transitional period of historical recording utilized, but also at every point of extended scientific inquiry into human relations and group behavior in living societies. This seems that instead of ignoring the great body of classical knowledge or of rejecting the "great books" concept of universal learning as irrelevant to advanced scientific inquiry, we must incorporate the translated social facts into the total continuum and integrate them with the abundance of interconnected current concepts into our "all-inclusive speculations comprising a master conceptual scheme from which it is hoped to derive a very large number of empirically observed uniformities of social behavior." This is consistent with Alfred Weber's dictum that "sociological concepts are so abstract that they have to be corrected by individual concepts adequate to the various historical realizations," and with Charles Horton Cooley's theory well-balanced between his thorough study of historical and cultural backgrounds and his own empirical study of individuals and groups.

TESTING GROUNDS FOR HYPOTHETICAL CONCEPTS

This brings us, then, to the supreme task of providing testing grounds for the hypothetical concepts and conceptual schemes so abundantly catalogued in the premises of folk sociology. The available testing grounds are primarily of two sorts. One is found in the source materials of authentic literature relevant to the subject field; and the other is found in the working hypotheses tested in empirical research in which concepts and norms of measurement and description are applied to contemporary groups. The source materials previously cited in five categories of authentic literature again are of two main sorts, the classical theories of total society and the general treatises and empirical studies of special cultures, peoples, and group behavior, by sociologists, anthropologists, and other behavioral social scientists. Each of these, again, reflects a twofold category. The classical theories include, first, those in the frame of reference of the historical process and philosophical systems, and, second, the system builders on the level of generalizations and conceptual analysis, including theories of social change and treatises on social process.

Of the special studies of cultures and peoples there are several categories. One comprises varied studies of pre-civilized or pre-city groups of primitive cultures, both through records of the past and current studies of contemporary "primitive" societies. Another comprises treatises on the level of frontier and earlier stages of evolving civilizations. Still others include writings on peoples and nations as cultural entities, ethnic groups and races, and contemporary communities and small groups. So, too, empirical studies of special societies and folk groups are primarily of two sorts. One consists of primary groups or component societies capable of reproducing themselves both biologically and socially, being representative of the determinate folk elements of population and organization in all human societies. The other consists of constituent societies and small secondary groups representative of the determinate elements of special purpose associational groups and technological units in all civilization. Empirical studies, again, may be classified according to the disciplinary and interdisciplinary identification of the authors.

IDENTIFICATION OF SOURCE MATERIALS WITH CONCEPTS

Numerous inferences from some of these sources have already been suggested in the reference notes for this preview. Further extended documentation will be provided in a book-proportioned bibliography appended to a text on Folk Sociology now under way.* It is, therefore, necessary at this point only to identify such references in the categories we have listed as are sufficiently relevant to the several concepts of folk sociology as to insure effective integration and general conceptualization. For illustration, it is possible to cite authors in each of the varied categories whose conclusions afford documentation concerning the validity of the polarity concept of folk culture and state civilization.

Thus, George Homans, studying a very specialized, constituent, small group on the level of interpersonal labor-management writes that "at the level of the small group, society has always been able to cohere. We infer, therefore, that if civilization is to stand, it must maintain, in the relation between the groups that make up society and the central direction of society, some of the features of the small group itself."[63] But he quotes Emile Durkheim, representative of the classical sociological theorists, as protesting the consensus of modern leaders that civilization has reached a stage at which it can be held together only by force (state civilization) contrasting the folk solidarity with the mass civilization, in which "a society made up of a boundless dust heap of unrelated individuals, whom an over-developed state tries to hem and hold in, is a true sociological monstrosity."

No less relevant are the verdicts of others widely separated in the time and conceptual level of their work. For Oswald Spengler,

* Dr. Odum died while this manuscript was still in the early stages. This article outlines, to some extent, the material which he contemplated developing in the text.

about as different from George Homans as possible, "the civilization is the inevitable destiny of the culture . . . civilizations are the last, the most external and artificial states of culture." For Arnold Toynbee, societies "passed out of the equilibrium of an existence without or before civilization . . . from the integration of custom to the differentiation of civilization."[64] Of the system makers, Alfred Weber's distinction between civilization and culture was also achieved through approximate empirical studies of the historical process as interpreted through the study of, first, primitive societies, and later of great civilizations. According to Weber, the folk culture reflected more spontaneity, more creativeness, more freedom. For, "the process of civilization is based upon the continuity and irreversible progress of reason. Civilization represents the human effort to conquer the world of nature and culture by means of intelligence in the spheres of technology, science, and planning." "Culture . . . is based on the realization of spirit, on philosophical and emotional self realization."

OF ANTHROPOLOGISTS AND SOCIOLOGISTS

Of the contemporary anthropologists whose studies of folk culture have validity for folk sociology, Robert Redfield defines and identifies his folk society largely in terms of the contrasting polarity with civilization. Thus "societies before civilization," "societies not affected by great civilization," "exhibit certain characteristics that distinguish them from civilized societies." Of the other anthropologists whose work has characterized earlier folk cultures in the continuum of societal development, A. L. Kroeber has documented a long list of postulates on the uniformities of cultural evolution; Robert Lowie has diagnosed "social organization," and George Murdock has described "social structure" through the study of many folk cultures.[65] Ralph Linton has constructed a relatively new history of culture through the continuum from early societies and through the concepts of culture and personality and the ritualization of custom.[66] V. Gordon Childe has substituted a logical continuum of societal development for the earlier stereotyped evolution of culture.[67] All these, again, differ in approach and intensity of conclusion from Lewis Mumford who, in four volumes undertaking a systematic story of cultural development, challenges contemporary society to reconstruct its latest stages of civilization or else be destroyed. Different again, yet relevant, is the presentation of Robert MacIver, representative of the middle range of sociological and political theory, that culture and civilization reflect definitive polar differences. Still different in method and concept was Franklin H. Giddings, MacIver's forerunner at Columbia University and an earlier system-maker who posited the zoögenic, anthropogenic, ethnogenic, and demogenic stages of socio-cultural development with civilization evolving as the ethnogenic passes into the civil or demogenic order of social relations.[68]

Of the anthropologists whose work may be identified with the continuum in terms of both ideal type polarities and the long exhaustive inquiry into the uniformities of the total configuration of culture, Kroeber illustrates best the validity of such work as testing grounds for the conceptualization of social process. Both Redfield and Kroeber also posit dichotomies of succession and concepts of folk traits, but Kroeber's comprehensive work goes further in identifying many interrelated situations with transitional societies and seeks a line or scale along which cultures can be arranged nearer one end than another. Redfield's polarity of rural and urban, sacred and secular, simple and complex compares with Kroeber's local and sophisticate, while Redfield's characterization of the solidarity and cohesiveness of the folk society compares with Lowie's revivification of the earlier Giddings' "consciousness of kind" as the core of the folk concept.

From this point on, however, Kroeber's work compares in comprehensiveness with the elaborate work of the cyclical and linear theorists, many of whose oversimplified assumptions he negates. So thorough and comprehensive is Kroeber's work that Pitirim Sorokin, whose theories are popularly quoted alongside those of Toynbee and Spengler, considers Kroeber's work the best of all and nearest his own conceptualization of the three-phase socio-cultural rhythm of ideational-idealistic-sensate cultures which have flowered into the magnificent structure of contemporary civilization now passing again into a new ideational, altruistic and cooperative culture. Sorokin lists 25 axioms from Kroeber, 14 of which appear relevant to the folk culture and state civilization continuum, and thus challenges the validity of all these concepts for realistic diagnosis.

F. R. Cowell, associate educational commissioner of Britain, writing in 1952 of "history, civilization, and culture," recapitulates the concepts of cultural changes as identified with rhythm, tempo-periodicity, oscillation, and fluctuation by reference to theories as they reflect polar concepts in pairs, in three-phase, four-phase, five-phase and six-phase constituent units in the total continuum. Samplings of the two-phase, in addition to those already identified, would include a mixed cavalcade: Maine's status society and contract society; Becker's sacred and secular; Tönnies' *Gemeinschaft* and *Gesellschaft;* Durkheim's mechanical and organic and also his simple and compound; Spencer's militant and industrial; Wilson and Kolb and MacIver's communal and associational; Zimmerman's localistic and cosmopolitan. Somewhat different but comparative would be Buckle's physical laws and mental laws; Wundt's natural and cultural polarity; Ward's natural and cultural; Gobineau's pure and unequal races and blended and equal races; Ratzenhofer's conquest state and culture state; and many other lesser authorities, in which the dichotomy infers certain constants and uniformities.

Of the three-phase rhythm the most notable are those of Comte's theological-metaphysical-positive stages; Tarde's invention-imitation-opposition; Hobhouse's kinship-authority-citizenship; Morgan's savagery-barbarism-civilization; Buecher's self-sufficing community—the city—the nation; Danilevsky's historico-cultural-ethnographic and early-middle-civilized; Hildebrand's *naturalwirtschaft-geldwirtschaft-creditwirtschaft;* Berdyaev's barbaric-medieval, Christian-humanistic, secular. Of the four-phase concept Spengler's twofold analogy of seasons and chronological age and Toynbee's growth and decay are most commonly cited. Walter Schubart's harmonious-heroic-ascetic-messianic is typical. Spring, summer, autumn, winter and childhood, youth, manhood and old age, organic analyses as utilized by Spengler, were also inferred by many other writers, while growth-decay-disintegration-decline, as utilized by Toynbee have been inferred by Ortega, Röpke, Danilevsky, Schweitzer, Mumford, Henry Adams, Machiavelli and ibn-Khaldun of the Arabian philosophy, the four Yugas of the Hindu, the four metal ages of Lucretius and many others.[69]

ORGANIC THEORIES OF SOCIAL STRUCTURE AND PROCESS

Reference is made also to the long and distinguished heritage of what has usually been called analogical organic theories of social structure and process, many exponents of which also interpreted society in some sort of succession or continuum. The most commonly cited reference is to Herbert Spencer's classical "from an indefinite, incoherent homogeneity to a definite, coherent heterogeneity" with a progressively growing differentiation and integration of human personality, culture, and society. All of this was in the framework of a quasi-biological organism with the individual as the cell or unit. So, too, Lilienfeld, holding society to be analogous to a biological organism but the highest form of organic life, identified process in a continuum from decentralized and unregimented political groups to regimes of centralized, autocratic, and regimented control. De Roberty, in the framework of an energistic theory, with superorganic elements of thought and abstract knowledge, saw a central trend of the historical process through scientific, philosophical, or religious, aesthetic and rationally applied thought.

Winarsky also identified process in an unusual continuum of social evolution. Positing society as a mechanistic system of points with individuals in perpetual movement he envisaged a law of social entropy leading progressively to greater socio-cultural equalization of castes, orders, classes, races, and individuals, with the final state a dead socio-cultural equilibrium and the end of mankind's history. This continuum was also similar to that of Gobineau's historical process from the pure and unequal races to the progressively blended and equal ones and again the end of civilization. For de Lapouge the peak of civilization, comparable to a biological organism, was reached with eugenics insuring fullest development and decay setting in with regress of eugenic forces.[70]

These references are adequate to indicate the range and nature of this large body of special learning which has its core in the search for uniformities in process, in the frame of reference of some sort of continuum from the beginning of human society up to the special period for which knowledge of "social facts" might be sought. The very diversity of concepts, the extraordinary quantity of theoretical explanations, and the persistent power of their logic, are evidences of the need of some unifying concept and flexible reference with which to frame each unit of inquiry.

COMPARATIVE CONCEPTS OF THE FOLK

In addition to their inferences with reference to the societal continuum, many of the theories of the system-makers were rich in
comparative concepts of the folk, the folk culture, the folk society,
and the composite character or personality of ethnic, racial, national,
or other special folk groups. These comparative concepts, again,
tend to be of two sorts, namely, the abstract concept such as Wundt's
classical "the most important collective concept of mental life," and
the more particularized concept of Tönnies' *gemeinschaft,* the natural
community as the living organism of human society. Both Wundt
and Tönnies expanded and identified their concepts to integrate the
general and specific meanings. For Wundt, the final integration was
the collective concept of humanity, easily identified with the contemporary one-world concept of society. For Tönnies, the polarity
from *gemeinschaft* to *gesellschaft* with the transitional social processes,
as growth from the youth of society to maturity, is easily identified
with the assumptions of contrast and balance between the folk culture
and state civilization.

Among the other comparative concepts for testing the validity
of the folk concept, citations are abundant in the writings of sociologists and anthropologists. Mannheim's "substantiality and completeness of the living process" and Cooley's primary group society
and "the essence of human interaction" may be paired to reflect the
concepts of two favorite sociologists. Paired anthropologists would
include Ralph Linton's "core of universals" and Robert Lowie's
"center of feeling," along with George Murdock's universal laws of
relationship and the common denominator of culture and Clark
Wissler's blending of people with culture and nature in the culture
area concept. Giddings' component societies and his collective concept of "consciousness of kind" and Mannheim's "common core of
culture," paired with Adam Smith's theory of sentiments and Kropot-
kin's mutual aid, reflect a core of cohesiveness inherent in the folk
concept.

Similar inferences are inherent in such concepts as Gumplowicz'
der Rassenkampf, and Huntington's "kith and kin" and again Maine's
classical kinship group, particularized by Murdock's in the social
structure of familial groups. These and many others identified in

the rich source references are measurably consistent with the Linton dictum that "the difference between folk cultures and modern civilizations . . . is primarily a matter of the proportion which the core of universals and specialities bears to the fluid zone of alternatives." Or, again Linton's concept of the social heredity of the human species in the continuum of human experience is not inconsistent with the popular concept of the folk such as Mary Austin's "to be shaped in mind and social reaction and to some extent in character and so finally in expression by one given environment, that is to be folk," which in turn corresponds well with Weber's concept of the social fact.[71]

THEORIES OF PROGRESS AND CHANGE

Inherent in most of the classical theories of societal structure and process were concepts of progress and change, illustrations of which have been given. In addition to the inferences in that large body of literature, however, the concept of social progress has continued to be a central theme of sociologists. These treatises are valid for testing assumptions, again in two ways. The surveying of concepts of progress is basic to an understanding of all value systems of man and the knowledge gained serves as testing grounds for revision of assumptions. Bury's earlier treatise on progress, with its fivefold elemental concepts, has been supplemented by Hildebrand and Teggart in summaries of the many theories of progress, while Carle Zimmerman has outlined the main facets of the concepts of social change and progress.[72] Hornell Hart's cataloguing of the techniques of progress and Arthur Todd's analysis of theories of progress may be paired with W. F. Ogburn's and F. Stuart Chapin's treatises on social and cultural change, and Pitirim Sorokin's voluminous records of the classical theories of socio-cultural change.[73] In addition to the sociologists' formal treatises on progress and change there is a very large body of popular writings by publicists, educators, philosophers, literary writers, and others listed subsequently, the main core of which is found in the challenge and crisis involved in modern changing civilizations. Others like John Dewey and Wesley C. Mitchell, in different disciplines, have tended to interpret progress and change as synonymous with process, more or less independent of primal causal factors.

Their concepts are still being tested in the crucibles of contemporary groups.

Continuing the documentation of sources for both strengthening and providing testing grounds for the main premises of folk sociology, the concepts of F. S. C. Northrop and Ralph Turner may be paired together to represent the work of contemporary philosopher and historian whose work may be identified with the societal continuum and with comparative concepts of the folk and also with interdisciplinary approaches to the main inquiry. Northrop's identification of the aesthetic and scientific with Eastern and Western cultures and his use of the dichotomy of theories of value and theories of fact, in both content and method, reflect long and patient inquiries into major civilizations as testing grounds for the search for uniformities. Ralph Turner, utilizing concepts of other disciplines as well as of history, finds the core of societal evolution in the concepts of structure and process in which urbanism reflects the beginning of all modern cultural traditions. The traits of liberalism, secularism, and intellectualism reflect the character of Western civilization in a continuum from the beginning of human culture up to the elaboration and accumulation of culture through invention and discovery. Both Northrop and Turner may be said to bridge the distance between the earlier single-discipline sociologists, philosophers, and historians and the later interdisciplinary anthropologists, sociologists, and social psychologists who are experimenting with empirical inquiries in concrete groups, communities or folk cultures. These in turn are valid both as a body of knowledge for testing premises of folk culture growing out of studies already made and for paving the way for continuing studies which may initiate and expand new technics of inquiries based upon those assumptions of folk sociology most needing verification.[74]

The abundant sources from recent special community studies, empirical inquiries into group behavior, and special treatises on national and ethnic cultures, again provide a three-way approach to the testing of assumptions. For, in the first place, they have re-examined many of the older concepts and revised some of the commonly accepted findings. Then in their observations growing out of empirical inquiries they have not only tested the validity and limitations of empirical methods but as a result of their findings have both confirmed some earlier theories and contributed new concepts of their own. Of the anthropologists, the recent contributions of Murdock, Lowie, Lewis, and Childe are excellent examples. Murdock, applying special methods to the study of social structure in 250 sampled societies but also building upon some of the findings of Sumner, Keller, and Wissler, finds inferences from internal evidence of the "single original type of organization" in folk culture. Murdock concludes that "Historical and comparative tests thus offer favorable parallel confirmation of the essential validity of the hypotheses advanced." Lowie, studying social organization with a view to seeking uniformities in all types of social units, confirms the Giddings' "consciousness of kind" but tests the concept in terms of concrete inferences of solidarity, territorial and ethnic factors in relation to institutions. Lowie writes that sociologists generally agree that "the community is a subjective but self-sufficient group united by a consciousness of kind; it is essentially a center of feeling."[75] Lewis, revising the study of Tepoztlán and utilizing different schedules and methods, confirms Redfield's general concepts of polarity from simple to complex cultures but expands the range to include a more complex continuum than merely rural-urban or sacred-secular traits.[76] V. Gordon Childe, questioning the validity of the analogy between cultural evolution and organic evolution, modifies Tylor's assumptions of uniformity of institutional development independent of race and language and questions the "threads and patches" theory of culture as well as Morgan's oversimplified stages of savagery, barbarism and civilization.

INTERDISCIPLINARY STUDIES

From among the interdisciplinary group representing anthropology, psychology, and sociology, special community studies are increasingly abundant in both published and unpublished works. Of the published books, the Warner studies of social life in communities, the Dollard, Davis, Gardner, Powdermaker, Hollingshead volumes and the Yankee City series and others such as the first-hand study of factory folkways by Ellsworth, may be paired with Homans' and Brownell's treatises on human groups and with many borderline studies by Lawrence K. Frank, David Riesman, Laura Thompson, Trigant Burrow, Paul Meadows.[77] From the special empirical studies of communities or special group cultures, there is again an abundance of testing grounds for the observation of traits, personality, uniformities, and diversities in group behavior and process.

Of the special field studies in which the premises of folk culture and civilization, folk quality and mass quality, have been tested in schedules approximating objective observations, there are again three main categories. One is the application of the folk culture-state civilization yardstick, with detailed field schedules of identification, to the rich source materials of anthropologists whose findings have been concentrated within the core of folk culture, such as Murdock's familial and kinship structure. A second is the application of these special measures to abundant samplings of studies that have been made independently of each other in all parts of the cultural world, such as John Embree's *Suye Mura: A Japanese Village;* Raymond Firth's *We, The Tikopia;* John Gillin's *Moche: A Peruvian Coastal Community* and *The Culture of Security in San Carlos;* Clyde Kluckhohn and Dorothea Leighton's *The Navaho;* Olen Leonard's *El Cerrito: The Culture of a Contemporary Rural Community;* Laura Thompson's *The Hopi Way;* and a solid catalogue of others easily available, including comparable numbers of inquiries made by sociologists, rural sociologists, and psychologists as well as anthropologists. The more than a score of such applications that have already been made indicate a high degree of validity.

CHARACTER STUDIES OF NATIONAL GROUPS

Of the remaining categories of published sources, the first comprehends an extraordinary range and quality of general treatises on national folk cultures, race and regional groups, and special ethnic threads in the fabric of composite cultures and civilizations. In addition to such studies as Benedict's on national character, Mead and Kroeber's on American traits, Kardiner's basic personality types, and Riesman's "Lonely Crowd," there are many major authors writing on national folk character. These include such works on Russia as Berdyaev, Best, Doob, Strong, Gray, Lamont, Maynard, and Vernadsky's the Russian people; Havelock Ellis on the genius of Europe and Andre Siegfried on "Nations have Souls"; Thorstein

Veblen's Germany in relation to the folk and the industrial revolution; Roth, Rodnick, Reinhardt, Kirkpatrick, and Becker's studies of Germany; Robin Williams' dynamics of American society, alongside the English anthropologists and psychologists, Gorer and Brogan's characterization of American character and people; Ross's people of Canada; Wise, Ziff, Bernstein, Cohen, Engleman, Finkelstein, Gaster, Ginzberg, Janowsky, Kastein, Koestler's studies of Jewish culture; Coon, Fisher, Horton, Keesing, Michener, Mitra, Newman, Payne and Young's studies of Asia, the East and the Middle East; Fei, Gerth, Wang, Yang, and White's studies of Chinese culture; Bisbee, Notestein's studies of the Scotch people; Arensberg, Jackson and O'Faolain's studies of the Irish; Weyer's studies of the Eskimos and their folkways; and many others.[78]

CONTEMPORARY POPULAR DIAGNOSES

The last category of sources, again in two main groups, consists of contemporary diagnoses of civilization, problems, crises and dilemmas from which a great body of both solid and fugitive literature has emerged. One category includes the natural scientists, again in two categories, namely the literature of facts and description about science and civilization and the literature of alarm and fear of catastrophe in modern civilization. The other group consists of a large body of diagnostic writings by publicists, educators, political leaders, ministers, and scholars, on the character and hazards of contemporary civilization.

The contributions dealing with science and society run the whole gamut from great philosophers and scientists such as Whitehead and Russell, paired with Conant, Sarton, and Urey, to panels of scientists appraising midcentury civilization in scientific journals led by J. R. Oppenheimer, and special treatises on atomic energy. Bertrand Russell and Aldous Huxley's multiple discussion of science and society may be paired with Lundberg's "Can Science Save Us?" and Mumford's satire on cities. Of the natural scientists, Harold C. Urey's "Survival or Suicide" and "I am a frightened man. All the scientists I know are frightened—frightened for their lives—and frightened for your life," and Vandiver Bush's "ruin and suicide" may be paired with Ralph Linton's "In the Götterdämmerung which overwise science . . . is preparing for us the last man will spend his last hours searching for his wife and child."

Of the educators, politicians, ministers and literary folk primarily from the United States writing on the level of alarm and warning, the roll call of university presidents includes: Sproul of California, Dodds of Princeton, Hutchins of Chicago, Fackenthal of Columbia, Conant of Harvard. The warnings of Thomas Dewey, Robert Taft, James Byrnes, Bernard Baruch, among the political leaders, may be paired with the warnings of the Pope, bishops, and ecclesiastical leaders in many denominations, and with a host of lay leaders, historians, and columnists. Henry Steele Commager and Stuart Chase of current vintage may be paired with the earlier Beard's "whither mankind" and questioning, or William McDougall's diagnosis of world chaos, or Henry Adams' law of civilization and decay, or Lombroso's and Freud's "tragedies" and "discontents" of civilization. Burchard's inquiries into the implications of scientific progress and Butterfield's tracing the origins of modern science may well be paired with Alexander's and others' challenge to reason and unreason and Burrow's characterizations of man's neuroses in contemporary civilization. Haldane, Haskins, and Heard[79] have written of heredity, politics, morals and human society in the new contemporary world while Janeway and Joad and many others challenged survival and decadence. From the wider horizon of world leadership, the consolidated consensus of international science, from UNESCO and other facets of United Nations, and from political and social leaders from the Orient and Africa, as well as from Americans who survey those areas, came powerful documentation of warnings, diagnosis, and fear.

ESSENTIALS FOR CONCEPTUALIZATION

From the foregoing references to literature, concepts, and situations, we now have a substantial body of cumulative inferences clearly identifiable with the main premises of folk sociology as they are relevant to the needs of both social science and human society. Insofar as the main emphasis is upon general sociology, the major needs are comprehended in the construction of a theoretical folk sociology as a basic subject field useful for testing the validity of the great body of historical knowledge and recorded experience, and also for achieving scientific results from empirical studies, again integrated with both historical facts and with the researches of other social sciences. Insofar as the emphasis is primarily upon problems of contemporary society in transition and travail, the major needs will be found in the diagnosis and identification of crucial problems and the necessary concrete studies and action research divorced from the inferences of moralistic orientation and well within the frame of reference of the theoretical conceptualization of folk sociology. All this assumes an acceptable documentation and general methodology capable of comprehending alike inquiries into the cultural-historical processes of societal evolution and empirical studies of great range and variety of interaction in "precivilization" groups, in "primitive" groups of the contemporary world, and in all manner of groups and societies in contemporary civilization.

The range and nature of needed documentation have been indicated in preceding pages. . . . So, too, something of the nature and methods of applying the concepts of folk sociology to empirical studies of special groups and cultures has been illustrated in the case of selected published works. [A] schedule of folk traits, basic to the folk sociology construct of human relations and tested for validity in group study, [would] include no less than one hundred and fifty identifiable traits catalogued under a dozen main categories of social interaction and presented in dichotomies of polarity for comparative traits of civilized culture. The dichotomy of traits for the folk culture and the state civilization assumes measurement either by observation or by identification with objective indices. Included are comparable traits in man's interaction with nature; his interpersonal interaction within the group; his interaction with leadership and with the main institutional modes of order and control: the family, religion, education, industry and economic institutions, government and state control, and the community itself. Other levels of measurable interaction include those with science and technology; with intercultural situations and ethnic groups; with social change and cultural configurations; and with values and attitudes.

Inherent in the processes of change from the folk culture to state civilization are always the determinant transitional stages of societal development. These are identified and measured primarily by means of prevailing technicways in the setting of a cross-cultural interconnected continuum from folkways and mores to technicways and the consequent problems of adjustments. The schedules for identification and measurement of technicways provide for the description in each category of selected traits, in time and spatial settings; the corresponding folkways prevailing; a catalogue of what transpired in science, technology, and material changes; the resulting technicways, transcending the folkways; the emergence of consequent problems of adjustment; and the documentation of sources essential for authenticating the results.

NEW RESEARCH OPPORTUNITIES

We come finally, then, to the task of appraising the nature and range of new research needs inherent in the discovery and diagnosis of the pyramiding "problems" of to-day's and tomorrow's civilization. The main problems may easily be identified with the dilemmas of transitional readjustment on the level of all the categories of traits and behavior in the dichotomies of folk culture and state civilization and all along the continuum of changing processes and products of transitional societies. The number of problems is limited only by whatever selective processes may be applied to particular areas of research delimited by available resources and relevant needs. Research areas and programs are, by the same token, identified with the total problem-field as envisaged or selected. And for purposes of clarification and for distinguishing between research and action programs, total "problems" are identified as (1) "societal problems" as applying primarily to long-time universal situations needing scientific "solutions," and (2) "social problems" primarily applying to concrete, local, here and now situations, needing immediate adjustment. Or the twofold identification may be designated as "scientific problems," and "ameliorative problems."[80] Florian Znaniecki makes the distinction in terms of "sociological problems" and "social problems."[81] It must be clear that the primary focus of folk sociology is upon sociological problems, although the study of social problems is often fruitful for scientific as well as societal "solutions."

Before turning to a tentative research frame of reference, there is one over-all situation easily identified with both the sociological and the social problems concepts which challenges folk sociology's best for both diagnosis and interpretation as well as for valid contributions to fruitful directions of social action. This is the challenge to answer fundamental questions being asked by scholars, publicists, and common man alike. This obligation is especially heavy for folk sociology since one of its main objectives is the identification of the folk with the heart of all human society in process and growth and with the character definition of the aspirations and ideals of every people. F. S. C. Northrop's concept of "the normative inner order"[82] of each people as basic to their whole philosophy of living is symbol of need when in transitional periods of crisis the people require a social morale for an age of science and technology.

The greater responsibility, therefore, rests upon folk sociology which recognizes that, inseparable in interaction and in the functioning of society are the reasonable demands of the articulate folk to understand and to have a part in the new directions of civilization. From East and West, from North and South, and from all the hinterlands and way-places of the earth where the folk are articulate, men and women, elders and youth, mass and class come asking for answers to their troubled questionings about the complexity and dilemmas of this contemporary world of ours. And they want answers that satisfy. They not only want to know what civilization is and how it has come to be what it is but they want to know what our prospects are for tomorrow and how we shall go on from today. And they want somehow to understand the long succession of human strivings and achievements of such vast unevenness in time and place, in some continuum which explains not only the ways in which we have come to now but in which also there is consistently enough to guide us well into peaceful paths of the future.

In their searchings for truth and ways, the people ask many specific questions. Why is there so much confusion and crisis in this most enlightened era of all mankind? Why is it that, just as man has achieved the miraculous and civilization has flowered into beauty, abundance, and security, there is all of a sudden so much questioning about the survival of the human race? What is all this we hear about man destroying himself, living on borrowed time, committing suicide? Is it true that both the morality revealed by religion and morality, nurtured and sponsored by the powerful folkways and mores and moored to the institutions of the people, no longer prevail? Is it true that low moral standards abound in high places? Surely men are not intentionally evil, nor madly rushing headlong over the steep places to destruction? Or are they rather confused in transitional periods of catastrophic change?

SPECIFIC QUESTIONS OF THE PEOPLE

More specifically, people begin to ask if it is true that contemporary civilization really is in such crisis as to indicate sure decay, on the one hand, or sure destruction, on the other? And many are asking whether science can save us, after having made us what we are. Why is it, some ask, that science moves toward substituting machines for men or the study of interplanetary life for the mastery of human life on this earth? Why is it that the most intelligent and skilled men in the world devote their highest energies and abilities to means of destroying man? Does it reflect intelligence for science to seek a bridgehead upon another planet from which the men of earth could be attacked? Why do men kill each other in multiplied ratios and why has the cost of killing a fighting man risen from 75 cents in Caesar's day to $50,000 in modern war? Why is it that production, the civilized index of rich living, is channelled so much into tragic dying? Why is it that peoples with the highest moral codes and ideology consent to the wholesale slaughter of masses of people in rationalized peace crusades?

Why is it again that men of intelligence, through social science and social inventions, have done so little in the realm of human relationships? Is it possible that intellectualism, which has played so powerful a role in the development of civilization, is failing to meet the needs of man? What of the assumptions of the need for spiritual renewal and what does that mean anyway? Can sociologists ignore the questionings of any group or the assumptions of those who make diagnoses and propose remedies?

PRIORITY SCHEDULES AND ACTION PROGRAMS

We have indicated something of the almost limitless range and variety of research areas and problems available within the total subject field of folk sociology and something of the ways in which its concepts may be tested and implemented when applied both to theoretical historical data and to current empirical studies. The task of selection, of perfecting priority schedules, and of identifying appropriate methods of research, is inseparable from the main task of conceptualization and testing the necessary hypothetical concepts which serve to delimit the subject field. Within this total framework, flexible categories of research areas and problems may be identified through the incidence of urgency, timeliness, relatively uniform consensus of needs, and trends. Categories comprehend expanding catalogues: long-time major programs of planned research, smaller unit-items of purposive research, concrete studies of small groups, comprehensive inquiries into national and racial cultures, special inventories of group conflict and crisis, studies of folk cultures functioning within state civilizations, studies of national character in terms of their "living laws" and "positive law," the dilemmas of the new nationalism, the continuous study of transitional societies the world over, together with special-purpose sponsored research identified with organization, management, planning, and experimentation.

Something of the logical order of priority schedules has been inferred in the several recent writings of many authorities in many disciplines in what is almost a clamor for sociology and the other social sciences to become more dynamic in meeting stated needs. "The solutions of problems of human interaction in community life, national affairs, and international relations, is, in fact, primary for continuation of our civilization," wrote one as recently as 1952, in the *Bulletin* of the American Association of University Professors. In somewhat similar interpretation F. S. C. Northrop in his latest volume, *The Taming of the Nations,* identifies the needs of international relations with scientific objectivity which "specifies the normative inner order of each nation and the relation between these national inner orders." Manifestly these and a thousand other implications indicate the urgency of a more comprehensive and definitive analysis of the changing structure of society everywhere through the special avenues of adequate studies of behavior, organization, administration, conflict, cooperation, and adjustment on the community level. Equally urgent is the unfinished task of diagnosis of nations and peoples in conflict and travail to the end that local, regional, and total society may be integrated on the enduring basis of sound sociological theory. A thousand vivid samples appear at every turn from every man's community in the place where he lives to every other man's community in other places; from so concrete an example as the adjustment in the southern United States of America to Supreme Court influence upon racial segregation, or South Africa's seemingly insolvable crises, to the integration and cooperation of diverse and conflicting concepts and action of the United Nations. In such a polarity construct, folk sociology, then, seeks not so much to become a new or different sociology but to focus, utilize, and integrate much of the best that general sociology may contribute to the dynamic science of human relations.

Notes and References to the Text

1. The problem of delineating a well-integrated subject field clearly identified with sociology and usful for both theory and research in contemporary society is a difficult one. For such a subject field is not just an area of special sociology or an exclusive methodological approach, or an all-inclusive frame of reference. It must not be too large and must be delimited by special concepts and yet it must be adequate to utilize many of the general concepts basic to sociological inquiry and must comprehend in its range such "floating" general subjects as the community, the city, rural life. The subject field must be methodologically oriented and adapted to effective integration with researches in other disciplines. In terms of total sociology, the subject field is identified more as representative of sociological *theories* than as all inclusive sociological *theory,* the distinction being that of Robert K. Merton, made in his discussion of Talcott Parsons, "The Position of Sociological Theory" in the *American Sociological Review* for April 1948.

For simple comparison and illustrative purposes, two other examples are here identified as "subject fields." One is the structure-function approach more specifically illustrated by Levy's study of comparative societies delimited by concepts and conceptual schemes with empirical referents only. See *The Structure of Society* by Marion J. Levy, Jr. Parsons' structure-function would be identified probably with three subject-field methodologies. The other illustrates the difficulty of delimiting a subject field in sociology, by comparing it with the subject field of *ecology* in the natural sciences, which seems relatively simple when defined as "the biological science of environmental interaction." It thus comprehends fewer concepts as the study of "the structure and temporal processes of populations, communities and other ecological systems and the interaction of individuals composing these units," than the involved study of folk society on these levels as well as on the upper levels of humanity itself and its processes and products of culture and civilization. See especially *Ecology* by Eugene P. Odum; *Principles of Animal Ecology* by W. C. Allee and others.

In the case of folk sociology, the conceptualization and utilization of a subject field broaden the meaning of a too limited concept of "folk," delimit the field within conceptual workability, integrate its many interconnected concepts so as not to multiply too many entities, and reverse the order of inquiry by focusing upon the contemporary end of the continuum and working back to the beginnings. See "Folk and Regional

Conflict as a Field for Sociological Study" by Howard W. Odum, *Publication of the American Sociological Society* (May 1931), pp. 1-17. See "System Building in Sociology" by Roger Nett, and "Is Theory for Demographers?" by Rupert Vance in *Social Forces* (October 1952), pp. 9-13. "Rural Sociology and the Folk Society" by Robert Redfield, *Rural Sociology* (March 1952); "Suicide and Crime in Folk and Secular Society" by Austin Porterfield, *American Journal of Sociology* (January 1952), p. 331.

2. Much will be said later and many references cited relative to (a) the inseparability of the total and historical society from its constituent units, and (b) the exclusive interrelationship between empirical study of particular phenomena in the world of experience and theoretical principles and hypothetical generalizations. See *Fundamentals of Concept Formation in Empirical Science* by C. G. Hempel, pp. 1, 2, 39-45; *The Logic of the Sciences and the Humanities* by F.S.C. Northrop, chaps. I, II, III, and XIV; *Logic: The Theory of Inquiry* by John Dewey; *Whitehead and This Modern World* by Lowe, Hartshorne and Johnson, pp. 3-24; *The Rules of Sociological Method* by Emile Durkheim, pp. xiv-xx; see also *Social Theory and Social Structure* by Robert Merton, and *Essays in Sociological Theory,* and *The Social System* by Talcott Parsons. It is not only in the social sciences that the historical process is considered determinant in theoretical generalizations but in the natural sciences as well. Thus, Sarton insists that science "is indeed a history of human civilization, considered from its highest point of view. The center of interest is the evolution of science but general history remains always in the background." See *The Life of Science* by George Sarton, p. 33; see especially *Modern Science and Modern Man, Science and Common Sense,* and *Understanding Science,* by James B. Conant; and the panel on "Fifty Years of Science" in *Scientific American* (September 1950).

3. For sociology's expected determinant role in contemporary research where major inquiries must be made in a world laboratory now more than ever identified with patterns of the past and inevitable changes of the future, the frame of reference commonly designated as *social change* appears over-simplified on the one hand, or on the other, as too much identified with the ideologies of Western civilization or the one-way inevitable direction of progress. A more comprehensive frame of reference appears to be found in the dynamics of a societal continuum so formulated as to comprehend the traditional concepts of social change and cultural evolution but also, and more, the concept of constant polarity and transitional society in which universals may be identified and reduced to constant societal denominators and identifiable norms capable of applying to all societies. Since the core of the most needed inquiries appears to be identified with our most recent and current situations and since the methodological orientation of folk sociology seeks to balance historical evidence and normative approaches with the measured facts of contemporary experience, the focus is more often than not on the present or most advanced terminus of the continuum, studying complex

current situations and working back to earlier simple forms. See *Evolution* and *Man Makes Himself* by V. Gordon Childe; *Darwin: Competition and Cooperation* by Ashley Montague; *Evolution and Human Destiny* by Fred Kohler; *Culture in Crisis* by Laura Thompson and others; the catalogue of empirical studies cited on pages 336-39 of this paper; *The Taming of the Nations* by F. S. C. Northrop; *The Primitive World and Its Transformations* by Robert Redfield; *The Tree of Human History* by A. H. Brodrick.

4. The documentation of stated needs of sociology would include a sweeping consensus by sociologists, other social scientists, natural scientists, educators, literary artists, and columnists. Sociologists have themselves contributed more than one hundred relevant articles in the *American Sociological Review, The American Journal of Sociology,* and *Social Forces,* in the last twenty years. See also *American Sociology* by Howard W. Odum, especially chaps. 4-13, for the catalogued needs as seen by the presidents of the American Sociological Society. See also chaps. 24 and 25. See *Continuities in Social Research* in which Samuel Stouffer's contribution features the "pay off" opportunities of sociology. The American Association for the Advancement of Science offers a thousand dollar prize for new sociological theory featuring what many natural scientists assume to be the primary need of sociology, namely, a closer approach to a naturalistic science. See *Science,* September 6, 1952. See also E. W. Lever and J. J. Brown, "The Need for General Laws in the Social Sciences," *Science* (October 12, 1951), p. 379.

As for the multiplying social and societal problems of contemporary society that need the sociological approach, both specific and general references are so numerous here and throughout this work that full documentation may be found in the considerable bibliography of more than a thousand titles in the forthcoming volume, *Folk Sociology.* See footnote p. 329. Even so, the extraordinary periodical literature from interdisciplinary journals can be sampled only alongside selected books. So, too, the references are cumulative so that, just as latest concepts are utilized to complete the identification and preliminary definitions of earlier ones, the final interpretation of needs and situations in current sociology will rest on cumulative inferences from many citations. Thus, the earlier query of Franklin H. Giddings asking "What is sociology and what is it good for?" is answered in many devious ways by such references as those of Angell, Parsons, MacIver, Merton, Lundberg, Lynd as are cited in note 5 and elsewhere.

5. For concepts and recent discussions of sociological theory by sociologists see the symposium on sociological theory in the *American Sociological Review* for April and October 1948 and also "The Prospects for Sociological Theory" by Talcott Parsons, for February 1950. See "Contributions to the Theory of Reference Group Behavior" by Robert K. Merton in *Continuities in Social Research,* as well as Merton's *Social Theory and Social Structure* and Parsons' *The Social System* and *Essays in Sociological Theory.* See *American Sociology,* chaps. 15, 24, and 25, by Howard W. Odum; *The History of Sociology,* introductory chapter by

Harry Elmer Barnes;*Sociological Theory and Social Research* by C. H. Cooley.

6. The need for the acceptance and clarification of major concepts does not imply inflexible uniformities or a limitation in number and kinds of special concepts useful for various purposes. Nor does it necessarily mean that, if two or more theorists define the same concepts differently, only one is "right" and the others "wrong." Marion J. Levy's identification of "system" as "two friends meeting on the street" and Pitirim Sorokin's with the total sensate Western culture may be mutually useful, the one as a concrete concept with empirical referents only and the other as the general conceptualization of process in societal evolution. Or again Levy's definition of society as "the most general concept of a concrete structure with which this study is concerned" has a different focus from Robert MacIver's "every kind and degree of relationship entered into by men" or Tylor's classical identification of culture primarily with artifacts, or the more than one hundred characterizations, and sometimes definitions, of culture available for cataloguing from many sources. The need emphasized here is for general agreement upon a reasonable number of major concepts which in turn may be either defined in terms of minor concepts or so interconnected with other concepts as to permit identification with varied situations and settings useful for consolidation and integration. Concepts as over-specialized ends in themselves or concepts multiplied primarily for distinctiveness reflect immaturity more than validity or usefulness. See pp. 87-89 of *Social Theory and Social Structure* by Robert Merton. See the definition of culture in Elliott Jaques' *The Changing Culture of a Factory*. See also "Social Ontology and the Criteria for Definitions in Sociology," *Sociometry* (December 1951), p. 355.

7. See *Social Philosophies of An Age of Crisis* by Pitirim A. Sorokin. See also "Sociological Theory and Its Historical Roots," Part I of *Essays in Sociological Theory* by Talcott Parsons.

8. See *The Logic of the Sciences and the Humanities* by F. S. C. Northrop, chaps. I-III.

9. See pp. 323-32 for references and further details.

10. Charles Horton Cooley's dictum to "make it total and make it human," might be compared with Robert Redfield's concept "as if humanity were one man" or as "the story of a single career, that of the human race." See *Primitive Societies and Their Transformations,* chap. I, by Robert Redfield; Levy, *op. cit.,* specifies *Homo Sapiens* as the only frame of reference for his study of comparative societies.

11. See especially James B. Conant, *Modern Science and Modern Man,* p. 109.

12. See pp. 302-6 for discussion and references on social change. As new references for applied identification see *The Big Change* by Frederick L. Allen, chap. 12, "Faster, Faster." See also *Outline of Social Change and Progress* by Carle C. Zimmerman and *Social Change,* rev. by W. F. Ogburn. As applied to empirical studies, see *The Changing Culture of a Factory* by Elliott Jaques.

13. See pp. 328-32 for discussion and identification with special studies.

14. See especially *Fundamentals of Concept Formation* by C. G. Hempel; *The Structure of Society,* chap. III, by Marion J. Levy, Jr.; *Social Theory and Social Structure* by Robert Merton, pp. 87-90; E. W. Lever and J. J. Brown, "The Need for General Laws in The Social Sciences," *loc cit.*

15. *Science and Common Sense* by James B. Conant, p. 25; and also his *Modern Science and Modern Man,* p. 62.

16. See *Primitive Societies and Their Transformation* by Robert Redfield.

17. See "Basic Concepts of Sociology" by N. S. Timasheff, *The American Journal of Sociology* (September 1952), pp. 176 seq.

18. From the work of Franklin H. Giddings whose *Scientific Study of Human Society* presented perhaps the first comprehensive version of this general definition of society, more than fifty attributes of sociology went into the making of his final definition; Lester F. Ward utilized more than a score; and Albion W. Small employed nearly as many coordinate definitions.

19. The early texts of E. A. Ross, C. H. Cooley, and Park and Burgess catalogued the longest and earliest authentic classification of processes and interaction. See *Understanding Society* by Howard W. Odum, chap. 30.

20. Until recently culture and civilization were commonly associated together as alternative aspects of the same thing. For another viewpoint see "The Distinction of Civilization from Culture in American Sociology," pp. 13-18 in *Culture: A Critical Review of Concepts and Definitions* by A. L. Kroeber and Clyde Kluckhohn; *Understanding Society* by Howard W. Odum, chaps. 14, 15.

21. See "Folk and Regional Conflict as a Field for Sociological Study" by Howard W. Odum, *loc. cit.;* also *Understanding Society,* chaps. 14 and 30.

22. See *Regionalism in the United States,* edited by Merrill Jensen, concluding chapter by Howard W. Odum; *American Regionalism* by Howard W. Odum and Harry Estill Moore.

23. See N. S. Timasheff, "Basic Concepts of Sociology," *loc. cit.,* and Marion J. Levy, Jr., *op. cit.* See also W. I. Thomas, "definition of the situation," in *The Polish Peasant.*

24. Perhaps Tönnies comes nearer to utilizing the exact equivalent of *State Civilization* in his *Gesellschaft,* although Spengler's and Ortega's *Mass Civilization* are almost analogous.

25. See *Mechanization Takes Command* by S. Giedion; *Machine Unchained* by Leo Hausleiter. See Lewis Mumford in *Technics and Civilization* and *Culture of Cities;* and special emphasis upon the machine world in most of the current popular books on crisis and change, e.g., *Mid-Century: The Social Implications of Scientific Progress,* edited by J. E. Burchard. Others include Arnold Toynbee's *The Study of History;* Oswald Spengler's *Decline of the West;* Brooks Adams' *Law of Civiliza-*

tion and Decay; Pitirim A. Sorokin's *Man and Society in Calamity;* Wilhelm Röpke's *The Social Crisis of Our Time;* Ortega y Gasset's *The Revolt of the Masses;* Lewis Mumford's *Technics and Civilization, The Culture of Cities, The Condition of Man,* and *The Conduct of Life;* Bertrand Russell's *The Impact of Science on Society* and *A History of Western Philosophy;* Sigmund Freud's *Civilization and Its Discontents;* along with Ralph Turner's *The Great Cultural Traditions;* F. S. C. Northrop's *The Meeting of East and West.*

26. One of the best acknowledgments of the dilemma of definition is that on p. 5 of *A Dictionary of Biology* by Abercrombie, Hickman and Johnson: "Many unfamiliar terms especially the rarer ones, are defined with the help of other technical terms, perhaps equally unfamiliar. . . . There is nothing for it but to follow up the terms until you come to an entirely intelligible definition." See also p. 149 of Kroeber and Kluckhohn's *Culture* for a remarkable catalogue of 164 definitions of culture and their conclusion that it was not necessary to construct another definition in order to utilize the central idea formulated by social scientists.

27. Kroeber and Kluckhohn, *op. cit.,* p. 181 and all of Part II, "Definitions," pp. 41-78. See also *The Science of Culture* by Leslie White.

28. These reflect the consensus of nearly all of the more than twenty elementary introductory textbooks in sociology, published within the last decade.

29. Talcott Parsons, for instance, *The Social System.*

30. See chap. 1, pp. 5-11, *Understanding Society.*

31. Cf. Alfred Weber, R. M. MacIver, Robert K. Merton, Howard W. Odum in Kroeber and Kluckhohn, *op. cit.,* pp. 14-15. Also Odum, *Understanding Society,* pp. 260-61.

32. Kroeber and Kluckhohn, *op. cit.,* pp. 44, 45 and Odum, *Understanding Society,* chaps. 6, 13, 14.

33. See V. Gordon Childe, *Evolution* and "Organic Evolution and Cultural Progress," chap. II, pp. 20-36 in *Man Makes Himself.*

34. See *Understanding Society,* pp. 260, 267, also 122, 123.

35. See Childe, *op. cit.;* Fred Kohler, *op. cit.,* pp. 107-11; *The Clock of History* by Alvin Johnson; *The Dynamics of Social Change* by B. Malinowski.

36. See *The Idea of Progress* by George Hildebrand and the earlier *Idea of Progress* by J. B. Bury; also *Technique of Social Progress* by Hornell Hart; *Outline of Social Change and Social Progress* by Carle Zimmerman.

37. See especially *Social Philosophies of an Age of Crisis* by Pitirim A. Sorokin; *The Uses of the Past* by H. S. Muller.

38. *Understanding Society,* pp. 636-37.

39. *Ibid.,* p. 639.

40. See *The Human Group* by George C. Homans; *Group Life* by Marshall C. Gresco; see recent texts in introductory sociology and anthropology.

41. See *Social Process* and *Social Organization* by C. H. Cooley; "The

352   *Folk Sociology as a Subject Field*

Small Group," unpublished doctoral dissertation, University of North Carolina, by Winfred Godwin.

42. See Kroeber and Kluckhohn, *op. cit.*

43. See *Religious Perspectives of College Teaching in Sociology and Social Psychology* by Talcott Parsons, p. 5.

44. See "The Promise of Regionalism" in *Regionalism in America* edited by Merrill Jensen. See *Understanding Society;* see also, *Geography in the Twentieth Century,* chap. XV, 345-72, by Griffith Taylor.

45. See *Ecology* by E. P. Odum. Also chap. 4, H. W. Odum, *Understanding Society,* pp. 83-86.

46. *Understanding Society,* pp. 260-61.

47. *The Social System* by Talcott Parsons.

48. *Primitive Societies and Their Transformation* by Robert Redfield.

49. *Understanding Society,* pp. 5, 35.

50. See *Folk Culture of Yucatan* and "The Folk Society" by Robert Redfield, *The American Journal of Sociology,* LII (1947), 293-308.

51. See *Social Change* by W. F. Ogburn for the elementary definition of *cultural lag.* See also *Society in Transition* by H. E. Barnes.

52. See "The Natural History of the Folk Society" by Robert Redfield, *Social Forces,* 31 (March 1953), pp. 224-28.

53. See again Kroeber and Kluckhohn, *op. cit.,* p. 44, for conclusion that the element of "totality" is almost universal in definition of culture.

54. *Understanding Society.*

55. See "Sacred and Secular Societies" by Howard Becker, *Social Forces,* 28 (May 1950), p. 361.

56. See *Marx, Darwin, and Wagner* by Barzun.

57. *Understanding Society.*

58. See *The Logic of the Sciences and the Humanities* by F. S. C. Northrop.

59. See "Postponement of Social Decision in Transitional Society" by Alvin Boskoff, *Social Forces,* 31 (March 1953), pp. 229-34.

60. See *Don't Resign from the Human Race* by Norman Cousins.

61. "A Theory of Synchronous Culture Cycles," by F. Stuart Chapin, *Social Forces,* 3 (May 1925), pp. 596-604.

62. "A Survey of the Cyclical Conceptions of Social and Historical Process," by Pitirim A. Sorokin, *Social Forces,* 6 (September 1927), pp. 39-40.

63. *The Human Group* by George C. Homans, p. 468.

64. See *Social Philosophies of an Age of Crisis* by Pitirim A. Sorokin.

65. *Social Organization* by Robert Lowie and *Social Structure* by George Murdock.

66. See especially *Tree of Culture* by Ralph Linton and his *Culture and Personality;* also chap. 6 in his *The Science of Man in the World Crisis.*

67. *Social Evolution* and *Man Makes Himself.*

68. See *Principles of Sociology* and *Inductive Sociology* by F. H. Giddings.

69. These are catalogued well in *Social Philosophies of an Age of*

Crisis, by Pitirim A. Sorokin. See also *History, Civilization, and Culture* by F. R. Cowell.

70. See "The General Analogical Approach" in *An Introduction to Social Research* by Howard W. Odum and Katharine Jocher.

71. The references here are to the main works of each author from which comparative concepts have been sought to substantiate the assumptions of the folkstate polarity concept.

72. Note identical titles of Bury and Teggart and Hildebrand, *The Idea of Progress.*

73. *Technique of Social Progress* by Hornell Hart; *Social Change* by W. F. Ogburn; and *Contemporary Social Theories* by Pitirim A. Sorokin.

74. See *The Meeting of the East and West* and *The Taming of the Nations* by F. S. C. Northrop and *The Great Cultural Traditions* by Ralph Turner.

75. See Lowie's *Anthropology* and *Social Organization* and Murdock's *Social Structure.*

76. See *Life in a Mexican Village: Tepoztlán Restudied* by Oscar Lewis.

77. See *Society as the Patient* and *Nature and Human Nature* by Lawrence K. Frank; *The Lonely Crowd* by David Riesman; *Culture in Crisis: A Study of the Hopi Indians* by Laura Thompson and others; *The Neurosis of Man* by Trigant Burrow; and *The Culture of Industrial Man* by Paul Meadows; *The Malays: A Cultural History* by Richard Winstedt.

78. See *The Russian Idea* by Nicholas Berdyaev; *The Soviet State and Its Inception* by Harry Best; *Soviet Economic Development Since 1917* by Maurice Doob; *The Soviet World* by Anna Louise Strong; *Soviet Land: The Country, Its People, and Their World* by D. G. B. Gray; *The Peoples of the Soviet Union* by Corliss Lamont; *Russia in Flux* by Sir John Maynard; *A History of Russia* by George Vernadsky; *The Genius of Europe* by Havelock Ellis; *Imperial Germany and the Industrial Revolution* by Thorstein Veblen; *The House of Nazi: The Duke of Naxos* by Cecil Roth; *Postwar Germans* by David Rodnick; *Germany 2000 Years* by Kurt F. Reinhardt; *Nazi Germany: Its Women and Family Life* by Clifford Kirkpatrick; *German Youth: Bond or Free* by Howard Becker; *American Society* by Robin Williams; *The American People: A Study in National Character* by Geoffrey Gorer; *The American Character* by D. W. Brogan; *The Land and People of Canada* by Frances Aileen Ross; *The New State of Israel* by Gerald de Gaury; *The Jew in American Life* by James Waterman Wise; *The Rape of Palestine* by William B. Ziff; *Jew-Hate as a Sociological Problem* by Peretz F. Bernstein; *Judaism: A Way of Life* by Samuel S. Cohen; *The Rise of the Jew in the Western World* by Uriah Zevi Engleman; *The Jews: Their History, Culture, and Religion* by Louis Finkelstein; *Passover: Its History and Traditions* by Theodore Herzl Gaster; *Agenda for American Jews* by Eli Ginzberg; *People at Bay: The Jewish Problem in East-Central Europe* by Oscar I. Janowsky; *History and Destiny of the Jews* by Josef Kastein; *Promise and Fulfillment: Palestine 1917-1949* by Arthur Koestler; *Caravan: The Story of the Middle East* by Carleton S. Coon; *The Middle East* by W. B. Fisher; *The*

Blight of Asia by George Horton; *Native Peoples of the Pacific World* by Felix M. Keesing; *The Voice of Asia* by James A. Michener; *The Vision of India* by Sisirkumar Mitra; *Turkish Crossroads* by Bernard Newman; *Near Eastern Culture and Society* by Cuyler Young; *Red Storm Over Asia* by Robert Payne; *Peasant Life in China* by Hsiao-Tung Fei; *The Religion of China* by Hans H. Gerth; *The Chinese Mind* by Gung-Hsing Wang; *A Chinese Village* by Martin C. Yang; *Thunder Out of China* by Theodore H. White; *The New Turks* by Eleanor Bisbee; *The Scot in History* by Wallace Notestein; *The Irish Countryman* by C. M. Arensberg; *The Burden of Egypt* by J. A. Wilson; *Ireland Her Own* by T. A. Jackson; *The Irish: A Character Study* by Sean O'Faolain; and *The Eskimos, Their Environment and Folkways* by Edward Moffat Weyer.

79. See *Heredity and Politics* by J. B. S. Haldane; *Of Societies and Men* by Caryl P. Haskins; and *Morals Since 1900* by Gerald Heard.

80. See *American Social Problems* by Howard W. Odum, Introduction and chap. I.

81. See *Cultural Sciences* by Florian Znaniecki.

82. See *The Taming of the Nations* by F. S. C. Northrop.

PART FOUR

Sociology in the Service of Society

Savoir prevoir et prevoir pouvoir

Auguste Comte

INTRODUCTORY NOTE

As a practical theorist, Howard Odum recognized the close relationship between theory and action as well as that between theory and research. He had a favorite saying: "If it won't work it isn't sound theory." As with theory, his was an applied research through which he worked toward a solution of specific problems. In the selected papers in this section, Odum points to: (1) the need for a practical social theory; (2) theory in its relation to public welfare and to national, regional, and state planning; and (3) education as the way forward in the social sciences. As early as 1924, in an editorial on "Dependable Theory and Social Change," Odum wrote, "Present-day social theory has no excuse for existence except as it becomes a scientific mode to meet the needs of social change." And again, "Social theory is nothing short of an adequate blueprint for social building." So in order to make practical theory effective, he early saw the need for a closer cooperation between the physical and the social sciences, the unity of which he emphasized as a "new keynote" to practical social theory. And in his address before the Harvard Alumni in 1939, he developed the thesis that such cooperation should be the coming major stategy of university research and realistic learning which might result in founding "an enduring society" through achieving "a better balance between the civilization of the state and the machines, on the one hand, and the culture of the folk and of learning, on the other."

In a discussion of Odum's theory of the relation of national, state, and regional planning, a logical starting point might well be his "Ideals of Government," written in 1926. Here he points out the fallacy, often found in formal theory, as well as in popular impression, "that the state and government constitute society itself, and that democracy is only a matter of political opportunity. Nothing could be further from the truth. . . . Democracy is more than a form of government; it is as broad as life . . ." and embraces all the major social institutions. "Hence we may say that a good democratic society is one in which the institutions are strong enough to guarantee each individual an opportunity to grow into normal development and to have full expression of personality and livelihood." In the selection on "The New Public Welfare," Odum's philosophy and technique of government are reinforced in the inclusive nature of the term "public welfare," which he defines broadly as "that very service of democratic government which provides organization, technique and means for making democracy effective in the unequal places—effective in extended application as well as ideals, written laws and statutes, and in constitutional provisions." Therefore, ". . . the alternative to present American democracy will be orderly transitional democracy, with more than ever the titanic struggle for equilibrium and balance between conflicting forces, such as individuation and socialization, and between theory and practice."

Social planning in this context is no longer an academic matter. Its organization and function must be set in the framework of American democracy. Then, "planning American style, becomes a sort of balance wheel to make possible the new technical, national planning, while at the same time preserving the American form of government." Regional development ("Regional Development and Government Policy") becomes an essential measure for the enrichment of the American whole. But there can be no regional planning without national planning. In fact, national, state, and regional planning boards, functioning together in a coordinated attack upon the most important needs alone can bring about a balanced culture and economy through the democratic process. Accordingly, "the heart of regional balance is found in the search for equal opportunity for all the people through the conservation, development and use of their resources in the places where they live, adequately readjusting to the interregional culture and economy of the other regions of the world or of the nation. . . ."

To Howard Odum the way forward was through education. His "Education in the Secondary Schools of the South" serves to show how he presented the cause of regional development to more popular audiences. Odum must have made hundreds of such addresses throughout the South, talking to teachers wherever he could and varying each speech enough to justify publication whenever this was demanded by various official groups who served as sponsors. But he also saw the need for an expanding higher education in which the university would make every effort to adapt itself to a modern world of technology and change. Here is the rare opportunity for the social scientist to take the leadership in coordinating the social sciences with the humanities and the physical sciences since they themselves are a part of the scientific revolution. Only in this way can and will the social sciences move forward to build in America a "society at its best."

K. J.

1. *Practical Social Theory*

Dependable Theory and Social

Change [1924]*

If it won't work, it isn't sound theory" was the effective and informal reply of a distinguished sociologist some years ago to a critic who affirmed that social theory was not "practical." By this simple statement he may have meant a number of things. He may have intended a good-natured definition of theory or a careful distinction between the real and the false. He may have meant simply that if a plan or scheme is to become dependable theory it must, as a matter of course, be based upon principles verifiable by experience or observation; or if a body of fundamental principles underlying a science be offered, such principles might also be verifiable by the application of that science; or if a vast amount of abstract knowledge be organized as theory, then such knowledge is the result of the measurement of specific facts; or again if the theory proposed be an explanation of social phenomena, forces, or action, it must be based upon analysis of "societal facts." This much is merely a Websterian sort of definition of theory. But much that is set forth as "theory" or that is reputed to be "theoretical" is merely personal opinion out of social perspective, or utopian generalization based upon subjective evidence. On the other hand, much of the best "theory" may not appear to "work" because of its delayed and imperfect application or because of the imperfect medium through which it must act. Tragedy and ridicule lie athwart the paths where academic theory has preceded social action or where scientific theory has awaited its day to transform varying aspects of world contacts.

* Editorial notes from *The Journal of Social Forces,* II (January 1924), 282-86.

Illustrations are legion. But they add *to* rather than detract *from* the value of real social theory—theory which stands its turn to meet the challenging demands of a changing social order. . . .

DEFINITIONS AND LIMITATIONS

And yet strictures of social theory there are, violent and vocal, popular and academic. They are not to be ignored, both because it is important to reinterpret the meaning of social theory for the everyday man and to revitalize it for the pure academician; or again because the present time is especially in need of scientific social theory, long wrought out, adequately interpreted and applied. With many of the viewpoints, partially representative, it is not difficult to sympathize.

*   *   *   *   *   *

WRONG INTERPRETATIONS

As a matter of fact most of the popular criticisms of social theory are based upon a misunderstanding of the facts and a sentimental impatience which lacks faith in the efficacy of truth. Professor Giddings' statement in the May [1923] *Journal* [*of Social Forces*] offers an adequate comment upon this situation. "For practical reasons even more than for merely intellectual ones, we need rigorously scientific studies of human society and of our individual relations to it. In particular we need such studies of the societal interests that are labelled 'public policy,' 'education,' 'missions,' and 'social work.' I am aware that this proposition is resented by men and women who suffer from an anti-'academic' complex and worry lest 'the human touch,' 'the ways of the neighborhood' and the naïve thinking of 'plain people' shall have spontaneity squeezed out of them by theory. This is an unfortunate misapprehension of what science is and what it does for us. It ought not to be necessary at this late day, but it is necessary, to tell the general public that science is nothing more nor less than getting at facts, and trying to understand them; and that what science does for us is nothing more nor less than helping us to face facts. Facing the facts that the physical and biological sciences have made known to us has enabled us to live more comfortably and longer than men once did. Facing the facts that the social sciences are making known to us, and will make better known, should enable us to diminish human misery and to live more wisely than the human race has lived hitherto. In particular it should enable us to take the kinks out of our imperfect codes of conduct. It will be discovered one day that the chief value of social science, so far from being academic, is moral."

*   *   *   *   *   *

BLUEPRINTS OF PROGRESS

But there are other factors than the common misunderstandings of what scientific theory is. There has been a constantly increasing opinion that social theory has passed the metaphysical stage or that social theory consists merely or primarily of discussions *about* social theory. But, as Professor Barnes points out, there has been a "gradual trend away from the transcendental and metaphysical generalizations toward a realistic consideration of the actual facts and processes of institutional life and growth, of the real activities of men living in conflicting and coöperating groups." For the purpose of this discussion, I would go as far as to say that present-day social theory has no excuse for existence except as it becomes a scientific mode to meet the needs of social change. But as such it is essential, not only for the measurement of the important factors in social life but also for the direction of social organization and the development of social statesmanship. Or again, at the risk of using a partial analogy, social theory is nothing short of an adequate blueprint for social building. No real builders will do without the best possible specifications and blueprints; and they must go on paper before they go into brick and mortar; but they are based upon "precise observation," accurate "measurements and accountings," and "systematic checking up." And for this reason they are good "theory" such as will become the forerunner of substantial, durable, and artistic edifices. For this sort of social theory there is great need; and for the making of it there is great dearth of social architects.

*   *   *   *   *   *

CURRENT CRITICISMS

Indeed one ventures to wonder just how much of such social theory is being developed at the present time. . . . The criticisms [of such theory] are these: That the constant substitution of talk, study, and discussion merely *about* social theory of the past may be calculated to do for sociology what the German philological method did for the classics; that the study of historical sociology, no matter how thorough, if it has not a view to social development, is a poor substitute for adequate modern dependable social theory; and that, after all, it is poor and incomplete scholarship. Furthermore, that the competitive effort of the professor of sociology to evolve some theory—purely for the theory's sake—which will outrank some other professor's theory, or which will save his face—a "contribution" having been made—stands a poor chance to rank among the immortals as compared with genuine theory brought forth in the ecstasy of a victory after long study, exhaustive research, and desperate search after truth. There is, further, an over-abundance of discussion and opinion being set forth as theory, substantiated neither by precise observations and accurate measurements on the one hand, nor systematic "checking up," on the other. While some of these opinions, to come back to the blueprint analogy again, may make attractive pictures, they furnish nothing of specifications or measurements whereby the social engineer, the social builder or the common worker of whom society is made can rear a superstructure of progress. The pictures are sometimes attractive—so attractive indeed that their "dreamy contemplation" is far pleasanter than the plain specification, the choice of which means the labor of years, the faith of the builder, the vision of the prophet. There is yet one other query: Where are those who have set themselves to the search after truth and the performance of study-tasks, the first fruits of which are to be expected only after one score—two score years? Rather, do we not count a single year as a watch in the night?

*   *   *   *   *   *

THE SCIENTIFIC BASIS

After all is said, there still remains the fascinating and unending tasks ahead, with always the return to the original basis of fact, scientific method of study, and adequate organization for effective application. . . . Perhaps nothing at this time is more important to the sociologist . . . than the recognition and attainment of better standards and methods of measuring the results of work done and observations made.

A New Keynote and Emphasis in

Social Theory [1928]*

Three observations concerning the present trend in the social sciences are important. One is more recognition of an emphasis upon the essential unity between the social sciences and the physical sciences; another is the increasing emphasis and value placed upon social theory; a third is the more effective integration of the theoretical, quantitative and scientific with the practical in social study.

Now these might at first glance appear to be a revival of earlier organic analogies between the physical and social sciences; of the over-emphasis upon theorizing, or of the type of provincial tie-in of early classical economic theorists with problems and policy. As a matter of fact the present trends are in striking contrast to the older tendencies. The present alignment represents a very real unity of basic relationship and of essential law and development. Social psychology, social biology, social anthropology, social ethics, social statistics are so far from being mere analogies that they derive their scientific validity from the fact that they are *different* from the physical branches and attain their "science" from their contribution *to* the science of society through the integration of background, method, content, and objectives. In this newer and more sane interrelation between the social and the physical sciences is found considerable

* *American Social Science Notes* (featuring the *American Social Science Series,* Howard W. Odum, General Editor. New York: Henry Holt and Company, November 1928), pp. 1, 6, 7.

promise of really effective synthesis in the future study of human society.

Again, there is perhaps an even greater contrast between the old "theorizings" and speculation and the present premium placed upon synthesis and scientific theory which derive their validity from the fact that they actually grow out of social situations and factual problems. Such theory is developing because of and in accord with the demands made upon modern social science, and their interrelations grow logically out of the need for cooperative attack with the best methodology which all the social sciences can produce. There is indeed a high value set upon political theory, or economic theory, or sociological theory, or any social theory which is comprehensive, concrete, scientific, and permanent enough to serve as working "blue prints" rather than as mere artistic pictorial "elevations" of society and its relationships.

It must be admitted that the situation is still one of trend, and that much of the coherent scientific theory desired is in the future. Yet the trend is accredited as being full of promise and not without considerable evidence of its successful products. A kingdom for the scholar who can really produce such theory—so acclaim the economists, the sociologists, the political scientists, the anthropologists, and the others whose university departments, whose research groups, and whose teaching and technical demands are yet unfilled. It so happens, therefore, that the vigorous attacks upon concrete places of research, the critical review of past literature and cultural development, and the search after *new* materials in region, case, in method, and in scientific analysis and correlation, afford the exact procedure through which may be expected genuine scientific synthesis and social theory. To his present tasks, as never before, the social scientist must bring a far better equipment in scholarly backgrounds of literature, of cultural heritage and of theory, alongside acquaintance with and participation in the dynamics of concrete research, quantitative method and case study. The waiting years of teaching, research and professional work, made full of this sort of search for equipment and contribution, will not be lean years.

Of a Closer Cooperation between the

Physical Sciences and the

Social Sciences [1939]*

In so distinguished a company of scholars and alumni, symbolic of the best of the past and the present in America's quest for reality in the modern world, perhaps the most that a visiting "professor" could venture would be the asking of certain rhetorical questions; and, after the manner of the professor, venturing the answers in a series of premises after the professor's own liking. For you recall that in the classroom the professor usually insists that his students must not accept what he says as fact without the most careful checking up; but that also he usually implies that when the students do check up they will find what he says just about right!

Now, it is not quite so easy to carry this assumption over into the alumni audience. Yet, it is in something of this spirit that I am inclined to think that the professor and the alumnus of the present day are in need of both a greater understanding and a greater sympathy than formerly, since the professor is called upon to answer more difficult questions and the alumnus is strained ever more and more to hold that loyalty and implicit faith in the professor that he used to have in his college days.

* Remarks before Harvard alumni in connection with his being awarded the honorary degree of Doctor of Laws by Harvard University at Commencement, 1939 (*Harvard Alumni Bulletin*, XLI [July 7, 1939], 1124-28). Reprinted by permission.

And professor and alumnus alike are solicitous of the university's welfare—the professor lest its lamp of learning and liberty be dimmed; the alumnus lest his *alma mater* take the wrong turning of the road in the crises of America today.

Thus, it is with a sort of plea for a mutual understanding and working together that I respond to your generous invitation today by asking whether or not one supreme task of the university, both for creative work and for survival value after the ideals of both professor and alumnus, may not be found in new reaches in the coöperation of the physical sciences and the social sciences on new frontiers not yet mastered.

You may recall the distinguished psychologist's illustration of two boys carrying a log. This was an example of how two in coöperation can do what neither alone can accomplish, yet each was still himself. Without coöperation much of the energy and strength of each might be wasted. With coöperation we have the equivalent of an effective social achievement.

I recall a story my father told me just a few weeks ago down in Georgia about one of these new pioneers, the farm tenant, exploring new frontiers of farm ownership. This man, long landless and list-less, had by means of the Farm Security Administration bought a farm near where he had been living all of his life on rented land. In time, yea, in a very short time, the place prospered; fields were green, houses and fences repaired, food crops, livestock, money crops seemed to give promise of a fine balance between the man and his land.

And in due time the church pastor came to visit and was loud in his praise of what God had wrought. Said he, "Brother, you and God in partnership have been rewarded with the fruits of faith, and you should give thanks night and morning to God for this partner-ship."

"Well, Reverend," answered the man, "you ought to have seen this farm when the Lord had it all by hisself!"

Many of you recall that the social scientists and the public at large quarrel with what the physical scientists are doing with the world. Some of you may recall also the report of a Nobel prize winner in words to the effect that the social scientists have had this world in charge lo these many years and look what it had come to!

Manifestly, the implication is that no one of these alone—the physical scientists, the social scientists, the public—have found the answers.

Is it probable, therefore, that in the closer coördination of the physical sciences with the social sciences, working hand in hand, on new cultural and physical frontiers, with the results of their work made available to the public through skills and the professions, may be found the next major strategy of university research and realistic learning?

Is it probable that this new frontier upon which these joint forces will meet may be found in an enduring society which may be attained only through a better balance and equilibrium between the civilization of the state and the machines, on the one hand, and the culture of the folk and of learning, on the other?

Now, I do not wish just to be projecting a series of stereotyped, academic assumptions, because I believe these constitute two of the most practical and realistic questions that can be asked of university men everywhere. For, whatever the phrases may mean, we are constantly being told that there are new frontiers to be mastered, and that man in the modern world must master the industrial and technical forces of the age or be mastered by them. From English Royalty to American common man, leaders of science and learning are challenged to meet the crisis.

Civilization is destroying society, they say.

Machines are masters of men.

Modern civilization is top-heavy with science. Science is lopsided; technology is a runaway.

The spirit of man, the inner worth of the individual, the spark of liberty are all endangered by this modern totalitarian civilization.

Now, even though this is "old stuff" and we are tired of hearing it, by the same token that is all the more reason why we must not only attempt to say something new, but to do something different.

All over the land, in commencement addresses and in learned journals and in the great literary magazines, the universities are heralded as torchbearers to rescue modern culture from this mad civilization.

I doubt if, on the projection of their present trend, the universities constitute the sure guarantees that we proclaim.

For, on the one hand, university science and technology, brilliantly going their own way and often scornful of societal objectives and the social sciences, point unerringly to more and more artificial society and supertechnology, whose demands exceed the capacity of living institutions and people to absorb and adjust.

And, on the other, the intellectuals, the humanists, and the social scientists, again often brilliantly going their own way, point again and again to a super-civilization as the *summum bonum* or the supreme end of society, with the social sciences too often substituting the imitation of the physical sciences for their utilization and implementation in realistic research and work.

Yet, one has only to examine recent issues of *Science,* the *Popular Science Monthly,* and the learned journals in biology, chemistry, and physics to note the extraordinary volume and quality of new exploration into the relation of science to society in such fields as engineering, biology, farm chemurgy, plant and animal ecology, plant and animal genetics, agricultural science, and many others; or to note the new emphasis of the American Association for the Advancement of Science upon the social implications of science; or the major features of the venerable American Philosophical Society.

So, too, in the field of the social sciences heroic efforts for scientific discovery, for realistic social inventions in the form of social planning, in which the assistance of the engineers and mathematicians, the chemists, physicists, and biologists is assumed, are evidence of the work of pioneers here.

Yet, it must be clear that many of the ambitious schemes of the scientists appear immature, unrealistic, and even dangerous; the social scientists appear unable even to get started; the intelligentsia stand afar off, perhaps meting the pity, rather than the censure, of a mature and intelligent world; and all are hesitant in the sweep of time, technology, and the new realism of mass man.

A hundred years' recording of the United States Patent Office shows a little more than 2,142,000 patents on inventions with a consistent diminution of output immediately after each great crisis; could we portray a similar record of attempted social inventions, the pathetic story would reflect again the old adage about necessity being the mother of invention. Yet the physical scientists and the social scientists were far apart here, and the world of science was too skeptical of social experimentation. Mr. Justice Brandeis has pointed out that in view of the fact that great triumphs of science have been in large measure due to experimentation, "to stay experimentation in things economic and social is a grave responsibility." Yet society has neither believed in nor been prepared for such social progress.

Something of the sensational advance in the marginal land between physical science and social science is reflected in the extraordinary sweep of inventions relating to biological matters, the total number of which, added to the patented inventions, reveals an extraordinary upturn since the 1920's.

Yet, these are only a part of the explanation of why civilization is top-heavy with scientific inventions. One does not have to subscribe to the Spenglerian cyclical law of civilization to distinguish between super-civilization and enduring society, which must be attained through a working equilibrium between civilization and culture. For this impending super-civilization, in all its totalitarian trends, stands in many bold contrasts to the new culture: of the state, super-state over against the folk and learning; organization over people, mass over individual, power over freedom, machines over men, quantity over quality, artificial over natural, technological over human, production over reproduction.

The verdict is one for too much civilization and too little culture.

Now I venture to suggest two testing grounds for university exploration into the study of this new balance between civilization and culture. The first lies within the framework of a greater Americanism approximated through the new regionalism, the theme of which I have characterized as essentially that of a great American Nation, the land and the people, in whose continuity and unity of development, through a fine equilibrium of geographic, cultural, and historical factors, must be found not only the testing grounds of American democracy, but, according to many observers, the hope of Western civilization. Manifestly, this is a task for all that all groups of scientists can do.

The second is found in the search, not for what science and technology are doing to society, but what the processes are, through which such tremendous transformations are being wrought. We have voluminous reports on the effects of invention and technology on society, but little on how they come to pass. I venture to predict, therefore, an entirely new area for the combined inquiries of the physical and social sciences. This will be research into the startling new phenomena of the technicways, which, in contemporary civilization, transcend the old folkways and supplant the mores, thus so modifying human behavior and institutions as to outmode the earlier rate of societal evolution.

Now this new frontier of the technicways does not seem to me to be merely a new series of jargon and terminology, for just as the old folkways and mores were practical ways of meeting needs in the long, cultural road of evolution, ultimately leading to the development of institutions, morals, and learning, so in this hectic world of bigness, speed, technology, super-organization, the technicways are the new ways of meeting the needs of a technological world. One only needs to look at the new technicways of war which violate all of the old folkways and agreements with reference to women, children, hospitals, institutions of learning, art; or the swift-changing episodes of our own science, economics, learning, morals, changing behavior patterns, and the demands upon our institutions which are accelerating the whole rate of our cultural evolution.

Perhaps in all of this I am appealing for a new opportunity for the social sciences, in which, working upon the great results of the physical sciences and working with them, we may attain results in some of the fields of social inventions and social technicways, which may match the flood tide of technology now sweeping down upon us. Here is a task adequate for any university and for all that the new social sciences can muster.

Perhaps I may close by comparing the younger of the social sciences to an incredible, bushy-headed, country bumpkin come to Paris, destined to usher in a new romanticism and to divert "the stream of French letters from its narrow channel into a wide and rushing river." To young Alexandre Dumas came five friendly influences—four friends and a notable company to urge him on. One friend was forever impressing upon the youth the shame of his abysmal ignorance. Another was ever opening the doors of living literature. A third relentlessly spurred him on to constant achievement. A fourth assured him resources, time, and leisure. And a fifth provided him with a finishing school or university for his artistry.

It is in some such spirit that we venture to hope that alumni everywhere will prove to be five friendly forces to make effective the new and realistic social science. Or I may make simpler comparison, this time using the quaint wisdom of one of our grand old Negro women who insisted that "when a puhson ain't got no education, they sho has to use their brains." It would be our wish that in return for these friendly forces and helps, in these days of great opportunity, we should try to use both our education and our brains.

2. National, Regional, and State Planning

Ideals of Government [1926]*

The mistaken idea is sometimes found both in formal theory and in popular impression that the state and government constitute society itself, and that democracy is only a matter of political opportunity. Nothing could be further from the truth, unless it was the other and somewhat similar false doctrine that the church was the sole determining social institution of power. The state itself has been shot through and through with the influence of other institutions. And just as the great social philosophies of the world have been colored with political theory, so almost all the great political theorists have found data and arguments from religion, natural law, the concept of justice, community organization, and a democracy more comprehensive than merely political democracy.

To trace the influence of Christianity upon the state is not a simple process but one of considerable perplexity, involving the correlation of the state with other institutions and other forces. What are the nature and functions of these institutions and forces that have shaped the destinies of individuals? How have these institutions and forces been related to each other, how related to the state and government, how influenced in the course of recent centuries by Christianity? How, in short, has Christianity affected, both indirectly and directly, the present cumulative status of political democracy as the chief mode of social progress? Such an inquiry brings into view the importance of the changing emphasis placed upon the individual, and the part which the several institutions and forces in question have had in placing this emphasis upon the individual and in making or marring

* Chap. XIX, pp. 230-43 in "Christianity and Modern Thought," Vol. IV in *An Outline of Christianity: The Story of Our Civilization* (5 vols.; New York: Bethlehem Publishers, 1926).

his life and happiness. By what attempts and vicissitudes, what philosophies and concepts, has the institution of state and government gradually evolved?

A list of the larger influences which mould the individual and direct social progress would include six major social institutions: the home and family, the school and education, the church and religion, the state and government, industry and labor, community and association.

Each institution shows, in the history of its development, a two-fold nature. The one is the form of social organization through which it functions, and the other is its generic social value and quality. The type of home may vary widely within the standard family. The school of yesterday differs widely from the school of today, although the great generic process of education is fundamental. The Catholic Church differs widely from the Protestant, although the institution of religion is continuous. Forms of state in at least four great nations were changed incidentally in the recent World War [World War I], but the processes of government must go on. Industry is a comparatively new institution, although the institutional law of life found in labor is as old as Adam. Finally, the communities of the Middle Ages and our present rural communities and cities have differed widely, but the essential process of association and of living together in group units is a minimum essential for society. These institutions depend for their effectiveness and unity upon one another. They stand as a buffer between the individual and the great processes of social change. If well builded, nurtured, and strengthened they promote normal growth and development instead of abnormality and revolution.

In addition, these institutions serve to direct and control the great dominant forces, among which we should include personal leadership, geographic environment, individual differences and heredity, and general social complexes and casual groupings. The institutions may develop or retard strong leadership. They fit in with the processes of individual adaptation and social inheritance. They help mankind to organize and marshal its forces to master the physical environment. They stand together as protection against the mass mind and as receiving-stations for mass influence.

From an examination of these institutions it is clear that political democracy is only a part of the whole. Democracy itself is more than a form of government; it is as broad as life and will be found to include the following forms.

Corresponding to the home and family there is that most important democracy, *organic democracy,* by which is meant the right to equal opportunity; the right of the child to be born well, to be nurtured and educated; the right of the mother and the women of a family to enjoy opportunities for normal expression and for devotion to humanity and the family; the right of race and nations to become a part of the world's system of justice. What shall it profit a child, or an individual crippled in his early stages of development, if he shall gain the whole opportunity to vote?

Corresponding to the school, there is the more largely accepted principle of *educational democracy,* which has generally been conceded to be one of the great contributions of the nineteenth century.

Corresponding to the church and religion is the principle of *religious democracy,* which has been a dominant note in the development of government and other institutions.

Corresponding to industry and work there is the principle of *industrial democracy.* For long years industry and labor were considered to be a matter of private concern; but if society and the state could have come to recognize industry as one of the great major social institutions, much of the strife, struggle, and present-day perplexity might have been avoided. This problem of industrial democracy is no more all of democracy than is religious freedom and political suffrage.

Finally, we find the principle of *social democracy.* Opportunities that may come through such institutions as the family, church, school, state, industry can scarcely be conserved unless the larger institution of community shall become the essence of social organization and international community.

In addition to its correspondence with the influential institutions democracy shows the influence of the dominant forces we have listed. Democracy must have its leaders; it must tend to develop every individual into a potential leader and into one capable of following other leaders as well. Democracy must take into consideration geographic influences and whatever there is of inequality in nature, as well as differences in age, sex, and race.

Throughout all this cumulative course of democratic tendency and theory the individual has become more and more the chief social objective. This may seem a commonplace now, but it has not always been so. The changing emphasis upon the individual has been a product of long struggle and costly evolution. There are many sides to this emphasis. With the purely educational or the physical or the abstractly philosophical sides we are not here concerned. But the principle of individual opportunity is fundamental to all our modern concepts of democracy. As Professor John Dewey says: "Democracy has many meanings; but if it has any moral meaning, it is found in resolving that the supreme test of all political institutions and industrial arrangements shall be the contribution they make to all-round growth of every member of society." Hence we may say that a good democratic society is one in which the institutions are strong enough to guarantee each individual an opportunity to grow into normal development and to have full expression of personality and livelihood. We may go further and say that whenever in the long road of human history individuals have failed, whether through poverty, ignorance, crime, vice, or premature death, some one or more of the institutions have failed him in his hour of need. It is a part of the sovereignty of government to take care that institutions do nurture and develop the individual. The contrast today between the old idea that the citizen exists to serve the state, and the idea that the state's sole purpose is to serve the citizen, is as marked as it was victorious, in theory at least, in the World War.

The abolition of slavery, the abolition of exploitation of man by man, and the abolition of primary antagonisms that have made a perfect human association and organization possible, have grown out of these great epochal concepts.

It can easily be seen that, in the development and control of social institutions and forces, the key institution is that of state and government. It is equally clear that the problem of measuring the influences acting upon government involves today more factors than ever before. We have, for instance, legislation and social service for such purposes as the nurture and protection of the home and family, the promotion of more comprehensive social education, the protection of religious liberties, the guarantee of civil and political rights, the recognition, promotion, and control of great economic processes, unifying of groups and peoples, and the promotion of universal peace. All of these are important concerns of the state. On the other hand, it is quite clear that the home and family, the technique and processes of education, the history and development of Christianity, the growth of the whole community organization and of the world peace movement —it is plain that their evolution, form, and ideals have challenged the institution of the state: government is now not simply a policing force but a social servant. How the great institution of government has evolved through its various stages and how the elements of Christianity have affected it, both indirectly through the other institutions, and directly since the Reformation, is one of the most interesting stories of human institutions. Some of the story is like a mystery with the outcome ever uncertain, and some of it features the villain; nevertheless it is a great story, with promise of the happy outcome.

For the larger democratic form and ideals of our present-day government have evolved through slow and varying processes. In a single hurried survey of the writings of some four score philosophers and social theorists one may find approximately fifty different concepts of government. Hegel would call it a spiritual essence. Lilienfeld, Schäffle, Spencer, and others might call it the trend of the social organism. Cole would refer to it as a unique entity, while Duguit would label it purposive association. And so other theories include the concept of a coercive institution, a social organism, a psychological organism, a means of defense, an aggregation of purposive groups, the supreme human association, the microcosm of the whole human process, the organized control of the minority, the determinate creature of community, the collective policeman, the creature product of social evolution, mutual aid, the voluntary contract, the essence of race struggle, contractual society, the social compact, and the restraint of conflicting interests.

Some of these may well be mentioned briefly in connection with the general evolution of government and the specific influence of Christianity upon theories of government. The forms of state have constituted a notable and varied series. With varying form they have embraced monarchy, aristocracy, democracy, the democratic republic, the democratic empire, the representative democracy, the attempt at pure democracy; forms of bureaucracy, absolutism, expansionism, imperialism, oligarchy, plutocracy, theocracy, physiocracy, clericalism, militarism, sovietism, and the like; theories of the federal state, the city state, the world state; the tyranny of the individual, the tyranny of the crowd; various concepts of sovereignty, including personal sovereignty, class sovereignty, mass sovereignty, property sovereignty, rational or intellectual sovereignty. Similarly, theories of liberty have been set forth accounting for civil liberty, fiscal liberty, personal liberty, racial or national liberty, international political liberty. James Bryce listed four kinds: civil liberty, or the exemption from control in respect to person and property; religious liberty, or the exemption from control of religious opinions and practices; political liberty, or the participation of the citizen in government of the community; and individual liberty, or the exemption from control of things not directly related to the welfare of the community as a whole.

These references to concepts and forms of government are given only to indicate something of the scope of political theory and the complexity of its development. Such a brief list does not, of course, attempt to enumerate technical political theories or to include the purely philosophical speculations. There are, too, many of these including contrasting conflicting speculations relating to idealism, naturalism, pragmatism, or those of monism and pluralism, moralism, and non-moralism, and the purely philosophical aspects of aristocracy versus democracy. There are also the legalistic theories centering upon jurisprudence. There are the proletarian political theories, enumerated by Professor Douglas—collectivism, anarchism, syndicalism, guild socialism, consumers' co-operation, agrarian distribution, the single tax, and bolshevism. There are also the contributions of the newer social psychology to political theory, as well as those of anthropology and various race and ethnic factors. Most of these are recent in their manifestation and show more clearly the present indications that political theory is still forming, with manifold branches of influence difficult to isolate completely. They will appear in excellent perspective, however, if placed alongside the earlier history of ideas of state and government.

What have been the influences making for progress in popular government in the modern world, and especially since the Reformation? To what extent has each of these been effective? What are the new forces or causes affecting modern political theory and practice? Bryce gives four causes of the progress of popular government since the obscure Italian beginnings. The first is the influence of religious ideas; the second is discontent with oligarchic misgovernment; the third is social and political conditions favoring equality; the fourth is abstract theory. It is, of course, difficult to estimate the influence of religion on the last phase. The question may well be raised as to whether or not a fifth cause could be found in the modern crises that have followed the World War [World War I] and in the very great social change and upheaval the world over. Professor Merriam, in his discussion of recent tendencies in political thought, lists three outstanding social features of this era. These are the further development of industrialism and urbanism, the new contacts of diverse races or nationalities, and the rise of feminism. From present indications it would seem that there is a fourth outstanding element, observable in that feature of the popular controversy over religion and evolution which manifests a tendency toward the domination of government by religious forces. How destructive this influence will be must depend, as it has depended in the past, upon the degree to which the religious factor becomes narrow, intolerant, and superstitious, or the degree to which the elements of true Christianity come to be applied to all the institutions and forces enumerated and thus indirectly to influence the state for good.

Let us turn now to the consideration of the influence of Christianity, one of the largest factors involved, upon the state and government. With the other influences we are concerned here only indirectly, as they are inseparably bound up with the theory and technique of governmental procedure and the origins and growth of democratic ideals. There are still other forces which are specially important in the period before the Reformation in the later periods of development, and in our own time. How Christianity picked up the thread, and persistently succeeded in weaving a fabric which has served as a background for many modern efforts, and now awaits final touches, is a theme worthy of many chapters. Says Professor Dunning, after tracing the history of political theory from its earliest stages, "Then came Christianity upon the scene. As this faith rose to influence and power its teachings transformed political as well as other philosophy. God and His scheme of creation gradually became recognized as the first cause of man and all human affairs. The divine will fixed the character and operation of social institutions." That is, if Rome ruled nations, God ruled Rome; if nation ruled men, God ruled nation; if there were human rulers, they ruled by the will of God. If, again, there were human laws, they were sanctioned by the divine law. Law and institutions made by man were indirectly from God. There were two distinct systems of rules for mankind: that of the temporal was from man, and that of the spiritual from God. Man must be subject to man, ruler, or government, sometimes church, sometimes state, but always with authority from God. There could be no questioning of the right of God, and consequently government found its sanction and emphasis in the ruler's right derived from God rather than in consent of the people.

In the fourteenth and fifteenth centuries arose the doctrine that by nature—God's nature, it is true—all men are free and equal; and if equal, then God's authority must not operate through any one superior being, but must reside in all the people. For two centuries thereafter the interpretation of nature on the one hand, and the quarrel of creeds on the other, brought about a lessened regard for divine authority. This was followed by an enhanced individualism and democracy, forerunner of more modern tenets of government. The nineteenth century found one of its main tasks in the attempt to harmonize the two doctrines of authority and sovereignty on the one hand, and of individual freedom on the other. Neither nature nor God seemed directly adequate, so that the influence of Christianity was exerted indirectly through interpretation, reason, righteousness, morality, history, liberty, justice. Finally, the larger concept of society was held to be the arbiter. What sort of society, then, became the question of importance? In the last of the nineteenth century we find abstract theories developed—the inherent power of society as an organism, the natural rights of the individual, the separateness of state and government from religion.

But at various periods there remained underlying in the minds of the foremost theorists the great idea of God, which was assumed to be dominant as the basic concept. Even Rousseau, who sometimes attacked Christianity as an anti-social force because it separated men from the things of this world, defended the fundamental values in Christianity, such as belief in God, a future life, happiness for the good and punishment for the wicked, the sanctity of social laws and contracts, and "no tolerance of intolerance." Hobbes, who thought that political sovereignty was supreme, felt that "the truth of God's word must prevail in the long run without recourse to restraint"; he was convinced that the Christian virtues of complaisance or pardon, modesty, mercy, forgiving disposition were all conducive to peace, which after all was the purpose of law—to substitute peace for war. Bodin, who believed that God and justice were factors controlling political life and institutions, considered, according to Professor Dunning, "a belief in a supernatural being important for the welfare of the State." In his estimation, however, the details of creed were of little importance, and force at best could be but an indifferent instrument for the maintenance of uniformity of religion among citizens. Locke, who thought that, since the worship of God was a means of eternal salvation, it was entirely outside the realm of the state, nevertheless declared that the atheist is not reliable when it comes to promises, contracts, and oaths which bind human society. Montesquieu reasoned that religion was outside the bounds of human compulsion; yet he discussed Christianity in a spirit of reverence as "unquestioned divine truth." Calvin asserted that the duty of secular leaders "begins with piety and religion," and the very spirit of the Reformation had to do with the relation of man to God. Luther preached the doctrine of passive submission to the established political and social order, though in a different way from the later Tolstoi. In Luther's view secular power was sanctioned by God as controlling those who were not Christians; Christians themselves did not need it. Melanchthon held that natural law included those principles of the human mind which concern the existence of God, our obedience to Him, and the principles concerning "civil institutions which promote His glory." "The first object of all government is the knowledge and glory of God." And so with others. The doctrine of the divine right of kings grew out of the doctrine of the divine character of secular government which was held by most of the greater reformers. Later the divine right of the people came in through the same channel. God sanctioned royalty as a convenience to the people—kings by divine right of the people. Thus the underlying concept of God and of the principles of Christianity went on and on, continuously interwoven with the secular theories.

Bryce states that four outstanding contributions of the Gospel to democracy are discernible. These are that the Creator has given each individual a special divine worth; that in the Creator's sight all souls are equal; that the inner life or "kingdom of heaven" within the individual is supreme; and that it is the duty of God's creatures to love one another. The first of these, he says, applies to freedom of conscience or spiritual liberty, obedience to God being greater than to man; the second implies human equality or equal rights to "life, liberty, and the pursuit of happiness"; the third has to do with purity of life and motive; and the fourth with the Christian community or brotherhood of man. Each of these influences has been used well and used badly.

Aside from these commonly recognized influences of Christianity upon the state, there are at least two other types that must not be omitted. The first of these is the general influence which Christianity has had in giving the individual his newest place in the world of equal opportunity, and its influence upon the other institutions—the family, the school, the church, industry, and the community. When the state comes to pass its laws for the protection and nurture of the family it does so because the family and the ideals thereof have shown the need. When the state comes to legislate for universal education it does so not because it simply wants to educate, but because it recognizes what education means to a democracy and assents to the democratic practice of giving every individual an equal chance in life. When the state legislates with reference to industry it is for the same general reason. The whole modern fabric and technique of government have changed because of the demands of these institutions upon it. In the same way the ideals of these institutions have colored and strengthened the policies of the state in many ways, and in respect to many human activities, government itself thus being a fine complex of all the institutions, guarding their rights, nurturing their needs. The fact, therefore, of Christianity's having had much to do with present standards and forms of the family, of education, of community and neighborliness, and with Christian principles in industry and race relations, is further evidence of a very great total influence upon government.

How the spirit of Christianity works out in actual practice, as for instance in "mothers' aid" [forerunner of Aid to Dependent Children], may become an important inquiry to those who wish to study further. All that the student of history and government needs to do is to classify and analyze the different elements in order to get some idea of the vast influence exerted. In Western democracies, like the

United States, he will find the influence writ large in every state constitution and in the laws of the nation, as well as in the vast pioneer work of the churches, the circuit-riders, and the great hosts of early settlers and later promoters. The Christian influence has not always been apparent in dealing with the American Indians and Negroes; but the deficiency has been due more to theological interpretations than to a wilful violation of Christianity.

The next general influence is one that cannot be measured objectively. It has to do with the innate progressiveness of Christianity. We do not mean the progressiveness of dogmatic theology but of the very spirit of the Christ-founder himself. If it is not progressive it is not Christian. Says Dr. Streeter: "If we believe that we find in Christ a unique revelation of the divine, it follows from that very fact that the Christian revelation is necessarily a progressive one, and that Christianity in proportion as it ceases to be progressive ceases to be Christian. Theology has commonly ignored this inference, but history supports it." And again, "There has come upon the world a supreme crisis, a crisis clamorous with the need for reconstruction—reconstruction all along the line, political, social, moral, religious. The world is looking for guidance; but the guide must be one who has the courage to discard what is obsolete and the insight to create what is new." This, Dr. Streeter thinks, is Christianity—the real Christianity of Jesus. Whether in the midst of our very complex situations and problems, it shall take its place in molding standards and ideals which shall be translated into modern methods of government, depends upon the church and what its interpretation and guidance prove to be.

For there are dangers ahead, of which two appear strikingly prevalent. The one is to go back to the purely naturalistic and purely intellectual philosophy, heedless of the ethical, moral, and social values that lie at the very heart of human life and association. The other is to revert to narrow dogmatic religion, intolerant, persecuting, ignorant, as far from the Christ ideal as paganism. This danger is apparent in both Catholic and Protestant intolerance, whether it be in America, with its cult of orthodoxy, or in Russia, with its war on the church in general. Neither of these extremes seems fitted to avail or survive in the modern complexity of civilization. The new period must be a period of technical government wrought out to survive, and in surviving to promote a greater civilization in the most complex society the world has known.

There are the enlarged factors of race; no longer can the clear-cut conviction stand that any people are the chosen of God in the sense that they are given power to subjugate others. This problem applies to situations existing within nations, and also to the world situation. The time has now come to attempt the application, to race situations, of the greatest contribution which Christianity has made: that of community—loving one's neighbor as one's self. Then there is the problem of industry, in which the spirit and laws of Christianity are but beginning to be challenged. Shall it be a Tolstoian literalness, or a Nietzchean antagonism, or the interpretation of community and cooperation? Here is the great problem of justice in urban areas —how can it be met without tyranny or paternalism? This is the age of science and research. Anthropology, biology, sociology, government seek to find the truth. It is an age of technical and administrative details, which can translate ideals into practice.

Into these situations comes the problem of internationalism, of revolution, of the challenge of world community. And through it all we face the reproach that government never yet has adequately provided for the wants of all men in all stations. If government, taking into its ideals the spirit of Christianity which suffers little children, can establish mothers' aid and juvenile courts; if in the spirit of the peacemakers it can work out a program of world community and eliminate war; if in all the manifold principles of Christianity it can, without ecclesiastical bigotry and selfishness, establish a form of government which shall apply these principles in all the hard places: then Christianity shall have exerted its supreme influence, and both government and democracy will be safe.

The New Public Welfare [1925]*

In the history and development of public welfare two strange anomalies appear. One is the almost universal tendency of human society to neglect the study and promotion of its own welfare and adequacy until it has first studied and promoted all things else. The other is the similar uniform habit and tendency toward carelessness, inefficiency, and even graft in the administration of public relief and corrections. Both are absurd and unreasonably illogical. Nevertheless, these are the facts which we have had to face. Just as the study of society was the last of the sciences to develop, so the scientific study and treatment of social deficiencies seems to be the hardest of all tasks to get under way. And, like the police departments of our large cities, traditional breeding grounds for inefficiency, waste and corruption, so public charities and public welfare seem most prone to catch up the straggling threads of loose thinking, non-progressive inertia and stubborn attitudes towards the normal evolution of democratic ideals.

There is now at last, however, a vigorous turn for the better. What was a decade ago a new ideal in the form of departments of public welfare is now coming to be a matter of fact. The burdened taxpayer is coming to realize something of the importance of having self-support in public institutions and of effecting economies in their administration. The public is also coming to realize that self-respect, earning capacity, rebuilding of character and fortune are the normal

* From Howard W. Odum and D. W. Willard, *Systems of Public Welfare* (Chapel Hill: The University of North Carolina Press, 1925), Chap. I, pp. 3-14.

and logical expectation of society's unfortunates. The taxpayer as well as the social worker is learning that it is more economical to keep people out of institutions than to put them in and try to reduce cost after they are in. In all of these processes, together with many others, the old ideas of charities and corrections with their manifold opportunities for waste and inefficiency have given way to the better concepts of public welfare in which protection, preservation and development, through preventive methods, take the place of the old remedial and endless processes. In all of these processes there will be found a very definite philosophy and important technique of government.

At the outset the fact should be emphasized that by "public welfare" is meant, not simply "welfare" or "human welfare" or "social welfare"; but that very definite service of democratic government which provides organization, technique and means for making democracy effective in the unequal places—effective in extended application as well as in ideals, written laws and statutes, and in constitutional provisions. Like "public education," "public welfare" constitutes a very distinctive concept and service. What public education was to the last half of the last century in the development of the democratic ideal, public welfare may well be to the first half of this century. Indeed it seems very probable that progress in the field of public welfare will constitute the outstanding contribution of the half century toward progress in American democracy. But like public education, long considered unnecessary, dangerous and bringing the stigma of charity to its recipients, public welfare must needs take its time to get under way, and must be misunderstood, misinterpreted and surrounded by limitations that impede its progress. It so happens, therefore, that there is perhaps no aspect of public service today that needs interpretation more than public welfare.

Public welfare is a definite part of government. No student of modern conditions will doubt the need of classifying with governmental efforts a division of public service upon which approximately one-fifth of the total general state funds and appropriations is being expended. Nor will he doubt the advisability of working out effective organization and technique for bringing about a larger service and a greater economy in the expenditure of these public moneys. If, on the other hand, the organization and administration of public welfare on efficient and scientific bases can actually save the government money and increase its efficiency in connection with its other divisions of service, the appeal for recognition is twofold. It is very clear that the old "charities and corrections" have been transcended by the newer reasonable, democratic, constructive and preventive, as well as remedial, service to all the people within the state's domain. It is equally clear that the obligation to make good in these newer steps of progress rests alike upon formal government and civil community; upon public officials and public service departments; and upon private voluntary agencies and social workers.

The scope and meaning of public welfare may be stated in other illustrative ways. Public welfare may be the last and perfecting stage in an effective democracy. Or again, public welfare may be to the ideals of a modern complex industrial American democracy what the first constitution was to the ideals of the early pioneers—a definite organization and means to give form and effectiveness to the ideals which they sought to make good. Democratic ideals, and even democratic laws and statutes, writ well in the capitols of state and nation, or embodied in the literature of a growing people—apart from life—will scarcely become permanent enactments if they do not reach the unequal places and the unequal folk. In a nation of very large and rapidly growing population of heterogeneous elements; of a very large and complex industrial development; of a very large and complex urban evolution; and of still larger areas of isolation and rural regions standing out, not as formerly alongside similar areas the country over, but in contrast to more developed sections, the inequality of "equality of opportunity" is likely to become the dominant characteristic unless there be developed a definite organization and technique to take care of such evolution and change. The great state papers of Washington and Lincoln and the others of the past have been great because America has "made them good" through enacted government. The ideals and objectives expressed in later periods can become great and effective only in proportion as they are "made good" by an enacted government and citizenship keeping pace with normal social growth and change.

The problem of the unequal places and unequal folk may be illustrated in scores of incidents and conditions in the very natural and normal development of American life today. The fault is not with growing America but with the inability or lack of disposition to have governmental and community services keep pace with inevitable progress. In past generations the assumption has seemed a natural one that inequality of opportunity was inevitable alongside inequalities in nature and nurture such as a normal life and society everywhere manifest. The newer ideals of democratic government were set forth in opposition to such assumptions. And yet these newer ideals will be without form and void, and inequality of opportunity will grow rather than decrease unless there be worked out perfecting steps through which such ideals may be interpreted and enacted for all the people in whatever areas and in whatever conditions. There may be at the national capitol or at the state capitol most excellent laws on compulsory school attendance, for example; laws designed to give all children an equal opportunity for education and development. But if there be outside and remote areas in which the people are not even aware of such laws; in which they do not and cannot know the meaning of such laws; or in which educational facilities are unequal; or in which social surroundings and inheritance are such as to make impossible the enactment of stated ideals of equality of opportunity, the attempt to enforce such a law but engenders a bitter minority, honestly and pathetically wondering what it is all about. This is true in other matters, such as the treatment of crime and minor criminals; in the matters of poverty and ignorance; in the matters of public health, of industry and of many matters pertaining to the freedom and the pursuit of happiness. It is true not only in isolated rural areas, but in congested city and industrial areas; it is true in the case of foreign elements of the population, and it is true in the case of great complex industries and city populations; and it is true wherever there is not a balance as between agriculture and commerce, capital and labor, big business and community life, town and country, the people and government, extremes and means.

In proportion to the increase of this minority in the unequal places, whether in numbers or in the degree of inequality, it would seem a fair hypothesis to affirm that the ideals and enactments of democratic government were not being made effective. This is true in more ways than one. It is true because the very principles of the democratic ideal, or, if you please, the democratic religion or philosophy, are being violated in both theory and practice. But it is true in an even more definite and forceful way. Whenever this minority of inequality tends to become a majority of discontent and of unknowing representatives of state or nation, existing government will tend to be overthrown and the age-long cycle begins over again. Herein lies the great contribution of community to government.

It may well be assumed that no state or national government, no matter how sincere and active in its endeavors to render democratic services, can succeed by the mere enactment of laws and statutes on its legislative pages. Nor can any large and modern state or nation hope from a centralized and formal headquarters alone to interpret and enact its government. This is true, if for no other reason, because of the physical impossibility of reaching all the elements within its domain. It is true further, because it violates the whole principle of civic cooperation and citizen participation in government, which is the essential basis of democracy. What is needed, therefore, is a guarantee that each social unit—state, county, smaller community —shall say in substance and in fact to the larger governmental unit: "We underwrite for this area and this people, through local government and civic cooperation, the task of both interpreting and carrying out the ideals and standards of democratic governmental services."

This principle has been assumed, of course, in our own government in its great approximation of the democratic ideal; and we have approached the ideal more nearly than has been the case in other times and by other governments. The problem now is to work out such definite organization and administrative means as will complete the services heretofore represented through public education, public health, public protection, and other forms of govermental coöperation as well as governmental coercion. Public welfare in its attempt to minister to the socially deficient, on the one hand, and to the unequal places to prevent social deficiency on the other, offers a next step. Public welfare, therefore, instead of becoming a form of centralized and paternalistic government, emerges as the opposite contribution of community to government, provided it has, of course, adequate organization, technique and standardized methods of operation. To state the problem negatively, the question may well be raised as to what, if not public welfare, in this sense, will prevent our own efforts in democracy from going the way of past efforts or of fulfilling the predictions of the pessimists as soon as our civilization reaches its more complex and difficult stages.

There is another important way in which public welfare may contribute largely to effective democracy. It has been the custom to consider democracy under two general divisions: The general philosophy of equal opportunity and the technique of government through which the ideals of such a philosophy are to be attained. But too often in the philosophy itself and in the social machinery for its effective achievement the whole concept has been too largely limited to political democracy. To seek political equality and equality of social opportunity for adults whose heritage, family life and opportunities for development have been woefully deficient is to offer a poor substitute for the fullness of life. To offer only a representative part in government through the ballot to those whose lives may be handicapped or broken through unequal struggles in industry is to offer a substitute for democracy. To violate the original American principles of religious freedom through intolerance and persecution or through constant religious conflict and strife, even though political representation may be unimpaired, would be going backward and not forward. To offer as a substitute for democratic government a centralized bureaucratic service or dictation by an intellectual aristocracy, or "super legislation" and censorship, is un-American, and also violates the principle of community participation in government. And thus it is with educational democracy and its several aspects. The important fact is that democracy is as many-sided as is life, and that to attain it, not only a philosophy, but a social organization adequate for life must be developed.

... Public welfare [therefore] may be said to contribute to a six-fold democracy of equal opportunity corresponding to the six major institutional modes of life: organic democracy, conforming to the home and family; educational democracy, conforming to opportunities offered through the school and education; political democracy, representing the state and government; religious democracy, representing the church and religion; industrial democracy, representing industry and work; and social democracy, representing the ideals of community and association. It seems clear that no one of these alone can be adequate, either for itself or for the development of the component parts. Industrial democracy can no more be taken for the whole, than can work be counted all of life. Religious freedom is worth little if children may not be born well, grow in health, develop in stature; if mothers and wives in isolated or congested areas must toil in an unequal distribution of life and labor as between men and women, as between neighborhood and families. The great American boast that men may rise from simple beginnings to greater leadership amounts to little if communities may poison youth with vice or idleness or injustice in the courts. Freedom to go to school, or compulsory laws to enforce attendance are pitifully weak in comparison with an effective family welfare service which instructs and leads into the knowledge of what education means and into the desire to attain it. Labor proclamations about participation in the government of industry are worth little compared to the cooperative enactment of an industrial welfare which prevents child labor, unsanitary conditions and the other inequalities which may arise because of the lack of understanding and co-operation on the part of all concerned. In all these aspects of human endeavor public welfare may be expected to make great contributions to progress; and it may be affirmed equally that without an effective public welfare service of this sort, there can be no maximum achievement toward the attainment of human development and human freedom.

The most outstanding example of the new philosophy and technique of public welfare will be found in the organization of state departments. City departments are important, but as yet they represent only special cases and special situations. County organizations are important as a part of the organic system underlying state organization and administration. It would seem most important, therefore, that larger efforts be undertaken to see that the state systems of public welfare in the United States be put upon some such substantial basis as are the state departments of education, of which every state has its definite organization and its definite administrative head. To study more fully, therefore, as much as possible of the present situation and of present organizations in the United States becomes an important task to which social workers, students of politics and public policy will more and more devote themselves.

Orderly Transitional Democracy [1935]*

PROBLEMS OF INEQUALITY

A little more than a decade ago I had the honor to edit a special issue of *The Annals* in which the Academy was pioneering in the field of "Public Welfare in the United States."[1] In this number we characterized public welfare as "the last and perfecting stage in an effective democracy," in that it was "that very definite service of democratic government which provides organization, technique, and means for making democracy effective in the unequal places." The problems of the unequal places and unequal folk were represented as multiplying so rapidly in the fertile soil of unprecedented change and technology that it was predicted that "the inequality of 'equality of opportunity' is likely to become the dominant characteristic" of the changing Nation. And in accordance with the Jeffersonian mandate, it was pointed out that whenever that growing minority which represents gross inequality tends to become a majority, then existing government is likely to be overthrown.

Since that time the sweep and the speed of change, technology, science, and invention have augmented the unequal places by ten million unemployed and their families, begrudged the common satisfactions of wholesome living and loving; by millions of youth in school and out, with no outlook worthy of American ideals; by two million pre-handicapped depression babies; by five million marginal

* The Annals of the American Academy of Political and Social Science, CLXXX (July 1935), 31-39. Reprinted by permission.
1. Vol. CV (January 1923).

folk on land and in urban fringe; and by ten more million of minority groups growing more articulate as the years go by. From the viewpoint, therefore, of the visible ends of democratic achievement, it would appear that we are rapidly approaching the margin of limits beyond which democracy does not and cannot exsit. For these reasons and because of social tensions and of multiple currents and forces now at work, it is imperative that we examine as critically as possible not only the probability of bridging the chasm between the concepts and ideologies of what has been called the American dream and its successful implementation through political democracy, but also to explore the availability of whatever alternatives may be possible.

For the purposes of this paper and under the limitations of time, data, and equipment for the task, we can do little more than approach the assignment through a series of assumptions, which may serve as an introduction and a framework for the further consideration of alternatives to democracy. The first series of assumptions relates to certain definitions and backgrounds basic to our premises; the second to the present status of democracy in the United States; the third to the nature and the areas of our transitional society; the fourth to what appear to be basic social and psychological currents or forces now operating to remold our culture; and the fifth to the movement and motivation for an orderly transitional democracy.

FIRST SERIES OF ASSUMPTIONS

1. The general premises of our discussions assume specifically the American democracy of the United States, rather than merely a general concept and philosophy of democracy. They assume some sort of answer to that critical current questioning as to what really is Americanism. The American characterization, however, applies to the underlying philosophy as well as to the historical recording of actual practices of democracy.

2. The American ideology seemed to assume first of all a political democracy with economic freedom. Within the framework was the "American dream" of every man with his opportunity for development, the lowest to the highest, the highest with only the limits of genius or skill. The American ideal seemed to have implied, therefore, the sociological ideal of superior mankind which sets a premium

upon individual variates from type, upon developed personality, upon the contribution of the genius or superior person who was to attain eminence through these self-same channels of opportunity which in turn was to be made possible through freedom and through the nurture of well-equipped institutions.

3. The setting and the procedures for American democracy, however, seemed to comprehend other definitive elements from which the present status is derivative. These include the assumption of limitless frontier areas and resources; of a magnificent agrarian culture later to be well balanced with industry; a ruthless exploitation of nature and the unquestioned mastery of a chosen people over racial minority groups; a group analogy to individual freedom in sectional achievements; the assumption of continuing strong genetic stocks of people in generous reproduction rates with no planned population limits in view; and the assumption of a certain national isolation and self-sufficiency.

4. Within these American premises there is still the assumption of a distinction between the concept of democracy which represents attainable ideals, and the actual visible ends of organized democracy which represent at most direction and approximation. This means a full recognition of the difference between theory and practice, between dominant ideas and actual institutions. It is assumed further that no matter what the present chasm between the theory and the practice of democracy may be in fact, the concept must be preserved as constituting the greatest promise of the ultimate attainment of the reality of the democratic process. Our definition therefore must be found somewhere within the limits of a merging of concept and theory with the reality of social process, in which will best be approximated the attainable ends of an enduring democracy.

SECOND SERIES OF ASSUMPTIONS

1. On the basis of such distinction between the concept and theory of democracy and the reality of the process and measuring practical results in the social ends of equality rather than in ideals or mere political framework, the present United States does not approximate the democratic ideal in practice. It is not so necessary to cite commonplace evidence to support this assumption as it is to indicate a sort of framework of inequalities and how they have grown up from

the earlier American days. For here is a nation in which the per capita wealth of the highest group is a thousand times that of the lowest; the per capita personal income tax of the highest state is more than a hundred times that of the lowest; and if personal and corporate income be considered, the highest state is 120 times that of the lowest; while if the per capita income as measured by net incomes of $50,000 or over be considered, the highest state is more than four hundred times that of the lowest. The states with the largest number of children to be educated have less than one-tenth the money for this purpose that the states with the smallest number have. And so on and on, measured by more than two hundred ordinary gauges of status, the index of inequality in the states and regions ranges anywhere from two to five hundred.

2. To cite more specific samplings, there is scarcely approximation to democracy in the life of many of the minority people in America. There is little semblance of democracy, either cultural or political, for twelve million Negroes in the United States, or for eighteen million white folks in the South who must educate more Negro children than all the children of all races in the wealthier Far Western region. There is no equality of opportunity for tenant farmers and their children, or for the millions of families who, for no fault of their own, submerged below the American standard, are told that they cannot have children. There is no semblance of equality and fraternity in the millions of displaced folk turned adrift from farm or mine or factory or shunted from one age group to another. There is no democracy for the millions who, following the American dictum to save, have lost everything they had and have broken under the strain. There is no equality for the millions of depression handicapped children already being conditioned to un-American standards and ideals. And there is little in current American democracy to appeal to the college youth who can look forward to very little in prospect for the immediate future.

"Is it true?"

3. We may venture a sort of recapitulatory series of syllogistic premises—questions to be answered "yes" or "no" somewhat as follows: Is it true that the United States has ample natural resources and wealth to meet all the needs of all the people now and for many generations to come? Is it true that in the wealth of

American technology there is to be found ample technical organization and managerial skill to derive from these resources such abundance of goods and services as would provide all the people with not only the bare necessities of life but abundant comfort, convenience, leisure, and high standards of living?

Is it true in reality, however, that millions of Americans are not only without these comforts, conveniences, and luxuries, but also without the essentials for survival of body, mind, and morale, in spite of the great abundance of technical skill and natural wealth?

Is it true also that the Nation is still possessed of money and abounding in wealth enough to make possible the utilization of this technology and natural wealth in such way as to turn production capacity into adequate channels of distribution and consumption? There are factories enough and more, with available capital for still more factories. There are houses and stores and banks and office buildings and schoolhouses and churches, even as before 1930.

Is it true, however, that this wealth is not available for adequate use; that most of it is concentrated in a few places and persons; that millions of Americans are becoming poorer and poorer through loss of home and farms which had been their fruits of a life-time of work and saving; and that millions of other Americans are on the verge of poverty?

Is it true that these conditions are resulting in multiplied inequalities of opportunity for the majority of the people; in increasing injustice throughout the Nation; in well-nigh universal lack of security; and in widespread confusion, unrest, distrust, and despair?

Is it true, therefore, that the Nation has reached a stage where it is in nowise guaranteeing to its citizens that perfect union, justice, domestic tranquillity, general welfare, and blessings of liberty vouchsafed in the preamble to the Constitution, or the safety, happiness, and rights specified in the Declaration of Independence?

Is it true, again, that the Nation cannot continue to survive under conditions so inalienably contrary to the foundations of its democracy, and under circumstances which are draining the vitality of its people and destructive of the ends of democratic government? Is it true also that nobody believes the Nation can long survive with such a burden of gross inequalities and injustice?

It is conceivable, therefore, that the American people will continue much longer not to heed the Jeffersonian injunction that it is not only their right but their duty to provide through new government "new guards" for their future security?

Is it true further that there is no general agreement on the part of the American people as to next steps, whether to alter or abolish the current economic system, or how best "to institute new government" such as would "seem most likely to effect their safety and happiness?"

Democracy has functioned

4. Why then do we talk about alternatives to democracy, if there is no democracy? The answer is that there has been political democracy and the approximation to social democracy in America, and that the framework of this democracy is still available, and in its new applications, largely untried. Undoubtedly the United States has been the nearest exemplification of the democratic ideal. The ideals set forth in political democracy and individualism have constituted a national faith in which the people have consented to what has been going on. The mass achievements and technology which have brought chaotic inequality have been the pride of the people. In so far, therefore, as it was theirs by intention and vote, no matter what the consequences, it was representative democracy. The "big man" pattern and the ambition of every man's man child to attain wealth, eminence, and comfort have motivated the people. They wanted and admired conquest and mastery. To return to . . . Mississippi democracy, if we consider the white race alone, theirs is a genuinely political democracy; for in the legislative halls of that state have been nearly a hundred different occupational combinations represented in the duly elected representatives of the people. And no matter what they have, it is what they have voted for. It is of, by, and for the people.

5. And to return to the crest of American achievement, the Nation was apparently coming nigh unto the goal of abolishing poverty under the grand technico-economic economy of unlimited production, the maximization of credit and consumers' power of the 1920's. The ideology, for instance, of the Century of Progress was that invested capital devoted to the expansion of science and invention would make possible standards for the common man which no period before had afforded kings and potentates. And undoubtedly

this was what the people wanted. And under a political democracy which could so order its governmental services to the people as to guarantee scientific and expert advice and insure against exploitation incident to the weakness of human nature, and could muster its science and social engineering together, Mr. Hoover's magnificent Americanism would have come much nearer to ending poverty in America than the pathological ideologies of a mass-minded world of discontent. The limitation there, as elsewhere, was the lack of workable ways to bridge the chasm between theory and practice.

Alternatives are not promising

6. Another fundamental reason for the continuing of this American faith as exemplified in democracy is the increasing conviction, arrived at from much observing and gathering of evidence, that the present alternatives being tried in the rest of the world do not appear to approximate the ideals of equality and opportunity even so much as the American system; and even though they succeed in lands of their peculiar conditioning, their ideologies and form do not carry with them the basis for social organization competent to achieve the highest American human welfare. Furthermore, preliminary experimentation in regional problems and special areas of American dilemma have not indicated their availability at the present time for successful application. Within the framework of our American premises, even though the goals of these alternatives conform to the ideologies of the greatest good to the greatest number of people, the difficulties in the way of their implementation are greater than those of our own democratic organization.

THIRD SERIES OF ASSUMPTIONS

1. Moreover, the great deficiencies of American democracy and inequality are explainable in terms of logical and inevitable sequences to circumstances, policies, and action which will not continue to obtain in the American picture. Consequently, there is yet the supreme challenge for American institutions to achieve qualitative results in the next era as they have achieved quantitative results in the past.

The hypothesis of this discussion is that the present gross inequalities and chaos are due to failure to achieve orderly transition from the old America to the new, and that in all probability the motivation and the attainment of such orderly transition in the present period will constitute the sole definitive democracy of the next few years. Inherent in the period will be the essence of both the democratic problem and any alternative solution which may prove necessary. It is likely that in the transition period and its motivation will be found not only crisis, tension, and travail, but also the supreme experiment of Western civilization.

Under such premises it is not possible at this time to predict what the new forms of our democracy may be or what substitutes may be available. The further premise of our discussion is, therefore, that the alternative to present American democracy will be orderly transitional democracy, with more than ever the titanic struggle for equilibrium and balance between conflicting forces, such as individuation and socialization, and between theory and practice.

Transitions, past and continuing

2. This problem of transitional democracy, like the other aspects of the American experience, is reflected in the past history of the Nation as well as in the current dilemmas which condition future economic and social arrangements. There was first of all the transition from the Jeffersonian small nation of rural states, of one or two regions of simple motivation, of homogeneity of people, of few occupations, with small individual fortunes centered chiefly in farm and forest, in land and homes, to the present very large nation of urban and industrial majorities, in greatly differing regions with complex motivation and heterogeneity of population, with hundreds of varied occupations, with large individual fortunes, with fabulous salaries, with corporate holdings and wealth not only in farm lands and commodities but also in city real estate, factories, railroads, traction and steamship lines, coal and iron, stores, banks, utilities, amusements, food, tobacco, textiles, furniture, rubber, leather, glass, machinery, automobiles, metal, petroleum, power, soap, drugs, and multiplied consumers' goods.

There was a transition from slaves to free men in sectional realignment, and it was not orderly.

There was and is a transition from agrarian culture and rural folk to industrial life and urbanization; from isolation to international contacts and back to nationalism; from lack of education to universal education; from illiteracy to a new literacy fearfully and wonderfully fabricated.

There was the transition from the rule of the few to the dominance of the many; from a man's world to a new world in which women assume increasingly larger influence; from the authority of the elders to the questioning of youth; from state and local priority to Federal centralization; from the human, man-land, man-labor emphasis to technology; from ideologies to science.

And there was the greatest of all transitions to be made between primary individuation and primary socialization.

And there was and is finally the transition from depression and emergency to recovery and reconstruction.

3. The significance of these fundamental premises is accentuated by the fact that these transitions are still to be made, and that in the history and the theory of society the transitional society is reflected as the most definitive of all social processes, conditioning the whole future evolution of each culture. The tests of orderly transitional society will be found in measures of realism and equilibrium as opposed to artificiality and confusion; of rationality and stability as opposed to pathology and confusion. Within the framework of American ideals and of the visible ends of social achievements, these objectives may well constitute the motivation for all our unified social and political techniques and coöperative endeavor.

FOURTH SERIES OF ASSUMPTIONS

1. In the present transitional period, partly as a result of the elemental factors mentioned and partly responsible for them, there appear to be certain parallel complex forces or movements, sometimes almost merging the one with the other, sometimes in conflict and cross currents. These multiple forces may be the guarantee of continuing democratic processes; or if subtly utilized by demagogue and mass pathology to merge the folkways with new and powerful stateways, they might easily result in the destruction of the American ideal.

2. One of a half-dozen such major forces may be assumed to be the movement toward violent revolution, in which the restless, resistless tides of dissatisfied folk are focused upon the overthrow of

present institutions. In America the catalogue of possible constit-
uents here is relatively long. In the Nation at large there are agrarian
discontent, labor restlessness, minority groups, and the intellectual
discontent of the professional agitator. In the regions roundabout
there are the Negro, other minority groups, the disinherited tenant
or miner, the industrial worker, the local demagogues, and the extra-
regional agitator.

3. On the other side is the movement toward fascism and dictatorship. In the failure of "recovery" or of a better planned and
ordered democracy would inhere the strength of fascism or its
equivalent. In such a move, so the argument runs, would appear
ways and means of satisfying youth, "solving" economic problems
for the businessman, fighting "communism" and "radicalism,"
giving the feeling of power and importance to the multitudes, releasing sufferers immediately from poverty and despair, releasing the
public from thinking, encouraging the protest against highbrowism,
realizing the hopes of a great nationalism, and producing action now.
Toward the attainment of these ends the pattern of dictatorship, if
the planned democratic order is rejected in the United States, would
bring to bear the subtle and almost irresistible combination of a quick
mass spiritual transformation and a quick, almost complete regimentation of the people, such that the folkways would come mys-
teriously and suddenly to coincide with the stateways.

4. A third powerful force is what appears to be a sort of mass
pathological and messianic current which sweeps along a mixed
company of idealists and discontents, a chief characteristic of whose
programs is flight from reality in constantly shifting expediency
programs.

5. There is then the powerful current of folk allegiance to the
demagogue, whose power is in his technique rather than in his
principles, and whose influence may be turned at any time in whatever direction appear to be merged the greatest number of forces
capable of being utilized by him.

6. There is, again, the great current directed by the playboys,
super-technologists, who seek new experimentation every morning,
new games of human direction every night. With little economic
or cultural background, they appear to be oblivious of the fact that

there has been a past, or that society evolves through equilibrium and balance. They are the ideological dictators de luxe.

7. There is, then, the great, deep current of laissez-faire millions who represent the logical product of a great and wealthy nation perpetually hoping for peace and prosperity, without doing anything about it.

8. There is finally a possible major current in the regional discontents and motivations of the different parts of America whose orderly integration into the American democracy of the new era may well constitute the balance wheel, or whose disintegration might permit of chaotic movements subversive of American ideals.

9. This situation, however, we must remember not only represents a typical American paradox, but is symbolic of the realities of a complex societal evolution. The presumption would be that the multiplicity of these movements, together with the two-party system in the United States, would militate strongly against either communistic revolution or fascistic dictatorship. Yet the combination of demagogic leadership and mass social pathology working in the framework of gross deficiencies and discontent may easily result in anything but orderly transitional democracy.

FIFTH SERIES OF ASSUMPTIONS

1. Our last series of assumptions will continue the mixed picture of American paradox. The first of these is that because of the extraordinary complexity of the situation the requirements of the next few years appear to be relatively clear. That is, because of our peculiar American conditioning and cultural equipment, because of the bigness, the speed, the complexity, and the technology of modern civilization everywhere, because of the sheer enormity of the Nation's wealth and resources, because of the limitation of experience, training, and character of its mixed peoples and divergent regions, because of the sweep of its tragedies and dilemmas and the irreconcilable nature and the immaturity of its epidemic of "isms," panaceas, propaganda, rumors, claims, interests, demands, ideologies, motivations, and plans, the specifications of next steps appear relatively clear. There seems to be only one way to provide for the rational regimentation of irrational society, and that is through the orderly planning of societal organization.

2. The specifications of such social planning appear to be four-fold. First of all, of course, there must be some sort of mastery—mastery of resources and forces. Second, such mastery implies knowledge of these forces and scientific work in their inventory and direction. This means realistic, hard-boiled adaptation to the spirit and technique of the age. It means further that there must be balance and equilibrium: between the individual and the group, between the old and the new, between folkways and stateways, between the Nation and states, between rural and urban, between agriculture and industry, between production and distribution. In the third place, there must be some sort of referendum to the people such as will recognize diversity of interests, parties, states, regions, and races. This means that an orderly planned society for America will provide for the reintegration of its several diverse regions into the national economy in order to obtain both unity and adequacy of economic and social life. These conclusions are based, furthermore, upon observations relative to the evaluation of society in general and especially of recent developments in Europe, as well as upon American premises.

3. In simple language, finally, our assumption seems to be that there will be no democracy or formal alternative to democracy in the United States for the next period, say twelve years of two six-year priority schedules, but that the definitive nature of our political and cultural activity will be found in the gigantic struggle of the American people to evolve an orderly democracy through the planned mastery of its great transitional period. In other words, the exact form of democratic organization strong enough to meet the needs of our present confused American civilization does not now exist. It is therefore the task of the social sciences and their techniques to help discover the basis and form for such organization. The assumption seems warranted, therefore, that the concentration of all major efforts of all parties and regions should be focused upon such orderly planned procedure as may reasonably be expected to receive the general sanction of the people. This, I submit, is the supreme test of democracy set in competition with the other alternatives of chaos, revolution, super-corporate control and centralization, socialism, communism, or fascism.

Regional Development and Governmental

Policy [1939]*

The assumptions of this paper, namely, that governmental policy
will include programs of regional development and planning,
are based upon what we should like to think of as self-evident facts;
if not facts, then premises, in support of which our several propositions may be considered in the light of hypotheses basic to whatever
final conclusions may emerge.

In the first place, the subject of regional development and governmental policy does not represent merely an abstraction or a metaphysical concept superimposed upon the working realities of modern
government. On the contrary, these assumptions of governmental co-
operation in regional development "grow out of the day's work."
They represent living realities and next steps. They represent fundamentals. They represent tools and techniques, not only in government
but in the multiple approaches to decentralization and redistribution.
They reflect needs and emergencies, popular questionings and technical exploration, and are both symbol and reality of the new Americanism. More than this, these assumptions rest on the solid foundation of
the new regionalism which serves both as an exploratory science of
cultural development and as a practical means of political and economic administration.

Most of our assumptions, therefore, not only follow logically as
next steps in the scientific study and planning of a great and complex

* The Annals of the American Academy of Political and Social
Science, CCVI (November 1939), 133-41. Reprinted by permission.

nation, but also grow naturally out of a great majority of the premises set forth in the papers constituting the body of this volume, as will appear from a critical examination of their contents and arrangement.

We referred to our assumptions as growing out of the day's work; that is, as being vitally realistic in that they have emerged from study, experiment, needs, and experience. There are two principal backgrounds in which this emergence is reflected. One is that of social research experimentation within the frame of reference of a major region of the United States; the other is the emergence of regional planning in the Nation as it has evolved from the earlier concept of metropolitan planning into both a philosophy and a technique of national development.

The first example was somewhat in the nature of a laboratory and testing ground; the second was reflected in the logical attempt to meet emergencies and to comprehend in practical ways the length and breadth and power of a great nation in transition. The special regional experience cited below to illustrate the scientific approach to American regionalism refers primarily to a twenty-year program of social research in the southern regions of the United States, long since recognized as national, economic, and cultural entities of great importance.

A REGIONAL LABORATORY

First, it seemed fair to assume that social study and social planning, in order to be realistic and responsible, must find their laboratory and their data within the region where the greatest reality abounds. Thus, we set up a sort of living regional laboratory where social phenomena could be studied and social planning explored. Such a laboratory, however, was not to be interpreted as provincial or local, but rather a concrete laboratory for testing generic premises. Problems selected for study and areas chosen for planning were to be those which would have generic value throughout all parts of the country. Thus, agricultural reconstruction, social-industrial relationships, the reintegration of agrarian culture in American life, race relations and prospects, the redistribution of opportunity and wealth, the techniques of making democracy effective in the unequal places, the organic nature of the folk life and the new realism of the people, were universal problems, finding their reality, however, in the living laboratory in which they grew.

It soon became clear, however, in the next place, that so far from being provincial or limited, these regional efforts required a more thorough background and wider knowledge for successful accomplishment than did the ordinary historical or theoretical approaches which focus merely upon principles, concepts, abstract laws, and the like. That is, it was necessary to reinforce our equipment in methods and approaches to the study of social problems, to study more comprehensively the cultural backgrounds involved in history and anthropology, and to supplement our knowledge with geography and other physical sciences. All this meant that it was necessary also to have a closer alignment and co-operation with and among all the social sciences. Not only this, but here was a frame of reference for the study of culture and economy which, without any doubt, set the tempo for a new era in the co-operation of the social sciences with the physical sciences, and in the co-operation of the so-called academic institutions, the professional schools, and the great land-grant colleges with governmental agencies.

Thus, work in this regional laboratory for social study and planning led to two relatively new methodological approaches. One was co-ordination and co-operation of the various sciences including the social sciences. The other was regionalism as a methodological approach, in which the attack upon universal problems could be made by all the sciences, and in which it became clear that the folk-regional society or culture constitutes the supreme unit for social study and the smallest unit in which all the factors, including those of natural resources, human resources, and cultural conditioning, may be found.

FACTORS NECESSARY TO UNDERSTANDING

There emerged, therefore, an important theoretical conclusion as to the role of regionalism in national analysis and planning. Yet the chief value, after all, was practical. It became clear that the understanding of one region, with its backgrounds, limitations, and prospects, could be attained only through a sort of science of the region, which may be likened unto a *gestalt,* in which all factors are sought out and interpreted in their proper perspective. That is, not only in each part related to every part, but also, planning for one aspect cannot successfully be done without adequate consideration of all aspects. Seen in the light of such a premise, a region—in this case the South—reflects everything that goes into the architecture of civilization, and its problems and prospects are reflected mirror-like in such ways as to enable us to stand off and look on them objectively and work towards a better mastery.

Further than this, however, it became very clear that it was not possible to characterize one region in terms of useful measures unless and until we had characterized the rest of the Nation and the other regions by similar comparisons. The regional approach, therefore, became a dynamic tool in the attempt to understand the living geography of the Nation and to place each of the great regions in their proper setting in the whole.[1]

This led still further to the conclusion not only that it is not possible for one region to develop without the co-operation of the other regions and of the Federal Government, but also that only through strong regional development can the Nation as a whole be enriched. Thus, through the newer reaches of regionalism as opposed to the old sectionalism, and through the almost universal trend toward centralization in government and economy, we came to a logical and scientific interpretation of the obligation of the Federal Government to co-operate with each of the regions. This obligation, of course, has been reinforced by the background of historical and political action and of cultural and economic differentials, in addition to these fundamental trends.

This still is not the end. Immediately with the movement to have regionalism transcend sectionalism and with the trend toward Federal centralization over state rights, there arise fundamental issues and

1. The essentials of this regional-national and national-regional approach are set forth in *American Regionalism* [Howard W. Odum and Harry Estill Moore, New York: Henry Holt & Co., 1938] and *Southern Regions of the United States* [Howard W. Odum, Chapel Hill: The University of North Carolina Press, 1936]. The six major regions are the Northeast and the Southeast, the Northwest and the Southwest, the Middle States and the Far West. In historical reality, there are two Norths, two Souths, and two Wests. There are two "Easts" and four "Wests." That is, the Northeast and Middle States are considered "North" by Webb in his *Divided We Stand;* [W. P. Webb, New York: Farrar and Rinehart, 1937], the Southeast and Southwest would be two Souths; while the Northwest and Far West would be "Wests." To go further back historically, however, the "East," Northeast and Southeast, was always set over against the many Wests, first the great Northwest, then Middle West, then Far West.

many points of conflict. These issues again are of universal and generic interest to peoples everywhere, to the end that centralization and totalitarian patterns may not transcend democratic form and retard progress. Thus, regionalism becomes the tool for decentralization, the buffer between Federal and state conflict, and if there is any way to prevent totalitarianism in a great complex, urban and industrial civilization of standardized tendency and to retain a quality civilization in a quantity world, it is through regionalism.

FEDERAL EQUALIZATION

Again, with reference to the case for Federal co-operation in regional development as basic to regional planning, the concrete illustration of the needs and experience of the Nation in relation to specific regions offers our most logical evidence. Thus, what is the logical basis upon which national planning might project the ideal of Federal aid to the states in education, health, highways, and agriculture? As has been pointed out often of late, the premise is that an economic, social, and cultural lag in any part of the country is an economic, social, and cultural menace to all parts of the country. Forty per cent of the young people 10 to 20 years old on farms in 1920 were in cities in 1930, and most of this net migration was from rural areas. The quality of the education in these rural areas is therefore a matter of vital concern to the industries, the cities, and the people of the whole country.

The Federal Government is the only agency that can redress this economic and educational imbalance between the metropolitan areas of the greatest concentration of wealth and rural areas of the greatest concentration of children in relation to adult population. Since all sections, all resources, and all the people combine to produce the wealth concentrated in the great centers, and since all the people as consumers help to pay the taxes on this wealth, it is just that a small part of the income from this wealth should go back to the states whence it came, for it is in the poorest states that is found the largest proportion of children whose equality and quality of education will determine the future of democracy in America.[2]

2. See *A Working Economic Plan for the South*. Recommendations adopted at Atlanta, Georgia, January 15, 1939, and distributed by the Southern Policy Committee.

It should be emphasized, of course, that the issue of Federal equalization is a national one; and further, that it is not a new one, since the practice is well established in such avenues as agriculture, road building, public health, social security, Federal relief, Public Works Administration, Works Progress Administration, and many other activities of the Federal Government.

NATIONAL ASPECT OF THE SOUTH

Let us look at the situation from the national viewpoint as it relates to the South. Here a creditor region sends most of its money elsewhere, and the surplus wealth of the Nation is in nowise available within the home border of the Southern States. The South is poor, and partly for this reason. But the South does contribute millions of dollars to the rest of the Nation, not only in its trade but also in its internal revenue payments to the Federal Government, one single state, for instance, paying more than twenty times what it gets back. But more than this, the South furnishes to the Nation millions of workers and replacement people for the cities and for industry and commerce and the professions. The South must educate these people, and even with their inadequate education it is an expensive proposition, so that the total cost and value of these people reaches into billions of dollars.

The South has contributed since 1900 nearly four million people to other regions of the Nation, and these people have carried with them their education and some of their heritage, and have worked for the rest of the Nation during the time of their highest productivity. Thus, the cost is not only in their equipment, but also in what they take away from the South and what they might contribute to the development of the region if they remained. The Nation, therefore, from any point of view, owes something to the region.

From still another viewpoint, the problem is pre-eminently a national one. It is generally agreed among all population experts that the South will continue to be the seedbed of the Nation's population and will provide the surplus people for many years to come. To this extent, therefore, the character of the people of the Nation will depend upon the character of the people of the South. In the present economy it is not possible for the South to provide facilities equal to those of the rest of the Nation, and therefore to give equal educational opportunity to all its children. Not only, therefore, is this problem one of democracy and equal opportunity as a national philosophy, but such unequal opportunity penalizes the whole Nation through these interstate migrations.

SOME ASSUMPTIONS OF REGIONALISM

The second background illustrating how the new regionalism has grown out of the day's work is still more impressive. First, the regional approach to many problems of adjustment in administration has become a logical "must," or next step, in practical affairs. This is reflected in the extraordinarily wide range of regional administrative units in all phases of governmental activity.[3] Yet, more than this, the assumptions of regionalism have emerged from the total cumulative experience and philosophy of contemporary civilization. We may look at some of these assumptions.

The first assumption is that there will be a continuously increasing role of government in both its range and its function in the modern world of bigness, complexity, and technology. The trend is already very marked, of course. . . .

It follows, therefore, that there is danger in this tendency towards expanded government and overcentralization. This danger may be primarily bureaucratic, or it may be a more serious threat of totalitarianism. One of the chief objectives of modern students and planners, therefore, is to seek ways and means of attaining modern efficient government without the accompanying handicap of the totalitarian government.

This is all in line with certain other assumptions of the present era, which may be examined from several viewpoints. One is on the hypothesis that there is at the present time a general crisis in modern society, resulting from changing civilization the world over, and in

3. See especially *Regional Factors in National Planning and Development* and J. W. Fesler's "Federal Administrative Regions," *American Political Science Review,* 30 (April 1936), pp. 257-68. See also the publications of the National Resources Committee, especially the eight publications on regional planning, Part I being Pacific Northwest; Part II, St. Louis Region; Part III, New England; Part IV, Baltimore-Washington-Annapolis Area; Part V, Red River of the North; Part VI, Upper Rio Grande; Part VII, Alaska, Its Resources and Development; Part VIII, Northern Lake States, another "economic problem" area.

particular a changing Western culture. Another is that there is at the present time a conflict in the more specific realm of free institutions such as nations have not faced for several centuries. The third assumption is that there is still emergency and crisis in the United States such as will continue for some time to test the endurance of American institutions.[4]

Other basic elemental assumptions are that science and invention, in this modern world of technology, have resulted in the outmoding of the old tempo of cultural development, whereby the folkways and mores permitted of gradual and slow evolution. The new *technicways* tend to transcend the *folkways* and supplant the mores, and thus accelerate the whole rate of societal evolution, throwing out of gear not only morals and manners, but also the economic and societal relationships of peoples and nations.

SOCIAL PLANNING

The next logical assumption, therefore, is that social planning, more than any other trend, combines the best efforts of all who seek to match physical science with social science, and will receive an increasing emphasis. Moreover, social planning is no longer an academic matter. It is here.

The assumption with reference to America, however, is that social planning must be set in the framework of American democracy, comprehending a working equilibrium in the whole cultural process and function. Such planning will utilize the full capacity of a social engineering competent not only to build new structures for the Nation but also to carry in the meantime the traffic of all the institutions in a transitional society, and within these institutions to permit of orientation, spontaneity, and flexibility.

This means that planning, American style, becomes a sort of balance wheel to make possible this new technical, national planning, while at the same time preserving the American form of government. This balance wheel is equivalent in both theory and practice to an advisory fourth division of government, called recently by Tugwell,

4. Some of these postulates were first stated in Odum's *The Regional Approach to National Social Planning,* published jointly by the Foreign Policy Association, New York, and The University of North Carolina Press, Chapel Hill, 1935.

the Directive Agency. This means that planning through duly constituted planning boards will serve as buffer between the several divisions of government—administrative, judicial, and legislative—and between Federal centralization on the one hand and state isolation on the other. If, so the assumption runs, it is possible to have a powerful and effective democratic government functioning in a world of conflict without becoming totalitarian, it can be done through this sort of planning.

Immediately, however, the next premise is that, due to the bigness of the Nation, to its cultural backgrounds and motivation, and to technological and sound theoretical considerations, the regional approach to national planning and development is absolutely fundamental to any successful, permanent, social planning program or procedure. This assumption, questioned vigorously only a few years ago, appears now to be generally accepted.

The assumptions that governmental policy will provide for ways and means of promoting regional development rest, of course, primarily upon the premises of greater national development and unity. Regional development becomes an essential measure for the enrichment of the American whole. It is in this sense that we have insisted that the theme of American regionalism is, after all, essentially that of a great American Nation, the land and the people, in whose continuity and unity of development, through a fine equilibrium of geographic, cultural, and historical factors, must be found not only the testing grounds of American democracy but, according to many observers, the hope of Western civilization.[5] The very definition of the region connotes a constituent part of a national whole; without the concept of the totality, there can be no region.

NATIONAL PLANNING BOARDS

Yet we cannot have regional development and regional planning without national planning, and it is not likely that we shall have any realistic, enduring planning procedures until the public has understood the sound theory and the imminent need of the whole process. Such a system of planning would necessarily comprehend the national, state, and regional planning boards functioning together in a coordinated attack upon the most important needs.

5. Odum and Moore, *American Regionalism*, p. 3.

The functions of these boards would be threefold. The first would be to act in the service of the President and of the Congress and provide information, facts, and planning programs in special projects initiated by the President or the Congress.

The second function would be to carry on a continuous social inventory of the Nation somewhat after the manner of *Recent Social Trends,*[6] so that there would be an authentic research-planning group working all the time, not only in designing and planning research, but also in utilization of the vast research agencies and statistics of the present Federal organizations and departments.

The third function would be to make contacts and co-operate with the regions and the states, and to carry on adult education and promotion and continuous referendum and publicity to the people. Some members of the planning board would continuously be sensing the various situations in the different states and regions, as well as interpreting the Nation to the President and Congress, and vice versa. It would be understood that research and plans would result in recommendations, action upon which would, however, always come through the regular administrative, judicial, or legislative function of government, and through the several regional and state agencies within which they were appropriate.

In this third function of promoting regional planning and co-operating with state and regional agencies, the national planning board should have available a moderate amount of funds for allocation to state and regional planning boards in accordance with definite and common-sense co-operative arrangements within each of these. Although the suggestion is clearly "academic,"[7] such a planning board might well save the Nation a great deal of money, in so far as it would be competent to undertake the research and investigation now provided for in the scores and scores of Congressional investigating committees and of isolated, overlapping, and duplicating research

6. *Recent Social Trends in the United States* (2 vols.; New York: McGraw-Hill Book Co., 1933).

7. It must be re-emphasized, of course, that this framework of national-regional planning is partly "academic" in that it is not possible to achieve so complete a program except through a referendum of the states to the people. The continuous reorganization of what is now the National Resources Planning Board is one evidence of the limitations of such a plan.

agencies within the Nation. Here would be opportunity better to implement the work and training of the expert in government without turning the government over to scientists and students.

STATE PLANNING BOARDS

The second type of planning board in logical order is the state planning board, the general specifications and functions of which would in analogous measure tend to follow the general provisions set forth in the national planning board. The functions of the state planning board would tend to have the same threefold objectives as the national planning board; that is, its first function would be to assist the governor in the work of planning and directing his state program; the second, to carry on a continuous program of study and planning for the state itself; and the third, to co-operate with city and county planning boards within the state, and with regional and Federal planning boards outside the state.[8]

REGIONAL PLANNING BOARDS

The third major type of planning board is the regional planning board, which should be less formal and less active than the national and state planning boards. In general, desired objectives could be attained by division of the Nation into a minimum-maximum number of major regions which would possess the largest possible degree of homogeneity measured by the largest possible number of economic, cultural, administrative, and functional indices, for the largest possible number of objectives. These areal divisions having been determined, the major regional planning boards might well be constituted as follows: one ex officio member from each state planning board; one representative from the national planning board; two representatives from the region at large; and one ex officio representative from each of the specialized, technical, subregional planning groups already at work in the region, such as the T.V.A. or special river-valley or interstate compact groups.

The function of the regional planning board would thus be even more advisory and general than that of the others, still following the

8. See *State Planning—A Review of Activities and Progress; State Planning, Programs and Accomplishments; The Future of State Planning.* Publications of National Resources Committee.

general threefold objectives. That is, it would first of all focus upon its regional problems and planning, serving particularly as a buffer between the national planning board and the state planning board. Secondly, it would seek to keep continuously a preview of facts and situations and a preview of trends in the region, with a view of co-ordinating the work of the states with that of the Nation. In the third place, it would have the peculiar task of co-operating with state and subregional planning boards.

THE PRESENT TENDENCY

We referred to some of these specifications as "academic" in that it is not likely that they can be made effective at this time. With an extraordinary opportunity such as the Nation has rarely experienced, namely, the beginnings of state planning boards in practically all the states, and with a national group ready to co-operate and co-ordinate, the present tendency seems to be gradually to abolish or to neglect the state planning boards, without which it is not possible to have regional planning boards effectively at work. Much of this trend, it seems to me, is due to the fundamental failure to co-ordinate planning with development; governmental operations with economic processes; physical planning with cultural planning; governmental planning with civic co-operation. It has thus come to pass that social planning has come to connote the opposite of development. A re-examination of the whole field of planning and development in the light of the Nation's policy with reference to the regions and to its greater wealth and welfare would seem now to be necessary.

Proposal for a United States Planning

Agency (1943)

CONTINUING AMERICAN DEMOCRACY THROUGH STATE AND REGIONAL PLANNING AGENCIES AS ORGANIC MANDATORY UNITS OF THE TOTAL NATIONAL PLANNING

THE UNITED STATES PLANNING AGENCY

(The State and Regional Agency inherent in the whole program)

CONSTITUTION

Authorized by Congress as a regular American constitutional form of procedure. Appropriations from Congress to include cooperative arrangements with State and regional agencies on the basis of precedents of federal service to agriculture, highways, public health, and social security. A major agency implying the prestige and distinguished service analogous to the Supreme Court. Members nominated by the President and approved by Congress.

PERSONNEL

Nine members, full time, whose qualifications and distinguished services correspond to members of the Supreme Court, heads of major commissions or members of the Cabinet. In general, major parties represented and one member from each of the regions and one or more at large.

A central office with a staff of research and planning experts and adequate administrative and secretarial service.

1. To insure a continuous scientific inventory of the state of the Nation and to provide essential information for the President, the Congress, the Supreme Court, and special needs; to co-ordinate research and approximate a clearing house; to reduce overlapping and economize on congressional committee investigations.
2. To act as buffer between the President and the other branches of government and to provide a safeguard against overcentralization and power through government by persons.
3. To act as buffer between the national government and the states and regions, and provide the necessary Federal centralization necessary to effective decentralization.
4. To serve as total unified advisory board in times of emergency and war.

THE STATE PLANNING AGENCY

(The Federal and Regional Agency inherent in the whole program)

CONSTITUTION

Authorized by the State legislature as a regular constitutional form of procedure. Appropriations from State legislature to include cooperative arrangements with national and regional planning agencies. A major agency implying the distinction and service comparable to the "highest" courts and commissions.

PERSONNEL

Nine members constituting a board large enough to insure a working quorum and adequate geographic representation of the State; small enough to guard against promiscuous council. Not more than four to be heads of State departments.

A central office with small staff of research experts and planning technicians.

FUNCTION

1. To provide essential information for the governor and different divisions of State government; to coordinate research and approximate a clearing house; to reduce overlapping and economize on State legislative committee investigations.
2. To act as buffer between the governor and house of representatives and other branches of government and to provide a safeguard against overcentralization and power through government by persons.
3. To act as buffer between the governor, counties, cities, and local government.
4. To cooperate with the regional and national agencies on problems of extra-State concern.

THE REGIONAL PLANNING AGENCY

(The State and Federal Agency inherent in the whole program)

CONSTITUTION

Authorized by the national legislation creating the United States Planning Agency, the State and regional boards being an organic part of the national agency. The regional agencies representative of the region being primarily composed of ex officio members of the State planning agencies. State cooperation authorized also by legislation creating State planning agencies.

PERSONNEL

One ex-officio member from each State and planning agency; one ex-officio member from each regional planning or interstate compact group already functioning, such as Tennessee Valley Authority; one member ex officio from the United States Planning Agency; one member at large. In the Southeast, for instance, this would mean eleven ex officio members, one from TVA, one at large, and one from the national agency, making a total of fourteen. In addition to fair representation, such an arrangement would insure a good chance for adequate quorum on emergency call.

A central office with an executive officer and secretarial and administrative assistance.

FUNCTION

1. A clearing house of conferences and procedures rather than research, enabling the States within the region to keep mutually informed and to avoid conflicting procedures.
2. To act as a buffer between the States, on the one hand, minimizing the trends toward extreme State rights and interstate barriers, but, on the other, also advising and protecting individual States in fundamental matters.
3. To act as buffer between the Federal, centralized government and the individual States; to avoid conflict between States and Federal authorities and to create wholesome understanding and relationships between the States and Federal Government.
4. To cooperate with the United States Planning Agency in special planning and development involved in river valleys, water resources, and other areas overlapping State boundaries.

REGIONS

Six Regions:	or	*Eight Regions:*
The Northeast		New England Northeast
The Southeast		Industrial Northeast
The Middle States		Middle States
The Southwest		Southeast
The Northwest		Central Southwest
The Far West		Pacific Southwest
		Central Northwest
		Pacific Northwest

If Six Regions:	*If Eight Regions:*
The Northeast	New England Northeast
Maine	Maine
New Hampshire	New Hampshire
Vermont	Massachusetts
Massachusetts	Rhode Island
Rhode Island	Connecticut
Connecticut	Vermont

New York
New Jersey
Delaware
Pennsylvania
Maryland
West Virginia

Industrial Northeast
New York
New Jersey
Pennsylvania
Delaware
Maryland
West Virginia

The Southeast
Virginia
North Carolina
South Carolina
Georgia
Florida
Kentucky
Tennessee
Alabama
Mississippi
Arkansas
Louisiana

The Southeast
Virginia
North Carolina
South Carolina
Georgia
Florida
Kentucky
Tennessee
Alabama
Mississippi
Arkansas
Louisiana

The Middle States
Ohio
Indiana
Illinois
Michigan
Wisconsin
Minnesota
Iowa
Missouri

The Middle States
Ohio
Indiana
Illinois
Michigan
Wisconsin
Minnesota
Iowa
Missouri

Central Southwest
New Mexico
Oklahoma
Texas

The Southwest
Oklahoma
Texas
New Mexico
Arizona

Pacific Southwest
California
Nevada
Utah
Arizona

The Northwest
North Dakota
South Dakota
Nebraska
Kansas
Montana
Idaho
Wyoming
Colorado
Utah

The Far West
Nevada
Washington
Oregon
California

Central Northwest
Montana
Wyoming
Colorado
North Dakota
South Dakota
Nebraska
Kansas

Pacific Northwest
Washington
Oregon
Idaho

Fundamental Assumptions

1. That democratic planning is organic and not merely incidental and, therefore, must be commensurate with the ideals and magnitude of American development. That is, the Planning Agency is a major, and not an incidental, tool.
2. The role of the States to be organic as in all fundamental aspects of American democracy.
3. Regional representation fundamental in accordance with the essentials of regional planning and the folk-interest not only in the United States but throughout the postwar world. The number of regions scientifically and realistically agreed upon is fundamental.
4. The planning and administrative *region,* for purpose of scientific delineation and practical planning, is a major, composite, multiple-purpose, group-of-states societal division of the Nation, delineated and characterized by the greatest possible degree of homogeneity, measured by the largest practical number of indices available for the largest practical number of purposes and agencies, and affording the least possible number of contradictions, conflicts, and overlapping.
5. Special functional, centralized planning for resources develop-

ment, conservation and use, such as in river valley planning, to be provided within the framework of the United States Planning Agency and its cooperative State and regional arrangements, rather than as separate independent agencies.

6. The planning agency to be the tool of all branches of government rather than of the Executive alone.

Special Note

The particular details of the above framework are not exclusively important as such. They are presented to indicate specific items as opposed to mere generalities.

Most "plans" and planning programs elaborate on what should be done; that is relatively easy to do. What is needed is a way to do it commensurate with reality and the American Democratic System.

Functional Levels of Social Planning in

American Democracy (1943)

CONTINUING THE DEMOCRATIC PROCESS THROUGH NATIONAL, STATE, REGIONAL, AND LOCAL PLANNING FOR A BALANCED CULTURE AND ECONOMY

LEVELS OF PLANNING

PHYSICAL PLANNING

Planning which seeks the best possible balance and equilibrium between people and the places where they live, the resources which they use, and the natural environment by which they are conditioned. Sometimes it is the land and the relation of man to its situation and use. Sometimes it is rivers and waters, forests and minerals, and what they mean to the development and economics of the people. Sometimes it has to do with wildlife sanctuaries, parks, and scenic places. Sometimes it has to do with the beauty of nature and the aesthetic aspects of towns, cities, and highways. Sometimes it has to do with national domains and publicly owned lands and sometimes with private properties and national communication lines. Sometimes it has to do with State, sometimes with counties, sometimes with cities, and sometimes with villages and rural communities. But always planning for the physical foundations has to do with the great organic, natural bases upon which happiness, culture, prosperity, and human welfare rest in their most elemental forms.

Selected Divisions

Land planning in its general aspects.
Land use for towns and cities.
Land use for State and national domain.
Land use for rural life and agriculture.
Rivers and drainage in their general aspects.
Flood control and power.
Navigation and transportation.
Sanitation and recreation.
Wildlife conservation and use.
Ocean, gulf, lake, and water fronts.
Minerals in their general aspects.
Discovery and development of new mineral resources.
Climate and regional variations.
Transportation and situation.
Inventory of total resources.

General Purpose and Functions

Planning for the best utilization of land and its adaptation to the largest number of purposes and needs.
Planning for the best utilization and situation for business, institutions, residence, highways, industries, parks, playgrounds.
Planning for the conservation and use of great forestry areas, parks, forestry and mineral conservation, recreation.
Planning for balanced agriculture, forestry crops, increasing production capacity and value and conservation of agricultural lands.
Planning for river valley development in relation to total national and State areas.
Planning for reservoirs of water for power and for prevention of flood.
Planning for the best use of rivers for commerce and recreation as a part of the transportation system.
Planning for the purification of waters both for the purpose of health and recreation.
Planning for the conservation and enlargement of fish and game, including the development of small streams, lakes, and ponds.
Planning for the utilization of fish and oyster resources, of transportation and recreation, and for harbors and shipping.
Planning for the conservation, development, and wiser use of mineral resources.
Research and planning for new uses of minor minerals.

Planning for the best possible use of climate in relation to culture and economy.

Planning for the wisest utilization of situation through highways, railways, airways, and other communication and transportation arrangements.

Research and planning to insure an adequate knowledge of all resources with a view to their wider and more effective use on behalf of the people.

ECONOMIC PLANNING

Economic planning as a specialized planning which involves the relation of government and economics necessitated as such by trends and needs. First of all is the essential universal demand for postwar planning, looking to the transition from war economy to peace economy. The two major areas here are the conversion of war industries and activities into normal peace-time work and the very special planning to avoid unemployment. The still more special planning to see that the millions who have been in war services have opportunity for occupation or occupational insurance and training in periods of transition. Economic planning is special in the sense that the ratio between government and politics, on the one hand, and business and industry, on the other, becomes a technical problem of adjustment, critical in modern life.

Selected Divisions

Postwar planning in general.
Conversion of war activities into peace-time channels.
Widening the range of occupational opportunity.
Individual business and industries in the postwar period.
Rural and small industries.
Agricultural development and diversified farming.
Selected special industries.
A type of special southern industry.
Banking and finance.
Public works programs.

General Purpose and Functions

An almost universal trend toward planning by individual businesses, by towns and cities, by States and the Nation for economic adjustment in the postwar period at home and abroad.

Planning for the quickest possible conversion of war industry into normal industry with the least possible confusion and with the largest amount of activity by industry itself.

Planning specifically in each community, industry, and State to give jobs to returning service men.

Planning by individual industries and business concerns for expansion, development, new markets, labor.

Planning for increasing emphasis upon rural industries, part-time industries, arts and crafts, and special development of industries for processing fibers, farm products, etc.

Planning especially for the small farmer and for balanced farming, including livestock and dairying.

Planning for certain special industries appropriate to the State, region, or locality, such as housing, air cooling, new industries.

Planning for a new era in farm fencing in the South, including the development of the steel industry for wiring, posts, and of concrete and forests products, developing an almost major industry overnight.

Planning for financing industry and cooperative arrangement between private banking and Federal Government.

Planning for special public works programs in support of needed industry and demobilization of business.

SOCIAL AND CULTURAL PLANNING

Although the objectives of all planning look to the development of the people and their welfare, there are certain types of planning often neglected in the over-emphasis on physical planning and business planning. Such planning emphasizes the social institutions and agencies and looks toward population policies with reference to the people themselves. In this field planning seeks to bridge the distance between research, resources, and the like, on the one hand, and the solving of problems and the adjustment of difficulties of the people, on the other. In this field, too, are many of the major services of government to the people—local, State, Federal.

Selected Divisions

Governmental public works programs.
Special programs for agriculture and rural life.
Programs of recreation.
Public welfare programs.

(Selected Divisions, cont.)

Public health programs.
Public education programs.
Population policies.
Race and minority groups.
Balanced economy and culture.

General Purpose and Functions

Planning through the cooperation of local, State, and Federal Government for construction of necessary buildings in institutions of learning, public service agencies, or housing facilities.

Planning for agricultural development and for cooperative efforts in strengthening country life and balanced agriculture.

Planning for community, State, and Federal programs of leisure-time activities and recreation.

Planning for more adequate and well balanced programs of services for the handicapped and the deficient and for preventive measures.

Planning by local, State, and Federal authorities for more adequate health services, including especially health education.

Planning for channeling research and theory into more practical educational work, with special reference to elementary and high schools.

Planning for wise distribution and optimum population programs.

Planning for local and regional adjustment and opportunity for race and minority groups.

Planning for well balanced communities, industry, and agriculture in relation to high standards of cultural development.

The Assumptions of Regional

Balance [1945]*

I

Our assumptions with reference to the regional balance of people and resources and of culture and technology are couched primarily in terms of the functional definition of regionalism and social planning rather than in terms of exact delineation or in terms of economic or ecological specialisms, although the concept is susceptible to definition in terms of the special attributes on these levels.

Our assumptions, further, tend to feature illustrations from realistic contemporary situations and operational strategy rather than the specialized attributes of the ideological concept or metaphysical "isms."

But before these, there is the broader, more general assumption that the key problem of all our postwar reconstruction and planning centers around the quality and balance of the people and culture, of economy and technology the world over. More appropriate for our purpose, the problem is one of regional equality and balance in the total integration of world order.

For it seems clear that a great deal, perhaps most, of the tragic situations of maladjustment, disorganization, and pathology in the world, are due to imbalance whether in terms of the lack of natural balance between plant and animal resources or between man and nature or whether in terms of the "haves" and "have-nots" in advanced civilization. Inherent in the waste and weakness of any region,

* *World Economics,* III (October-December 1945), 57-66.

in the conflict and lack of unity of the people, and in hazards of regional imbalance and pathology are lurking dangers and dilemmas capable of swelling to floodtide mass emotion, confusion and revolution in the immediate postwar world and after.

And by the same token, the main strategy of planning will be found within the framework of regional balance and equality which must include not only economic opportunity but cultural development and the thing now so much stressed, namely justice in world organization. Yet justice, admittedly basic to adequate and enduring arrangements, is not primarily something on the level of abstract morality or moralistic principles, but of the essential regional equality and balance of opportunity in the places where people live set in the framework of world standards and interrelationships.

As relating to the functional aspects of this thing we call the regional balance of man and culture, it seems demonstrably clear that many of the conferences for racial, religious, and world unity became in effect forces for disunity, centering on abstract demands on the one hand and concrete pleas for special priorities on the other, rather than realistic strategy for regional and racial balance and harmony within the framework of the people, their resources, situation, technology *and* high moral principles.

II

Now we turn to our main assumptions on the basis of the functional definitions of regionalism and planning and our illustrations from world regions and from the quest for the regional balance of America.

In the first place, the assumptions of balance comprehend a great deal more than the technically defined balanced economy with its factors of balanced agriculture and industry and the other factors so well defined by the economists. These are assumed as basic to what Buckle a long time ago called order and balance in a country and what administrative authorities have been seeking in balanced parities and parity programs. For the purposes of this syllabus the heart of regional balance is found in the search for equal opportunity for all the people through the conservation, development and use of their resources in the places where they live, adequately adjusted to the interregional culture and economy of the other regions of the world or of the nation. The goal is, therefore, clearly one of balanced culture as well as economy, in which equality of opportunity in education, in public health and welfare, in the range of occupational outlook, and in the elimination of handicapping differentials between and among different groups of people and levels of culture prevail.

With reference to the functional definitions of regionalism, it is necessary to re-emphasize the fact that the primary objectives of regionalism are found in the end product of integration of regions more than the mere study and development of regions themselves. The regions are studied and planned to the end that they may be more adequate in all aspects of resources and culture; yet regionalism itself is primarily interested in the total integration and balance of these regions. In the world order it is not so much a problem of conflict between universalism and regionalism as it is one of world order and organization brought out through the representation, initiative, and balance of world regions. In the case of American society it is not so much a question of centralization of authority in conflict with state rights as it is developing an adequate federalized central authority capable thereby of achieving realistic decentralization. In other words, it is necessary to have some sort of world order or organization before the world's regions can be integrated and before they may be co-operatively developed at their best. In American society there must be strong national character and organization before the Nation can be made strong through the strength and integration of its diverse regions so that regionalism may supplant the older separatism and isolationism of sectional development.

So, too, the global situation with reference to races, minority peoples and nationalities has made increasingly clear and vivid the organic significance of this regional quality and balance of the people everywhere. The assumptions of regional balance here are both culturally theoretical and administratively practical since it seems likely that one of the key tasks of the postwar planning world will be to rediscover and recognize the folk personality of millions of people who give new emphasis to *vox populi, vox dei* or to the realistic verdict that only the people count. All this means that regional balance assumes a healthy diversity; that the way of each region is the way of its culture and that each culture is inseparably identified with its regional character.

This is not only nothing new but has always been recognized as a definitive part of understanding peoples and their institutions. It has always been recognized by the common people in their loyalties and devotion to their own customs and institutions and in their criticism of others. It has always been recognized by anthropologists and sociologists in their study of cultures. Regional attitudes and *mores* are so definite and powerful that they constitute rights and wrongs; they determine the nature of behavior and institutions. Intolerance, therefore, of the *mores* of a people reflects narrowness and provincialism of outlook. In the contemporary America there has recently developed an increasing tendency among urban intellectuals to belittle and to characterize as bad many of the *mores* of rural society and for intellectuals everywhere to dictate the ways and means of living for minority peoples wherever they are. Manifestly, however, this is one source of conflict and imbalance in the world, for consider the facility of the United States to dictate cultural order for Poland or the conflicting folk of the Balkan States or the South American Republics. Or, consider the over-simplified plans for the reintegration of the cultures of India or the conflicting claims of Palestine. This reflects a strange backwardness in an age of communication and intellectual liberalism. The depth and width of the growing chasm and threatened imbalance and the reasons for it would be unbelievable if the situation were not actually true.

This regional quality of culture, behavior and institutions is, of course, universally applicable to all regions of world society. The recognition of this regional quality of world society, of its imbalance, and of the need for regional arrangements for world organization and peace, while relatively new, is rapidly becoming the basic consideration in nearly all plans for stabilizing world organization. Symbolic of the swelling tide of regionalism is the conviction of Sumner Wells "that an effective international organization can be constituted only through the creation of regional systems of nations . . . under an over-all international body representative . . . of all regions." But in whatever instance the point of emphasis is that it is through cooperative arrangement and the integration of diversified cultures that strength and stability are to be found.

Such a functional regionalism thus becomes a tool for attaining balance and equilibrium between people and resources, men and machines, the State and the folk. It is a tool of the democratic process in that it provides for the redistribution of the good things of life and of the opportunity to work within the framework of every people's geography and of their inherent cultural equipment. It is a tool for democratic world reconstruction in the postwar world, because it is through cooperative regionalism rather than economic nationalism that the society of tomorrow can be organized for human welfare instead of for military achievements. It is a tool for social planning, because it takes into consideration the rights, privileges, resources of people and areas, and stresses self-government and self-development as opposed to coercive centralized power. It is a tool for social planning, also because it offers specific technical workable ways of developing and conserving resources for human-use ends. Since regionalism, as the opposite pole of sectionalism, isolation, and separatism, is as true of international as well as of national affairs, it wants no self-sufficiency in economy. It wants no isolationism and separatism, and it wants no totalitarianistic tragic imbalance between the folk and the state or between power and the people.

III

There are other assumptions of regionalism which it is not necessary to discuss in relation to our main premises. Assumed are the specifications of administrative regionalism, regional planning, regional mercantilism and the science of the region which delineates regions, defines its terms, and sets up its adequate methods. There is the final point of emphasis which is that regional balance is essentially synonymous with the ends of social planning. There are many satisfactory definitions of planning in terms of its attitudes. Two of these I like especially. One is a commonly used one which makes the objectives of planning the attainment of balance and equilibrium between competing factors and the substitution of effectiveness and abundance for inefficiency and scarcity. The other is one utilized by Patrick Geddes which assumed planning to be the bridging of the distance between science and knowledge and practical problems. In both of these, as in all efforts toward world regional balance, are implied skills, science, expertness through which the facts and specifications are provided and through which then the distance is bridged.

I am well aware of the assumptions of those pure theorists who affirm that since everything is in flux and change is a law of process that, therefore, there can be no such thing as balance. But it is not the statics of a laissez faire society that we are talking about. We know a lot about change and social process and social interaction. It is exactly in the problems and processes of social values, social progress and social change and the adaptation of men and culture to resources and time and situation that the inherent power of balance is sought. We know also a great deal about the grand old doctrine of mankind being in the state of sin but I see no reason why something shouldn't be done about it in the great process of adjusting man to doing things in the right way—sin being the essence of doing the right things in the wrong way and the resulting maladjustment and pathology.

IV

We have then to make brief application of this thing we call regional balance. Naturally the first application at this time is to world order and international relations. We need only recapitulate the essential premises of regional balance and then look at the map of the world with its ill-distribution of people in relation to resources and living relationships. You can see on a map, for instance, the wide range of income closely related often in the lower brackets to the densest populations. Similar applications may be made by reference to the different resources, land, minerals, water, power, labor, machinery. Manifestly, here are the measurable ways of indicating need of and attaining regional balance in a world where accounts are now sadly out of balance. Manifestly, too, the technical problems of tariff, free trade, of money and exchange and especially of transportation and organization are among the technical, workable ways of doing the job.

In the assumptions of the regional balance of America there are, of course, two major aspects: one is that of a better balance between and among the Americas and the other is that of the regional balance of our own Nation, with which, of course, we have been here concerned. We may illustrate briefly with three aspects of the situation, namely the overall importance of regional balance, some specific aspects of planning that need correction, and the Southern regions as illustrations of imbalance.

With reference to the national character we need only say that to understand the significance of regional balance in America we need only recapture the epic of the Nation's powerful heritage of resources set in the midst of every region and of every folk at work at every occupation in which democracy has been made enduring because of the diversity of people, place, work, wealth; and to measure the tragedies of imbalance in waste and weakness, in conflict and isolationism. Yet there is another aspect of great importance and that is America's success in attainment of regional balance in its effect upon the world. America can adopt the procedures of planning and interregional and interracial organization and cooperation and be ready to join the world in international organization and cooperation for peace. Or America can join the conflicting nations and races in perpetual warfare and violence and lose its place in the leadership of the world of international organization for peace. This problem is no more a one-way obligation in the United States, with its opportunity for interregional and interracial balance, than is the obligation of nations and races and folk in tragedy and travail the world over.

Finally, it seems well to illustrate the nature of imbalance by referring to a specific level of planning which often forgets the essentials of regional balance and therefore negates the idea of national strength and unity. How national planning might *not* contribute effectively to the regional balance of America may be illustrated in two sample cases. There was, for instance, in the depression 1930's an earlier publication at the time when America's consumer purchasing power was scarcely more than sixty billion dollars prepared by a national planning agency looking toward full employment. In the program, recommended under the title "Resource Utilization," it was pointed out that when the total purchasing power of the Nation reached seventy or eighty billion dollars the Nation could give full employment to all of its employables. Yet it was stated that even if the total consumers' purchasing power should rise to ninety or ninety-five or even one hundred billion dollars there would be need for scarcely any increase in agricultural workers. As applied to the agricultural regions and their mode of farmer folk, it would thus come to pass that, when the rest of the Nation was reaching its peak of prosperity on the basis of industrial America, they would be in depression straits with too little employment and having the necessity of paying high prices for commodities made on the basis of high prosperity. The original program not only failed to plan for regions and their farm populations, but on the contrary assumed that the logical thing would be for the rural folk to migrate to industrial centers, where already people were congested mainly in one or two regions.

This brings us to the second type of planning which accentuates regional imbalance and works to the detriment of the regions. That is, the procedure which takes the youth from one region to another, trains them, and concentrates them in the same urban industrial centers that already exist, results inevitably in the impoverishment of the region from which they are drained and is not a sound policy for the Nation or the region. Such programs fail to provide training and work opportunity for the youth of that region, and this inevitably results in deficiency areas. It assumes an uneven regional distribution in terms of "the have" and "the have-not" regions with the corollary that such regions can best be provided for through Federal aid and should be expected only to come as near self-support as possible.

V

With reference to the *Southern Regions of the United States* as an illustration of the opportunity for attaining genuine regional balance, we have often pointed out that perhaps the South affords the best testing ground for regional planning in the United States. This is true for several reasons. In the first place, the measure of regional imbalance is more marked in the South than in any other region. This imbalance is found in many aspects of life. It is found in the realm of educational opportunity on all levels. It is found in the field of research where science and research, as they may be applied to resources and regional development, have made a relatively small contribution and play a relatively small role as compared to other regions. It lacks a balanced economy as between agriculture and industry, as well as a balanced agriculture itself. The population and its use need new balance both within the region and without and further distribution throughout the other regions of the Nation. Particularly, the South is out of balance in its ratio of Negro to white and in its capacity to render equality of opportunity in this field. The South, therefore, seeks a better balanced culture and economy to the end that it may have a wider range of occupational opportunity and a better balanced institutional service.

In all these aspects of regional imbalance, the problem of planning is a national one rather than a Southern one. The problem also is a two-way one, since the problem of seeking regional equality and balance is the number one postwar domestic problem of planning and since much of the South's imbalance is due to national procedures and national economies that have developed since the Civil War.

The achievement of regional equality and balance of America is, however, not only of the greatest importance to the South and to America but to the world of international order also. For, in relation to specific problems—tariff, exports, good neighbor policy, and the like—the South will have increasingly large possibilities; but also in proportion as the United States of America can solve its problems of regional balance in the total culture and economy, the rest of the world will be reassured and will profit by the technique which America uses.

3. Education the Way Forward

Education in the Secondary Schools of the

South [1940]*

Readers of books used to have a way of saying that the purpose of a preface was for the author to explain why he did not include in his discussion the things that he should have included and why he did include those things which he should not have included. My own feeling is that the purpose of the preface to a book or an introduction to a talk is not that, but to point out that the subject being discussed is about the most important topic which it is possible to consider. It is with some such attitude that we approach the subject of education in the secondary schools in the South. This seems true both because of the basic importance of the subject in a changing education and because of the role which the secondary school plays in this changing drama of American education. There are certain other, perhaps self-evident, assumptions which appear basic to our consideration.

One of these is that American Youth and their realistic education in close living harmony with their American and regional environment constitute one of the key problems, considered by many the chiefest of all problems in American education. Another assumption which seems universally accepted by school people throughout the country, as well as by publicists and statesmen in general, is that the

* An address delivered before a joint meeting of the Commission on Institutions of Higher Education and the Commission on Curricular Problems and Research, Atlanta, Georgia, April 10, 1940. Published in *The Southern Association Quarterly,* IV (August 1940), 523-29.

objective of this education must be mastery of the physical, technical, and cultural forces which sweep down upon us, and that this mastery must be turned to human-use ends through a regular democracy which shall guarantee the continuity of human development through a superior mankind and more adequate human society.

If this is true, another assumption follows: namely, that education for youth must mean education and preparation for their participation in the American dream commensurate with the guarantees of American democracy. This means that there must be a revitalized interpretation of Americanism to understand and to utilize our great resources and our regional diversity through the development of which only can the greatness of America be continued. This means that youth must understand the twofold basis of Americanism: one, the living geography and resources of a great continent which distinguish it from Europe or Asia or Africa; and the other, the living background of our political, historical, and cultural ideals.

Before the American Dream was Nature, primal in its grandeur and abundance, primeval in its years of as many seasons as the mind of man can contemplate. Before Man and his Society, before Plymouth and Jamestown, was the American continent, later symbol and reality of a new world apart from Europe or Asia or Africa. In the ever-resurging quest for "Something to prove this puzzle, the new world," it is good to remember that before Man on this continent was this Nature, prolific and powerful, kind in its nurture, ruthless in its laws, alike merciful and merciless, the eternal creator and creature of living societies.

Before there were men to hear and see and feel there were crashing thunder and forked lightning, frigid cold and torrid heat, eastern sunshine and western rains, storms over a thousand mountain tops, floods in countless valleys. And there were growing things in limitless abundance, millions of quick, heart-throbbing beasts of the fields and birds of the air and countless symbols of glory and brilliance in the flowering colors of trees and plants. And there was abundance of fruits and harvests, seasons of springtime and summer, of autumn and winter. And there were the successions of living things, millions following millions, in the life and death of the ever-cycling nature-world. And there were such variety and abundance, such vastness and expanse, such glory-vistas and mystery as had not been hitherto recorded in the annals of the earth.

With reference to that Americanism, grounded in the high purposes of American institutions and democracy, it is important for us to renew our intentions to make of America a society at its best, as an age-long ideal in which God, man, and nature, working together, create a society at its best. This means, of course, America at her best, each region at its best, each state at its best. In particular, therefore, we should come ultimately to examine education in the secondary schools of the South with a view to a program of education, through which Southern youth would develop the South at its best.

I find myself tempted to venture a twofold approach to the discussion of this most important topic, combining the methods of the professor and the politician. This, of course, would seem to be a difficult undertaking. The professor, you know, always knows exactly how it should be done, and the politician always promises something good in the end!

In the case of "The South at Its Best," it is very clear that we have a difficult situation, on the one hand, to say what is best and, on the other, to say how we shall bring it about. Who, for instance, is to be the judge of what is the best?

It must be clear, therefore, that our statement of desirable and attainable ends of Southern regional development must be in terms that are flexible, comprehensive, enduring, and commensurate with the cultural, economic, and social framework of our American democracy. Our attainable standards must be stated in terms of capacities of growth, of development of natural resources and people, of the devotion of the people and their wealth to institutional services through which we seek a balance and equilibrium between the people and wealth, between men and technology, between culture and civilization. We do not, therefore, say "The South at Its Best" is a wealthy South, or an industrial South, or an agrarian South; but we say that "The South at Its Best" is a growing South, a developing South, utilizing, developing, and conserving all of its resources in a balanced economy, of, for, and by the people, and of, for, and by all of the institutions. Its specific objectives and its specific needs will then be worked out in relation to each diversified phase of life, each changing situation, and in the combined and cooperative work of all acting together. Now, if I may, I shall continue our discussion after the manner of the professor by asking a few questions. And I propose to answer them, too, if you accept my verdict. Here are the questions:

What is the nature of the regional economy of the South at the present or in the very recent past?

What is the difference between the present economy and the desired optimum?

What are attainable standards and developments of the immediate future?

What resources, producers, and facilities will be required to make up this difference?

How may the region acquire the resources and facilities to make up this difference?

And finally what are the best ways, the best steps, of going about obtaining these resources?

If we oversimplify these questions and restate them in a way which apparently will appeal to the popular motivation of the South, they would read something like this:

What is it that we now have?

What is it that we want?

What is the distance between what we have and what we want?

What will it take to bridge this distance?

How can we get what it takes to bridge the distance?

What is the best way to go about getting what it takes?

Now we come again to emphasize the fact that our statement of what the South needs to be at its best is not something very specific in the field of education or industry or labor or capital, but it is the development of all of its people and capacities. We may, therefore, examine a simple framework upon which to project our questions and answers.

The Southern regions of the United States are a component part of a great nation, whose development and welfare depend upon the corresponding development and welfare of all of its regions adequately integrated and coordinated. For the purpose of this little discussion, we assume that there are five major types of wealth and resources which go into the making of a rich civilization. These are natural wealth and resources; technological wealth—science, skill, organization, and management; capital wealth—invested capital and means for the development of resources; human wealth—the people, symbol and reality of all wealth; institutional wealth—means for developing human wealth.

Now, our studies have shown that the South excels in two of these types of wealth, but lags in three. That is, it has a super-abundance of natural wealth and of human wealth, having a great range and variety of climate and resources, on the one hand, and being the seedbed of population, on the other. It lags, however, in technological wealth—skill, science, and management; and because of this, therefore, it is short in capital wealth and is, therefore, poor; and because of this it is not able to support its institutions for the development of its people as it would desire to do. In addition to these technical limitations, there has been a large measure of waste in both natural resources and human resources, so that it has been customary to think of the South in terms of a certain mode of low economic and living standards and of a relatively large number of marginal folk living on eroded land without resources enough to reach the American standard of living. The most common illustrations of this have been in recent years in terms of farm tenancy, of certain limited opportunities of the Negroes, and of the dilemma of the cotton and tobacco money-crop economy. In general, this is the basis for characterizing the South as the Nation's number one problem.

Now we have answered our question as to what we now have in the South. We shall now look at the answer to the next question as to what we want. You will see the extraordinary importance of education here from our next assumption; namely, that if the South can provide education, skill, science, and management, through which it can translate its natural wealth into capital wealth and income adequate to support its institutions, forthwith the South would excel in all five of these great resources, and would, therefore, constitute "The South at Its Best." That is, if we can translate our natural resources into capital wealth, I have the feeling that the South is sufficiently highly motivated to devote a great portion of this wealth to our institutions, which in turn would develop and enrich the people, conserve their interest, and contribute to that American democracy which makes wealth and weal synonymous. This is the South that we want.

From the viewpoint of the schools and those who support the schools, there are three immediate tasks which, if accomplished, together with the other planning and rapid progress that is being made, would justify the enthusiastic statement of many Southerners that the South is the Nation's *opportunity number one*. First is the problem of educating the new generation of the South to sense the meaning of natural wealth and its relation to the living realities of the people and their welfare; this includes a sensing of the value of work and high standards of achievement. Second, is the problem of widening the range of occupational opportunity, through new developments, to the end that the superabundance of Southern youth may have a chance to work, and thus to develop and use our resources. The third task is, then, actually to train and equip these youth so that they may function adequately and in competition with workers everywhere.

Manifestly, more capital wealth is necessary for the undertaking of these tasks. This wealth must come from several sources: from the South's own economic gains in line with the extraordinary progress that has been made in the last few years; from the investment of wealth owned by Southerners who are joining in the new frontiers of Southern development; from investments of those who live outside the region, but who see in it an opportunity for regional and national development; from national foundations whose monies in research and experimentation can give leverage to regional support; and from the Federal Government in equalization programs—agriculture, roads, health, education, public safety, and the like.

It must be clear that although some of these tasks belong to the institutions of higher learning, to technical schools, to industrial research, to farm chemurgy, to lawyers and businessmen, it is essentially a problem of public education to be achieved through the increasingly dynamic and realistic school system, for it is evident that our youth at the present time do not have a sense of the real meaning of natural wealth, of standards of work, of achievement. It has not been fashionable either for boys or girls to be interested in soil erosion, natural resources, conservation, waste of men and waste of soil, or in social problems. One of the most pathetic spectacles of our whole situation is that of the most attractive youth in the world literally hanging around drugstores and wayplaces, wondering what it is all about and what to do next.

With reference to the widening range of occupational opportunity, it must be clear now that scarcely more than half of our Southern youth can hope to have equal opportunity in the old sense of the American dream—opportunity to work, to create, to have families, and to find security. There must be new avenues through increasing industry and the balance between industry and agriculture and increased opportunity for trained leaders. We must work out the answers to some such questions as this: how many and what sort of new and old industries will give occupations to how many people from the farms and villages, who in turn will create purchasing power to enable how many more people to remain on the farm to produce commodities of that sort, in turn to help support industries which make for a balanced economy?

It must be clear also with reference to the third need that at the present time our Southern youth are not trained to do anything very well. In an age of scarcity and need for work, for engineering, for skills, for farming, for dairying, it is not possible to find personnel equipped to do the jobs that must be done and in reality jobs that the youth themselves would want to do if they knew about them and were so equipped.

Public education has been one of the pillars of the faith and the hope of American democracy. In this new sense it must become increasingly the key to the development of new American frontiers. When, therefore, we say that it is incumbent upon us all to devote the next ten years as a measuring space to achieve the South at its best, we must begin with public education and with youth, and with that great body of teachers who must be educated to sense this new power and realism of education. Education, then, in the secondary schools in the immediate future must be synonymous with this ideal of "The South at Its Best" in a nation which finds strength in the diversity and richness of its regions.

This "South at Its Best" being a young South, a growing South, less impeded by technological determinism than other regions, may also seek in its education that balance and equilibrium between culture and civilization, which must undoubtedly mark the survival of any democratic nation in the modern world. This cultural education must somehow recreate and reincarnate the natural folk society of the people in harmony with nature and resources. "The South at Its Best" as wrought out through the educational program, must have harmony and balance between the genuine, realistic culture of the people and the mechanical civilization of urbanism and technology, which will insure an enduring society. This is not to talk about what is right and what is wrong, what is best and what is worst, but it is to point out a scientific margin of survival for a superior mankind and adequate society.

As symbolic of some of the differences between culture and civilization as they are reflected in the appraisal of the past, the present, and future prospects, we may present sampling of those contrasts which will challenge education in the future.

For instance, culture is the folk society, and civilization is the state society.

Culture is democratic, while civilization is autocratic and totalitarian.

Culture means growth and development; civilization means merely progress and decline.

Culture connotes survival; civilization, achievement.

Culture is evolutionary and slow moving, while civilization is revolutionary and highly accelerated.

Culture is human, striving, personal, and individual; civilization is the machine, the mass, and the class.

Culture is natural and realistic; civilization is artificial and utopian.

Culture is ethnic and societal, while civilization is civil and technological.

Culture is adolescent and growing; civilization is mature and senescent.

Culture is moral-purposive, while civilization is scientific-technical.

Culture seeks the best quality and value, while civilization achieves the maximum, the quantity, money and power.

But in all this search for societal culture, we must keep in mind that we mean the total cumulative heritage of the people in the larger societal, anthropological sense, and not the superficial, artificial form and technology, whether it be of the machine, of utopia, of intelligentsia, or of art. For it is a social axiom that whenever the demands of artificial society, of super-technology, of super-specialism exceed the capacity of the people to adapt and whenever the means, whether as institutions or as machines, come to take on the civilized nature of ends in themselves, where ends justify the means, then society begins to deteriorate, and unless living culture is recreated through a new and dynamic and realistic education, sooner or later there is disorganization and decay.

Expanding Higher Education: Which Way Is Forward in the Social Sciences? [1955]*

It seems peculiarly appropriate that I have this opportunity to discuss fundamentals, basic needs, and redefinition of the American university, just fifty years after I had the rare opportunity of participating in G. Stanley Hall's bringing together perhaps the most distinguished group of European and American scholars on his occasion of presenting Sigmund Freud and many other German and American educators, among whom were Jung, Ebbinghaus, William James, Franz Boas, and John Dewey.

Stanley Hall, having studied in Germany, thought he saw, first at Hopkins and then at Clark, the dream and the maturing of university as the one institution which would stand forever upon the rock of freedom to study, to research, to teach, to write. "University," he thought, "was the highest essence of the intellect, the finest expression of the spirit, the surest road to liberty, and the most satisfying achievement of those who search for truth, mastery, and understanding." Just a little later, Woodrow Wilson wrote eloquently in the same spirit and dream. "University spirit is intolerant of all the things that put the human mind under restraint. It is intolerant of everything that seeks to block advancement of ideals, the excellence

* This paper was prepared by Dr. Odum for the annual meeting of the American Council on Education, Chicago, Illinois, October 1954. It was read by Dr. Gordon W. Blackwell and published posthumously in the *Educational Record*, XXXVI (January 1955), 49-55. Reprinted by permission.

of truth, the purification of life." Unfortunately, concept and definition, partly because they were so stubbornly grounded in the ideal, did not prove so simple of either definition or attainment.

This was the dream of G. Stanley Hall, which he tried so hard to translate into American reality from the first days of Hopkins to his last days in Clark University, where it is sometimes said he died of a broken heart when his beloved German scholars signed the Hymn of Hate and prostituted their science and learning to totalitarian ruthlessness. President Wilson's bitterness was no less devastating than Hall's And yet, in many ways, these were the first morning and evening of a titanic struggle between universities and the strange spectacle of university goals and ideals and practices defeating their own ends, unless indeed contemporary man can come to terms with some approximation of consensus and core.

The goal and meaning of university are the same today as fifty years ago, with the main specific core always seeking to maintain university as its own integer. In the popular reference of Professor Douglas Bush, the burden is upon the humanities as the bearer of the original sin complex; the causal factors rest with science and invention; what to do about them rests primarily with the social sciences, and the total dilemma bears down upon the ambition and dynamics of an America which has been full of movements, trends, and eras. Thus, the setting in which the university must survive is immeasurably more complex than could be even imagined back in the first decade of the century. For even a half-century ago, there was the great continuum of cultural development pulling two ways—from the sacred to the secular, from the individual to the mass, from freedom of the individual to considerations of the majority, from culture to civilization, and always the threatening primary competition between the moral order and the technological order. And besides these, there are the amazing *facts,* astronomical in numbers, of cultural and economic development and pressures that are causal factors generally overlooked.

A preview of our future tasks, I think, must be well bottomed in an understanding of the major backgrounds and traditions upon which our American universities have grown great. There is no substitute for the facts, although facing the facts is not enough. A half-dozen of the levels of university achievement will reflect a better understanding of the great work which our universities have done, their natural conflicts and limitations in a dynamic, growing American society, some of the hazards which they faced, and the current dilemmas which multiply.

First of all, we recall, of course, the earlier religious bottoming of our American universities from those days when Harvard was founded to give deeper understanding and learning to the religious leaders of the New World on through the founding of King's College, Columbia, Princeton, Yale, down through the notable roll call of denominational colleges in every state, and all along the long road of chartering our state universities. There was always the thread of religion and piety and humility running through the fabric of scholarship and learning. This was what the people wanted and what the leaders of those days, conforming to the early American pattern, wanted and voted.

So effective was this work of the people that the earlier colleges multiplied rapidly within the framework of religious endowment and atmosphere. And in some regions there grew up sturdy colleges for men and for women in each of the major denominations, and their graduates often constituted perhaps the major influence in our college education of the time.

There was then the powerful influence of European culture and the example of European universities in the classics, in science, in philosophy, molding and conditioning the ideals and patterns of America's growing college and university life.

From these influences the development of our colleges and universities tended to become, even as European universities, more and more exclusive in their assumptions that university education and culture found their definition limited to something very precious and special that could be obtained by only a relatively small number of the people. It was assumed that university must be bottomed in the learning of the past and the pureness of the laboratory which saw science for science' sake, although for a long time even science had to fight hard for its laboratory in the curriculum.

Now, no matter how realistic and true that level of university education and culture might have been, it was only a part of the basic assumptions of the "American dream" which was to make public education a sort of *religio poetae,* which was to be the open sesame to good citizenship and equality of opportunity for all men. Consequently, there developed another level of university education, symbolized in the rise and rapid development of our great state universities, starting in the great Middle West, spreading southeastward, and then farther to the other wests of expanding America. This was a movement in the direction of democratizing university education. As Frederick Jackson Turner has pointed out, through the state, "the university offers to every class the means of education, and even engages in propaganda to induce students to continue. It sinks deep shafts through the social strata to find the gold of real ability in the underlying rock of the masses. It fosters that due degree of individualism which is implied in the right of every human being to have opportunity to rise in whatever directions his peculiar abilities entitle him to go, subordinate to the welfare of the state. It keeps the avenues of promotion to the highest offices, the highest honors, open to the humblest and most obscure lad who has the natural gifts, at the same time that it aids in the improvement of the masses."

Nothing in our educational history is more striking than the steady pressure of democracy upon its universities to adapt them to the requirements of all the people. From the state universities of the Middle West, shaped under pioneer ideals, has come leadership in the fuller recognition of scientific studies, and especially those of applied science devoted to the conquest of nature; the breaking-down of the traditional required curriculum; the union of vocational and college work in the same institution; the development of agricultural and engineering colleges and business courses; the training of lawyers, public health and public welfare personnel; development of politics and public men and journalists—all under the ideal of maturing democracy, rather than of individual advancement alone.

Yet the development of these great American state universities founded on the basis of democratic service to the people in many ways followed the same trend and level of university education in the great endowed eastern institutions and later in other great universities, such as the University of Chicago and Stanford. They tended, therefore, to become again aristocratic in the sense that their enrollment and their curriculum tended to follow the earlier pattern of America's leading universities. So much was this true that when the second level of democratic state university education was set in the form of the land-grant colleges of agriculture, engineering, and mechanics, it became the common mode to seek legislative funds for these newer schools on the ground that the earlier state universities had become instutions for rich men's sons and for classical education. And in those states where the land-grant colleges were merged with the state university, the new college took on the name of "cow college," and the standards of the university were considered greatly lowered, in contrast to the mid-century powerful contributions to the enrichment of the rural American culture.

Then followed the further extension of the democratic education policy in the establishment of teacher-training institutions, normal schools and colleges, and special technical institutions for women. Most of these, in the effort to feature the humanities, later were to seek full recognition and rating as standard colleges and universities, just as the special designation of Negro colleges came to be omitted, thus multiplying the units of state higher education on different levels and complicating the problem of the university.

It was perhaps logical, therefore, if not inevitable, that the next trends in university development were to be set on the quantitative level, seeking to give university instruction in all the multiple fields demanded in the modern world by both the people in general and by special interests of varying sorts. This quantitative level of university education tended to make increasingly greater and greater demands upon the financial support of the people, thus bringing the university system nearer to the other fiscal procedures of economy and efficiency in the use of public funds.

The universities had already moved naturally into what might be called a popular level in two ways. First, they sought to provide ways and means for every high school graduate to attain that university education which the people had come to consider an open sesame to success; and secondly, they undertook in competitive processes to appeal for popular support of the people and to develop alumni loyalties through adult education, extension work, and public athletics.

Now, manifestly, these several levels of university trends were not necessarily exclusive one of the other, nor was there always a clear index of demarcation. Rather, they represent university's effort to adapt itself to a modern world of change and technology which also reshaped all of our other institutions. In the midst of these levels and interwoven in between them in the fabric of American college and university education were still the hundreds of notable private institutions, seeking nobly to maintain standards and yet to adapt themselves to the qualitative needs of the people and particularly their religious constituencies.

Once again the cumulative heritage of these university levels of achievement reflected an extraordinary body of learning in the humanities, the sciences, and the social sciences, and a qualitative and quantitative contribution to knowledge and to method never before approached in the history of learning and education.

And notable in this heritage was the extraordinary personnel of the faculties and research staffs of the universities and colleges of the nation. Grand professors and scholars they were, devoted and fearless, self-sacrificing and indefatigable, beloved of a vast body of students, symbolic of the people that America could produce.

And there was that lesser body of men, the presidents, chancellors, deans, and other technical administrators, who made possible the functioning of college and university life on a scale never before approached. Many of these were notable leaders not only in the field of education but also in the general culture and public esteem.

Now manifestly, there have been limitations and deficiencies in each and all of these levels and in the cumulative results. It could not be otherwise. No one nor all of these levels have failed and to no one or even to several of them can be ascribed what has often been called the "failure of our college and university education." But they have not failed. Our realistic examination of their limitations, on the contrary, has for its purpose the assurance that they shall not fail, but that the university of the future, building upon them, noting their limitations and mistakes, following their trends, will find its promise and prospect in the better coordination and integration of these institutions in an increasingly effective adaptation to the needs and institutions of the American people.

We have thus far analyzed situations, movements, and trends to which we have pointed with pride, but we have not yet sensed their relevance to the total present dilemma of university. What we have said in the attempt to sense the meaning of history and the dynamics of changing structure of civilization is true, but we have failed to ask, "What else is true?" and especially, "What else is true?" for university's current situation. So we come once again to analyze the startling changes which have been mastering our destiny.

We do not catalogue with fear or dread these revolutionary changes that shake the pillars of our world. Rather, we look upon them as the real challenge and response which bring us to a need for diagnosis and direction; a need which can be met if we bring to bear upon this challenge the same initiative, power, and support which we currently give to our newer atomic and interplanetary research. In the contemplation of these facets of the total university problem, we must do two things: namely, stop our routine cataloguing of the startling and sublime as if we were merely chattering statistical units in a new methodological approach, and then come to a sense of the meaning of all that we face.

To begin anew our enumeration of change, consider that fifty years ago university was the main core of what we called starry-eyed science, with relatively small amounts of research done by government and industry. Now, university is a poor third to governmental and industrial research, which are literally transforming the earth's profile on all levels. Yet with even the limited amount of university research, in science alone a single laboratory for a specific purpose may now spend five times the total Jeffersonian price of the great Louisiana Purchase. From our simple college laboratory we move to a single observatory with a million-pound telescope that will peer a million light years into space, a light year being the distance that light crosses in one year—5,805,696,000,000 miles.

And from where do the costs of these and other more startling atomic laboratories come? Well, we have usually quoted Thomas Jefferson with humanistic approval when he inclined to urge that we leave all industries to Europe; that cities are to the body politic what sores are to the human body; and that that government is best which governs least. The facts are that perhaps 75 percent of the people now at work get their incomes from occupations that did not even exist a half-century ago. This is the fruit of industry, urbanism, and governmental cooperation in the great industrial expansion of the United States, the unquestioned leader of the world's resources, industry, and production. It is for this reason that we proclaim ourselves the hope of the world. How, then, can the humanities, or other facets of university, prepare new millions for new work that never existed in the great heydey of the humanities? Nor existed scarcely yesterday, when the social sciences began.

We have not even mentioned the common everyday varieties of dilemmas that stem from the floodtide of new students, the shortage of teachers and equipment. We have not noted that university has rediscovered the elementary and secondary schools, against which universities complain bitterly, but on behalf of which most faculties have done little. We have not mentioned many of the clichés, such as the radio, "television fish-bowl culture," the role of football and other athletics, or that the freedom of the intellectuals may have failed because it was primarily focused upon their own personal concepts and subjective values of liberty, advocated for themselves but not for the common man.

Nor have we catalogued the amazing ignorance and isolation apparently necessary to academic specialization. Many of our social scientists and humanists so teach their specialties as to put their subject matter beyond the pale of the average student, who indeed has been provided few great teachers in these fields. Much of the hopeful, flowering researches are still often atomistic, and the semantics of their presentation often make them appear as ends in themselves instead of means to the greater understanding. Our bulwarks of university have let the defense of freedom slip behind the call for security. Perhaps now we merely record with sorrow and ineffectiveness how the financial rewards of our liberal arts folk fall behind those of the professional folk, and have long since quit wondering whether education leads or follows economic, cultural, and technological development.

What can the social scientist say or contribute? We must repeat that the inventory of all the prevailing complexities and difficulties offers a challenge here as in no other great sphere except that of war and peace and the uses of science for human society. On this assumption it seems possible that several things can be said. But even so, we must remember that the numerous and specialized personnel of the social sciences cannot always agree in the earlier stages of their many-variegated efforts, and no one or two can speak for them all or even a mode. I would like to see a baker's dozen Barzuns and

Reismans and others available devoting a span of years to a realistic and relentless analysis of the American university as such, even though they might have to go through the hot and cold war of general education.

It seems likely that the social sciences might do more in the study of organization, structure, and processes of university. For we still find it difficult to induce all the faculties and the governing boards and the people to realize that university now constitutes not only a complicated structure of its own, but in actual function and control it is closely connected with state and public. There are really four cornerstones to the modern university: the humanities and the liberal arts college; the graduate and research program; the technical and professional personnel engaged in teaching and in meeting expanding service demands; and the administrative, public policy, and educational leadership of the total university. And if these are the four cornerstones, then let's not just talk about them, but make them cornerstones of power, with each having its due share and role. I do not know of any university which functions fully and freely with the full support of this fourfold base. Perhaps the analysis of structure and organizational aspects will help.

The social scientists have tried hard to devise and schedule new series of social science courses that will bring closer the humanities, the social sciences, and the philosophy of science. In this and his other work, the social scientist may come closer to analyzing the total situation in frames that provide a living reference of working achievement for the university president, who must bear an increasingly greater burden.

Of university's main dilemma, freedom is the core, and not how many courses of what kind are taught. In the modern world, either to demand freedom, or to profess it, is virtually futile, unless we can locate freedom in the structures of our institutions. And, of course, all our structures have changed and are changing. There is a rare opportunity for the social scientist to study the structure of freedom in the mountainous case material made available, for instance, in Columbia's current celebration.

Then, it might be that the social scientist can, in the words of Charles Horton Cooley, "make it total and make it human." We have apparently learned that science can destroy humanity; but is that the purpose of education? We know also that if all science is taught, and our systems of education sufficiently indoctrinated as to indicate that the human mammal may have no more expectation to survive than any other mammal, then that doctrine will prevail in contradistinction to the total noble record of mankind. But is this the purpose of university as human society's own most cherished integer of cultural development? Now as never before there is consensus that the social and moral order should survive the threatening technological order; and if there is a consensus that the total emphasis is upon human society as an entity of its own, it would seem that the social scientists are about ready to join with the great scientists and philosophers of the American Philosophical Society, or to be committed to special assignments therein.

For, above all things, we must understand that the social sciences are of human creation, part of the ceaseless questing of humanity for knowledge and understanding and, even, palliation. If, in objective analysis, the social sciences have not yet learned to measure in every respect the range and power of the human spirit, they do tell abundantly of universal time and process in human affairs. Themselves part of the scientific revolution, they restore to man both humanity and dignity, whether he has lost these to the machine, to swift social change, or to the totalitarian state. For all of their jargon, the net result is that the social sciences are humane voices, whose tracery of "what is" and "how it became so" to millions of students must inevitably raise the level of social maturity. And, we may ask, to what other voice is the youthful product of modern civilization so likely to listen?

The Bibliography of Howard W. Odum

Books and Monographs

Religious Folk-Songs of the Southern Negroes (Clark University Doctoral Dissertations, 1909). Adapted and published in the *American Journal of Religious Psychology and Education,* III (July 1909), 265-365.

Social and Mental Traits of the Negro: Research into the Conditions of the Negro Race in Southern Towns. ("Columbia University Studies in History, Economics and Public Law," Vol. 37, No. 3.) New York: Longmans, Green and Company, 1910. Pp. 302.

"Public Welfare in the United States" (ed.), *Annals of the American Academy of Political and Social Science,* CV (January 1923). Pp. 282.

The Negro and His Songs: A Study of Typical Negro Songs in the South (with Guy B. Johnson). Chapel Hill: The University of North Carolina Press, 1925. Pp. 306.

Southern Pioneers in Social Interpretation (ed.). Chapel Hill: The University of North Carolina Press, 1925. Pp. 221.

Systems of Public Welfare (with D. W. Willard). Chapel Hill: The University of North Carolina Press, 1925. Pp. 302.

An Approach to Public Welfare and Social Work. Chapel Hill: The University of North Carolina Press, 1926. Pp. 178.

Negro Workaday Songs (with Guy B. Johnson). Chapel Hill: The University of North Carolina Press, 1926. Pp. 278.

American Masters of Social Science: An Approach to the Study of Social Science through a Neglected Field of Biography (ed.). New York: Henry Holt and Company, 1927. Pp. 411.

Man's Quest for Social Guidance. New York: Henry Holt and Company, 1927. Pp. 643.

Rainbow Round My Shoulder: The Blue Trail of Black Ulysses.

Indianapolis: Bobbs-Merrill Company, 1928. Pp. 323. Reprinted by Grosset and Dunlap in their series, "Novels of Distinction." Listed by the American Library Association in "Forty American Books of 1928" (*Journal of the National Education Association,* XVIII [December 1929], 313-14).

Wings on My Feet: Black Ulysses at the Wars. Indianapolis: Bobbs-Merrill Company, 1929. Pp. 309.

An Introduction to Social Research (with Katharine Jocher). New York: Henry Holt and Company, 1929. Pp. 488.

An American Epoch: Southern Portraiture in the National Picture. New York: Henry Holt and Company, 1930. Pp. 379.

Cold Blue Moon: Black Ulysses Afar Off. Indianapolis: Bobbs-Merrill Company, 1931. Pp. 277.

Collaborated in *Prospecting for Heaven: Some Conversations about Science and the Good Life,* by Edwin R. Embree. New York: Viking Press, 1932. Pp. 185. *Passim.*

Arranged and edited *Civilization and Society: An Account of the Development and Behavior of Human Society,* by Franklin Henry Giddings. New York: Henry Holt and Company, 1932. Pp. 412.

Recent Social Trends in the United States. 2 vols. Findings of the President's Committee on Social Trends (Assistant Director of Research and Co-editor. Also contributed Chap XXIV, "Public Welfare Activities"). New York: McGraw-Hill Book Company, 1933. Pp. 1568.

Southern Regions of the United States. Chapel Hill: The University of North Carolina Press, 1936. Pp. 664.

American Regionalism: A Cultural-Historical Approach to National Integration (with Harry Estill Moore). New York: Henry Holt and Company, 1938. Pp. 693.

American Social Problems: An Introduction to the Study of the People and Their Dilemmas. New York: Henry Holt and Company, 1939. Pp. 549. rev. ed., 1945. Pp. 549.

American Democracy Anew: An Approach to the Understanding of Our Social Problems (with Harold D. Meyer, B. S. Holden, and Fred M. Alexander). New York: Henry Holt and Company, 1940. Pp. 614.

Alabama Past and Future: The States at Work Series (with Gladstone H. Yeuell and Charles G. Summersell). Chicago: Science Research Associates, 1941. Pp. 401.

Race and Rumors of Race: Challenge to American Crisis. Chapel Hill: The University of North Carolina Press, 1943. Pp. 245.

In Search of the Regional Balance of America (edited with Katharine Jocher). Chapel Hill: The University of North Carolina Press, 1945. Pp. 162 (A publication commemorating the Sesqui-Centennial of the University of North Carolina. Reprinted from *Social Forces*, XXIII [March 1945]).

Understanding Society: The Principles of Dynamic Sociology. New York: The Macmillan Company, 1947. Pp. 749.

The Way of the South: Toward the Regional Balance of America. New York: The Macmillan Company, 1947. Pp. 350.

American Sociology: The Story of Sociology in the United States to 1950. New York: Longmans, Green and Company, 1951. Pp. 501.

Articles, Brochures, Chapters, Pamphlets

"Folk-Song and Folk-Poetry as Found in the Secular Songs of the Southern Negroes," *Journal of American Folk-Lore*, XXIV (July-September 1911), 255-94; (October-December 1911), 251-396.

Hygiene in the Schools of Philadelphia. Philadelphia: Bureau of Municipal Research, 1912.

"Negro Children in the Public Schools of Philadelphia," *Annals of the American Academy of Political and Social Science*, XLIX (September 1913), 186-208.

"The Relation of the High School to Rural Life and Education," *High School Quarterly* (April 1914), pp. 139-47.

"School Values in Boys' and Girls' Club Work," *Girls' and Boys' Club Work*, Georgia State College of Agriculture, 1914, pp. 5-10.

The Place of Animal Husbandry in the Schools. University of Georgia Extension Publications, 1914.

Practical Community Studies. University of Georgia Extension Publications, 1914.

"Standards of Measurement for Race Development," *Journal of Race Development*, V (April 1915), 364-83.

"Some Studies in Negro Problems of the Southern States," *Journal of Race Development*, VI (October 1915), 185-91.

"What the Universities Are Doing for Rural Education," *High School Quarterly* (January 1916) pp. 108-15.

"Introduction," in "Civic Co-operation in Community Building," *Bulletin of the University of Georgia*, XVI (June 1916), 3-4.

"Negro Home and Health Conditions," *Southern Workman* (December 1916), pp. 691-97.

"German Education and the Great War," *Bulletin of the Board of Education of the Methodist Episcopal Church, South* (November 1919).

"University Cooperation in Public Welfare," *Bulletin of the North Carolina State Department of Charities and Public Welfare*, III (July-September 1920), 38-43.

"Constructive Ventures in Government: A Manual of Discussion and Study of Woman's New Place in the Newer Ideals of Citizenship," *The University of North Carolina Extension Leaflet,* IV (September 1920), No. 1. Pp. 95.

"Community and Government: A Manual of Discussion and Study of the Newer Ideals of Citizenship," *The University of North Carolina Extension Leaflet,* IV (January 1921), No. 5. Pp. 106.

"Health and Housing," pp. 41-44, *Cooperation in Southern Communities: Suggested Activities for County and City Interracial Communities,* edited by T. J. Woofter, Jr., and Isaac Fisher. Atlanta: Commission on Interracial Cooperation, 1921.

"Attainable Standards in Municipal Programs: A Partial Report of the First Regional Conference of Town and County Administration Held at Chapel Hill, September 19, 20, 21, 1921" (ed.), *The University of North Carolina Extension Bulletin,* I (December 1921), No. 7. Pp. 130.

"A University Plan," *Journal of Social Forces,* I (November 1922), 49.

"The Journal of Social Forces," *Journal of Social Forces,* I (November 1922), 56-61.

"Effective Democracy," *Journal of Social Forces,* I (January 1923), 178-83.

"Newer Ideals of Public Welfare," *Annals of the American Academy of Political and Social Science,* CV (January 1923), 1-6.

"Attainable Standards for State Departments of Public Welfare," *Annals of the American Academy of Political and Social Science,* CV (January 1923), 137-43.

"Positions for Trained Social Workers in the Field of Public Welfare," *Annals of the American Academy of Political and Social Science,* CV (January 1923), 182-84.

"Fundamental Principles Underlying Inter-racial Co-operation," *Journal of Social Forces,* I (March 1923), 282-85.

"Democracy and Life," *Journal of Social Forces,* I (March 1923), 315-20.

"Reading, Writing, and Leadership," *Journal of Social Forces,* I (March 1923), 321-35.

"Comprehensive Social Work," *Journal of Social Forces,* I (May 1923), 471-76.

"The Search After Values," *Journal of Social Forces,* I (May 1923), 342-43; (September 1923), 506-7.

"The Transfer of Leadership," *Journal of Social Forces,* I (September 1923), 616-20.

"An Attainable Rural Standard," *Journal of Social Forces,* II (November 1923), 111-14.

"Public Welfare and Rural Adequacy," *The Rural Home* (Proceedings of the Sixth National Country Life Conference, St Louis, Missouri 1923), pp. 96-103.

"The Search After Values," *Journal of Social Forces,* II (November 1923), 3-4; (January 1924), 142-43; (March 1924), 318-19; (May 1924), 478-79; (September 1924), 638-41.

"Dependable Theory and Social Change," *Journal of Social Forces,* II (January 1924), 282-86.

"Toward a More Articulate South," *Emory Wheel* (March 20, 1924), pp. 1, 2, 7.

"A More Articulate South," *Journal of Social Forces,* II (September 1924), 730-35.

"The Search After Values," *Journal of Social Forces,* III (November 1924), 2-5; (January 1925), 200-3; (March 1925), 400-2.

"G. Stanley Hall: Pioneer in Scientific Social Exploration," *Journal of Social Forces,* III (November 1924), 139-46.

"The New Public Welfare," *Proceedings of the Ohio State Conference of Social Work, 1924.*

"Masters of Work," *Journal of Social Forces,* III (January 1925), 337-39.

"Public Welfare and the Community, as It Relates to the North Carolina Plan of Public Welfare: A Statement for the North Carolina Federation of Women's Clubs," *University of North Carolina Extension Bulletin,* IV (February 1925), No. 10. Pp. 53.

"University Research and Training in Social Science," *Journal of Social Forces,* III (March 1925), 518-24.

"A Southern Promise," *Journal of Social Forces,* III (May 1925), 739-46.

"The Duel to the Death," *Social Forces,* IV (September 1925), 189-94.

"The Discovery of the People," *Social Forces,* IV (December 1925), 414-17.

Sociology and Social Problems. Chicago: American Library Association, 1925. Pp. 32.

"Public Welfare and Democracy," *Proceedings of the American Country Life Association, 1925,* pp. 117-22.

"The New Negro," *Modern Quarterly,* III (February-April 1926), 127-28.

"Swing Low, Sweet Chariot," *Country Gentleman,* XCI (March 1926), 18-19, 49-50.

"Down That Lonesome Road," *Country Gentleman,* XCI (May 1926), 18-19, 79.

"The Promise of the Social Sciences," *Social Forces,* V (September 1926), i-iv.

"Frontiers of Social Work," *Social Forces,* V (December 1926), 268-69.

"Governmental Responsibility for Social Work," *Proceedings of the Maryland State Conference, 1925-1926.*

"Ideals of Government," Chap. XIX, pp. 230-43 in "Christianity and Modern Thought," Vol. IV, *An Outline of Christianity: The Story of Our Civilization.* 5 vols. New York: Bethlehem Publishers, Inc., 1926.

"Changing Requirements for the Doctor's Degree," *Social Forces,* V (June 1927), 600-2.

"The Science of Society," *Social Forces,* VI (September 1927), ii.

"Introduction," pp. ix-x in *Citizens' Reference Book: A Textbook for Adult Beginners in Community Schools,* Vol. 2, by Elizabeth Morriss. Chapel Hill: The University of North Carolina Press, 1927.

"Increasing the Circulation of Social Forces," *Social Forces,* VI (March 1928), ii.

"The Search After Values," *Social Forces,* VI (June 1928), ii.

"How New Is the South in Social Work," *Survey,* LX (June 15, 1928), 329-30.

"Editor's Introductory Note," pp. v-vii in *American Marriage and Family Relationships,* by Ernest R. Groves and William F. Ogburn. New York: Henry Holt and Company, 1928.

"Foreword," pp. 3-4 in *A Decade of Negro Self-Expression,* compiled by Alain Locke. Charlottesville, Virginia: The John F. Slater Fund, 1928. Occasional Papers No. 26.

"A New Keynote and Emphasis in Social Theory," *American Social Science Notes.* New York: Henry Holt and Company, 1928. Pp. 7.

"Social Resources and Social Waste in the South," *Georgia Educational Association,* 1928.

"Regional Social Research," *Vassar College* (January 1929).

"The 'Scientific-Human' in Social Research," *Social Forces,* VII (March 1929), 350-62.

"Regional Portraiture," *Saturday Review of Literature,* VI (July 27, 1929), 1-2.

"Black Ulysses Goes to War," *American Mercury,* XVII (August 1929), 385-400.

"Black Ulysses in Camp," *American Mercury,* XVIII (September 1929), 47-59.

"The Sociological Viewpoint in Rural Social Research"; "The Sociological Viewpoint in Rural Social Organization," *Ohio State University* (October 8, 1929).

"Folk and Regional Conflict as a Field of Sociological Study," *Publications of the American Sociological Society,* XXV (May 1931), 1-17.

"The Sociological Viewpoint on Education and Racial Adjustment," *Education and Racial Adjustment: Report of the Peabody Conference on Dual Education in the South* (November 1931), pp. 56-59.

"Lynchings, Fears, and Folkways," *Nation,* CXXXIII (December 30, 1931), 719-20.

"Notes on the Study of Regional and Folk Society," *Social Forces,* X (December 1931), 164-75.

"Trends in Public Welfare," *Proceedings of the National Conference of Social Work, Minneapolis, 1931,* pp. 441-50. Chicago: University of Chicago Press, 1932.

"The Epic of Brown America," *Yale Review,* XXI (Winter 1932), 419-21.

"Sociology and the Study of the Modern World," *Roads to Knowledge,* edited by William A. Neilson. New York: W. W. Norton, 1932. Pp. 326-49.

"New Frontiers of Leadership in Public Affairs," *Bulletin of Emory University,* IX (March 1933), 52-71.

"Notes on Recent Trends in the Application of the Social Sciences," *Social Forces,* XI (May 1933), 477-88.

"New Frontiers of American Life," *Southwest Review,* XVIII (Summer 1933), 418-29.

"Public Welfare Activities," *Recent Social Trends in the United States,* pp. 1224-73. New York: McGraw-Hill Book Company, 1933.

"The New Setting for English Teaching: I. Industrial-Economic Life," *English Journal,* XXII (November 1933), 711-19.

"The New Setting for English Teaching: II. Social Changes," *English Journal,* XXIII (January 1934), 19-30.

"Regionalism vs. Sectionalism in the South's Place in the National Economy," *Social Forces,* XII (March 1934), 338-54.

"An Approach to Race Adjustment," *Woman's Press,* XXVIII (April 1934), 196-97.

"Social Planning and the New Deal," *News and Observer* (Raleigh, North Carolina), May 20, 1934.

"Where the Sociologist and Social Worker Begin," *Social Forces,* XII (May 1934), 465-72.

"A New Deal Popular Bookshelf: How Much Social Realism, How Much Social Science, How Much Grinding Grist?" *Social Forces,* XII (May 1934), 601-6.

"The Case for Regional-National Social Planning," *Social Forces,* XIII (October 1934), 6-23.

"A Sociological Approach to National Social Planning: A Syllabus," *Sociology and Social Research,* XIX (March-April 1935), 303-13.

"Orderly Transitional Democracy," *Annals of the American Academy of Political and Social Science,* CLXXX (July 1935), 31-39.

"Promise and Prospect of the South: A Test of American Regionalism," *Proceedings of the Eighth Annual Session of the Southern Political Science Association, December 26, 1935,* pp. 8-18.

"A Tragedy of Race Conflict," *Yale Review,* XXV (1935), 214-16.

The Regional Approach to National Social Planning: With Special Reference to a More Abundant South and Its Continuing Reintegration in the National Economy. New York: The Foreign Policy Association; and Chapel Hill: The University of North Carolina Press, 1935. Pp. 31.

"Social and Economic Trends as Affecting the Education of Tomorrow," *Educational Responsibilities of Today and Tomorrow,* pp. 36-47. Philadelphia: Twenty-Second Annual Schoolmen's Week Proceedings, 1935.

"Cotton and Diversification," *Problems of the Cotton Economy,* Section III (Proceedings of the Southern Social Science Research Conference, New Orleans, March 8, 1935), pp. 50-71. Dallas, Texas: Arnold Foundation, 1936.

"Testing Grounds for Social Planning. The Promise of the South, a Test of American Regionalism," *Plan Age,* II (February 1936), 1-26.

"Realistic Premises for Regional Planning Objectives," *Plan Age,* II (March 1936), 7-21.

"Despite Potentialities the South Is an Area of Scarcity Instead of a Land of Abundance," *South Today* (published in 12 southern newspapers through the Southern Newspaper Syndicate, August 1936).

"Planning for the State's Social Welfare," *Public Welfare News Letter,* No. 14 (Raleigh, North Carolina, October 1936), pp. 1-6 (mimeographed).

"Six Americas in Search of a Faith," *Independent Woman,* XV (October 1936), 309, 334-36.

"The Way of a Wealthy Nation in the Modern World," *Proceedings, Institute of Public Affairs,* University of Alabama, 1936.

"The Southern People: Their Background, Their Resources, and Their Culture," *Proceedings, Institute of Public Affairs,* University of Alabama, 1936.

"Alabama's Place in the South," *Proceedings, Institute of Public Affairs,* University of Alabama, 1936.

"Toward Regional Social Planning," *Proceedings, Institute of Public Affairs,* University of Alabama, 1936.

"Social Security and Public Welfare in the '30's," *Minutes and Materials, Second Annual Institute, North Carolina State Employment Service and National Reemployment Service,* pp. 61-64. Raleigh: North Carolina Department of Labor, 1936 (mimeographed).

"The Implications of Radio as a Social and Educational Phenomenon," *Educational Broadcasting 1936: Proceedings of the First National Conference on Educational Broadcasting, Washington, D. C., December 10-12, 1936,* edited by C. S. Marsh. Chicago: University of Chicago Press, 1937. Also printed in *Educational Record,* XVIII (January 1937), 24-27.

"The Errors of Sociology," *Social Forces,* XV (March 1937), 327-42.

"These Southern Regions," *Alabama School Journal,* LIV (May 1937), 12.

"From Sections to Regions," *Saturday Review of Literature,* XVI (June 12, 1937), 5.

"Notes on the Technicways in Contemporary Society," *American Sociological Review,* II (June 1937), 336-46.

"A New Realism of the People," *Education and Human Relations* (Read before the Second Southern Area Institute of Human Relations, Chapel Hill, North Carolina, July 1, 1937, Report of the Institute).

"Industrial Relations and the Social and Economic Life of the South," *New Factors in Industrial Relations,* pp. 67-74 (Summary of the 18th Annual Industrial Conference, Blue Ridge, North Carolina, National Council of the Young Men's Christian Association, July 15-17, 1937).

"The Human Aspects of Chemurgy," *Farm Chemurgic Journal,* I (September 17, 1937), 60-71.

"Regional Planning," pp. 35-44 in *Library Trends,* edited by L. R. Wilson. Chicago: University of Chicago Press, 1937.

Security and Welfare: Which Way Is Forward for North Carolina? Marking a Twenty-fifth Anniversary (assisted by Harriet L. Herring and Don Becker). Raleigh: North Carolina Conference for Social Service, 1937. Pp. 24.

"American Regionalism: The Implications and Meanings of Regionalism," *Progressive Education,* XV (1938), 229-39.

"New Sources of Vitality for the People," *Journal of the American Dietetic Association,* XIV (June-July 1938), 417-23.

464   *Bibliography of Howard W. Odum*

"The Promise of Graduate and Research Work in the South," *Inauguration and Symposium at Vanderbilt University, Nashville, Tennessee,* pp. 99-108. Nashville: Vanderbilt University, 1938.

"What about the Federal Equalization Fund for Education?" *Southern Newspaper Syndicate,* 1938.

"America: States and Regions," *Social Forces,* XVI (May 1938), 584-86.

"The State of Sociology in the United States and Its Prospect in the South," *Social Forces,* XVII (October 1938), 8-14.

Problems of the South: A University of Chicago Round Table Broadcast, September 4, 1938 (with Earl S. Johnson and William H. Spencer). Chicago: University of Chicago Round Table, 1938. Pp. 12.

"What Is the Answer?" *Carolina Magazine,* LXVIII (February 1939), 5-8.

"The Meaning and Significance of Democracy," *Eleusis of Chi Omega,* XLI (May 1939), 210-13.

"The South as Testing Ground for the Regional Approach to Public Health," *Proceedings of the Annual Congress on Medical Education and Licensure,* pp. 14-17. Chicago: American Medical Association, 1939. Also in *Journal of the American Medical Association* (Spring 1939).

"Of a Closer Cooperation between the Physical Sciences and the Social Sciences," *Harvard Alumni Bulletin,* XLI (July 7, 1939), 1124-28.

"The Position of the Negro in the American Social Order of 1950," *Journal of Negro Education,* VIII (July 1939), 587-94.

"Of New Social Frontiers in Contemporary Society," *Frontiers of Democracy,* VI (October 1939), 15-17.

"Regional Development and Governmental Policy," *Annals of the American Academy of Political and Social Science,* CCVI (November 1939), 133-41.

"On the Southern Frontier," *Southern Frontier,* I (January 1940), 1, 4.

"Is the South the Nation's Number One Economic Problem?" *Scholastic,* XXXVI (March 25, 1940), 8-9, 16.

"Education in the Secondary Schools of the South," *The Southern Association Quarterly,* IV (August 1940), 523-29.

"Three-fold Task Awaits South's Development," *Southern Frontier,* I (October 1940), 1, 4.

"Fundamentals of Americanism," *High School Journal,* XXIII (November 1940), 297-98.

"Foreword," pp. vii-xi in *Southern Industry and Regional Develop-*

ment, by Harriet L. Herring. Chapel Hill: The University of North Carolina Press, 1940.

"Towards the South at Its Best," *Mississippian* (Spring 1941).

"Introduction," pp. 9-10 in *Get More Out of Life: How Troubled People Can Find Help,* by Catherine Groves. New York: Association Press, 1941.

"The Role of Regionalism and the Regional Council in National Planning," *National Conference on Planning, 1941,* pp. 316-26. Chicago: American Society of Planning Officials, 1941.

"Implications of the Emergency for Schools," *News Letter,* Southern Association Study in Secondary Schools and Colleges (February 1942), pp. 1-2 (mimeographed).

"Regionalism—A Technique for Large-Scale Social Planning and Democratic Checks," *New Leader* (February 28, 1942), pp. 3, 6.

"Three-fold Task Awaits South's Development," *The Need to Eat Is Not Racial,* pp. 10-11. Atlanta: Commission on Interracial Cooperation, May 1942.

"A Sociological Approach to the Study and Practice of American Regionalism: A Factorial Syllabus," *Social Forces,* XX (May 1942), 425-36.

"The Way of the South: A Regional Approach to the Promise of American Life," *Christendom,* VII (Summer 1942), 377-89.

"Patterns of Regionalism in the Deep South," *Saturday Review of Literature,* XXV (September 19, 1942), 5-7.

"The South at Its Best," *Baptist Student,* XXII (October 1942), 3-5.

"The University, Scholarship and the People," *College of Education Record* (University of Washington, Seattle), IX (November 1942), 1-9.

"The Glory that Was, and the Southern Grandeur that Was Not," *Saturday Review of Literature,* XXVI (January 23, 1943), 9-10, 35-36.

"The Upper Old South: An Editorial" (with Virginius Dabney), *Saturday Review of Literature,* XXVI (January 23, 1943), 3.

"Sociology in the Contemporary World of Today and Tomorrow," *Social Forces,* XXI (May 1943), 390-96.

"A Study of War," Critique of *A Study of War* (2 vols.), by Quincy Wright, *Social Forces,* XXI (May 1943), 472-73.

"Introduction to Race Tensions," *University of Chicago Round Table,* No. 276 (July 4, 1943), pp. 1-2.

"Toward a New Era in Race Relations," *Pulse,* I (November 1943).

"Crisis in the Making," *Crisis,* L (December 1943), 360-62, 377-78.

"The American Heritage" (Proceedings of the Twentieth Annual Educational Conference and the Ninth Annual Meeting of the Kentucky Association of Colleges and Secondary Schools, University of Kentucky), *Bulletin of the Bureau of School Service,* XVI (December 1943), 51-59.

"Towards a More Dynamic Regional National Planning," *Planning, 1943* (Proceedings of the Annual Meeting, American Society of Planning Officials), pp. 66-71.

The North Carolina Jersey Book. Swannanoa: North Carolina Jersey Cattle Club, 1943-1944. Pp. 26.

"A New Era in Race Relations," *Pulse,* I (January 1944), 6-8.

"The Legend of the Eleanor Clubs," *Negro Digest,* II (February 1944), 17-22.

"Patrick Geddes' Heritage to 'The Making of the Future,'" *Social Forces,* XXII (March 1944), 275-81.

"Problem and Methodology in an American Dilemma," Critique of *An American Dilemma, The Negro Problem and Modern Democracy* (2 vols.), by Gunnar Myrdal, *Social Forces,* XXIII (October 1944), 94-98.

"Americans All," *Negro Digest,* III (November 1944), 44.

"The Challenge of Public Welfare," *Public Welfare News,* VII (Raleigh, North Carolina, December 1944), 24-27.

"Towards the Future," *Southern Frontier,* V (December 1944), 1, 3-4.

"Folk," "Folk-Regional Society," "Folk Society," "The Region," "Regional Planning," "Regionalism," "Technicways," *Dictionary of Sociology,* edited by Henry Pratt Fairchild. New York: Philosophical Library, 1944.

"The Sociologist Looks at Resource Education," *Nation's Schools,* XXXV (February 1945), 50-51.

"From Community Studies to Regionalism," *Social Forces,* XXIII (March 1945), 245-58.

"The Way of the South," *Social Forces,* XXIII (March 1945), 258-68.

"The Regional Quality and Balance of America," *Social Forces,* XXIII (March 1945), 269-85.

"The Way of the South," *Southern Frontier,* VI (August 1945), 1.

"The Assumptions of Regional Balance," *World Economics,* III (October-December 1945), 57-66.

"In Interracial Tensions," chap. XVIII, *Making the Gospel Effective,* edited by William K. Anderson, pp. 170-80. Nashville: Commission on Ministerial Training, the Methodist Church, 1945.

"The South at Its Best, the South at Work: Part I," Chap. 4; "The South at Its Best, the South at Work: Part II," Chap. 5; "Administrative Levels of Social Planning Agencies in American Democracy," Chap. 9; *Marshaling Florida's Resources,* edited by

Charles T. Thrift, pp. 30-37, 38-45, 65-68. Lakeland: Florida Southern College Press, 1945.

"The Social Sciences," *A State University Surveys the Humanities,* edited by L. C. McKinney, pp. 108-17. Chapel Hill: University of North Carolina Press, 1945 (A publication commemorating the Sesqui-Centennial of the University of North Carolina).

"Permanent Institutes" (with Katharine Jocher), *The Graduate School Research and Publications,* edited by Edgar W. Knight and Agatha Boyd Adams, pp. 155-72. Chapel Hill: The University of North Carolina Press, 1945 (A publication commemorating the Sesqui-Centennial of the University of North Carolina).

"Ernest R. Groves and His Work," *Social Forces,* XXV (December 1946), 197-206.

"Towards Tomorrow," *Understanding Marriage and the Family: A Symposium in Honor of Ernest R. Groves,* edited by Ray V. Sowers and John W. Mullen, pp. xv-xix. Vol II of the American Family Magazine Book Foundation. Chicago: Eugene Hugh Publishers, 1946.

"Social Morale in an Age of Science," *Southwest Review* (Winter 1947). Pp. 7.

"Tasks for Sociology," *Social Forces,* XXVI (March 1948), 373-75.

"On Definition and Measurement," *Social Forces,* XXVI (May 1948), 497-98.

"Social Change in the South," *Journal of Politics,* X (May 1948), 242-58; reprinted in *The Southern Political Scene, 1938-1948,* edited by Taylor Cole and John H. Hallowell. Gainesville, Florida: Kallman Publishing Co., 1948.

"The Unchanging South," *Torch,* XXI (October 1948), 10-11, 20.

"Tribute to Dr. Roy M. Brown upon His Retirement from the Faculty of the University of North Carolina," *Public Welfare News* (Raleigh, N. C.), XI (December 1948), 1-2, 12.

"F. H. Giddings," "E. A. Ross," "Lester F. Ward," *Collier's Encyclopedia.* New York: Crowell-Collier Publishing Co., 1948.

"This Is Worth Our Best," *The Southern Packet,* V (January 1949), 1-7.

"Linebreeding for Perfection," *Jersey Bulletin* (May 10, 1949), pp. 719, 766-88.

"The American Blend: Regional Diversity and National Unity," *Saturday Review of Literature,* XXXII (August 6, 1949), 92-96, 169-72.

"Edwin H. Sutherland, 1883-1950," *Social Forces,* XXIX (March 1951), 348-49.

"Laboratories for Peace," *Saturday Review of Literature,* XXXIV (May 12, 1951), 9-10.

"Toward the Dynamic Study of Jewish Culture," *Social Forces,* XXIX (May 1951), 450-52.

"Luther Lee Bernard, 1881-1951" *Social Forces,* XXIX (May 1951), 480-81.

"Edward Alsworth Ross, 1866-1951" *Social Forces,* XXX (October 1951), 126-27.

"The Promise of Regionalism," Chap. 15, *Regionalism in America,* edited by Merrill Jensen, pp. 395-425. Madison: University of Wisconsin Press, 1951.

"The Ph.D. Degree and the Doctor's Dissertation in Sociology and Anthropology," *Social Forces,* XXX (March 1952), 369-72.

"The Social Scientist Looks at Public Health," *Proceedings of the First Institute of Public Health, Veterans Administration Hospital, Tuskegee, Alabama, March 16-19, 1952,* pp. 137-54.

"For a Richer and Better Balanced Resource Development: Summary and Interpretation of Findings," *Conservation and Development in North Carolina,* II, pp. 356-71. Raleigh: Conservation Congress, November 17-19, 1952 (mimeographed).

"Folk Sociology as a Subject Field for the Historical Study of Total Human Society and the Empirical Study of Group Behavior," *Social Forces,* XXXI (March 1953), 192-223.

Symbol and Reality of Consolidation. Acceptance of the Fifth Annual O. Max Gardner Award, Anniversary Dinner, Woman's College of the University of North Carolina, March 22, 1953. Asheville: The Stephens Press, 1953. Pp. 7.

A Clear Vision for North Carolina. An Address Delivered at the 40th Annual Meeting of the North Carolina Conference for Social Service, Asheville, May 5, 1953. Raleigh: North Carolina Conference for Social Service, 1953. Pp. 6.

"On the Definition of Literature," *Shenandoah,* V (Winter 1953), 13-21.

"On Southern Literature and Southern Culture," *Southern Renascence: The Literature of the Modern South,* edited by Louis D. Rubin, Jr., and Robert D. Jacobs, pp. 84-100. Baltimore: Johns Hopkins Press, 1953. Also printed in *The Hopkins Review,* VII (Winter 1953), 60-76.

"Ellsworth Faris, 1874-1953," *Social Forces,* XXXIII (October 1954), 101-3.

"On Diagnosis and Direction in Certain National and Southern Issues in the United States," *Journal of Social Issues,* X (1954), 4-12.

"An Approach to Diagnosis and Direction of the Problem of Negro

Segregation in the Public Schools of the South," *Journal of Public Law,* III (1954), 8-37.

"Expanding Higher Education: Which Way Is Forward in the Social Sciences?" *Educational Record,* XXXVI (January 1955), 49-55.

General Editor

Social Forces. Baltimore: The Williams & Wilkins Company, 1922-1954.

North Carolina Social Study Series. Chapel Hill: The University of North Carolina Press, 1924-1935.

American Social Science Series. New York: Henry Holt and Company, 1925-1933.

This bibliography is not definitive. Book titles are complete, but copies of some of Dr. Odum's earlier publications—bulletins, pamphlets, articles—are at present not available. Copies not at hand are also responsible for incomplete listings of some references. In addition, book reviews, of which Dr. Odum contributed many, especially during his earlier professional life, are not included, but critiques are.

The chronological arrangement has been followed in order to show development in Dr. Odum's thinking over the years. This, it seems to us, places his work in clearer perspective than would an attempt to classify his writing under several fields. Accordingly, we have used but two categories: (1) Books and Monographs; (2) Articles, Brochures, Chapters, Pamphlets, each arranged in chronological sequence.

Index

Of Persons

Of Subjects

American democracy, place of planning in, 422-26

Black Ulysses, his mother, 19-24; his father, 20-22; and broken homes, 22-23

Christianity, 372, 376-77
Civilization, as state society, 225-26, 282-84, 289; technological aspects of, 226-27; artificial, 227-28; as intellectualism, 227, 289-90, 320-22; as power, 227; and culture, 281, 285-86; as concept, 284; characterized, 285-87; cumulative, 286; as urban society, 287-88; American and European compared, 290-92; as scientific humanism, 291-92; in Hitler's Germany, 292; differences in contemporary, 303-4; and culture as contrasting concepts, 317-18; interconnected processes of, 319-20; and a-chievement lag, 320-22; uncultured, 320-22; popular diagnosis of, 339-40
Commission on Interracial Co-operation, 47
Conflict, social, 241, 252; religious, 246
Cultural lag, 248
Cultural studies, empirical documentation of, 336-37
Culture, concept of, 300-1

Democracy, more than political opportunity, 372-74; varieties of, 373-76; social, 374; in depression, 391-94ff.; in transition, 391-402; and poverty, 393-94; minority groups in, 394; economic failures in, 395-400; alternatives to, 397, 400; deficiencies in

American, 397-98; experiments in, 400-1; need for social planning in, 401-2
Desegregation, crisis of, 67; and social change, 68ff; pressures of, 69-70; the South and, 74; and science, 76; and religion, 77; and the Federal government, 78-79; South resists, 79-81; South's resources for, 92-96; place of courts in, 99-101; dilemma of, 102-5; next steps in, 105-7
Domestic servants, shortage of, 60-66

Education, as way forward in South, 436-44; of youth in depression, 436, 441-42; and regional development, 439-41; pillar of democracy, 442; and the search for societal culture, 443-44. *See also* Higher education
Eleanor Clubs, rumors of, in South, 60-66
Environment, and the writer, 206-18

Faulkner, William, as example of literary regionalism, 202-18; as regional writer, 213-16
Federal equalization, 407-8
Folk, the, and mass, 316-17; comparative concepts of, 334-35
Folk culture, and cultural cycles, 231-34; in historical development, 231-33; and trend to civilization, 233; characterized, 315
Folklore, importance of, 8
Folk mind in folk songs, 7
Folk society, as definitive society, 223; as informal, 224-28; as natural, 224-25, 228; decline of, 234-37; in the United States, 237-38; defined, 241-46; concept of, 243-46. *See also* Society
Folk sociology, study of transitional society, 231; field of, 293ff; concepts in, 296-98; his-